D0204856

AMERICAN IMMIGRATION & ETHNICITY

A 20-Volume Series of Distinguished Essays

EDITED BY
George E. Pozzetta

A Garland Series

TITLES IN THE SERIES

VOLUME 14

AMERICANIZATION, SOCIAL CONTROL, AND PHILANTHROPY

EDITED BY
George E. Pozzetta

GARLAND PUBLISHING, INC.
New York & London
1991

Introduction Copyright © 1991 by George E. Pozzetta
All Rights Reserved

Library of Congress Cataloging-in-Publication Data

Americanization, social control, and philanthropy/ edited by George E. Pozzetta
p. cm.—(American immigration and ethnicity; v. 14)
Includes bibliographical references.
ISBN 0-8240-7414-9 (alk. paper)
1. Immigrants—United States—Social conditions.
2. Americanization. 3. Minorities—United States—Social
conditions. 4. United States—Emigration and immigration—History.
I. Pozzetta, George E. II. Series.
E184.A1A6734   1991
305.8'00973—dc20   90-49267

Printed on acid-free, 250-year-life paper
Manufactured in the United States of America

INTRODUCTION

Once I thought to write a history of the
immigrants in America. Then I discovered
that the immigrants were American history.

Oscar Handlin,
The Uprooted (1951)

When it first appeared forty years ago, Oscar Handlin's startling observation occasioned disbelieving reactions; today, changes in historical scholarship have moved immigrants much closer to the central position posited by Handlin than perhaps even he ever considered possible. Once relegated to the fringes of historical investigation, immigrants now speak to the main themes of American history with an eloquence that belies the lack of attention they received earlier. In large part this is true because of what has happened to the field of immigration studies. Drawing from the momentum of the new social history, with its perspective "from the bottom up" and its insistence on exploring the experiences of ordinary people, the scholarly inquiry into immigration and ethnicity has produced an astounding outpouring of books and articles over the past several decades.

This rich and complex historical literature has drawn heavily from the methodologies and insights of the other social sciences and humanities, and the wider investigation into immigration has criss-crossed disciplinary boundaries at a rapid pace. The major journals of History, Political Science, Anthropology, Sociology, and Geography, for example, regularly carry essays dealing with the immigrant experience, and hundreds of articles appear in the more specialized local, regional, and topical publications of each discipline. Simply finding the relevant essays on any given topic within the general field has become a substantial challenge to researchers. This collection, therefore, represents an effort to bring together a selected cross section of the most significant articles on immigration and ethnicity. It is not definitive, no compilation treating with such broad-ranging and dynamic topics can ever be, but it is indicative of the scholarship that has shaped—and continues to shape—these important subjects. The major themes and issues of the field are discussed below, and each volume contains an individualized listing of supplemental readings for additional guidance. Taken together the collected essays contained

APR 9 1991

within these volumes explore the manifold ways in which "immigrants were American history."

The liberation of immigration studies from its previously marginalized position has flowed from a number of critical interpretive and conceptual advances. One of the most important of these has been the effort to place immigration to America in the context of broader patterns of movement. Alerted by Frank Thistlethwaite's pioneering work, which showed how European migration to America was only part of a much larger transatlantic population and technological exchange, researchers now realize that an American-centered perspective is too restrictive to comprehend the full dimensions of migration. Immigrants from all quarters of the globe often envisioned America as only one destination among many, and then not necessarily a permanent one. Outmoded conceptions of "America fever" and exclusive one-way movement have given way to more complex understandings of the various manners by which America attracted and retained immigrants. The best works have taken into account the ability of multinational labor markets, economic cycles, transportation networks, as well as individual familial strategies, to propel immigrants outward in multi-step journeys.

At the same time as Thistlethwaite called for attention to large scale movements, he also urged that scholars be sensitive to the highly particularized nature of small scale migrations. Instead of studying "an undifferentiated mass movement" of individuals from loosely defined nation states, he insisted that immigrants be seen as emanating from "innumerable particular cells, districts, villages, towns, each with an individual reaction or lack of it to the pull of migration." This perspective necessarily involved linking the homeland with the new land in very precise ways, accounting for the specific influences of such factors as chain migration, kinship networks, travel agents, steamship companies, and repatriation flows, as well as the highly individualized economies of local regions.

Rudolph J. Vecoli's seminal work on Italian peasants in Chicago has pushed the study of premigration backgrounds in new directions. By pointing out that old world cultures survived the ocean crossing and significantly influenced adaptations in America, Vecoli stimulated a broad-based inquiry into the various ways in which immigrant traditions articulated with new world realities. The resulting scholarship has shifted the emphasis of investigation away from attention to the forces of assimilation and cultural break-down to those of cultural persistence and ethnic continuity. Immigrants did not succumb passively to pressures for conformity, but rather followed patterns of resistance and accommodation to the new land by which they turned themselves into something new—ethnic Americans. The ethnic culture that they created has proved to be a dynamic quality that has had influence into the third and fourth generation and beyond.

Such a viewpoint has led to different conceptions of assimilation and acculturation. Less often have scholars viewed these processes as easy, straight-line movements from "foreign" to "American." Nor have they continued to be captivated by images of a vast "Melting Pot" at work that has thoroughly erased differences. Rather, newer studies have posited a syncretic outcome in which both immigrants and the mainstream society have been changed, and the overall process of immigrant integration has emerged as more contingent and unpredictable than previously imagined. Attempts to preserve immigrant languages, value structures, and tradition, for example, could not, and did not, result in the exact replication of old-world ways. In a process of "invention" and "negotiation," immigrants adapted their ethnic cultures to meet changing historical circumstances and to resolve the problems of duality inherent in their straddling of Old and New Worlds. At the same time, the host society was changing, or "reinventing," its own cultural traditions, in part because of the need to accommodate the presence of diverse clusters of immigrants.

Much of the most stimulating new research carried out along these lines has adopted the urban immigrant community as its setting. Community studies have not only examined the institutional structures of settlements, but have also typically attempted to penetrate into the "interior worlds" of newcomers to discover the mentalities, values, and life strategies that shaped immigrant destinies. Such inquiries have probed deeply into the families, kin groups, and neighborhoods that formed the core of immigrant districts. Their conclusions have revised older conceptions of immigrant neighborhoods that emphasized the social pathology of family breakdown, crime, and deviant behavior. Immigrant communities emerge as remarkably vibrant and complex entities that provided effective cushions between the often strange and harsh dominant society and newly arrived residents. They also were far from the homogenous bodies so often envisioned by outsiders, but rather were replete with various "subethnic" divisions based upon distinctions of class, religion, ideology, and local culture. The process of immigrant adaptation to America, therefore, was as often marked by tension and conflict *within* ethnic concentrations as it was by friction between the group and the receiving society.

Internal divisions were also features of immigrant communities in rural and small town locations. However, the distinctive physical and cultural contexts encountered in such settings meant that immigrants usually experienced different adjustment patterns from those of their urban-dwelling cousins. More isolated from mainstream contact and better able to establish a local hegemony, immigrant settlements in these settings often maintained traditional languages and folkways for longer periods of time and with less change than was possible in city neighborhoods. The ethnic culture that rural immigrants crafted correspondingly reflected these particular conditions.

Eschewing a reliance on sources generated by the host society and utilizing a broad range of foreign language materials, researchers have demonstrated the existence of a remarkable range of civic, labor, religious, recreational, cultural, and fraternal organizations created by immigrants. Each of these played important roles in mediating the difficult adjustment to new-world conditions, and the presence of these institutions points to the need of recognizing immigrants as active agents in determining their own futures. To be sure, they were often circumscribed in their actions by poverty, nativism, discrimination, and limited skills, but they typically responded with imaginative adaptations within the limits imposed upon them. Many formal immigration institutions such as labor unions and mutual aid societies, for example, employed collective strategies to overcome the constraints restricting immigrant lives. Informal familial and kin networks often assisted these initiatives with adjustments of their own to ease the process of insertion into America.

The most fundamental institution of all, the immigrant family, reveals these patterns clearly. Families did not disintegrate under the pressures of immigration, urbanization, and industrialization, but rather proved to be remarkably flexible and resilent. Family structures and values responded to the multiple challenges imposed by migration—both in urban centers and rural spaces—by expanding their roles to accommodate a variety of new demands. Immigrant women, in their capacities as mothers and daughters, played critical functions in these transformations. Recent work, however, has attempted to move the study of immigrant women beyond the family context and to view women as historical actors who were able to influence the larger society in many different ways. The broader challenge has been to reveal how women confronted the multiple dilemmas posed by migration, and, more generally, to insert the issue of gender into the wider interpretations of the immigrant experience.

Since most immigrants entered America in quest of work, and after the 1860s usually industrial work, their relationship to the labor performed assumed a special importance. The vast majority arrived with preindustrial cultural values and confronted a complex urban-industrial economy. This encounter was a crucial factor not only in understanding the patterns of immigrant assimilation and social mobility, but also in comprehending the nature of American industrialization and the processes by which an American working class came into being. Through their collective labor as workers, their actions as union members, and their varied responses to exploitation and insecurity, immigrants were critical elements in the shaping of a modern American economy and labor force. Researchers are continuing to explore the exact nature of this dialectical relationship as they attempt to link immigrant values and expectations with the demands of the workplace.

Just as scholars have pursued the immigrant into the factory, home, and mutual aid society, so too have they entered the doors of immigrant churches in their investigations. The denominational pluralism that has characterized American society is a direct outgrowth of the nation's ethnic pluralism. Older works concentrated on examining the institutional histories of different immigrant religions and on the conflict engendered by such issues as parochial education and the formation of national parishes. More recently scholars have moved the study of America's religious tapestry out of church buildings and diocesan boardrooms and into the streets and neighborhoods. By examining the "popular piety" of immigrants, researchers hope to understand more clearly the ways in which new arrivals integrated the actual practice of religion into their everyday lives.

Investigators have already learned much about the relationships between ethnicity and political behavior. Indeed, one of the most surprising findings of the "new political history" was the discovery that ethnocultural considerations—often in the form of religious indentifications—were critical influences in shaping American voting patterns. Election outcomes in many parts of the nation often hinged on such factors. Indeed, perhaps no aspect of the American political arena has been immune to the force of ethnicity. Currently, researchers have been interested in determining how immigrants shaped a political culture of their own as they adapted to the American environment. Arriving from dissimilar backgrounds and frequently containing within their ranks followers of many different political ideologies, immigrants cannot be neatly classified into simple categories. Whether as supporters of urban machines, leftist critics of American capitalism, or as second and third generation politicians pushing group demands, immigrants and their progeny have been essential ingredients in the American political equation.

The American educational system similarly underwent profound transformation due to the immigrant presence. Many newcomers approached this powerful institution with ambivalent feelings since education in America offered both an opportunity for future progress and a danger to valued traditions. For their part, schools and school officials were forced to cope with unprecedented problems of space, curriculum, rules of discipline, attendance, and staffing. Immigrants ultimately found it necessary to judge the worth of education defined in new-world terms, both in relation to themselves and their children. They reacted in various ways, ranging from the formation of separate educational initiatives that sought to maintaine cherished values to the avoidance of formal educational institutions altogether. One thing was certain: both sides of the equation were changed by the contact.

America responded to the immigrant presence in varied ways. During periods of crisis, the host society often reacted by promoting rigid programs of Americanization that sought to strip away foreign customs and values. Research has shown that even programs of assistance and outreach, such as those offered by settlement houses and philanthropic agencies, often contained strong doses of social control. Immigrants were not unaware of these elements and frequently reacted to these and such programs as bilingual education and affirmative action have engendered sharp public division. The present collection of essays, therefore, should be seen as providing the first installment of an important research agenda that needs to be open-ended in scope, responsive to new methodologies and interpretations, and cognizant of its relevance to contemporary American society.

The editor wishes to thank Leonard Dinnerstein, Victor Greene, Robert Singerman, Jeffrey Adler, Robert Zieger, and especially Rudolph Vecoli and Donna Gabaccia, for their helpful advice on this project.

GEORGE E. POZZETTA

SUPPLEMENTAL READING

Tomas Almaguer, "Racial Discrimination and Class Conflict in Capitalist Agriculture: The Oxnard Sugar Beet Worker's Strike of 1903," *Labor History*, 25 (Summer 1984), 325–350.

Mie Liang Bickner, "The Forgotten Minority: Asian American Women," *Amerasia Journal*, 11 (Spring 1974), 1–17.

Melvin Dubofsky, "Organized Labor and the Immigrant in New York City, 1900–1918," *Labor History*, 2 (1961), 182–201.

Melvin Dubofsky, "Success and Failure of Socialism in New York City, 1900–1918," *Labor History*, 9 (Fall 1968), 361–375.

Charlotte Erickson, "Emigration from the British Isles to the U.S.A. in 1831," *Population Studies*, 35 (1981), 175–197.

Frances H. Early, "The French Canadian Family Economy and Standard-of-Living in Lowell, Massachusetts, 1870," *Journal of Family History*, 7 (Summer 1982), 180–199.

Howard M. Gitelman, "No Irish Need Apply: Patterns of and Response to Ethnic Discrimination in the Labor Market," *Labor History*, 14 (1973), 56–68.

Philip Gleason, "Confusion Compounded: The Melting Pot in the 1960s and 1970s," *Ethnicity*, 6 (1979), 10–20.

Philip Gleason, "The Melting Pot: Symbol of Fusion or Confusion?" *American Quarterly* SVI (Spring 1974), 20–46.

Bruce C. Levine, "Immigrant Workers, 'Equal Rights,' and Antislavery: The Germans of Newark, New Jersey," *Labor History*, 25 (Winter 1984), 26–52.

Hubert Perrier, "The Socialists and the Working Class in New York, 1890–1896," *Labor History*, 22, No. 4 (Fall 1981), 485–511.

Thaddeus Radzialowski, "Immigrant Nationalism and Feminism: Glos Polek and the Polish Women's Alliance in America, 1898–1980," *Review Journal of Philosophy and Social Science*, 2 (1972), 183–203.

Robert Swierenga, "Dutch Immigrant Demography, 1820–1880," *Journal of Family History*, 5 (Winter 1980), 390–405.

Peter Temin, "Labor Scarcity in America," *Journal of Interdisciplinary History*, 1 (Winter 1971), 251–264.

CONTENTS

NEIL BETTEN

Polish American Steelworkers: Americanization Through Industry and Labor

Numerous American institutions affected immigrant workers. This essay, focusing on Polish steel workers in Gary, Indiana from 1906 to the early 1920s, deals with industrial influences on workers lives. It examines the way in which the American industrial employer—in this case US Steel—attempted to reform, help, and manipulate the immigrant worker while fostering Americanization. It also seeks to understand how many immigrant workers—especially Polish Americans—informally learned about American society from labor related experiences.

After the founding of Gary in 1906, Poles and Polish Americans came to the city from Chicago, and elsewhere, including the Polish areas of Europe, to work in the United States Steel Corporation mills. Poles and Polish Americans constituted the largest foreign language ethnic group working in the city's steel mills. With some minor exceptions, Gary's Polish steel workers spent half of their day on the job—almost all of their waking hours, from the establishment of the city until 1923. Therefore, much of what they learned about American society mirrored their work experience. Corporation officials who realized this attempted to structure a work environment that Americanized the immigrant to reflect industrial interests. But work oriented acculturation resulted from informal relationships as well as from formal programs. Any industrial work situation resulted in some learning about American society; the steel mills were no exception. Working in multinational crews made learning of English a necessity. Although a man might work under a foreman of his own nationali-

This paper was read at the meeting of the Polish American Historical Association in Washington, D.C., on December 28, 1976.

ty, such a convenience did not often last. At any rate, the fore-man would communicate in English as his work crew became more diversified. Likewise, learning safety rules and techniques for higher paying jobs led to gradual advancement in the English language.[1]

US Steel supplemented this unconscious aspect of ac-culturation with an overt program designed to Americanize the Polish immigrant. Although real patriotic zeal may have been an impetus, particularly during the Great War, immigrant accultura-tion served the corporation in several other ways. It would be less likely for the Pole who had adjusted to the United States to return to Europe during that portion of his life when his working capabilities remained high. The more stable the labor force, the lower the corporation's cost for recruiting and breaking in new workers. This became a particularly important consideration as the corporation up-graded workers to higher skills and invested in their training. In addressing US Steel workers the *Gary Works Circle,* a management publication, often presented the virtues of settling down in one place and laboring for one firm, US Steel. In one issue it typically suggested, "you can't get the best out of life living on another man's land, and moving around." The Americanization program could benefit the corporation in other ways. A speedy immigrant acculturation might deter nativist hostility by blunting some of the arguments of anti-immigrant forces. Keeping open the gates of entry provided the firm with a continual supply of labor thus fostering a lower wage-scale. In addition, the learning of English often improved safety records and thus lowered costs. The Polish worker could read warning signs and safety notices while he could no longer ignore the more complicated safety and rule booklets with impunity. Indeed, US

---

1 Unskilled and semi-skilled steel workers worked twelve hours a day between 1900 and the early 1920's. Before World War I, most firms reduced the hours to ten a day, but the twelve-hour day, seven-day week reemerged with the war. U.S. Steel established an eight-hour day in 1923. On the found-ing of Gary, see Raymond A. Mohl and Neil Betten, "City Planning by Private Enterprise: U.S. Steel and Gary, Indiana," *Journal of the Institute of Planners* (Fall 1972), pp. 203-15. For the best con-temporary examination, see Graham R. Taylor, *Satellite Cities: A Study of Industrial Suburbs* (New York: Appleton, 1915). U.S. Steel, which refused to cooperate with the study, would not make available any data indicating the relative proportion of ethnic groups the corporation employed. It is clear, how-ever, from the U.S. Census and from intensive surveys by the Gary International Institute (International Institute, Folder 1919: Study of the Foreign Born, 1908, 1919, 1932; International Institute Papers held in Gary, Indiana, at the Institute's office) that Poles constituted the largest foreign language ethnic group in the city. In addition, an intensive research study, "Entrepreneurship and Ethnicity" (in Gary), unpublished paper by Leslie Singer, illustrates in various ways that the category that was composed mostly of Poles had the lowest rates of entrpreneurial activity. Both factors indicate that when we are discussing male Poles in Gary, we are talking about steel workers. The impressionistic evidence also supports the view that Poles were primarily steel workers.

Steel English classes were taught using safety manual materials and the Americanization program entered US Steel by way of the safety and welfare programs.[2]

US Steel's Good Fellow Club illustrates the industry's occasionally subtle approach to Americanization. The club served the workers, cost the company very little, and, typically, provided an entry into the Americanization process. Many US Steel plants first established such groups during the 1914 recession. The Good Fellow Club in Gary began with a visiting nurse service financed by donations from steel workers. From the beginning, Club workers realized that dealing with various cultures meant special problems. "The work requires patience and perserverence besides knowledge of racial character traits and habits." The American born nurses, of course, reflected some of the biases of the day. They assumed that all immigrants were dirty and that their households had to become American replicas. Likewise, the *Gary Works Circle* commended the nurses for attempting to stem the "waste and extravagance" supposedly common in Polish and other working class families. To remold the immigrant remained an underlying motivation of the US Steel nursing program. "Among the women and children much of the Americanization work is in hands of the Visiting Nurses," a US Steel publication pointed out. It added that through children's clubs and homemaking advice, "the nurses are given opportunities to inculcate American ideals in the minds of boys and girls, and through them to reach the parents." Although the health program constituted its main thrust, the Club provided children's services such as summer camp and occasional parties. Those activities also had a conscious Americanization intent.[3]

The war witnessed an intensification of US Steel's effort to Americanize Polish and other immigrant workers. The corporation program took on a vigorous patriotic orientation. In a front page article, the *Gary Works Circle* pointed out that "a strong campaign is being made in Gary Works to help the foreigners learn the English language and to have them realize that they will in this way prepare themselves for higher citizenship." In becoming an American, the Polish steelworker indicated his loyalty, not merely to the corporation, but to the country. "It is our duty as Americans," the corporation publication added, "to

2 Untitled article, *Gary Works Circle*, June 1918, p. 1.
3 "The Good Fellow Club," *Gary Works Circle*, Sep. 1918, pp. 1-11; "Americanization," U.S. Steel Corporation Committee of Safety, *Bulletin*, 1918, p. 95; "Our Children's Christmas," *Gary Works Circle*, Jan. 1918, p. 7.

3

cement the people in our country into a homogeneous nation."[4]

In addition to such publishing ventures, the corporation sponsored patriotic parades and demonstrations. Steel Superintendent Gleason led such a parade in Gary in April 1917. A telegram sent to President Wilson stated that "Gary just now finished the greatest patriotic demonstration ever held in Indiana." Flag Day, 1918, constituted an even more memorable occasion. The celebration began on company property with a parade led by the Gary Works band followed by employees in work clothes. The procession meandered to "six rousing department meetings." Upon arriving at the first meeting, workers formally raised the American flag, with a bugle accompaniment. The pledge of allegiance and a "patriotic sermon" delivered by a local minister followed. After "patriotic selections by the Electrical Department Quartet," the participants solemnly read aloud the "American Creed," stating their belief in the United States as "a perfect union, one and inseparable, established upon the principles of freedom, equality, justice and humanity." Each worker then pledged, "it is my duty to my country to love it; to support its Constitution; to obey its laws; to respect its flag; and to defend it against all enemies." After the first meeting closed with the Star Spangled Banner, the participants reformed and proceeded to the next department meeting where the scene was repeated. After the last of the six meetings, the parade traveled through the main streets of the city and returned to the US Steel administrative office for a final ceremony. There, with a soldier and sailor assisting, an especially large flag was raised by a steelworker dressed as Uncle Sam. US Steel spokesmen concluded that the demonstration "could not fail to inspire all with a greater love of Our Country and Flag." Indeed, they added, the procession "established beyond a doubt that our men are patriotic and loyal."[5]

Patriotism also served to prod the Polish immigrant worker to produce more. "Men of Gary Mills" the corporation proclaimed, "you are building the wall of steel that holds back the mailed fists of our enemies." Significantly it went on: "you have broken many production records, there are many more to be taken. Make the sky your limit, the forced peace of the entire world your goal." A Cleveland steel official captured the thrust of management thinking when he told the workers: "I have got a message for

4 "Americanization," *Gary Works Circle*, Ap. 1917, p. 1.

5 David Brody, *Steel Workers in America. The Non-Union Era* (New York: Harper and Row, 1969), p. 191; Isaac James Quillen, "Industrial City: A History of Gary, Indiana to 1929," Diss., Yale University, 1942, pp. 271-72; "Flag Day, Gary Works," *Gary Works Circle*, June 1918, p. 2.

you direct from your government . . . that your greasy overalls . . . are as much a badge of service and honor . . . as the uniform of the army or navy."[6]

The citizenship campaign of Gary Works had its more mundane side as well. The firm enrolled workers into "opportunity classes." Over a thousand men attended these evening sessions in 1918 alone. The curriculum consisted primarily of the "Roberts method" of citizenship education. Designed by Peter Roberts for the YMCA, the curriculum consisted of three segments. The first part, which concentrated on language, utilized phrases used in home and work, buying, selling and travelling. Reading, geography and Roberts' version of history and civics followed the rudimentary mastery of English. This second sequence used "patriotic texts." The final phase prepared the worker for the naturalization exam. In 1916, US Steel's Committee of Safety *Bulletin* noted that Roberts' program instructed the foreigner in proper citizenship, "the principles of clean, wholesome living." The program also had the flexibility to satisfy a firm's individual needs. Historian Gerd Korman who analyzed such programs on a national scale found that "each of these industrial firms [which] incorporated the 'Y's program for immigrant workers with their welfare and safety efforts integrated it with their attempts to discipline their employees." In Gary, US Steel not only used the usual Robert units, but also taught special technical courses. The plan auditiorium, library and classrooms were in full use during evenings and sometimes during the day. *Gary Works Circle* concluded that the "far-reaching and great benefit derived by the 1200 employees in attendance at both the technical classes in steel-making and the classes in English for our foreign-born is beyond estimate."[7]

The corporation supplemented formal Americanization classes with the latest in media instruction. The US Steel Safety Committee produced a movie widely shown to steel workers in Gary and in fifteen other cities. Officially it purported to illustrate safety devices but the *US Steel Corp. Bulletin* clearly indicated the film's thrust. "It depicted an ignorant peasant, who if he had remained in his native land, never would have risen above the

---

6 David Brody, *Labor in Crisis, The Steel Strike of 1919* (Philadelphia: Lippincott, 1965), p. 47; no title, *Gary Works Circle*, 1918, p. 7.

7 U.S. Steel Corporation Committee of Safety, *Bulletin*, Dec. 1916, pp. 52-53; Gerd Korman, *Industrialization, Immigrants, and Americanizers, A View from Milwaukee, 1866-1921* (Madison: State Historical Society of Wisconsin, 1967), pp. 159-60. Gerd Korman, "Americanization at the Factory Gate," *Industrial and Labor Relations Review* (1965), pp. 339-40; "Safety and Welfare," *Gary Works Circle*, May 1918, p. 2.

dull worthless level of his surroundings." He went to work at Gary Works, attended corporation classes, and engaged in "innocent amusements in plenty at the clubhouse or at the YMCA." The firm did provide some material concerning safety devices: "to his astonishment he found numerous safety appliances were installed to make his work as free from danger as possible." Perhaps the crusading atmosphere of wartime made such an approach seem reasonable. US Steel echoed the sentiments of the country at large when it considered the Americanization of Polish and other immigrant workers as a "national problem of vital importance" which had to be met to achieve "a hundred per-cent America."[8]

Management tried not only to Americanize the immigrant but also to stimulate a narrow patriotism. One can only guess at the results of such campaigns. Undoubtedly, massive flag-waving demonstrations and propaganda films have their effects. In addition, the corporation's patriotic claims went virtually unopposed in the city's press, church sermons, and local labor literature. No one wanted to be declared traitorous. Yet, it is still impossible to measure the result and to separate the effect of US Steel from other forces promoting American nationalism. Historian David Brody has suggested that the patriotic campaigns had their effect, and by the war's end the workers "felt themselves of as well as in America." Not only did they believe the patriotic statements about liberty, democracy, and equality, but they felt they earned their acceptance in American society through hard work, physical sacrifice, and through the purchase of war bonds. This probably occurred, but it is difficult to substantiate. On the other hand, thousands of Polish Americans did attend local English, citizenship and technical US Steel classes yearly in Gary. That US Steel aided a large number of Poles in perfecting English and preparing for naturalization is quite obvious.[9]

In a sense, then, the Americanization program was a success; nevertheless, Gary's spokesmen for organized labor did not hold it in high regard. Labor did not oppose the corporation's Americanization program as such, but argued that "It has been proven beyond doubt that the best [Americanization] method to pursue is to pay American wages and grant American conditions of work." The *Central Labor Union News* pointed out that as soon as the war had curtailed the nation's labor supply and wages therefore rose, immigrant workers "became owners of homes, demanded the

8 "Motion Pictures," U.S. Steel Corporation Committee of Safety, *Bulletin*, 1918, pp. 5-6; Korman, "Americanization," p. 414; U.S. Steel Corporation, *Bulletin*, Dec. 1918, p. 95.

9 Brody, *Steel Workers in America*, p. 190.

food of an American, [and] bought good clothes." This was the kind of Americanization that counted, according to organized labor. After labor's loss of the 1919 steel strike the city's labor spokesmen declared, "Mr. Gary does not want the employees educated and Americanized. He does not want American standards to prevail in his industries or he would make them so." The *Central Labor Union News* argued that long hours of labor—a lack of time for study and recreation—were in fact antithetical to Americanization.[10]

The labor movement had its own interests and viewpoint regarding the immigrant and immigration. While diverse ethnic groups had jointly manned the picket lines, organized labor in Gary opposed continued large scale migration to the United States. The reason was economic; more workers meant a weaker bargaining position for those that were here. The *Central Labor Union News* asked: "Can this country absorb all this new labor without displacing those already employed . . . is this labor to be used to reduce wages?" Although the labor paper claimed it did not oppose immigrants, but "their exploitation by the industrial barons," it did call for "Just and wholesome laws . . . to prevent immigration to this country beyond the ability of the country to furnish employment for them." The *News* was likewise concerned that a flood of oriental immigrants might replace any lessening of the European tide.[11] But the *Central Labor Union News*, as the organ for the Central Labor Union of Lake County, also supported the values and aspirations of Gary's working class Poles and of other immigrants. It published articles stressing their heritage in the United States, urged immigrant workers to avail themselves of free government-sponsored English language programs, suggested that English should be used more at home, supported the struggle for Irish independence, opposed politically motivated deportations and generally defended the rights and the image of the foreign-born.[12]

Organized labor also stimulated Americanization in another, less overt, but perhaps more lasting way—through labor solidarity. To form a union and engage in a strike (as Gary's steel workers did in 1919), meant that workers of various nationalities had to work closely together in building an effective organization. The Union, for example, attempted to diminish Polish and Russian

10 *Gary Central Labor Union News*, Sep. 14, 1919, Mar. 7, 1920, Oct. 19, 1919.

11 *Ibid.*, Oct. 10, 1920, Aug. 17, 1917, Nov. 28, 1920, May 4, 1919, May 11, 1919, July 4, 1920.

12 *Ibid.*, Mar. 21, 1920, Oct. 14, 1919, May 20, 1920, Oct. 5, 1919, Nov. 21, 1920, Sep. 26, 1920, Ap. 18, 1920, July 6, 1919, Nov. 23, 1919.

differences which, over the centuries, had become imbedded in their cultures, (as well as Turkish-Greek and Serbian-Croatian differences). If workers could not set aside, at least temporarily, their ethnic based antagonism, management would easily continue to divide and control them. Once the worker planned and worked together for common union goals suspicions could lessen and myths could erode. As a Gary labor activist put it, "all were involved in a common cause. Working conditions prevailed above nationality conflict and antagonisms." Moreover, unionization and the strike taught immigrant workers much about American society.[13]

As a result of the 1919 steel strike many workers became permanently committed to unionism (although it took another fifteen years to successfully organize Gary's steel mills), served on union committees, and learned how unionism operated—not just in Gary, but in other parts of the country as well. They learned something of political procedures as well. Gary's union meetings were democratic; anyone could speak and the majority ruled, making a knowledge of parliamentary procedure necessary. The workers thus experienced how government was supposed to work in American society at large.

If organization helped introduce workers to local democracy and brought ethnic groups together, it also created fissures. US Steel imported southern blacks and Mexicans as strike breakers. It was long remembered by the immigrants of the city. Following the strike the *Central Labor Union News* attempted to heal some of the wounds inevitably resulting from the use of strike breakers. It deplored the Chicago race riots, and pointed out that "Only the poor white man and the poor black man suffer and die in these conflicts and nothing is gained." It continually pressed the argument that "Better by far that the white worker and the black worker join forces, each respecting the rights of the other, and work for the common good." It attacked politicians for "trying to spread race dissension" and merchants who "placed signs in their places of business which read 'White Trade Only!'" It vigorously told its primarily white readers that organized labor opposes this attitude. "Organized labor is for the colored worker and will support his every move for the advancement of his in-

13 *Ibid.*, Sep. 14, 1919; also, see David G. Saposs, "The Mind of the Immigrant Community in the Pittsburgh District," in Interchurch World Movement, Commission of Inquiry, *Public Opinion and the Steel Strike* (New York: Harcourt, Brace and Howe, 1921), p. 232; William Z. Foster, *The Great Steel Strike and Its Lessons* (New York: B. W. Huebsch, 1920), pp. 199-204.

terests," claimed the *CLU News*. Surprisingly the newspaper occasionally admitted racism in the labor movement but realized that "the autocrat capitalist is courting . . . the black wage slave against the white wage slave," and therefore the "union with its regrettable and unjust policy of the past, claims repentance and now says to the Negro, 'Come into our ranks.' " The worker's leadership apparently learned that racial unity would be necessary to win labor conflicts in the future but they had to persuade both white and black workers.[14]

Undoubtedly the immigrant also learned of management's power—how 250,000 workers could be defeated by a handful of powerful entrepreneurs. They learned how their immigrant status could be used against them.[15] The corporation depicted the union effort in Gary, and in virtually every other steel town, as an alien, European radical conspiracy that only the misguided and slow thinking foreign born would support. To disseminate this message in Gary, US Steel used the friendly press and revived the "Loyal Americans League," a nationalistic vigilante group organized during the war. The League subtly threatened Gary's citizens of "foreign birth" by pointing out that "the same opportunities are open to them that are available to the citizens whose ancestors arrived on the Mayflower," but only if the newer immigrants "are law abiding." The League soon claimed the immigrant workers were not law abiding, as it allegedly uncovered radical plots in the city. Its fullpage advertisements in both of Gary's daily newspapers found that "the Bolsheviks, IWW, Red agitator and wandering trouble-maker is in Gary."[16]

Although the Gary *Evening Post* accepted League advertisements, it disassociated itself from the League's position, and it reported the subsequent strike fairly objectively. The Gary *Daily Tribune*, on the other hand, promoted an anti-immigrant, anti-radical hysteria. The *Tribune*, for example, reacted to a labor meeting commemorating the Haymarket Affair by claiming it would be held by communists committed to violent revolution. The immigrants had their "Red Sunday," as the paper called it,

---

14 Gary *Central Labor Union News*, Aug. 3, 1919, Feb. 8, 1920, Sep. 25, 1920, Oct. 1, 1920, Oct. 12, 1919.

15 For an excellent study of similar strikes (i.e., the focus of the study is Americanization), see Hyman Berman's unpublished study on labor solidarity available from the Minnesota Historical Society.

16 Gary *Daily Tribune*, Sep. 13, 1919, Sep. 24, 1919; Gary *Evening Post*, Sep. 24, 1919, Sep. 29, 1919, Sep. 30, 1919, Oct. 3, 1919, Oct. 6, 1919, Nov. 7, 1919, Sep. 21, 1919, Oct. 8, 1919, Sep. 19, 1919, Sep. 16, 1919, Sep. 18, 1919, Aug. 9, 1919, May 5, 1919, Oct. 14, 1919, Oct. 15, 1919, Oct. 27, 1919, Nov. 19, 1919, Nov. 21, 1919, Sep. 23, 1919, Sep. 20, 1919, Sep. 30, 1919, Oct. 1, 1919, Oct. 20, 1919. For labor's discussion of the repression, see *Strike Bulletin*, Sep. 25, 1919, Sep. 30, 1919; Gary *Central Labor Union News*, Sep. 21, 1919, Oct. 3, 1920, Sep. 21, 1919, May 11, 1919.

9

without incident. The next day the *Tribune* reported that "Rampant Bolshevism was throttled in Gary . . . but not without a show of force." It applauded the manhandling of Polish and other immigrant workers as they left a meeting hall. The "treat-'em-rough squad," as the paper called it, was aided by an assortment of law enforcement officials, and led by Captain H. S. Norton of US Steel.[17]

. The newspaper equated, as did US Steel, radicalism with immigrants. "It is in the radical element, many of them aliens," the paper claimed "that the Union organizers found a fertile field." The day the strike began the *Tribune* reported, it was "a noticeable fact that most of the foreign born people are staying away from the plants while a great percentage of the American employees, including the colored men, are at work as usual today."[18]

The corporations used ethnic tensions and latent American nativism, in all the major steel centers, to divide the strikers and create hostility toward them. "Good red-blooded Americans" were urged to vote against the strike at International Harvester's Steel plant in Wisconsin, and in Pittsburgh workers were told "This is no ordinary strike. Rather it must be looked upon as the diabolical attempt of a small group of radicals to disorganize labor and plant revolution in this country." The AFL director of the nation-wide strike later pointed out that the companies clearly used the anti-foreign issue as they instilled fears of an immigrant worker uprising. Writing in 1920, he criticized corporation spokesmen for, "calling the walkout a 'hunky strike,' they told the Americans that if it succeeded the latter would have to give over to the despised foreigners all the good jobs and shop privileges they enjoyed. Their slogan was 'Don't let the hunkies rule the mills'. They openly circulated handbills inciting to race war."[19]

Federal troops occupied Gary supposedly to suppress this foreign uprising. The army accepted the corporation's analysis and assumed that a radical conspiracy of Polish and other foreign born workers existed. General Wood, writing to US Steel's George W. Perkins, suggested that the country must promptly get "rid of the alien or naturalized Reds . . . . The destructive group is small but well organized." The *Evening Post* reported that Colonel Mapes informed the press that military "raids show conclusively that the steel strike in Gary was fostered by Reds

17 Quillen, "Industrial City," p. 330; Gary *Daily Tribune,* Sep. 22, 1919.
18 Gary *Daily Tribune,* Sep. 22, 1919.
19 Brody, *Labor in Crisis,* p. 158; Foster, *The Great Steel Strike,* p. 199.

and Revolutionists in the hope of plunging the entire country in a nationwide revolt against the United States government." Although Mapes later claimed he was misquoted he was widely reported as saying "if the military department revealed the evidence it has gathered in Gary the strike would break at once." He promised, in the words of the *Daily Tribune*, that "every red agitator will be rounded up by the end of the week" and admitted that "IWW and Bolshevik literature by tons is being confiscated." Such statements reflected both the League and the corporation position. When a congressional committee investigated the strike sometime later, the army could not substantiate the allegations it made in Gary. An intelligence officer, Lieutenant Donald C. Van Burne, did reveal the assumption that foreigners, radicals and strikers were closely inter-related. In answering a question concerning the proportion of foreign workers on strike in Gary, the officer answered, "a large majority are foreigners. In my examination, sir, of those suspect radicals that have been brought to me or come to my attention, I have not seen a single American-born."[20]

Apparently the military intuitively believed that Polish immigrants and other foreigners, supposedly radical, sponsored the strike. The army then suppressed strike activities, arrested union leaders, and harrassed the local labor movement—all because of an imagined conspiracy. The suppression had its effect. Local strikeleader John Fitzpatrick described and analyzed the military occupation. He pointed out that most immigrants were in awe of government authority. When strike leaders were deported, or imprisoned it lowered morale and lessened strike effectiveness. Morever, US Steel gave the impression that it was a government owned corporation, "that any one interfering with the steel company's affairs would be deported or sent to Fort Leavenworth." He described mill officials calling at strikers' homes with squads of soldiers lined up outside to aid the workers in deciding whether or not to return to work. After a long and bitter struggle, the strike in Gary and elsewhere failed. Thus the Polish American steelworkers learned of management's awesome power, and how US Steel could use the condition of being foreign born, and therefore supposedly unpatriotic, against the immigrant.[21]

Polish immigrants came to America and entered the packing plants, mines, and mills in large numbers. American industrialists,

---

20 Quillen, "Industrial City," p. 368; Gary *Evening Post*, Oct. 15, 1919, Oct. 27, 1919; Gary *Daily Tribune*, Oct. 27, 1919; Brody, *Labor in Crisis*, p. 135.
21 Foster, *The Great Steel Strike*, p. 170.

in part, built their empires on profits made by paying immigrant workers low wages for the longest work-day in the land. Although the economic revolt of industrial unionism did not succeed until the mid-1930s (with the CIO), immigrant workers, such as Gary's Poles, still profited from their work experience and they gained important knowledge about the society of which they were becoming a part. The industrial experience transmitted this knowledge consciously through formal Americanization classes, patriotic propaganda, and corporation programs officially designed for other purposes; and less consciously through daily labor, the process of unionization and the effects of strike activities. The experience of Polish workers in Gary clearly demonstrated to them the parameters of economic activism within industrial society and accustomed them to the technique of survival through struggle, sacrifice, and hard work.

THE TRANSFORMATION OF WORKING-CLASS ETHNICITY: CORPORATE CONTROL, AMERICANIZATION, AND THE POLISH IMMIGRANT MIDDLE CLASS IN BAYONNE, NEW JERSEY 1915-1925

By JOHN J. BUKOWCZYK*

Despite America's darkening anti-labor climate after 1900, the decade prior to U.S. entry into World War I showed that industrial protest and labor radicalism had not disappeared. These years witnessed great strikes at McKees Rocks (1909), Lawrence (1912), Patterson (1913), and Akron (1913), and also saw an upsurge of labor militance in countless less celebrated incidents.[1] The significant part of this record, however, is the strikers' identity. They were not the same native-born tradesmen who had acquired a reputation for protest in the late 19th century, but unskilled immigrants. These men and women who so dramatically reshaped the American working class during the mass-production years had often remained outside the American labor movement. But as their attitudes hardened and their numbers grew, immigrant workers now posed the first serious challenge

* A version of this article was presented at the annual meeting of the Social Science History Association in Nashville, Tennessee, Oct. 23, 1981. The author would like to thank Alan Dawley, Herbert Gutman, Daniel Leab, John DeBrizzi, William Reddy, Chris Johnson, Bob Zieger, and Tom Klug for their helpful discussion and comments at various stages. He would also like to thank Di Miles of the Reuther Library—Wayne State University, Sigmund Woytowicz, formerly of the Bayonne Public Library, as well as Ron Grele and the New Jersey Historical Commission, which awarded a grant-in-aid which made the research for this article possible.

[1] See David Brody, *Workers in Industrial America*: *Essays on the Twentieth Century Struggle* (New York, 1980), 37ff.; James R. Green, *The World of the Worker*: *Labor in Twentieth-Century America* (New York, 1980), 67ff.; David Montgomery, *Workers' Control in America*: *Studies in the History of Work, Technology, and Labor Struggles* (New York, 1979), 91ff.

0023-656x|83-84|2501–054

to America's industrial capitalist order since the great labor up-heaval of the 1890s.

In this immigrant working-class revolt, American labor there-fore found a unique opportunity, but by 1919 that opportunity simply had evaporated. The opportunism of AFL leaders during the War isolated radical, militant, and often spontaneous protest. Repression—by corporate security forces, extra-legal middle-class "citizens" groups, and the enforcement arms of the State—crushed protest. Finally, "welfare capitalism" diffused or coopted working-class dissent, while Americanization programs suffused American society with ruling-class values that suffocated work-ing-class resistance. As a result, union-organizing and working-class protest fell into disarray, and the 1920s became "lean years" for American labor.

The major theme in the history of class relations in the late 1910s and early 1920s was thus the re-establishment of corpo-rate control over a heavily immigrant, "re-made" American work-ing class. Accordingly, much of the historical literature on the period focuses on the external process of cooptation and repres-sion.[2] Subsidiary developments *within* immigrant working-class communities, however, also similarly affected working-class his-tory during the period. If we look inside those communities, we discover a complicated social world populated not only by work-ers but also by assorted small proprietors, petty entrepreneurs, and ethnic professionals who, taken together, constituted the im-migrant middle class in process of formation.[3] Sometimes allied with their working-class co-nationals but often coupled with cor-porate managers and civic officials, middle-class immigrants in order to advance their own political and economic interest ma-nipulated malleable ethnic symbols. In the 1910s and 1920s,

---

[2] See for example, Irving Bernstein, *The Lean Years: A History of the American Worker, 1920-1933* (Boston, 1960); William Preston, Jr., *Aliens and Dissenters: Federal Suppression of Radicals, 1903-1933* (Cambridge, MA, 1963); Stephen Meyer III, *The Five Dollar Day: Labor Management and Social Control in the Ford Motor Company, 1908-1921* (Albany, 1981); Alan Dawley, "The State Made Visible: Policing Work and Loyalty in the United States, 1917-22" (paper presented at the Third Annual North American Labor History Conference, Wayne State Univ., Detroit, Oct. 8, 1981).

[3] More properly speaking, it was the *petit-bourgeoisie*, a *lower* middle class. See Arno J. Mayer, "The Lower Middle Class as Historical Problem," *Journal of Modern History*, 47 (1975), 409-436; John J. Bukowczyk, "Polish Factionalism and the Formation of the Immigrant Middle Class in Brooklyn, 1880-1929," *Immigrant Communities in America*, ed. John Bodnar (Urbana, IL, forthcoming).

these middle-class immigrants created an ethnic variant of the "American Creed" which also helped contain new co-nationals' labor militance.

The place to investigate this development is the burgeoning industrial towns and cities of America's Second Industrial Revolution, whose mass-production industries attracted unskilled immigrants from Southern and Eastern Europe who streamed into the country in search of work in the years before the Great War. Bayonne was such a place—a bastion of heavy industry in New York harbor, the site of major labor turmoil between 1915 and 1916, its population heavily Polish and foreign-born.

From the outset, Polish immigration to Bayonne mirrored developments in Bayonne's industrial economy, particularly in the oil refining industry. Poles first arrived in significant numbers between 1880 and 1885, as refining operations in the city expanded. In 1883, managers mechanized a large refinery barrel factory and hired Poles, Slovaks, and Ruthenians to break a strike by American and Irish coopers. In the next fifteen years, this pattern recurred. In 1885 and again in 1901, more Poles won places after factory enlargement and mechanization and because they were "available and made satisfactory laborers"; while in 1903 and 1904, still more entered as strikebreakers. From an estimated two hundred families in 1900, the Polish population in Bayonne thus climbed to about nine hundred families ten years later. Along with the Slovaks, Poles dominated the refinery barrel factories and held many of the unskilled jobs in the refineries, in the stills, and in other Bayonne industries. Occupationally, they had made inroads into semi-skilled fields too—as helpers, machine operators, coopers, headers, and occasionally as foremen.[4]

Factory work represented a great change for the vast majority of Polish refining industry workers who had been farm la-

---

[4] Reportedly they came to exceed 20% of the work force in that industry. This figure, however, is only approximate, as it includes only those employees for whom the Immigration Commission secured information. It is likely that, compared to the Irish, Poles were disproportionately undercounted and that they accordingly accounted for a far larger percentage of the total refinery labor force than Commission figures indicate. See U.S. Senate, *Immigrants in Industries: Reports of the Immigration Commission*, 61 Cong., 2 sess., no. 633 (Washington, DC, 1911), XVI, 751, 760-762, hereafter cited as *Immigration Commission*; *Our Lady of Mount Carmel Church, Bayonne, New Jersey, U.S.A., Seventy-five Years, 1898-1973* (n.p., n.d.), 30-32.

borers or small peasant proprietors in the old country.[5] Though working conditions in the refining industry compared favorably to those in other industries during the period, immigrants accustomed to the intermittent rural workplace still found the conditions extraordinarily taxing. Most refinery workers labored nine hours a day six days a week, but men in the refining department followed staggered-hour, day-and-night shifts for a weekly average of 84 hours. Moreover, despite so-called "excellent" general sanitary conditions, the industry still took its toll in broken health and shortened lives. Lead burners in the sealing departments chronically suffered from "lead colic."[6] Still-cleaning, another occupation heavily populated by Poles, posed hazards so graphic that it attracted the attention of radical journalist John Reed, who described it in chilling detail in a *Metropolitan Magazine* article:

> A gang of two to five men . . . are set to clean each still. Wearing iron shoes, and wrapped in layers and layers of sacking, they enter the still in turns to break out the red-hot "cokes" left by the oil. In a temperature of over two hundred degrees they work furiously—a man can only stand it for three or four minutes at a time—from three to four hours a day. Almost every day someone collapses in the still and has to be rescued, sometimes with his clothing on fire. When they come out, after their spell, they strip and throw themselves down in the snow, if it be winter, or dash buckets of water over each other. One man said they looked like "boiled meat."

In order to refresh themselves, still-cleaners usually downed buckets of beer after they emerged from this noxious inferno. About the men who endured this harsh regimen, one doctor commented:

> the average working-life of a still-cleaner is *ten years*. Take a twenty-year-old Polish or Lithuanian peasant who has worked out of doors all his life; a big, strong, healthy animal—the finest human material in the world. At thirty he will be a bent old man, with white hair. At thirty-two he will be dead.[7]

---

[5] Of the Polish men in the oil refining households reported on by the Immigration Commission in 1910, fully 80% had been farm laborers and another 8% had been independent farmers before coming to the United States. See *Immigration Commission*, XVI, 777-778.

[6] *Ibid.*, XVI, 789, 800-802.

[7] John Reed, "Industrial Frightfulness in Bayonne," *Metropolitan Magazine* (Jan., 1917), n.p., clipping in Bayonne Public Library Clipping File, hereafter cited as BPLCF.

Peasant fatalism, reinforced by the dolorious world-view of Polish Roman Catholicism, helped inure Polish immigrant workers to these harsh conditions. But it was the purpose that many Poles had in mind when they emigrated which actually encouraged them to endure industrial hardship. Many young Galicians and Russian Poles left behind families in Poland who struggled to hold on to undersized parcels of land.[8] Less immigrant than migrant, these Poles considered their sojourn in American factories a temporary expedient. They fully intended to return to Poland and use their American wages to buy land or to bail out debt-ridden rural households.

Yet however transient, Polish immigrant workers in cities like Bayonne could not afford to overlook some features of factory labor and urban life. The very precariousness of conditions in industrial America continually threatened to wreck all of their plans, since injury, sickness, lay-off, discharge, wage cuts, and industrial depression could unexpectedly disrupt immigrant financial calculations at any time. Other chronic problems also worried even the temporary sojourner. Without financial resources or skills, unable to speak English, sometimes unable even to read or write, immigrant workers found themselves vulnerable even when employed.

Against this insecurity, Bayonne's Polish immigrant working people took shelter within their own growing community. For many, immigrant families helped cushion the shock of uncertainty in a new and alien world. Here the unmarried immigrant also sought refuge as boarder or lodger.[9] Other immigrant institutions also helped working-class immigrants keep body and soul together. In 1898, Bayonne Poles founded the Roman Catholic parish of Our Lady of Mount Carmel which henceforth would shape the identity of Bayonne's Polish community.[10] As in other Polish settlements, Bayonne's Polish Roman Catholic church be-

---

[8] In 1909 Bayonne's Polish population numbered about 5500; 40% of the Poles came from Russian Poland, 50% from Austrian Poland, and only 10% from German Poland. See *Immigration Commission*, XVI, 758.

[9] Of the Polish families selected for study in the Immigration Commission's general examination of employees in the oil refining industry, 42.3% took in boarders or lodgers. *Ibid.*, XVI, 795.

[10] *Our Lady of Mount Carmel Church, 1898-1973*, 31-32. Shortly after its founding, a schism in the parish resulted in the short-lived St. Mary Carmelite Roman Catholic Polish Church.

came the religious, cultural, and social center of gravity for Bayonne's Polish neighborhoods.[11]

Yet Polish immigrant workers in Bayonne did not sit back content and passively accept pastoral assistance, religious comfort, and parochial aid. Drawing on the principle of mutual aid which already had taken root in the Polish countryside in peasant land banks and village cooperative societies, Bayonne Poles joined together in fraternal benevolent associations ". . . for mutual moral and material assistance."[12] Finally, working-class immigrants discovered still another institution which could shield them from industrial hazards and a host of alien laws, practices, and customs. Bayonne's Polish newcomers depended heavily upon assistance from the settlement's "go-betweens," i.e., from immigrant shopkeepers and small-business proprietors.

Despite dire predictions by European social critics that the development of industrial capitalism would push the lower strata of the middle class—including artisans and shopkeepers—into the growing industrial proletariat, by the early 1900s this had not happened.[13] Many skilled crafts dropped precipitously during these years while the autonomy of surviving artisans and shopkeepers often declined. But on the whole, the spread of capitalism often multiplied rather than shrank opportunities for petty enterprise and small business. One of the ways in which this occurred involved international mass migration. The great influx of European migrants to an alien United States between the 1880s and the 1920s created myriad opportunities for immigrant entrepreneurs—shopkeepers, fraternal insurance operators, agents, liquor dealers, small-time bankers, and occasionally confidence men—who together constituted a separate stratum within immigrant working-class communities like Bayonne.

In Bayonne, several Polish small proprietors achieved local prominence early during the mass migration years. Stanley Fry-

[11] *Ibid.*, 30-38, 52. On the clergy and immigrant community leadership, also see John J. Bukowczyk, "Factionalism and the Composition of the Polish Immigrant Clergy," S. Blejwas and M. Biskupski, eds. *Pastor of the Poles: Polish American Essays*, Polish Studies Program Monograph No. 1 (New Britain, CT, 1982), 37-47.

[12] See Victor Greene, *For God and Country: The Rise of Polish and Lithuanian Ethnic Consciousness in America, 1860-1910* (Madison, 1975), 39. Cf. Frank Renkiewicz, ed., *The Poles in America, 1608-1972* (Dobbs Ferry, NY, 1973), 62.

[13] See Bukowczyk, "Polish Factionalism and the Formation of the Immigrant Middle Class," ms. pp. 10ff.

czynski operated a provisions business, while Ignatius Fordonski ran a grocery-butcher shop. Men like Konieczny, Anthony Dworzanski, Leon Pejkowski, and John Mydosh built another pioneer immigrant institution: the tavern or unassuming grocery-saloon.[14] While practicing their trade, these immigrant proprietors provided necessary social services for Polish newcomers. Customarily, immigrant small shop owners and saloonkeepers wrote and translated letters, extended credit and advice, held money, brokered jobs, found housing, arranged steamship tickets, and served as general "agent" for their inexperienced countrymen and countrywomen.[15] In return for loyal patronage, immigrant shops and small businesses thus helped shelter working-class immigrants. From this reciprocal exchange developed extensive patronage/clientage networks and habits of mutual obligation, certainly different from—yet nonetheless reminiscent of—the reciprocal obligations and duties which had tenuously knitted together peasant and landlord in 19th century rural Poland.

At many other points the lives of immigrant working people and Polish small proprietors overlapped and flowed together during the early years of settlement. Residential proximity, kinship connections, and intermarriage strengthened the ties between the two groups. The composition of the proprietary stratum also remained highly fluid as upwardly mobile immigrants occasionally tried their hand at small business and unsuccessful proprietors of economically fragile undertakings slipped back into working-class jobs. This fluidity caused a continual circulation between the two groups which encouraged mutual empathy and forged more tangible links in personnel as well. Finally, the nature of immigrant small business reinforced these other bonds. The fact that a lively trade presumed an easy interaction between shopkeeper and customer, i.e., required the cultivation of "good will," discouraged immigrant proprietors from noticing a social distance between themselves and their working-class clientele.[16] Yet de-

---

[14] *Bayonne Evening Times*, Nov. 20, 1959, Oct. 17, 1961, BPLCF; *Our Lady of Mount Carmel Church, 1898-1973*, 29, 33, 34.

[15] Victor Greene, "Poles," *Harvard Encyclopedia of American Ethnic Groups*, ed. S. Thernstrom (Cambridge, MA, 1980), 793.

[16] In middle-class areas, Richard Hoggart has observed, the shopkeeper "... assumes, in manner at least, a lower status than his customers...," but in working-class districts, "...the shopkeeper is among his own class, though his income may sometimes be above the average of the neighborhood." See Richard Hoggart,

spite these connections, a social distance did separate the two groups, and it grew wider as the immigrant economy matured.[17]

Differences in their social and cultural backgrounds distinguished Bayonne Polish proprietors from immigrant workers.[18] Though Poles from both the Russian-held and Austrian-held Polish partitions would eventually enter the proprietary stratum, in the early years of mass migration most proprietors were German Poles. As a group, immigrants from the German-held Polish partition possessed more property, a higher level of education, and greater social status than the Russian Poles and Austrian Poles who clustered disproportionately in unskilled working-class occupations. Subsequent differences between Polish proprietors and immigrant workers grew out of their market relationship. A situation wherein Polish working-class customers tried to buy as cheaply as possible while Polish proprietors struggled to squeeze profits from precariously undercapitalized small businesses was fraught with incipient economic—and perhaps class—tensions.[19] Finally, middle-class ends and immigrant working-class social and cultural forms also sometimes collided. Immigrant entrepreneurs who organized fraternal benevolent societies illustrate how this typically happened. They diverted these working-class associations to self-serving ends and sometimes transformed them into de facto insurance companies.[20]

As middle-class immigrants strove for political power within the immigrant settlement, however, they tried to narrow the gap which separated them from their working-class co-nationals. Middle-class Poles entered immigrant politics during the early days of Polish settlement in Bayonne when they challenged pastoral authority and pressed their own claims for political leadership. Vying for control over parish administration and finances, two

---

The Uses of Literacy: Aspects of Working-Class Life, with Special Reference to Publications and Entertainments (London, 1957), 54.

[17] Cf. John J. Bukowczyk, "Steeples and Smokestacks: Class, Religion, and Ideology in the Polish Immigrant Settlements in Greenpoint and Williamsburg, Brooklyn, 1880-1929" (unpublished PhD diss., Harvard Univ., 1980), 168-171.

[18] See *The World* (New York), June 27, 1926, BPLCF.

[19] Cf. Bukowczyk, "Steeples and Smokestacks," p. 169. On the general fragility of small businesses, see the essays in Stuart W. Bruchey, ed., *Small Business in American Life* (New York, 1980).

[20] See Frank Renkiewicz, "An Economy of Self-Help: Fraternal Capitalism and the Evolution of Polish America," C. Ward, *et. al.*, ed., *Studies in Ethnicity: The East European Experience in America*, East European Monographs, No. 73 (Boulder, CO, 1980), 71-91.

lay trustees led a move which split Our Lady of Mount Carmel parish in August 1898, a mere seven months after its founding. According to a parish source, the two trustees ". . . were big donors and didn't want to divest control of their investment to the bishop." That parish leaders who opposed Mount Carmel's pastor met at Konieczny's Tavern underscored the growing role which Polish saloonkeepers in particular had come to play in immigrant politics. Their role—and that of other immigrant small proprietors—would not diminish, despite the fact that the parish rebellion had dissolved by 1903.[21] Indeed, by the 1910s these middle-class immigrants had further widened their influence in the Polish settlement's economy and politics. They drew upon traditions of middle-class leadership transplanted from late 19th century Poland and exploited their control of community patronage/clientage networks. But they also capitalized on the rising popularity of secular Polish nationalist ideology during the pre-war period. Because Polish nationalism emphasized ties of common language, culture, and origins which all immigrants shared, it reinforced middle-class efforts at building a working-class clientele and political constituency within the immigrant settlement.[22]

In the early 1900s, middle-class Polish immigrants thus tried to transform immigrant working-class ethnicity. To working-class Poles, Polish ethnicity was a bundle of cultural values and attitudes, beliefs and practices—informed by class—which knitted together families, neighbors, and friends, shaped everyday life, and shielded them from the hostile industrial environment. Now middle-class Poles taught them that ethnicity could be something more. To the immigrant middle-class, ethnicity was also *ideology* —a set of ideas, progressive reformist principles, and political sympathies which could transcend everyday experience, overcome class, regional, and cultural differences, and mobilize working-class immigrant loyalties.

---

[21] In that year, the New Jersey Superior Court awarded contested property to the Mount Carmel loyalist faction. See *Our Lady of Mount Carmel Church, 1898-1973*, 31-32, 34. A similar conflict pitting saloonkeeper against pastor is discussed in John J. Bukowczyk, "The Immigrant 'Community' Reexamined: Political and Economic Tensions in a Brooklyn Polish Settlement, 1888-1894," *Polish American Studies*, 37 (1980), 5-16.

[22] See Bukowczyk, "Steeples and Smokestacks," chapts. six and seven.

As it evolved, Bayonne's Polish immigrant settlement may have seemed a self-contained system to the casual observer who walked its streets and alleys or who peered into its church, saloons, and shops. But having grown up as an appendage of Bayonne's refining industry, Polish Bayonne was hardly self-contained. The refineries affected virtually every aspect of immigrant working-class life, including relations between Bayonne's Polish workers and shopkeepers. Moreover, though subtleties in the way Poles used their culture and defined their ethnicity escaped refinery managers, the latter developed their own attitudes about the foreignness of their work force and how it fitted in with sound managerial practice and industrial efficiency.

Bayonne's industrial managers held contradictory attitudes about their foreign-born workers. Officially, the refineries frowned upon foreignness and sought ". . . to eventually have only English-speaking labor in the establishment." In practice, however, refinery operators tolerated the foreignness of their work force. Owing to a shortage of cheap, English-speaking labor, managers hired workers despite their inability to speak English and accepted job applicants regardless of nationality. But ethnic stereotypes still did influence employment decisions. Some employers considered the "Slav races . . . more efficient as unskilled labor" because of their "docility and submission to authority." A Bayonne barrel factory superintendent judged Poles "very satisfactory laborers," while the general manager of one refinery thought them "more intelligent" than Italians and hence "more desirable as semi-skilled laborers." Yet stereotypes did not always agree. The manager of another Bayonne refinery considered Poles "untrustworthy and unreliable." They

> . . . do not apply themselves intelligently and are apparently without ambition to increase their efficiency. Social and religious duties interfere with their work to some extent, and their low standards of living render them physically unable to perform hard-labor work.[23]

Bayonne refinery managers regarded ethnicity inconsistently during the mass migration years, but did share one point in common: their toleration of foreignness evolved into a policy of control and manipulation. The Immigration Commission reported

---

[23] *Immigration Commission*, XVI, 800, 802, 805-806.

contradictory findings, that the refineries worked "... mixed gangs in all departments, as clannishness is thereby prevented, and ... better work secured," but that "the same races of immigrants ... [were rarely] employed in more than one establishment." Yet regardless which strategy they followed, managers sought to use ethnicity to deter workers from uniting. Into the 1910s, their efforts succeeded. Ethnically mixed gangs of newer immigrants produced "little association among races outside of work." Even more pronounced divisions separated the newer immigrants from the older immigrants and native-born workers. While the new immigrants lived in Bayonne's factory districts, the native-born and older immigrants—skilled and better paid—commuted to Bayonne from Newark, Jersey City, Elizabethport, and the surrounding area. Not surprisingly, the oil refinery worker households studied by the Immigration Commission in 1909 recorded a scant twelve union members—not a single Pole—while reports characterized the industry as "little affected by industrial disturbances."[24]

The corporate strategy of divide-and-conquer notwithstanding, aspects of Polish working-class culture already had helped make the immigrants into tractable, docile, obedient workers.[25] Transplanted peasant fatalism; Roman Catholic attitudes about suffering, martyrdom, and salvation; deep attachments to family and household which produced a preoccupation with "steady"

---

[24] *Ibid.*, XVI, 757, 800, 802, 804.

[25] In recent years, the literature on working-class Polish immigrants in the 1980-1920 period has grown appreciably. See, for example, Victor R. Greene, *The Slavic Community on Strike: Immigrant Labor in Pennsylvania Anthracite* (Notre Dame, IN, 1968); Greene, "The Polish American Worker to 1930: The 'Hunky' Image in Transition," *The Polish Review*, 21 (1976), 63-78; Edward Pinkowski, "The Great Influx of Polish Immigrants and the Industries They Entered," Frank Mocha ed., *Poles in America: Bicentennial Essays*, (Stevens Point, WI, 1978), 303-370; Dominic A. Pacyga, "Crisis and Community: The Back of the Yards 1921," *Chicago History*, 6 (1977), 167-176; Pacyga, "Villages of Steel Mills and Packinghouses: The Polish Worker on Chicago's South Side, 1880-1921," paper presented at Conference on Poles in North America sponsored by the Multicultural History Society of Ontario and the University of Toronto, Toronto, Canada (Oct. 23-25, 1980); Frank Renkiewicz, "Polish American Workers, 1880-1889," S. Blejwas and M. Biskupski, eds., *Pastor of the Poles: Polish American Essays*, 116-136; John Bodnar, Michael Weber, and Roger Simon, "Migration, Kinship, and Urban Adjustment: Blacks and Poles in Pittsburgh, 1900-1930," *Journal of American History*, 66 (1979), 548-565; Bodnar, Weber, and Simon, *Lives of Their Own: Blacks, Italians, and Poles in Pittsburgh, 1900-1960* (Urbana, IL, 1982), *passim*; John J. Bukowczyk, "Polish Rural Culture and Immigrant Working Class Fornation," *Polish American Studies*, 41 (Autumn, 1984), forthcoming.

work; and political interests directed away from conditions in America and toward affairs in partitioned Poland all tended to blunt class resentments among immigrant workers and to foster an acceptance of the industrial status quo.[26] Rapid turnover, return migration, and considering industrial labor in America a momentary opportunity or a temporary cross to bear had a similar effect. Yet not all such "traditional" and migrant attitudes meshed so easily with the industrial capitalist order. The Poles' belief in a customary social right to have work challenged patterns of cyclical unemployment and arbitrary discharge which played such a pivotal role in the American industrial economy of the period. Community cohesiveness likewise threatened managerial authority. Finally, a host of transplanted rural values and practices—viz., the observance of religious holidays, "pre-industrial" work rhythms, alcohol consumption—continually interfered with the factory regimen. As a result, beneath the apparent calm which prevailed in Bayonne's oil refineries subterranean tensions remained a more or less constant feature of immigrant working-class employment throughout the early decades of Polish migration to the city.[27]

By the early 1910s, the changing character and composition of Bayonne's working-class Polish immigrant community soon caused these chronic tensions to erupt. First, by the 1910s, the temporary character of Polish settlement in Bayonne had begun to fade as more and more immigrants sent for families or married, joined the parish, formed organizations, and otherwise set down roots in the oil refining city. When the outbreak of the World War in 1914 cut off the possibility of re-emigration, even more Polish sojourners postponed—or abandoned—plans to return to Poland. In the process, temporary migrants who readily had endured transitory hardships now suddenly became permanent settlers with a newfound concern about the character of the

[26] See Renkiewicz, "Polish American Workers"; John Bodnar, "Immigration and Modernization: The Case of Slavic Peasants in Industrial America," *Journal of Social History*, 10 (1976), 44-67; Bodnar, "Immigration, Kinship, and the Rise of Working-Class Realism in Industrial America," *Journal of Social History*, 14 (1980), 45-65; John J. Bukowczyk, "Polish Rural Culture."
[27] See Renkiewicz, "Polish American Workers;" Bukowczyk, "Polish Rural Culture;" Lawrence D. Orton, *Polish Detroit and the Kolasinski Affair* (Detroit, 1981), 174-180; Herbert G. Gutman, "Work, Culture, and Society in Industrializing America, 1815-1919," *American Historical Review*, 78 (1973), 531-588.

work and the conditions of employment and a deeper stake in community life.[28]

Second, while migrants from rural Poland had little acquaintance with radical ideologies or progressive politics in the 1880s, the opposite held true for post-1890 migrants. Leaving a rural society now gripped by popular agitation for peasant land reform, strikes by agricultural wage laborers, and a full-fledged rural socialist movement, they carried an assortment of democratic and egalitarian notions which hardly fitted contemporary —and latterday—stereotypes. Moreover, after the repression of the Revolution of 1905 by tsarist authorities in Russian Poland, Polish settlements in America also received an infusion of political radicals, trade unionists, and insurrectionaries who had fled literally for their lives. That many settled in New York City and environs is evident from the sudden rise of the Polish left there during the subsequent period. The Alliance of Polish Socialists (*Zwiazek Socjalistów Polskich*), founded in 1896, experienced a burst of support after 1905. Polish socialists also played a leading role in the Polish nationalist Committee for National Defense (*Komitet Obrony Narodowej*), which operated between 1912 and 1914 with much of its strength in the New York area. Blending Polish nationalism with a radical social and economic program, these Polish leftists appealed strongly to other working-class Poles and helped galvanize workplace tensions and class resentments into an upsurge of labor militance in the 1910s.[29]

In Bayonne, the spark which exploded the city's vaunted "industrial peace" soon came at the Standard Oil Company's works. Because company foremen functioned virtually as independent labor contractors, with broad power over hiring, discipline, workpace, working conditions, and firing, supervision in the plant operated on a direct, personal, and often arbitrary basis.[30] Polish

---

[28] Cf. Michael J. Piore, *Birds of Passage: Migrant Labor and Industrial Societies* (New York, 1979), 112-113, 154-157.

[29] A less nationalistic Polish socialist body, the Polish Section of the Socialist Party of America, also was active during these years. See Stefan Kieniewicz, *The Emancipation of the Polish Peasantry* (Chicago, 1969), 214-220, 226-235; Bukowczyk, "Polish Rural Culture;" Renkiewicz, "Polish American Workers," 123; Victor Greene, "Poles," 795; Greene, "The Polish American Worker," 78.

[30] George Sweet Gibb and Evelyn H. Knowlton, *The Resurgent Years, 1911-1927; History of Standard Oil Company (New Jersey)* New York, Vol. II, 135, 139-141.

migrants from an often still quasi-feudal Polish countryside might have accepted such supervisory relations as commonplace. But denied customary reciprocal rights in the workplace which typically had helped contain class tensions between laborer and landlord in rural Poland, immigrant workers now found the "pull-and-tug" of class relations in the Bayonne refinery brutal, capricious, and very lopsided: foremen took far more than they gave in return.[31] Polish immigrant workers chronically brooded about "being fleeced out of a portion of their earnings by unscrupulous 'bosses' and 'supervisors.'"[32] Ethnic differences between immigrant workers and native-born—often Irish—foremen only aggravated the problem, as did the intense wartime speed-up then underway in the plant.[33] Thus primed, Bayonne's industrial powderkeg merely awaited a match. On July 15, 1915, the heavily Polish gang of still-cleaners at the Standard Oil works complained that they were continually "cursed out" by the foremen, subjected to physical intimidation and ethnic abuse, and that, "to settle grudges, foremen were detaining cleaners in the hot stills, with temperatures up to 250°F." When refinery officials refused to hear their grievances, the still-cleaners—about 100 men—walked out, to be joined a few days later by about 900 workers in the cooperage and barrel departments.[34]

For a while, affairs in Bayonne hung in the balance. Intransigent refinery managers imported a crew of strikebreakers—mostly Italians—while the strikers, grown more resolute, began to organize. Soon picketing and similar grievances at other Bayonne plants spread the strike to the Tide Water Oil, Vacuum Oil, and Bergen Point Chemical companies. With 1500 of its 5000 employees now out, Standard Oil shut down its Bayonne operations on July 20. Later in the day, striking workers—joined by their wives—stoned local police guarding the plant and start-

[31] Renkiewicz, "Polish American Workers," 117.
[32] Our Lady of Mount Carmel Church, 1898-1973, 49.
[33] Immigration Commission, XVI, 759.
[34] Strikers reportedly demanded "a fifty-hour week, time and a half for overtime, a 15 per cent increase in wages, and no discrimination because of strike activity." See Stuart Chase, A Generation of Industrial Peace: Thirty Years of Labor Relations at Standard Oil Company (N.J.) (1947), 9-10; Gibb and Knowlton, Resurgent Years, Vol. II, 142. For recent accounts of the strike, also see George Dorsey, "The Bayonne Refinery Strikes of 1915-1916," Polish American Studies, 33 (1976), 21ff; Philip S. Foner, On the Eve of America's Entrance into World War I, 1915-1916: History of the Labor Movement in the United States (New York, 1982), Vol. VI, 41-64.

26

ed a fullscale riot. That evening a second—smaller—riot ensued after striking workers attacked a Polish non-striker. Shortly, an American Federation of Labor representative and Frank Tannenbaum, an IWW organizer, arrived in Bayonne to assist the strikers. The Bayonne refinery strike had entered a new phase.[35]

With its major factories closed and its streets swollen with striking Poles and other immigrant workers, Bayonne now faced open revolt by its working class; and its corporate and civic authorities responded decisively. The fact that Pierre Garven, counsel for the New York office of Standard Oil, also served as Bayonne's mayor, already guaranteed that the Bayonne Police Department would vigorously aid any corporation attempt to break the strike.[36] When the police proved inadequate to the task and their use seemed politically unwise, however, Mayor Garven himself urged refinery officials to hire private armed guards to protect company property and help pacify the city. Upon Garven's advice, Standard engaged the nefarious Pearl L. Bergoff, a recent resident of Bayonne and proprietor of a notorious New York City "industrial service" firm. Bergoff already had six labor spies planted at Standard Oil. Now Bergoff furnished Standard with a barge full of guards, guns, and ammunition and dispatched a second contingent to Tide Water.

For the next four days, Bergoff's private army of so-called "nobles" terrorized the strikers by sniping at pickets and launching armed sorties into the assembled crowds. No fewer than five strikers died and several more sustained gunshot wounds before the corporate reign of terror at the hands of Bergoff's "armed thugs" finally subsided. In the end, force—and persuasion—applied from another quarter finally restored order to the city of Bayonne. Hudson County Sheriff Eugene K. Kinkead broke up the strikers' organization, beat up their young socialist leader Jeremiah Baly, dispersed Bergoff's forces, arrested IWW organizer Tannenbaum, and banned the sale of the radical news-

---

[35] Dorsey, "Bayonne Refinery Strikes," 22-24. Tannenbaum, a 22-year old busboy and member of the Waiters' International Union, had only recently led an IWW drive to organize the unemployed during the winter of 1914. See Philip S. Foner, *The Industrial Workers of the World, 1905-1917*; *History of the Labor Movement in the United States* (New York, 1965), Vol. IV, 444.

[36] Contrast this with the 1939 Chrysler strike in Detroit, when the Hamtramck police responded to pressure from the city's heavily Polish-American working-class electorate and sided with the strikers. See *Union Town* (Detroit, n.d.), 21.

paper the *New York Call.*[37] Yet Kinkead also tried to mollify the strikers by manipulating ethnic sentiments. "I told them they were Poles and had suffered much at the hands of Russia," the Sheriff said, "and that I was an Irishman and my people had suffered at the hands of England." Also citing their common religion, Kinkead tried to make the strikers "feel that he was one of them."[38] Despite the absence of federal mediators, with whom Standard Oil refused to deal, Kinkead's iron fist, silver tongue, and relative impartiality brought the immigrant strikers back to work. Soon thereafter they received part of the wage increase they had sought—at a time when earnings of the Bayonne plant were rising from $332,000 in 1914 to $6,552,000 the following year.[39]

The way corporate and civic officials handled the 1915 refinery strike reflected the underside of their attitudes about immigrants. Moved by class consciousness, race hatred, and simple fear and convinced that outside agitators were manipulating ignorant foreigners, Bayonne's ruling elite resolved to teach the immigrant a lesson. The instructions which Standard Oil General Manager George B. Gifford gave Pearl Bergoff amply revealed the refiners' intentions. "Get me two hundred and fifty husky men who can swing clubs," Gifford told Bergoff. "If they're not enough, get a thousand or two thousand. I want them to march up East Twenty-second Street [Bayonne] through the guts of Polacks."[40] Bayonne's police harbored their own resentments against the striking Poles. One graphic strike vignette

---

[37] Dorsey, "Bayonne Refinery Strikes," 23-27; Edward Levinson, *I Break Strikes!*, reprint edition (New York: Arno Press, 1969), 158, 161-164, 166-168; Chase, *A Generation of Industrial Peace*, 9; Gibb and Knowlton, *Resurgent Years*, Vol. II, 141-142, 144-146. According to historian Philip Foner: "After his release from prison, Tannenbaum played little role in the IWW. The last mention of him as a participant in an IWW activity is in *The New York Times* of Sept. 2, 1915. He is listed along with Helen Gurley Flynn and Alexander Berkman as having been prevented from addressing a meeting of 1500 employees of the Standard Oil and Tidewater companies. Following this experience, Tannenbaum was helped to complete his education by several philanthropic-minded people. He abandoned the labor movement and later became a professor at Columbia University, specializing in labor relations, Latin America, and antiradicalism." See Foner, *Industrial Workers of the World*, Vol. IV, 448.

[38] *Survey*, 34 (Aug. 7, 1915), 415. Along the same vein, Kinkead had his deputies remove their hats when they passed Bayonne's Greek Catholic Church, the place of worship of many strikers. See *Literary Digest*, 51 (Aug. 7, 1919), 257.

[39] Gibb and Knowlton, *Resurgent Years*, Vol. II, 141-142, 144-146.

[40] Levinson, 162.

described how officers wrecked a Polish saloon frequented by strikers. According to the account, one policeman ". . . amused himself by shooting holes in framed paintings of the Kings of Poland and put a bullet through *the picture of Kosciuszko*— the Pole who fought so gallantly in the American Revolution."[41] This climate of repression affected Bayonne's foreign- and native-born residents alike. The United States Commission on Industrial Relations called the collapse of the strike "a complete victory for the Standard Oil Company as to its vital policies."[42] Even more important to bolstering Standard Oil's power in the city, the strike deepened anti-immigrant attitudes. Native-born residents interviewed in 1916 divided Bayonne's population into two classes: " 'white' men and foreigners."[43]

But repression failed to teach the Poles a lesson which would stick. The following year, in October 1916, the now far better organized immigrant workers again struck Standard and Vacuum, protesting wages, hours, the high cost-of-living, and abuses by some of the foremen.[44] In milder form, workers, officials, and police repeated the 1915 scenario. Once again, force eventually ended the strike. Yet the 1916 strike showed that force alone could not prevent still another such outbreak. The chronic volatility of the immigrants, Bayonne authorities believed, irrepressibly stemmed from their very foreignness.

Despite its racist overtones, a kernel of truth lay at the heart of this observation about immigrant working-class ethnicity: it did underpin both refinery strikes. As evident from the list of strike casualties and from the fact that *Poles* began both strikes, common language and culture fostered common action and widespread community support. In turn, the refineries' tactic of engaging non-Poles—mostly Italians—as strikebreakers reinforced the social boundaries of the ethnic working-class community. Class and ethnicity overlapped to provide a powerful bond for Bayonne's strikers which realized the worst fears of the refinery managers. "Clannishness"—cohesiveness arising from shared

---

[41] Reed, "Industrial Frightfulness in Bayonne," n.p.
[42] Levinson, 169.
[43] John A. Fitch, "The Explosion at Bayonne," *The Survey* (Oct. 21, 1916), 62; Dorsey, "Bayonne Refinery Strikes," 28.
[44] Gibb and Knowlton, *Resurgent Years*, Vol. II, 151-152; Dorsey, "Bayonne Refinery Strikes," 28-30; Levinson 169-170.

ethnic culture—was dangerous. Finally, those Polish strikers who wore buttons which read "Liberty for Poland" showed that rising Polish nationalism—viz., ethnicity-as-ideology—also was dangerous.[45] Instead of diverting immigrant attentions abroad, Polish nationalism—when fused with radical ideologies like socialism and populism—buttressed immigrant working-class militance here.

This working-class understanding of ethnicity wrenched social relations within Bayonne's Polish settlement. Striking Poles demanded that their middle-class countrymen and their priests live up to ideals of "community" cohesion and mutual obligation on which their patronage/clientage networks rested. During the 1915 strike, workers fired at Rev. Sigismund Swider, pastor of Our Lady of Mount Carmel parish; by urging strikers to return to work, he had breached community solidarity.[46] They also demanded that refinery officials dismiss ". . . a foreman, a fellow Pole named Anthony Jozwicki, whom they regarded as one of the most brutal bosses *and* who refused to go out with them." [Italics added][47] Jozwicki's *real* crime was not brutality, for that the men would have forgiven. Jozwicki's unforgiveable offense was disregarding the claims of ethnic cohesiveness which should have obliged him to go out. By demanding his dismissal, striking Poles insisted that mutual duties and obligations should accompany common nativity and should constrain foremen who expected obedience from their men.

Yet not all of Bayonne's immigrant middle class violated this assumed trust. Rushing to catch up with their radicalized working-class countrymen, Bayonne's Polish shopkeepers and professionals avoided Swider's and Jozwicki's mistake and supported the strikers. Local merchants extended credit which sustained the strikers' families throughout the conflict. Paul Supinski, a Polish attorney from neighboring Jersey City, translated speeches into Polish, presided over a strike meeting, and represented his striking countrymen to refinery officials. Polish saloonkeepers also lent critical support. In both years, strikers met at saloonkeeper John Mydosh's hall, while several saloonkeepers like Anthony

---

[45] Reed "Industrial Frightfulness in Bayonne." n.p.
[46] Gibb and Knowlton. *Resurgent Years*, Vol. II, 146.
[47] Dorsey, "Bayonne Refinery Strikes," 22.

Dworzanski actually helped lead the strikes. Dworzanski sat on the 1916 strike committee as a Standard Oil worker, while also running a grocery store and tavern business in the city. After the strike, the ambitious and upwardly mobile Dworzanski inspired the founding of St. Anthony Society for Mutual Aid and Benefit, a fraternal insurance operation which members appropriately named after his own patron saint. During the 1916 strike, police recognized the role of men like Dworzanski and arrested John Mydosh's son and five other saloonkeepers on charges of inciting to riot.[48]

Perhaps feelings of ethnic solidarity motivated these Polish proprietors and professionals, but they also stood to gain by supporting the strike. First, by backing the strikers middle-class Poles showed up Bayonne's Polish pastor and thereby won another small victory in their long-standing competition for political and social authority within the immigrant settlement. Second, by siding with the workers middle-class Poles also countered the small but vocal Polish socialist minority that had challenged their leadership in the last few years. Finally, supporting the strike reaffirmed ethnic ties which redounded to their economic benefit. At the time of the strikes, Polish saloonkeepers and small proprietors faced stiff competition from Irish-owned saloons and from Jewish immigrants "extensively engaged in small business enterprises."[49] As a result of the strikes, however, the precarious market position of Bayonne's Polish businessmen improved measurably.

The middle-class Poles' market position improved in two ways. First, strikers attacked the Poles' competitors. We may never know for certain why rioters sacked one Bayonne business street during the 1915 refinery strike. Perhaps rumors that one saloonkeeper harbored company guards and tipped off police touched off the violence. But the identity of the storeowners whose businesses were wrecked suggests that class antagonism alone did not motivate the rioters. Four men owned saloons which fell victim to the riot: Samuel Schwartzberg, Richard Flood, David Weinberg, and Samuel Greenberg—three Jews and an Irishman, ostensibly.

[48] *Ibid.,* 22, 24, 25, 27, 30; *Bayonne Evening Times,* Oct. 17, 1961, and *Bayonne Evening Review,* Oct. 14, 1916, BPLCF; *Our Lady of Mount Carmel Church, 1898-1973,* 50.
[49] *Immigration Commission,* Vol. 16, 759, 762.

Jacob Cohen, owner of a drygoods store which rioters sacked, obviously also was Jewish.[50] Interestingly, crowds attacked not a single Polish business during the two strikes. The prevalence of Jewish-owned businesses in Bayonne may account for this pattern of violence, but not entirely. Historic tensions between Poles and Jews in Poland conditioned immigrant working-class behavior. The fact that Pearl Bergoff and probably at least one of his lieutenants, John ("Jew Stoney") Speiser, both were part Jewish exacerbated intergroup resentments.[51]

Secondly, supporting the strikes aided Polish businessmen in a positive way: it strengthened their own claim to immigrant working-class patronage as against their Jewish competition. The rumor that Jewish lawyers conspired with Bayonne saloonkeepers to fleece arrested immigrant strikers of their savings in a bailbond racket may explain why mobs sacked Samuel Greenberg's saloon: he was one of Bayonne's notorious "bail sharks."[52] But it also may explain why strikers selected Paul Supinski of Jersey City instead of a local lawyer to serve as their counsel. Middleclass Poles were harnessing both ethnic *and* religious ties to cordon off immigrant business patronage during these turbulent years.[53]

Out of the two refinery strikes, ethnicity thus emerged as a far more complicated thing than Bayonne's refinery managers may have anticipated when they hired the first Pole into their plants in the 1880s. While ethnic differences did still divide the work force, foreignness proved increasingly difficult to manipulate. In both strikes, unskilled immigrants like the Poles be-

---

[50] *Bayonne Evening Review*, Oct. 10, 1916, BPLCF.

[51] Levinson, *I Break Strikes!* 35, 165. Bergoff was born of a Dutch Protestant mother and a German Jewish father.

[52] A proverb said to have circulated among Bayonne's "regular"—presumably non-Polish—attorneys held: "When a Polak comes around, get his money—or somebody else will." This professional tip found ready application in a bailbond racket allegedly used by Jewish lawyers to defraud immigrant strikers. According to one strike account, immigrants often carried their bank books with them "as a sort of 'talisman'." When arrested immigrants summoned Jewish lawyers, the latter secured the immigrants' release, but only for the price of the bank book. The practice, reportedly termed "stripping the bank-roll," sometimes netted fabulous sums, with one Pole losing $225 and another a staggering $450 to the bailbond gimmick. But the lawyers profitted less than would appear, for they allegedly shared their proceeds with co-conspirators—none other than Bayonne saloonkeepers—called in to provide the actual cash which secured the prisoners' release. See Reed, "Industrial Frightfulness in Bayonne."

[53] For a full discussion of this issue, see Bukowczyk, "Steeples and Smokestacks," chapt. six.

haved far more militantly than English-speaking workers.[54] Since it heightened labor unrest, Bayonne authorities therefore concluded, foreignness was a dangerous thing which they had to render harmless.

In the wake of the 1916 strike, Standard Oil managers instituted a wide range of welfare capitalist measures designed to wean immigrant workers from virulent foreignism. Wage increases, coupled with accident, sickness, and death provisions, sought to convince the immigrants that "capital and industry are partners" and led one local newspaper to conclude that Bayonne stood "on the threshold of becoming a workmen's paradise."[55] Standard also reformed its supervisory apparatus, organizing a "Foremen's Club" in order to impart loyalty and professionalism to critical frontline personnel and introducing its celebrated "Industrial Representation Plan." Designed at the behest of John D. Rockefeller, Jr., after the infamous Ludlow Massacre of 1914, the Industrial Representation Plan established a company union, work rules, a progressive system of fringe benefits, and a formal grievance procedure.[56]

To augment these efforts, Standard also sharpened ideological weapons. In September 1920, Standard established *The Messenger*, a company magazine "published every Saturday in the interest of the Employees of the Bayonne Refinery." Trying to build a rapport between labor and management, *The Messenger* inculcated a work ethos into working-class readers. Front-page editorials railed against "The Chronic Kicker," "The Anonymous Letter," and the "Industrial Drifter," while the magazine constantly extolled a version of the Protestant ethic: "Don't let any bewhiskered Bolshevik tell you that there is a royal road to success or that we can achieve success without work." In a notice for a corporation-sponsored recreational event, *The Messenger* revealed how Standard Oil viewed its relationship with its employees. "Old Mamma Standard Oil," the magazine advised:

---

[54] Dorsey, "Bayonne Refinery Strikes," 24; Gibb and Knowlton, *Resurgent Years*, Vol. II, 151-152.
[55] *Bayonne Evening Times*, July 13, 1918, BPLCF.
[56] *Evening Post* (Bayonne, N.J.), Nov. 8, 1919, BPLCF; *The Messenger*, I (Dec. 3, 1920), 2; Chase, *A Generation of Industrial Peace*, 12-14, 17-21; Gibb and Knowlton, *Resurgent Years*, Vol. II, 136.

is going to have big family gathering at Pershing Field, Jersey City,
tomorrow, where she expects to meet and greet all the thousands and
thousands of children. You being one of these you are, of course,
invited to attend and expected to accept the invitation.[57]

While the corporation flourished its mailed, motherly fist, other
benevolent constraints fell into place. In 1918, for example, corporate money financed a block of model apartment houses in
Bayonne.[58] This measure, like all the rest, encouraged working-
class loyalty and gratitude which could serve corporate purposes.

However effective, the carrot-and-stick blend of welfare capitalism and repression could remain only a stopgap so long as
one basic conclusion obtained: foreignness itself was dangerous.
That conclusion seemed increasingly true during the xenophobic
World War One years. Accordingly, as war with Germany
neared, Bayonne authorities acted to protect the city's large industries against sabotage. Standard Oil officials took a "census"
in their plant "with a view toward ascertaining the nativity and
sympathies of their employees." [59] If nativity and sympathies were
thus linked, saboteurs would be foreigners. And if foreignness was
dangerous, there followed only one logical next step: to stamp
it out wherever possible and Americanize the immigrants.

Already in 1915 at the end of the refinery strike, Bayonne
industrial leaders witnessed how Americanism could quell social
ferment among the foreign-born when Sheriff Eugene Kinkead
opened a meeting of strikers:

> [Kinkead] began by having two of his deputies unfurl a large Amer-
> ican flag, which started the workers cheering. Then, he told them to
> go back to work in the name of the United States, the flag, and him-
> self. "If there is any foreigner," he said, "who is dissatisfied with
> conditions in the United States, for God's sake let him go where he
> has came from."

Kinkead's performance impressed the Poles, who returned to
work and henceforth called the sheriff "godfather" ("*Kresni
Ocec*" [sic]) for his role in ending Bergoff's reign of terror in

[57] *The Messenger*, I (Sept. 11, 18, Oct. 2, Dec. 8, 1920; Jan. 28, June 24, 1921).
    The magazine was patterned after *The Lamp*, a corporation-wide organ which
    began publication in May, 1918. See Dorsey, "Bayonne Refinery Strikes," 30.
[58] *Bayonne Evening Times*, July 13, 1918, BPLCF.
[59] *Ibid.*, Feb. 5, 1917.

Bayonne.[60] Bayonne industrial managers, smarting from the strikes, themselves later instituted private efforts to Americanize the foreign-born. As early as October 1917, a committee of Bayonne manufacturers considered how to convert immigrants into Americans and thereby "help the immigrant work out his salvation."[61] During this time, Standard Oil and the International Nickel Company also sponsored "industrial classes" inside their plants, with respectively 180 and 160 "students" who posted an impressive 89% attendance rate.[62] These Americanization lessons not only sought to impart patriotism, but also to instill work discipline. Along with English and civics lessons, the Bayonne Chamber of Commerce lectured that, "it is necessary that [immigrants] be taught to realize the baneful influences of the saloon and the dance hall—not by means of enforced abstinence, but that they be taught to realize the virtues of moderation. . . ."[63]

Despite these efforts, civic officials complained that local industrial managers showed little interest in public Americanization work. It therefore remained for civic rather than industry officials to spearhead Bayonne's public Americanization drive.[64] Because the city depended upon Standard Oil for half of its revenues by 1881 and because Standard and Tide Water contributed to the police and firemen's pension funds "in appreciation of services rendered . . ." during the strikes, we might surmise that city officials merely did the bidding of the refiners.[65] But this was not the case. By trying to diffuse immigrant working-class militance, public officials promoted notions of law and order and private property rights which they too shared, strengthened their own influence over Bayonne civic affairs, and en-

---

[60] Dorsey, "Bayonne Refinery Strikes," 26-28.

[61] *Jersey Journal* (Jersey City, N.J.), Oct. 25, 1917, BPLCF; *The Messenger*, I (Dec. 24, 1920; April 8, 1921).

[62] *Bayonne Evening Times*, Dec. 5, 1919, BPLCF.

[63] *Jersey Journal*, Oct. 25, 1917, BPLCF. Cf. Stephen Meyer, "Adapting the Immigrant to the Line: Americanization in the Ford Factory, 1914-1921," *Journal of Social History*, 14 (1981), 67-82. I would like to thank the author for furnishing me with a copy.

[64] *Jersey Journal*, May 22, 1919; *Bayonne Evening Times*, Mar. 13, 1919, BPLCF.

[65] John A. DeBrizzi, "Class Formation and the State: Class, Status and the Political-Economy of an American Industrial Society," *Berkeley Journal of Sociology*, 26 (1981), 118; Alfred Davis, Fire Department Chief, Bayonne, to Henry Wilson, Director of Public Safety, Aug. 10, 1915, in *Minutes of the Board of Commissioners, Bayonne, N.J.*, Aug. 10, 1915; *Minutes of the Board of Commissioners, Bayonne, N.J.*, Nov. 14, 1916.

hanced the importance and autonomy of Bayonne's municipal bureaucracy.[66]

Bayonne officials relied upon persuasion and threat in order to Americanize the immigrants and settled upon citizenship as the most tangible measure of their own success. As the 1920 Federal census enumeration approached, Bayonne citizenship statistics gave cause for hope. While 30% of Bayonne's population was still "alien," during the past twelve months alone 5,179 aliens in Hudson County filed declarations of intentions to become citizens and over 2,900 petitioned for naturalization. Immigrants responded to the Americanizers' citizenship campaign for obvious reasons. Without citizenship, immigrants faced severe disabilities in post-war America. After a January 1920 Red Raid in New Jersey netted 68 Bayonne residents—"the largest number of any municipality in the country" with at least a third of them Poles—citizenship applications flooded into the Hudson County Bureau of Naturalization at the rate of 80-100 a day.[67] While citizenship offered protection, it also conferred positive benefits. These included preferment in employment, access to political patronage, and that most singular gift—according to American mythology—prized since the days of the Yankee yeoman farmer. That gift, of course, was the right to vote.

But that Bayonne's city fathers and refinery managers should have encouraged immigrant citizenship and thus enfranchisement raises a perplexing question. After immigrant strikers twice threatened corporate power in Bayonne, were industrial and political leaders not afraid that immigrant citizens now would use votes to accomplish the same end? Apparently they were not. Bayonne's Americanizers believed that foreign vices could be shed and American virtues learned through civic education. Still, education alone would hardly have ensured responsible immigrant voting had it not been for the immigrant middle class, which would soon play a powerful role in the Americanization drama.

Even as Bayonne's middle-class Poles aided their striking coun-

---

[66] DeBrizzi, "Class Formation and the State," 111-115, 118. DeBrizzi's article is especially helpful in relating these developments to the broader crisis over municipal finance.

[67] *Bayonne Evening Times*, Mar. 1, 1920; *Bayonne Evening Review*, Jan. 7, 1920, BPLCF.

trymen, they themselves were changing. And as they changed, they redefined their social position within the immigrant working-class world. In terms of the group's socio-economic composition, immigrant shopkeepers slowly gave way to ethnic entrepreneurs and professionals who shouldered the mantle of leadership as Polish Bayonne entered the 1920s. Business tied these men to the larger economy and society—via property law, government and financial bureaucracies, and electoral politics. In the process, it drew them beyond the working-class world which immigrant shopkeepers had inhabited. In terms of ideology, middle-class immigrants also changed. Disappointed with events in post-war Poland and increasingly absorbed in their own business affairs, middle-class Polish-immigrants adopted two slogans in the early 1920s which no longer invoked the progressive principles that had characterized Polish nationalism a few decades earlier. The two slogans were *"Wychodztwo dla Wychodztwa"* and *"Swój do Swego."* [68] The first meant "The Emigrants for Themselves" and signified a shift away from Poland's politics and toward Polish affairs in America—language maintenance, cultural preservation, political and ecclesiastical representation, resistance to nativism, and upward social and economic mobility. The second, loosely translated, meant "Patronize Our Own," i.e., Buy Polish. In middle-class hands, Polish nationalism —ethnicity-as-ideology—thus became a benign and malleable creed that buttressed political patronage and economic clientage networks and increased their influence over working-class immigrants.

Withal, Bayonne's middle-class Poles had found themselves in an awkward position during the recent refinery strikes. From one side, Polish socialists challenged their leadership. Yet as they jockeyed for their countrymen's loyalty by siding with the strikers, civic and corporate officials now menaced their fragile economic and political position in the city. Not only did Bayonne police wreck John Mydosh's saloon for his role in the 1915 strike—an obvious form of pressure—but authorities also coerced Polish middle-class strike sympathizers in more subtle ways. Bayonne officials equated support for the strikes with disloyalty and sub-

---

[68] Bukowczyk, "Steeples and Smokestacks," 374-380.

version, viz. the company's charge that one Polish lawyer—probably Paul Supinski—was "an agent of the German emperor" for the part he played in the 1915 strike.[69] Later the Americanization program attacked the economic underpinnings of the immigrant middle-class. By equipping immigrants to do for themselves it would eliminate many middle-class service occupations.[70] This accumulated pressure may clarify why local merchants finally withdrew credit from the strikers in 1915.[71] They did so amidst a wave of repression and as the strike turned steadily left.

Bayonne's middle-class Poles thus welcomed the overture that Bayonne's civic and industrial leaders now extended. Perhaps following the guidelines laid out by Peter Roberts, architect of YMCA Americanization work, Bayonne Americanizers invited middle-class Poles to join the Americanization campaign.[72] Their enlistment caused few pangs of conscience. Americanization could aid business and professional advancement. Moreover, as Polish nationalism itself had come to mean "The Emigrants for Themselves"—promoting Polish interest in America—that ideology already converged with the credo middle-class Poles soon would adopt: "Polish-Americanism."

Polish involvement in Americanization work in Bayonne already had begun before the War. In September 1912, Joseph Derowski, the son of a Standard Oil timekeeper and the first Pole appointed to Bayonne's Police Department, formed the Young Men's Democratic Political Club, the first such Polish organization in the city.[73] Though Derowski's club arose at a time when some national Polish-American fraternals urged Poles to become American citizens in order to lobby more effectively for Poland, Bayonne's Polish Democrats apparently promoted self-advancement.[74] After the refinery strikes and American entrance into the

[69] DeBrizzi, "Class Formation and the State," 130.
[70] Cf. *Americanizing a City* (Detroit, 1915), 8.
[71] Dorsey, "Bayonne Refinery Strikes," 27.
[72] Cf. Peter Roberts, *The New Immigration: A Study of the Industrial and Social Life of Southeastern Europeans in America,* reprint edition (New York: Arno Press, 1970), chapter 12. I should like to thank Thomas Klug for bringing the Roberts chapter and the National Americanization Committee pamphlet to my attention.
[73] *Our Lady of Mount Carmel Church, 1898-1973,* 39-46.
[74] Joseph A. Wytrwal, *America's Polish Heritage: A Social History of Poles in America* (Detroit, 1961), 232-233. In 1934, Derowski, who "acted behind the scene, prodding and motivating the club," became Bayonne's first Polish police lieutenant. See *Our Lady of Mount Carmel Church, 1898-1973,* 39, 48.

war, Bayonne's middle-class Poles grew steadily more involved in Americanization work and related activities which boosted their social, economic, and political standing in the city. The U.S. military intelligence department dispatched one young Pole to Bayonne on secret orders to "see how the Polish people are doing"; though he reportedly turned up no subversives, espionage among his countrymen nonetheless launched a future career in Bayonne Polish-American politics.[75]

From these beginnings, Bayonne's middle-class Poles soon plunged into less clandestine Americanization work. In February 1919, Bayonne Poles met at Mydosh's Hall to reorganize the Polish Democratic Club as the Polish Citizen's Club. Present and active were tavern keeper Leon Pejkowski, undertaker Stanley Fryczynski, and attorney Paul Supinski, the strikers' erstwhile counsel. Two months later, the club joined the Bayonne Board of Education in sponsoring a Polish Americanization rally. Held at Mydosh's Hall, the saloon sacked by police during the 1915 strike, the meeting feature several speakers including Superintendent of Schools Preston H. Smith, Mayor Pierre Garven, undertaker Stanley Fryczynski, and lawyer Paul Supinski. A later gathering in September 1919, however, best illustrates how much Bayonne immigrant affairs had changed. This "mass meeting in the interest of the evening schools and especially the Americanization classes" brought together Alexander Debski of the socialist newspaper the *Polish Daily Telegram* (*Telegram Codzienny*); Rev. W. Slominski of Our Lady of Mount Carmel Church; attorney Paul Supinski; and representatives from the Texas Oil Company in Bayonne and from the Standard Oil Company plant. Police officer Joseph Derowski provided musical entertainment.[76]

The careers of two Bayonne Poles reveal much about how

---

[75] Anonymous interview number one (Bayonne, N.J.). His assignment unknown to anyone except local police and, interestingly, Bayonne's Polish pastor, this Polish intelligence operative circulated in saloons, Polish clubs, and organization meetings and filed written reports to his military superiors. He probably worked under Alexander Bruce Bielaski, grandson of a Polish political refugee, who directed the investigation of pro-German activities in the United States and reportedly "hired secret agents of Polish descent to ferret out radicals with Polish backgrounds." See Edward Pinkowski, "The Great Influx of Polish Immigrants," 308.

[76] *Bayonne Evening Times*, Feb. 2, April 1, 24, Sept. 29, 1919, BPLCF.

middle-class Poles mixed professional ambition and American-ization work. Saloonkeeper and Standard Oil worker Anthony Dworzanski served on the refinery strike committee in 1916 and founded St. Anthony Society for Mutual Aid and Benefit in the aftermath of the strike. In 1923, Dworzanski joined Bayonne's police force, rising to the rank of lieutenant sixteen years later. Eventually Dworzanski became Bayonne's Commissioner of Public Works. Stanley Fryczynski's career parallels Dworzanski's. Working himself up through a series of manual labor jobs, Fryczynski opened a provisions business in 1911. After a stint in night school, in 1916 Fryczynski became an undertaker. Two years later, the ambitious Pole joined the Bayonne Elks, where-upon he won appointment to the Americanization Committee. In 1926, Fryczynski opened a private bank and in 1930 formally entered Bayonne politics. Through his Americanization and po-litical work, Fryczynski helped 2,700 immigrants become citi-zens.[77] One Polish lawyer in Bayonne suggested why Fryczynski performed so Herculean a task: "Well, you know, to pick up the business and at the same time to help out the Polish people."[78]

Polish middle class participation targeted Bayonne's Amer-icanization campaign for success. As trusted leaders, middle-class Poles had access to the heart of Polonia. As recruits to the Americanization cause, they opened that heart to Bayonne's na-tive-born Americanizers. Part seduced, part coerced, middle-class Poles thus bolstered the power structure in Bayonne during most difficult years. They did so by transforming Polish-American ethnicity from the vital core of the ethnic working-class commu-nity into an effective control mechanism. Yet we must not jump to the conclusion that the immigrant middle class in Bayonne—and probably in countless other American industrial cities dur-ing the period—was mere puppet or hireling in the piece. Mid-dle-class immigrants also advanced their own interests during Bayonne's oil refinery strikes and thereafter. The ideology of "Polish-Americanism" countered the dual threat of American-ization and assimilation.

What needs explanation, however, is why working-class Poles

[77] *Ibid.*, Nov. 20, 1959; Oct. 16, 1961, BPLCF.
[78] Interview with Casimir Tokarski (Bayonne, July 23, 1980).

followed the middle-class. Several factors seem to have influenced Polish working-class thinking. With the outbreak of the Polish-Soviet War in 1920, patriotic working-class Poles recoiled from Bolshevism because it endorsed traditional Russian territorial aims and therefore menaced their resurrected homeland, post-Versailles Poland. Drawn by middle-class anti-Bolshevism, they also identified with the middle-class Poles; upwardly mobile working-class immigrants themselves aspired to become small-business proprietors. Working-class Poles also found practical reasons to follow middle-class leaders. Because the defeat of the second refinery strike extinguished many other options, immigrant working-class interest now often did lie within the supportive patronage/clientage networks of the ethnic community. Finally, working-class Poles could have perceived a hidden benefit from middle-class politics. As strikers learned in 1915 and 1916, he who controlled politics ran the police, the fire department, and the courts. Through politics they might decide the outcome of future strikes.

The fragile control which Bayonne's corporate and civic leaders achieved with the cooperation of the immigrant middle class would prove recurrently susceptible to pressure from below. Even while Sheriff Kinkead repressed the 1915 strike, he had to underscore a hitherto unstated point. "It has got to be understood," the Sheriff said, "that these wealthy people with their palatial homes can't hire men to shoot down poor people just to protect their property. They can't be allowed to kill human beings to save mere plants and machinery."[79] If nothing else, Bayonne Poles had won an important concession in principle, however routinely reneged on in the years ahead. Thereafter, Poles intermittently asserted their rights in organizing efforts during 1920 and 1924.[80] With their votes, meanwhile, Polish working people purchased a measure of social responsiveness from their middle-class leaders and pressed for those legislative reforms which altered American capitalism during the 1930s. The great welfare state erected by the New Deal undoubtedly became a powerful new means of controlling social ferment, but

[79] *Survey*, 34 (Aug. 7, 1915), 415.
[80] *Bayonne Evening Review*, Jan. 10, 13, 1920; April 11, 1924, BPLCF.

it also brought significant improvement to working-class lives, improvement which only working-class protest could have made possible.

NOTES ON CONTRIBUTORS; *continued from page 2*

H. Keil and J. Jentz, eds. *German Workers In Industrializing Chicago, 1850-1910.* Forthcoming from the Univ. of Illinois Press is his study of working people and class consciousness in Detroit, 1875-1900. He is currently at work on a quantitative analysis of the electoral basis of local labor parties in the 1880s.

RONALD W. SCHATZ is Assistant Professor of History at Wesleyan Univ. He received his PhD from the Univ. of Pittsburgh (1977) where he studied with David Montgomery. Schatz is the author of *The Electrical Workers: A History of Labor at General Electric and Westinghouse, 1920-1960* (1983). His current research interests concern corporatist motifs in American working-class history. From 1977 to 1979 he was an Andrew W. Mellon Foundation Fellow in the Humanities at Standford Univ.

From Voluntary Association to Welfare State: The Illinois Immigrants' Protective League, 1908-1926

ROBERT L. BUROKER

WITH the decline in recent years of the welfare state as a major political issue, it is perhaps now time to trace its administrative history. American historians, fascinated by the partisan and ideological struggles of American liberalism, have produced a substantial literature on the intellectual and political movements which culminated in the New and Fair Deal. They know much less, however, about the social and technological changes which made a national welfare state possible, and they have little knowledge of earlier state and local contributions. This was a crucial phase in the modernization of American government, and social scientists and public officials as well as historians might profit from examining how bureaucracies began and what experiences prior to 1933 made such innovations possible.

What happened in early twentieth-century America to spur the development of public welfare bureaucracies? Modernization, after all, implies that certain types of changes have made other types of changes much more probable. Before a welfare state is feasible a society must have at least the following: (1) a permanent group of people who are continually occupied with social problems and who develop the expertise to deal with them; (2) provisions for the expansion and transmission of such expertise; (3) organization and techniques to integrate that expertise into public recognition and state action.[1] While not exhaustive, these three criteria are necessary

This essay received the Organization of American Historians' Pelzer Award for 1971. Mr. Buroker is a graduate student in the University of Chicago.

[1] These criteria were formulated after consulting a number of works, the most helpful of which were: Maurice Bruce, *The Coming of the Welfare State* (London, 1961); Philip Klein, *From Philanthropy to Social Welfare: An American Cultural Perspective* (San Francisco, 1968); Roy Lubove, *The Professional Altruist: The Emergence of Social Work as a Career 1880-1930* (Cambridge, Mass., 1965); Ralph E. Pumphrey and Muriel W. Pumphrey, eds., *The Heritage of American Social Work: Readings in Its Philosophical and Institutional Development* (New York, 1961); and Harold L. Wilensky and Charles

TABLE I

FOREIGN BORN IN ILLINOIS BETWEEN 1910 AND 1919*

Nationality	Foreign Born In Illinois, 1910	Admitted Aliens Giving Illinois As Their Destination, 1910–1919
German	311,680	45,875
Scandinavian	166,812	34,561
English, Irish, Scotch, and Welsh	214,161	44,207
Greek	10,487	24,088
Italian	73,085	77,489
Lithuanian and Lett	32,662	22,920
Polish	148,809	86,910
Russian	2,595	15,199
Slovak	13,722	11,507

* Grace Abbott, "Memorandum as to Work to be Immediately Undertaken by the Immigrants Commission (March 19th, 1920)," 1, Supplement II, Box 58, Records of the Illinois Immigrants' Protective League.

conditions for the development of a modern welfare state. How were they fulfilled during the Progressive era?

The years between 1900 and 1920 saw an enormous proliferation of voluntary associations to assist a variety of disadvantaged groups, including the impoverished immigrant with his unique set of problems. The history of the Illinois Immigrants' Protective League (IPL) during the Progressive era suggests how progressive movements contributed to the welfare state in America. What kinds of people were involved and why? How successful were their efforts to fulfill the three necessary conditions for a welfare state? What was the relationship between voluntary associations and subsequent government agencies?

Illinois, and Chicago in particular, experienced a massive influx of immigrants between 1890 and 1910 (see Tables I and II). In 1910 there were 974,013 foreign born in Illinois. Between 1910 and 1919 there were 362,756 new arrivals from abroad. The League was organized in 1908 in response to the problems encountered by immigrants in the Chicago area. The idea for such a league came from a committee of a women's trade

N. Lebeaux, *Industrial Society and Social Welfare: The impact of industrialization on the supply and organization of social welfare services in the United States* (New York, 1958).

TABLE II

IMMIGRANT ALIENS ADMITTED TO, EMIGRANT ALIENS DEPARTED
FROM, ILLINOIS, AND NET INCREASE OR DECREASE IN
POPULATION, FROM 1892 TO 1928*

Year	Immigrant Aliens Admitted	Emigrant Aliens Departing	Net Increase or Decrease
1892	46,012		
1893	45,686		
1894	22,783		
1895	16,798		
1896	22,093		
1897	12,067		
1898	12,129		
1899	18,795		
1900	27,118		
1901	30,509		
1902	45,845		
1903	63,378		
1904	57,457		
1905	72,770		
1906	86,539		
1907	104,156		
1908‡	58,733	28,725	+30,008
1909	63,379	14,485	+48,894
1910	93,340	13,165	+80,175
1911	76,565	21,157	+55,408
1912	67,118	28,355	+38,763
1913	107,060	24,178	+82,882
1914	105,811	23,637	+82,174
1915	19,062	11,682	+7,380
1916	418	6,612	−6,194
1917	10,690	2,182	+8,508
1918	2,748	3,488	−740
1919	3,951	4,638	−687
1920	16,964	17,951	−987
1921	48,358	17,652	+30,706
1922	22,410	14,039	+8,371
1923	35,612	4,582	+31,030
1924	46,254	3,977	+42,277
1925	20,382	4,557	+15,825
1926	20,176	4,377	+15,799
1927	20,723	3,911	+16,812
1928	19,165	3,802	+15,363

* "Immigrant Aliens Admitted to, Emigrant Aliens Departed from Illinois," Main Collection, Box 47. Records of the Illinois Immigrants' Protective League.
‡ No departure figures are available before 1908.

union group, which was formed to visit immigrant girls and women. One of the first efforts of IPL was to take over that work.[2]

Each year about 20 percent of the women and girls leaving Ellis Island destined for Chicago were unaccounted for at their destinations.[3] Most were never found. Women and girls who did arrive often had incorrect addresses; some were taken to saloonkeepers or houses of prostitution by cabbies and expressmen. Many were picked up by policemen and "placed" in the homes of Chicago residents who had contacted the police department for just that purpose. Quite a few officers were involved in the racket, and many girls never reached their families.[4] In 1910 Jane Addams wrote of the heartbreak these abuses caused:

> Every year we have heard of girls who did not arrive when their families expected them, and although their parents frantically met one train after another, the ultimate fate of the girls could never be discovered; we have constantly seen the exploitation of the newly arrived immigrant by his shrewd countrymen in league with the unscrupulous American; from time to time we have known children detained in New York and even deported whose parents had no clear understanding of the difficulty.[5]

A related problem was the protection of all immigrants upon arrival at Chicago's railroad stations. Unscrupulous cabbies and expressmen used official-looking costumes and badges and a stock of foreign phrases to lure immigrant families into their vehicles, usually to charge them exorbitant fares, but often to transport them to labor camps in the Chicago area. The League planned to assist immigrants at the railroad stations and to support proposals for a federal protective bureau for immigrants in Chicago.[6]

There were also flagrant malpractices by employment agencies which specialized in immigrant workers. Charging exorbitant rates, they often delivered men and women to employers in seasonal labor camps, many as far away as Wisconsin and Iowa. The immigrant was later discharged without any way of returning to Chicago. The League decided to investigate the situation and to recommend appropriate city and state legislation.[7]

In general IPL tried to help the immigrant adjust to American life. As an article in the by-laws of the League stated:

[2] Illinois Immigrants' Protective League, "Eleven Years of Community Service" (Jan. 1920), 2, Box 60, Supplement II, Records of the Illinois Immigrants' Protective League (IPL) (Preston Bradley Library, University of Illinois, Chicago Circle).
[3] League for the Protection of Immigrants, *Annual Report (1909-1910)* (Chicago, 1911), 6.
[4] Illinois Immigrants' Protective League, "Eleven Years of Community Service," 4-5.
[5] League for the Protection of Immigrants, *Annual Report (1909-1910)*, 4.
[6] Illinois Immigrants' Protective League, "Eleven Years of Community Service," 5.
[7] League for the Protection of Immigrants, *Annual Report (1909-1910)*, 27-29.

The objects of this organization shall be to apply the civic, social and philanthropic resources of the city to the needs of foreigners in Chicago, to protect
them from exploitation, to cooperate with the Federal, State and local authorities
and with similar organizations in other localities, and to protect the right of
asylum in all proper cases.[8]

Time and time again the League lamented its own and the public's colossal
ignorance of immigrant life. One purpose from the beginning was to collect as much information as possible on the problems of various immigrant
groups in Chicago. In this respect IPL was starting to develop the expertise
necessary to manage a social problem. Acting on its information, according to the first *Annual Report*, the League would welcome newcomers and
see that they reached their destination; guard them against wrongs at railroad stations, labor camps, and employment agencies; assist them in finding
work; advise and encourage them to take advantage of the many co-operating educational facilities furnished by night schools, settlements, churches,
YMCA, and others; supplement these when necessary; protect women and
girls from prostitution and the white slave trade; personally visit to assist
newcomers and to follow up assistance; confer with local, state, and national authorities, and especially with police.[9]

Among IPL's founders were Margaret Dreier Robbins, social economist,
suffragette, educator, and wife of the prominent progressive politician
Raymond Robbins; Ernst Freund, University of Chicago law professor and
later president of the American Political Science Association; Julius Rosenwald, chairman of the board of Sears, Roebuck and Company; Julian Mack,
a judge on federal circuit court of appeals; and Samuel N. Harper, professor of Russian language and literature at the University of Chicago and
son of William Rainey Harper, president of the University of Chicago.
The most active members were the social workers. Addams was instrumental in getting IPL started, although after that her other duties kept
her from being more directly involved. Sophonisba P. Breckinridge, a social
worker and professor of social economy at Chicago, was active as an advisor
to the League. Grace Abbott, later to become director of the Federal Children's Bureau, was the moving force behind the League. As executive secretary throughout most of its first twenty years, her professional approach to
social work, her valuable experience, and her influential contacts in Illinois
and throughout the country were indispensable to the League's operation.

These eight people were the most famous League leaders, but they represent only a small portion of the total leadership. Between 1908 and 1917

[8] "The Immigrants' Protective League in 1930," 2, Box 60, Supplement II, Records of
IPL.
[9] League for the Protection of Immigrants, *Annual Report (1909-1910)*, 5-6.

47

there were sixty trustees, officers, and executive committee members. Enough biographical information is available for forty of them to reveal definite patterns of occupation, age, religion, politics, education, and geographic backgrounds.[10] A majority were members of a profession or the wives of members of a profession (see Table III). The businessmen all worked for large-scale enterprises. Most were high-level managers in corporations, and not one worked in or owned a small business. The lawyers

TABLE III

Occupations of Forty League Leaders, 1908–1917

Occupation	Number	Percentage
Lawyer	7‡(1)*	20.0‡
Businessman	8 (1)	22.5
Professor	8 (1)	22.5
Social Worker	5	12.5
Physician	1 (2)	7.5
Journalist	3 (1)	10.0
Public School Administrator	1	2.5
Politician	(1)	2.5
Total	40	100.0

  * Parentheses include the number of wives whose husbands practiced each profession.
  ‡ Total number and percentages include occupations of the husbands whose wives served as League leaders.

either had successful private practices in commercial law or worked in corporate legal departments.

Of those whose politics are known, nine were Republicans and four were Democrats. They ranged in age from twenty-six to sixty-seven, the mean age being forty-five. In leadership this was not a young organization, although several young women worked on the staff throughout this period. Of the twenty-one leaders whose religious preferences are known, fourteen were Protestants, five were Jews, and two were Catholics. Among those whose place of birth is known, there were thirty native Americans and only five foreign born. Those who had been born in the United States came from a variety of geographic backgrounds. Seven had been born in Chicago,

[10] Biographical information was obtained primarily from John W. Leonard, ed., *The Book of the Chicagoans* (Chicago, 1905), and Albert Nelson Marquis, ed., *Who's Who in Chicago* (Chicago, 1926).

eleven in other large cities, four in rural or small-town Illinois, and seven in rural areas or small towns outside Illinois. It was a highly educated group (see Table IV). Almost two-thirds of them had a college degree, and over one-third of them had doctorates.[11]

A leader of the League was thus likely to be a Protestant, well-educated, middle-class, native-stock American. This is a familiar portrait of progressive reform, but while it discloses something about the people who participated in organizations like IPL, it does not explain why they chose to do so. Indeed, the most troublesome question for progressive historiography is

TABLE IV

HIGHEST EDUCATIONAL LEVEL ACHIEVED BY
THIRTY-THREE LEAGUE LEADERS

Level	Number	Percentage
High School Only	10	30.3
Some College	2	6.1
Bachelor's Degree	7	21.2
Master's Degree	3	9.1
Doctorate	11	33.3
Total	33	100.0

simply raised again. Why, beginning around 1900, did so many of the American middle class decide that their country needed urgent reform? By most standards those were prosperous times, and materially the middle class was doing well. Discontent among workers, farmers, and immigrants seems logical, but not within the ranks of the relatively well-to-do.

The traditional and most enduring explanation is that progressivism was their response to industrialism. Through the state they wanted to remove the evils of the city and factory, aid the underprivileged, to regulate a

[11] It is interesting to see how the social make-up of IPL differed from that of its most vociferous opponent on immigrant questions, the Chicago area Ku Klux Klan. No direct comparison is possible because the Klan figures do not distinguish between leaders and members. Nevertheless, Kenneth T. Jackson gives a useful occupational breakdown of those Chicago residents whom the Catholic magazine *Tolerance* reported to be members of the Klan in 1922 and 1923. Jackson found that 20 percent were businessmen, 29 percent were white collar clerical workers, and 39 percent were blue collar workers, while only 4.6 percent were lawyers and 5.4 percent were other professionals. The League reformer appears to have been a different social type from those who tried to exclude the newcomers from American society. Kenneth T. Jackson, *The Ku Klux Klan in the City, 1915-1930* (New York, 1967), 108.

capitalist economy, and democratize the American political system. It is a testament to the power of this thesis that over the years historians of widely divergent perspectives have reasserted it. Still, a crucial question remains unanswered. Why did some members of the middle class participate in progressive movements while others continued to support McKinley-Taft conservatism? An adequate explanation should be able to tell historians the relevant differences between these two groups. Moreover, the precise connections between aspects of industrialism and the responses to them are often left undefined. Several historians, including Samuel Hays, Robert Wiebe, Gabriel Kolko, and James Weinstein,[12] have explored those linkages for businessmen in the new corporate economy, but other dimensions of progressivism (and especially social welfare movements) have yet to receive such explicit treatment.

In 1955 Richard Hofstadter offered a persuasive interpretation. According to Hofstadter, anxiety over declining status often motivated progressives to reform efforts.

[T]he United States was a nation with a rather broad diffusion of wealth, status, and power, in which the man of moderate means, especially in the many small communities, could command much deference and exert much influence. The small merchant or manufacturer, the distinguished lawyer, editor, or preacher, was a person of local eminence in an age in which local eminence mattered a great deal. In the absence of very many nation-wide sources of power and prestige, the pillars of the local communities were men of great importance in their own right.[13]

After the Civil War this began to change, and the result was a severe sense of dislocation on the part of the social groups which had traditionally provided community leadership.

The newly rich, the grandiosely or corruptly rich, the masters of great corporations, were bypassing the men of the Mugwump type—the old gentry, the merchants of long standing, the small manufacturers, the established professional men, the civic leaders of an earlier era . . . . [T]he America [of the traditional groups] they knew did not lack opportunities, but it did seem to lack opportunities of the highest sort for men of the highest standards. In a strictly economic sense these men were not growing poorer as a class, but their wealth and power were being dwarfed by comparison with the new eminences of wealth and power. They were less important, and they knew it.[14]

[12] Samuel P. Hays, *The Response to Industrialism: 1885-1914* (Chicago, 1957); Gabriel Kolko, *The Triumph of Conservatism: A Reinterpretation of American History, 1900-1916* (Glencoe, 1963); James Weinstein, *The Corporate Ideal in the Liberal State: 1900-1918* (Boston, 1968); Robert Wiebe, *Businessmen and Reform* (Cambridge, Mass., 1962).
[13] Richard Hofstadter, *The Age of Reform: From Bryan to F. D. R.* (New York, 1955), 135-36.
[14] *Ibid.*, 137.

The status revolution thesis explains the behavior of many progressives. It is not so applicable to people like those who founded and directed the League. For one thing the status anxious progressives often resented the immigrant because he was a source of political power for the corrupt city machine. Moreover, it is unlikely that the people participating in IPL were experiencing status anxiety. The majority were well-educated professionals, and many were the first of their families to receive a college education. Several, instead of being replaced by the new plutocracy, were active participants in it. All but one of the lawyers worked for large corporations. Among the businessmen there was not a single small merchant or manufacturer. To a man they were part of the élite of the new economic order, and, in addition, several of them were self-made men, stock boys who became corporation presidents. The university professors and the social workers were members of professions which were rapidly growing as distinctive occupational groups. Thus, far from resenting the changes which industrialization and urbanization had brought to American society since the Civil War, the leaders of the League had every reason to feel self-confident since they were riding the crest of those changes. They represented the new occupations of corporate management and professional skill which were to become the élite strata of twentieth-century America.

Recent investigations of professionalism and bureaucratization during the Progressive era suggest another social basis for reform movements. The growing post-Civil War professional middle class is the subject of an important chapter in Wiebe's *The Search for Order: 1877-1920*. During this period most modern professional associations were organized, and those which practiced specialized skills became an integral part of urban-industrial America. Their self-awareness further accentuated rural-urban differences, and living primarily in the larger cities they understandably tried to focus increasing political attention on the problems of the city environment.[15] Roy Lubove's *The Professional Altruist* describes the growth of social work as a profession. After using recent refinements of the sociological literature on bureaucracy and professions to explain the history of both social work and the public welfare agency, he concluded:

Specialization and the idealization of expertise, the growth of an occupational subculture, and bureaucratization were instrumental in shaping the character of twentieth-century social work. These typical features of an urban-industrial society have affected not only the professions but most spheres of life, and their controlling influence will undoubtedly remain potent.[16]

[15] Robert H. Wiebe, *The Search for Order: 1877-1920* (New York, 1967), 111-32.
[16] Lubove, *The Professional Altruist*, 220.

Hays discovered an important political result of these developments when he analyzed the social bases of municipal reform movements. Professionals as well as businessmen dominated these groups, and Hays found that what distinguished these reformers from their less active colleagues in business and the professions was their relatively recent arrival on the social and political scene. The businessmen came from large-scale industries which were but a half century old, and the professionals were "in the vanguard of professional life, seeking to apply expertise more widely to public affairs."[17]

These insights suggest a more adequate explanation for why so many ostensibly comfortable people became at least social welfare progressives. By 1900 a social class based on specialized expertise had become numerous and influential enough to come into its own as a political force. Educated to provide rational answers to specific problems and oriented by training if not by inclination toward public service, they sensed their own stake in the stability of the new society, which increasingly depended upon their skills, and quite predictably turned their attention to the misery of the urban lower classes. In this sense they were responding to the evils of industrialism and urbanism. They were themselves, however, as much a part of the modernization process as the sweat shop and the tenement.

The history of the League is consistent with this interpretation. Clearly IPL was concerned primarily with integrating the immigrant into American society. The leaders were not fundamentally dissatisfied with the American system, and they urged no radical changes. They were trying to solve problems of limited scope. Social theorists have often commented on the stabilizing influence which professionals seem to exercise. Indeed, as Talcott Parsons notes, "The development and increasing strategic importance of the professions probably constitute the most important change that has occurred in the occupational system of modern societies."[18] A professional class can prevent serious conflict in a modernizing social system with glaring inequalities in wealth, status, and power. Professionals become experts at alleviating problems and adjudicating conflicts which might otherwise develop into significant disruptions.[19]

Prior to the Progressive era the professions had been growing at an unprecedented rate. Between 1870 and 1900 the number of professionals per 100,000 population almost doubled. The professional labor force increased

[17] Samuel P. Hays, "The Politics of Reform in Municipal Government in the Progressive Era," *Pacific Northwest Quarterly*, 55 (Oct. 1964), 160.

[18] Talcott Parsons, "Professions," David L. Sills, ed., *The International Encyclopedia of the Social Sciences* (17 vols., New York, 1968), XII, 536.

[19] Joseph Ben-David, "Professions in the Class System of Present-Day Societies," *Current Sociology La Sociologie Contemporaine*, XII (1963-1964), 249.

245 percent in contrast to a 125 percent rate of growth for the total labor force. The expansion was greatest in architecture, teaching, and journalism.[20] Most League leaders were members of the professional classes, and the plight of immigrants became a focus for their expertise. Whatever their differences, the social science professor, the journalist, the corporation lawyer, and even the corporate executive shared a belief that American society needed their special skills.

Another dimension to IPL leadership deserves special consideration. Thirteen among the forty IPL leaders were women, and most of the staff workers were young women in their twenties. Abbott was the moving force behind the League in its first two decades. A social worker, Marion Schibsby, directed the staff work throughout much of this period and stayed with her work during the financial crisis years of the early 1920s. The participation of women in reform movements is nothing new to progressive historiography.

Indeed, the suffragette and the female social worker had already become classic American types. One historian, however, has put these women in a most interesting perspective. Arthur Mann notes something fundamentally different between Addams' generation and generations of earlier female reformers. By 1900 the legal emancipation of women was almost completed, and a new social type was emerging. The career woman was replacing the feminist. Speaking of Vida D. Scudder, Addams, and their contemporaries, Mann states, "All these women the modern American will recognize as completely modern, whereas the feminists, whether Lucy Stone or Alice Stone Blackwell, Julia Ward Howe or Elizabeth Stuart Phelps, savor of an age unlike our own."[21]

Addams recalled in *Twenty Years at Hull House* how, when she graduated from Rockford College, her first concern was to find a useful purpose for her training. She went to Europe, discovered the settlement house concept, returned to Chicago, and found her role at Hull House.[22] With minor variations, her story is the story of many of these women. They were the first American generation of their sex to leave the household in large numbers and contribute significantly to the society outside the home. Women like Breckinridge and Abbott became highly competent social sci-

[20] Alba M. Edwards, *Comparative Occupational Statistics for the United States, 1870 to 1940* [Department of Commerce, Bureau of the Census, *Sixteenth Census of the United States: 1940 Population*] (Washington, 1943), 111.

[21] Arthur Mann, *Yankee Reformers in the Urban Age: Social Reform in Boston, 1880-1900* (New York, 1954), 227.

[22] Jane Addams, *Twenty Years at Hull House: With Autobiographical Notes* (New York, 1911), 65-88.

entists and administrators. Like the corporation lawyer, the industrial executive, and the university professor, they were, as Mann suggests, part of the first generation of modern America. Far from being anxious to preserve their traditional roles, they were assertive career women, a new and permanent type in American society. In Boston, Scudder spoke for all such women when she wrote:

Into this world . . . life with bewildering and contradictory theories, yet bent, as no other age has ever been, in the analysis of social evil and the right of social wrong—into this world we are born—we, the first generation of college women. In a sense, we represent a new factor in the social order. . . . Surely, I may at least say, that we make ourselves significant if we will.[23]

In Chicago, the organizers of IPL were part of the larger search by an emerging professional class for the expertise to direct the advance of the new order.

How successfully did the League translate its objectives into results? The evidence indicates that between 1908 and 1926 it managed an impressive quantity of private and public social work. Operating with a staff which rarely exceeded ten or twelve people, it collected information on Illinois immigrant groups, established a case work service, aided new arrivals, improved the employment agency situation, and pressed for state and federal legislation. Its work went a long way toward fulfilling many of the functions of a modern welfare state agency.

The League began in 1908 to locate lost immigrant girls. It obtained their names through private agencies in New York and later through the United States Immigration Service. Representatives of IPL who were familiar with the language and European backgrounds of newcomers made regular visits. It helped to locate missing family members. Girls who needed assistance were put in touch with night schools and various available social agencies. From 1909 to 1915 the League contacted and helped 19,512 immigrant girls.[24]

To protect all immigrants upon arrival in Chicago the League worked closely with newspapers to publicize the problem. In July 1910, the Chicago and Western Indiana Railroad donated a small building across the street from the Dearborn station. There the League established offices, reception rooms, bedrooms, and baths.[25] For the next eighteen months it was

[23] Quoted in Mann, *Yankee Reformers in the Urban Age*, 201.
[24] Illinois Immigrants' Protective League, "Eleven Years of Community Service," 3-4.
[25] *Fifth Annual Report of the Immigrants' Protective League (1913)* (Chicago, 1914), 8-9.

a well-matched battle between the female IPL workers and the cabbies and expressmen. There were numerous altercations, but the women won out, and the number of people aided by the League at the Dearborn station increased steadily through 1913.[26] Between July and December 1910, the League helped 1,903 people. In 1911 the number increased to 5,204. The next year it tripled to 15,537, and in 1913 it increased to 41,322.[27]

Throughout this period IPL negotiated with federal officials in an effort to obtain a federal bureau to protect immigrants in the Chicago railroad stations. In this effort they received the support of a number of influential Chicago civic associations, including the prestigious Commercial Club.[28] In 1913 Congressman Adolph J. Sabath of Illinois introduced a bill to establish federal bureaus at stations like Dearborn. It became law in July 1913. The government rented a building near the station which was equipped with reception rooms, baths, laundry, and beds. These facilities, however, were rarely used. The government's most frequent excuses were the decline in immigration beginning in August 1914 and the fact that there were no provisions for getting people from the station to the federal building. The League offered to transport the immigrants, but in the end it had to carry on most of the station work itself. Congress failed in later years to appropriate sufficient funds, and IPL continued as the sole protector of new arrivals from abroad.[29]

One of the first League projects was a thorough study of Chicago employment agencies. Abbott's research team discovered that of 289 licensed agencies in Chicago in 1908, there were 110 which specialized in immigrant workers.[30] On the basis of the published reports of malpractices by many of these agencies, the legislature in 1909 passed amendments to the employment agency licensing laws which provided for stricter standards and better enforcement.[31]

Besides these major activities, the League carried on a number of other projects designed to help immigrants adjust to American life. For several years, for example, until it persuaded the Bureau of Immigration to take over the task, IPL compiled a list of all children, aged six through sixteen, who came to Illinois by way of Ellis Island. These lists were furnished to

[26] Illinois Immigrants' Protective League, "Eleven Years of Community Service," 5.
[27] *Ibid.*, 6.
[28] League for the Protection of Immigrants, *Annual Report (1909-1910)*, 6.
[29] *Sixth Annual Report of the Immigrants' Protective League (1914)* (Chicago, 1915), 6-7.
[30] Grace Abbott, "The Chicago Employment Agency and the Immigrant Worker," *American Journal of Sociology*, XIV (Nov. 1908), 289.
[31] League for the Protection of Immigrants, *Annual Report (1909-1910)*, 6.

truant officers and school superintendents in Illinois communities.[32] During American participation in World War I the League handled 2,840 draft cases involving immigrant men. League members explained to alien registrants their rights and obligations under the laws and acted as interpreters in communications with draft boards.[33] Beginning in the autumn of 1918 the League began to assist aliens in connection with the new income tax laws. There were a number of ambiguities in the laws relating to non-citizens, and IPL was able to get some of the regulations clarified. Case workers also assisted immigrants in filing their forms.[34]

In 1918, at a time when the League was experiencing severe financial difficulty resulting from the war, the Illinois state legislature established the Immigrants Commission within the State Department of Registration and Education. The League had been publicizing the need for such a commission for some time. On July 1, 1919, the new agency began its work. Abbott was named director, and, for all practical purposes, the staff of the League became the staff of the new Immigrants Commission.[35] According to the authorizing statute, the new Commission was to:

Make a survey of the Immigrant, alien born, and foreign-speaking people of the State, and of their distribution, conditions of employment, and standards of housing and living. Examine into their economic, financial and legal customs, their provisions for insurance, and other prudential arrangements, their organization, and their education needs; keeping in friendly and sympathetic touch with alien groups and co-operating with State and Local officials, and with immigrant or related authorities of other States and of the United States.[36]

The Commission operated on a budget of $15,000 for the biennium. This sum did not compare favorably with the budgets for similar commissions in three other large states. For equal periods the California commission had $140,000; the New York commission had $51,200; and the Massachusetts commission had $56,000.[37] In the following two years, however, the Commission was surprisingly active. Under Abbott's direction two massive studies were completed and well-publicized by the press in 1921. One involved the educational needs of immigrants in Illinois, and the other reported the results of investigations on the immigrant and the coal mining communities in Illinois. Both studies prompted a variety of state actions.

[32] Illinois Immigrants' Protective League, "Eleven Years of Community Service," 8.
[33] Ibid., 8-9.
[34] Ibid., 9.
[35] Reprint of "Immigrants' Protective League," Social Service, 3:8 (Chicago: Chicago Council of Social Agencies, May, 1926), 3, in Box 62, Main Collection, Records of IPL.
[36] "The Illinois Immigrants' Commission," memorandum (April 8, 1929), 8, Box 47, ibid.
[37] "Memorandum as to Appropriations of other Commissions, Boards or Bureaus charged with duties similar to those of the Illinois Commission," ibid.

One, the attack on adult illiteracy, was especially productive.

Abbott's study of the immigrants' education first brought to light the problem of illiteracy in Illinois. The report noted that Illinois ranked twenty-third among the states in the amount of money spent on schools for each $100 of taxable wealth. As a result, Abbott commented, "It was not surprising that the commission found that 96.9 per cent of the women and 88.6 of the men interviewed in the course of its investigation . . . were not able to read and write English, and that 53.5 per cent of the women and 24.2 per cent of the men could not speak English."[38]

Following the Commission's report, both the Commission and the League, now just a paper organization, made a concerted effort to collect as much data as possible on the problem of illiteracy in the state. They compiled a memorandum, "Startling Statistics on Illiteracy in Illinois," which did, indeed, include some startling findings. Illinois, it was discovered, ranked twenty-second among the states in the percentage of illiteracy and twenty-fifth in the percentage of native white illiterates. In 1910 there had been 168,294 illiterates in the state, and by 1920 the number had increased to about 174,000.[39]

The most serious obstacle was a state law which forbade local communities from providing educational facilities for people over the age of twenty-one. The Commission, the League, and a number of other voluntary organizations including the Illinois League of Women Voters began a publicity campaign to amend the statute. Six years later they were successful. The legislature passed a bill that gave the communities of the state the power "to establish classes for the instruction of persons over twenty-one years of age, and to pay the necessary expenses of the same out of the school funds of the district."[40] At the end of the decade there was significant improvement. By 1930 the number of persons ten years of age and over unable to read and write English had decreased to 153,507. The percentage of illiteracy in Illinois had been 3.4 percent in 1920. In 1930 it was 2.4 percent.[41]

The illiteracy studies were only one example of the skill with which the League and the Commission collected statistics on social problems in Illinois. Abbott and her co-workers in IPL had long been known for their ability to conduct massive survey research. In 1914 Abbott and some other Chicago social workers were invited by the state of Massachusetts to conduct a statewide survey of immigrant problems. Their efforts were instrumental in

[38] Reprint from Chicago *Daily News*, March 23, 1921, *ibid.*

[39] "Startling Statistics on Illiteracy in Illinois," 1-5, memorandum, *ibid.*

[40] Mrs. Kenneth F. Rich, "Opportunity Under the New Adult Education Law," *Bulletin of the Illinois League of Women Voters* (Nov. 1927), 1, reprint, in *ibid.*

[41] National Advisory Committee on Illiteracy, *Illiteracy Statistics for the State of Illinois* (Washington, 1930), 1-3, in *ibid.*

the success of the Massachusetts Immigration Commission.[42] It would have been impossible for a national welfare system to develop without the now commonplace tools of social statistics. Their refinement was primarily a nineteenth-century development, and IPL leaders were no exceptions among social workers in Europe and America in recognizing the usefulness of the innovations in applied mathematics. The Chicago School of Civics and Philanthropy, founded in 1903 by Addams, Abbott, Breckinridge, and others, offered regular courses to those wishing to join the new profession of social service administration. From the very first year one of the required courses was "Methods of Social Investigation," a class taught by Abbott and Breckinridge. It dealt with a variety of social research techniques including "the application of statistical methods to social problems, the collection and tabulation of data, the use and misuse of averages, index numbers and weighting."[43] Since many IPL staff members were trained at this school, it is not surprising that the League and the Commission were able to ascertain both the quality and the magnitude of immigrants' problems in Illinois.

The Illinois Commission maintained a large and growing load of case work, primarily in the Chicago area. The Commission case load for a three month period increased from 332 in January-March 1920, to 874 during the same three months of the next year.[44] The Commission also carried on IPL's work in supervising the assistance of immigrants at railroad stations. In the last three months of 1920, 942 people received assistance, and 1,218 received Commission aid at Chicago railroad stations in the first quarter of 1921.[45]

Despite the Commission's successes, its functions were terminated by Governor Lennington Small's veto of its next biennial appropriation on June 30, 1921. In his farewell address the previous governor, Frank Lowden, had urged that the legislature continue to support the work of the Commission. The lawmakers had responded by voting a $58,000 budget for the years 1921 to 1923. Small's veto was part of a last minute economy move which included vetoes of appropriations for a number of state agencies.[46]

[42] Illinois State Department of Public Welfare, *Grace Abbott: November 17, 1878 to June 19, 1939* (Springfield, Illinois: Nov., 1940), 11, in Box 3, Supplement II, *ibid.*
[43] Chicago School of Civics and Philanthropy, *Bulletin*, 1 (July 1909), 23.
[44] "Protective Case Work in Chicago and its Immediate Vicinity," memorandum in Box 58, Supplement II, Records of IPL; Illinois Immigrants Commission, "First Quarterly Report of the Executive Secretary for January, February, and March, 1921," typewritten draft in *ibid.*
[45] Illinois Immigrants Commission, "Fourth Quarterly Report of the Executive Secretary, 1920," typewritten draft in *ibid.*
[46] "The Present Program of the Immigrants' Protective League and a Sketch of its Reorganization," memorandum (1926), 1, Box 57, Main Collection, *ibid.*

The Commission and League members were stunned on the evening of June 30, when they received word through the press that as of the next day, the beginning of a new fiscal year, the Illinois Immigrants Commission would cease to exist. At that time the Commission was working on about 500 cases, but it had to vacate its offices in Springfield and Chicago within a few hours.[47] On July 2, the trustees of the League met to decide what to do in the face of the veto crisis. There was enough money to pay two people to finish the existing case load. The Girls' Protective Bureau at Hull House donated office space, and through July 118 cases and 117 new ones were either handled or referred.[48] After August 1, Abbott and Schibsby handled case work themselves, and together during the next month they helped 145 new clients.[49]

The trustees decided to try to raise about $5,000 each year for casework and to wait for the state to reactivate the Commission which still retained its legal existence.[50] They had trouble raising the money, but by 1924 they were able to add four new case workers to the staff, making a total of six. During the next two years the League handled about 4,000 new cases. Finally, after five years of waiting and lobbying, the League decided to reconstitute itself as a private organization, a status which it has maintained to this day.[51]

What can be concluded about the work of the League and the Commission through 1926? The evidence suggests that IPL, in both its private and public capacities, fulfilled the necessary conditions for a modern welfare state agency. It constituted a group of people who were continually concerned with social problems and who became experts on such matters. Through the Chicago School of Civics and Philanthropy, several League members laid the groundwork for the growth of an expertly trained profession of welfare administration. They collected and analyzed mass data. They publicized problems and thereby facilitated public recognition and state action. Finally, they actually performed welfare service work on a surprisingly large scale. They set an example of the type of organization which was necessary to administer a modern welfare system.

The League was only one of hundreds of voluntary associations founded between 1900 and 1920. There is no reason to believe that its experience was unique within its own reform era or throughout the history of American reform. Alexis de Tocqueville wrote of Jacksonian America that,

[47] *Ibid.*, 2.
[48] *Ibid.*
[49] Ernst Freund to IPL members, Dec. 12, 1921, Box 47, *ibid.*
[50] Abel Davis, memorandum, July 31, 1925, *ibid.*
[51] "Present Program of the Immigrants' Protective League and a Sketch of its Reorganization," 2, Box 57, *ibid.*

"Wherever, at the head of some new undertaking, you see the government in France, or a man of rank in England, in the United States you will be sure to find an association."[52] This perceptive observer captured something essential to the growth of American government. In a country where decision-making was highly decentralized and where the natural impulse was always toward local autonomy and a suspicion of government, the voluntary association assumed a crucial role in developing the expertise and the organization necessary to manage social problems. When the state finally acted, the minimum requirements of knowledge, personnel, and procedure were already available in the experience of private groups.

Mann has noted the absence of thorough histories of a number of important voluntary associations.[53] Closer study of these groups might substantiate the thesis that in the United States voluntary organizations formed the basis not only for the welfare state but for the whole development of modern public bureaucracies. One can think of numerous examples of people involved in private organizations who assumed newly created government positions in areas where they possessed special skills. Perhaps this is only part of a larger pattern involving a characteristic if not unique American system of public administration, a system in which the voluntary association has usually laid the necessary foundation.

If this is so, the Progressive era deserves reinterpretation as a key transition period in American history. Historians have overemphasized the extent to which progressive reform was a reaction against industrialization and urbanization. Granted it was a response to the more severe evils of the city and the factory, but many progressive leaders were themselves a part of the emerging system. The corporation lawyer, the business executive, the social science professor, the career woman—all were the results of forces transforming a nineteenth-century nation.

If the experience of the League holds true generally, there were many influential progressives who were quite at home in urban-industrial America. They formed associations, and within those associations they developed and professionalized new skills. Max Weber saw professionalization and technical efficiency as two characteristics of the ideal type bureaucracy. Perhaps the Progressive era was among other things the era of the proto-bureaucratic association, a necessary link between agrarian, town meeting America and the America of the managed metropolis.

[52] Alexis de Tocqueville, *Democracy in America*, Richard D. Heffner, ed. (New York, 1956), 198.
[53] Arthur Mann, "The Progressive Tradition," John Higham, ed., *The Reconstruction of American History* (New York, 1962), 176.

Americanization as an Early Twentieth-Century Adult Education Movement

ROBERT A. CARLSON

THE AVERAGE middle-class American contemplated the turn of the twentieth century from his farmhouse or his home on the city's fringe with a smug complacency. The United States had just defeated what Americans viewed as the archetype of "backward" Europe—monarchical and Roman Catholic Spain—in a war that had led to easy victory, empire, and a vastly increased self-esteem and world esteem for the United States.

At home, despite some pockets of economic distress in the nation, (1) prosperity was general for middle-class Americans and contributed to their complacency. Of course, when they thought about it, some of these people probably experienced a vague uncertainty about the fast-growing cities with ghettoes of foreign-born inhabitants that seemed so out of line with the folk-image of a rural society based on the yeoman farmer. (2) Yet, true to the laissez faire, Darwinist philosophy then current, Americans assumed that these immigrants would be assimilated as earlier immigrants had been, with a finer American type resulting.

This belief in inevitable progress wrought by spontaneous forces, preached by such social Darwinists as William Graham Sumner of Yale, led to a benevolent apathy. Others contributed to the smugness. Historian John Fiske and political scientist John Burgess had studied the world as it then was, had seen England supreme, America on the rise, and they proclaimed this as empirical proof of the supremacy of the Anglo-Saxon race and its institutions of government and law. The

Mr. Carlson is Assistant Professor of Education, University of Saskatchewan.

new eugenics movement "scientifically" classified European nationalities into a "hierarchy of merit." (3) It described the blond, long-headed Teutons of the north, the so-called Old Stock immigration to the United States, as inherently superior to the round-headed or dark-skinned central and southern Europeans who were now the largest group coming to these shores. Earlier, American prejudice had accorded shabby treatment to the vast German and Irish immigrations. (4) Now, any American of northern European background could feel pride of race based on scientific evidence.

The complacency of the middle class—born of social Darwinism, general prosperity, nationalism, and race pride—was soon put to rout by a spate of "muckraking" journalists who struck fear and guilt into this group by spotlighting the changing conditions in the land. Jacob Riis' exposé in 1902 of slum conditions in *The Battle with the Slum* and the 1904 series of articles by Lincoln Steffens on *The Shame of the Cities* opened the way to a heightened national concern for Americanization education.

"The more the muckrakers acquainted the Protestant Yankee with what was going on around him, the more guilty and troubled he felt." (5) Protestant, Anglo-Saxon values—defined as American values—seemed threatened from within as the result of his own inaction. The very institutions Burgess and Fiske had praised were shown to be corrupt in the big cities. The muckrakers showed that Irish-American political "bosses" were sewing up the immigrant vote and ruling the cities as foreign princes were imagined to rule their fiefs. Big business itself—by its monopolistic methods—threatened the old Protestant anvil of competition upon which individual worth was to be hammered out.

Protestant, middle-class Americans determined to preserve what they viewed as the American way of life. (6) Their resolve gained reinforcement from Lester Frank Ward's new interpretation of social Darwinism. According to Ward, no longer should society simply let natural law work its "will." It should try to understand natural law and then take advantage of its knowledge to improve its lot. "The day has come for society to take its affairs into its own hands and shape its own destinies," Ward wrote. (7)

So the reformers—many businessmen, churchmen, academicians, farmers, and scions of old-line American families—involved themselves in politics and joined with the middle-class pioneers who had begun settlement work in the United States in the 1880s. (8)   This so-called Progressive Movement built rapidly to 1917, capturing a major part of the 1912 third party Progressive Party platform.

By 1916 Progressivism would succeed in embodying many elements of its social justice program into the law of the land. Its other main emphasis—the return of orderly, efficient government—would bring procedural reforms by 1916 to many states in the form of the initiative, the referendum, the recall, and the direct primary. Nationally, it would gain acceptance of the direct election of the United States Senate by the American people.

Progressivism wanted to get the control of government back into the hands of the people—the right people, that is—those who understood American values, i.e., the reformers' values. And they came to realize as they came in contact with the immigrant that their values were not his values.

Political economist John Commons of the University of Wisconsin epitomized the reaction of middle-class reformers to their experience with the immigrant. "The American has learned . . . that this is a free government . . . based on constitutional principles of . . . trial by jury, separation of powers, independence of the judiciary, equality of opportunity. . . . These abstract principles have . . . influence as a guide to his ballot. But the immigrant . . .," Commons wrote, "votes as instructed by his employer or his political 'boss,' because it will help his employer's business or because his boss will get him a job, or will, in some other way, favor him and others of his nationality." (9)

The reformers now began to question whether they could carry out their efforts without solving the growing "immigrant problem." (10) There was a yearly influx between 1905 and 1914 that was never less than three-quarters of a million, largely of central and southern Europeans. (11)   Many of the reformers were appalled by the conditions under which the immigrants lived and wanted to help ameliorate the situation. This was the extension to the immigrant of the social justice side of Progressivism. Advocates of national order, efficiency, and government operation according to Commons' "abstract principles"—the harsher side of the movement—often argued for restriction of what they called the New Immigration from southern and eastern Europe. For a time both these groups of Progressives, and other Americans as well, would find consensus in the traditional American faith in education as the means of solving "The Problem."

There were two sides to this educational endeavor. One was the effort to educate the general public. This at first was a battle betweeen restrictionists and antirestrictionists. Soon both groups were educating the American public to the need they felt to Americanize those immigrants who were already here. The education of the immigrant was the other side of the Americanization campaign.

Americanization had begun altruistically enough in the late 1800s. Those reformers who joined the social settlement movement and lived in the immigrant neighborhoods often learned a considerable amount about these peoples that helped temper the Americanizing ardor. The experiences and programs of Nobel prize-winning social settlement pioneer Jane Addams at Hull House symbolize this form of settlement work. (12)   Jane Addams was willing to learn:

> . . . last Thanksgiving Day, I spent some time and zeal in a description of the Pilgrim Fathers, [and] the motives which had driven them across the sea. . . . The audience of Greeks listened respectfully, altho I was uneasily conscious of the somewhat feeble attempt to boast of Anglo-Saxon achievement in hardihood and privation to men whose powers of admiration were absorbed in their Greek background of philosophy and beauty. At any rate, after the lecture was over, one of the Greeks said to me quite simply: "I wish I could describe my ancestors to you; they were different from yours." His further remarks were translated by a little Irish boy of eleven, who speaks modern Greek . . . into . . .: "He says if that is what your ancestors are like, that his could beat them out." It is a good illustration of our faculty for ignoring the past, and of our failure to understand the immigrant estimation of ourselves. (13)

In developing their programs, Hull House workers took into account the needs expressed by the immigrants and came to view the immigrant not merely as an empty vat to be filled with Americanism. (14)   Rather, they saw the immigrant as bearing his own unique gifts to his adopted land. To help the newcomers adapt to America, Hull House offered English classes and other practical types of training, such as homemaking and industrial arts. Programs gave opportunity to immigrants to utilize their old country craftsmanship skills which generally lay fallow in the working and housing conditions imposed by industrial America. The programs brought together immigrants of different backgrounds with Old Stock Americans, developed recreation and educational programs for children and adults, worked to build respect among the second generation for the parents' backgrounds and worked for community spirit and community organization.

The emphasis on the individual—with his involvement in program development largely on his own terms—was the approach most characteristic of the social settlement. Jane Addams believed the example and experience of American life would shape, or Americanize, the immigrant for better or for worse. (15) In her autobiographical writings, she showed deep concern over social conditions that forced immigrants into low-paid factory jobs and slum living conditions. She was concerned, too, with the tendency of many Americans to blame the immigrant for the conditions they saw surrounding him. And she worked to change the attitude of the general public and its government officials who seemed ready to harass all foreign-speaking or foreign-appearing people when one of their number engaged in some antisocial act. She showed how the 1886 Haymarket riots in Chicago, the assassination of President McKinley in 1901 by Leon Czolgosz, World War I, and the takeover in Russia by the Bolsheviks brought panic reactions by the American people and their government against the immigrants. "Good" Americans indulged in guilt by association and ignored the concepts of trial by jury and presumption of innocence—some of the very same "abstract principles" of Americanism that they wished to teach to the new immigrants.

In the work of alleviating poverty, involving immigrants in another side of American life, and in interpreting conditions to the American middle class, the small group of settlement workers was a humanizing influence in the Americanization drive. It must be pointed out, though, that settlements could engage in subtle, even unintentional, forms of compulsion, such as drawing people to perhaps undesired meetings on the basis of obligation for past favors. And many settlement workers continued to assume that they had much to teach the immigrant about the true American way of life. Many reformers, seemingly, were unaware that the foreign language press and other of the immigrants' own paraphernalia were helping them adapt to their new environment. Perhaps the reformers did have much to teach the immigrants, but often their approach—so characteristic of the smugness of American life at the time—tended to condescension which elicited only confusion or rebuff from the immigrant. (16)

Despite its faults, the social settlement approach was humanitarian in its desire to aid individual immigrants. This humanitarian aspect can be seen also in such early programs as free public school extension lectures and social center programs for immigrants, special public school classes in English and civics, and in the Americanization activities of the foreign language press in America. These were programs that developed largely as responses to requests from the immigrants themselves.

The humanitarian approach to Americanization reflected one side of Progressive reform as it applied to the immigrants. But there was the other side of Progressivism—the order and efficiency aspect. It was largely out of this other side of Progressivism that Americanization quite early in the twentieth century began to shift in approach toward "an imperious demand for conformity." (17)

Not all who operated in a manner consistent with the vision of Ward's melioration philosophy agreed with the humanitarian, individualized service concept of education. Sociologist Edward A. Ross, a leading reform thinker, articulated in 1901 the educational doctrine of social control as a means of building a better American society. (18) Fearing the decay of the church and other indirect means of maintaining the social order, Ross saw public education as the panacea. It would be "an economical system of police" to stamp the individual into his society so that he himself would not desire to do things out of step with his society. (19) Ross believed that the natural leadership of American society belonged in the hands of the elite of ideas and talent who would provide expert direction of the society on behalf of the people and would reject the class interests he felt often infected leaders of society. Although most of his followers seemed little worried about it, Ross did see dangers to democracy in his social doctrine. He felt, however, that the many disparate organizations in American society would keep the state and the leaders in check.

Generally in sympathy with this social control doctrine of education were such academicians as John Commons, Albion Small, Ross Finney, David Snedden, and Charles Ellwood. These were among the leaders in the rise of social science in America. The approaches toward the immigrant suggested by these academicians took two courses—restriction, and/or compulsory education for Americanization.

Ross, apparently deeply influenced by the "science" of eugenics, looked about him and saw evidence of vice, exploitation, and degradation in the big cities where the immigrants lived, and this empirical evidence combined with the teachings of eugenics to convince him by 1914 that ". . . the blood now being injected into the veins of our people is 'sub-common.' " (20) He told his readers to compare the faces of Labor Day paraders and to note differences between unions dominated by the Old Stock (teamsters, piano movers, and steam fitters) and those dominated by the New Immigration (cigarmakers and garment workers). "To the practiced eye," he wrote, "the physiognomy of certain groups unmistakably proclaims inferiority of type. I have seen gatherings of the foreign-born in which narrow and sloping foreheads were the rule. The shortness and smallness of the crania were very noticeable." (21) Using case histories of the actions of people in shipwreck disasters of different nations, Ross concluded that "Northerners seem to surpass the southern Europeans in innate ethical endowment" and warned that these American qualities would be lost "in proportion as they absorb excitable mercurial blood from southern Europe." (22)

In 1910 Charles Ellwood presented the arguments for restriction in a systematic fashion: the Industrial Argument—protect American workmen from depressed wages; the Social Argument—impossible to overcome the essential foreignness of immigrant "thought and actions"; the Political Argument—immigrants "incapable of understanding and appreciating our free institutions"; and the Racial or Biological Argument—danger of degenerating the "national Blood" as well as the national institutions. (23)

The efforts of these and other social control advocates to restrict immigration brought a number of successes. (24) In 1903 the United States increased the immigrant head tax from one to two dollars and outlawed the entry or naturalization of anarchists. In 1907 the United States doubled the head tax and excluded imbeciles, the feebleminded, and prostitutes. In 1907, too, restrictionists won a victory in the appointment of a Federal Immigration Commission to restudy the whole question of immigration. (25) And restrictionist efforts continued.

Different social control advocates, however, emphasized different approaches. While Ross, Ellwood, and some of the others tended to argue primarily for educating the American public to accept immigration restriction, John Commons in 1907 emphasized the need to educate the immigrant. He distinguished between amalgamation (creation of a common racial stock) and assimilation (a "union of minds and wills" enabling common life and action). (26) "To be great a nation need not be of one blood, it must be of one mind . . .," Commons wrote. "Race and heredity may be beyond our organized control; but the instrument of a common language is at hand for conscious improvement through education and social environment." (27) Commons found it impossible to think that immigrants could understand patriotism without proper Americanization.

Commons' thinking soon began to find expression at the action level. By 1912 the goal of national "one-mindedness" replaced the original social service motivation behind the YMCA's Americanization programs. (28) The Association's 1912 handbook emphasized fear and social control, warning that "America seems to be the melting pot for all nations of the world, but unless it really succeeds in melting, fusing and creating a more or less harmonized constituency —a Christian American nation—the chaotic mixture may destroy the melting pot." (29) The YMCA complained that the New Immigration was replacing the "wholesome, earnest, faithful citizens and nation builders" from England, Ireland, Germany, and Scandinavia with "masses of suspicious, clannish people from southern and southeastern Europe" who had "foreignized" the centers of congested American cities. (30) It warned that "Unless we can assimilate, develop, train and make good citizens out of them, they are certain to make ignorant, suspicious and un-Americanized citizens out of us. Unless we Americanize them they will foreignize us." (31) And the YMCA assisted in this effort to assimilate or homogenize the immigrant into American society by providing classes in English and citizenship. (32)

This society-oriented concept of Americanization would soon become the consensus in the United States, overriding the humanitarians' desire to maintain the immigrants' cultures within the American nation. An ideology like that of John Commons would have little interest in maintaining dissenting or minority values. Its interest was in preserving the values and institutions of the dominant element in the society and in gaining acceptance of these by all others for the sake of a single-minded nation. Although this philosophy seldom gained effective implementation in specific educational programs, its rhetoric became dominant in the thought of the country. Paradoxically enough, it was the advocates of humanitarian laissez-faire who led the nation into an acceptance of Americanization education based on this harsh ideology of social control.

A society-oriented Americanization campaign developed under the leadership of the North American Civic League, an organization founded in 1907 by those who wanted to continue America's tradition as haven for the dispossessed *and* by a number of industrialists who wanted to maintain a flow of cheap labor. The work of this group included fact-finding programs and demonstration projects in immigrant education, but it emphasized education of the general American public in behalf of continued immigration and support of humanitarian programs for the immigrants. (33) The league's educational efforts did help to maintain public support for continued immigration. But no longer could it hew to a laissez-faire line or to a purely humanitarian rhetoric if it was to hold public sentiment on its side. Americans were aroused about the source and numbers of immigrants, their religions, their political and economic thinking, and the conditions in which they lived. To allay these fears, pro-immigration forces, like the North American Civic League, developed—by experience—a policy highly successful in keeping America open to continued immigration. That policy, basically, was: "Not restriction, but Americanization." It was a position the restrictionists had difficulty in refuting.

And the "man on horseback" who virtually seized leadership of this campaign to "wake up America" to its "duty" to nationalize its immigrants was no man at all. It was "a crisp, authoritative young lady with an instinct for order and organization . . ., an apostle of industrial efficiency" who "in one breath . . . preached social welfare and national discipline." (34) This former settlement worker and muckraking social researcher—Miss Frances Kellor—led her New York branch out of the increasingly reactionary North American Civic League onto the national level in 1914 as a central clearing-house to assist, unify, and involve public and private agencies in the Americanization effort. (35) Her organization renamed itself the Committee for Immigrants in America to reflect the new national scope.

In her efforts to reach the American public with the twin Progressive messages of social justice for the immigrant and nationalization of the immigrant to the National Mind, she attached Americanization to the increasingly popular concepts of conservation and efficiency propounded by Theodore Roosevelt and by America's pioneer theoretician of business efficiency, Frederick W. Taylor. (36) A large body of literature had sprung up by 1914 advocating the application of business efficiency to schooling. (37) And efficiency criteria gained ruthless application in the nation's elementary and secondary schools in an effort to help children to fit into American life in a way thought to be the least costly and most desirable for the society.

Frances Kellor applied the concept of efficiency to the education of adult immigrants. Like John Commons, her interest was more in behalf of American society than in behalf of the immigrants. She argued that a nation, a community, and a factory would gain efficiency by requiring a single language for communication and by encouraging like-mindedness in thought. She was a latter-day Horace Mann in her zeal for homogeneity in American life and thought. Deeply disturbed by racial and labor-management "factionalism," she looked at Americanization as the science of nation-building. (38) Particularly in the earlier part of her work, she was deeply moved by the exploitation of the immigrant by both native Americans and foreign labor gang leaders, or padrones. (39) As a means of conserving human resources, she argued for Americans to ameliorate the conditions thrust upon the immigrants. (40) But it was to be a two-way street. The immigrant would have to learn to spend his wages more wisely, to eat the right kinds of food, to wear the right kinds of clothes, to understand what constituted fair wages and decent working conditions, and to spend in America the money he earned here. (41)

To bring about these humanitarian and smug middle-class blessings of Americanism, Frances Kellor worked to "rev up" the engines of society to pressure the immigrant for conformity to these more efficient patterns of life. "We are on the way to supplementing scientific management with citizenship management," Miss Kellor wrote. "Some of us believe that in this new spirit lies the hope of the nation." (42)

Frances Kellor worked to involve business and labor in this common endeavor of Americanization. On the basis of efficiency, she argued for employers to institute English classes for their immigrant workmen. It would improve the safety record and lead to a more stable work force. Aware of the increased interest in Americanization by employers following the 1912 Lawrence, Massachusetts, IWW-led strike of immigrant workmen, (43) Miss Kellor argued: "Strikes and plots . . . fostered and developed by un-American agitators and foreign propaganda are not easily carried on among men who have acquired, with the English language and citizenship, an understanding of American industrial standards and an American point of view." (44) She applauded the decision of Packard Motor Company and Paige-Detroit Company to pressure immigrants to become citizens by a policy of nonpromotion for noncitizens. (45) She rejoiced that this signified the end of the old industrial laissez-faire policy toward immigrant workers.

Aided by advice from Miss Kellor's organization the Detroit Bureau of Commerce, leading Detroit industries and the Board of Education, cooperated in an English-first program, or as it was soon termed, an American-first program. (46) This interest by the employers now enabled Detroit to expand its night school program and bring in YMCA adult education expert Peter Roberts to prepare the evening school teachers for their increased responsibilities. Roberts and the YMCA now adapted themselves to the efficiency approach. (47) It was not too difficult. Inside of ten years the YMCA had revised its Americanization goals from humanitarian service to social control and now to national efficiency.

To get attendance at the Americanization schools in Detroit, the Board of Commerce instituted a hard-sell advertising campaign that urged attendance at English classes for better citizenship and better jobs. The Americanizers posted signs to this effect on factory bulletin boards and at area gathering places of immigrants, put the message in pay envelopes, arranged for pastors of foreign language churches and editors of foreign language newspapers to advocate class attendance, and arranged for inserts to be placed in foreign language books borrowed from the library and in packages brought home from the stores by anyone "who looked like a foreigner." (48) The Saxon Motor Company made night school attendance compulsory for its non-English-speaking workers. The Northway Motor and Manufacturing Company required its non-English-speaking employees to attend either its own factory school, the public evening school, or face discharge. Cadillac Company and most other firms merely gave strong encouragement to their employees to attend the public evening schools. The paternalistic Ford Motor Company, however, discouraged attendance at the public schools and required it at its own school "where the pupils are told to 'walk to the American blackboard, take a piece of American chalk, and explain how the American workman walks to his American home and sits down with his American family to their good American dinner.'" (49)

Although this struck some Americanizers in 1916 as "grotesquely exaggerated patriotism," (50) Packard Company President Alvan Macauley justified the Detroit effort as paying off in terms of "industrial efficiency and organization." (51) Soon industry professional and trade magazines abounded with advice to managers and efficiency engineers to Americanize employees in the name of business efficiency and profit. On the basis of a careful investigation of factory Americanization programs for the Solvay Process Company in 1918, Charles Paull of Harvard University found that evening schools had generally failed to reach the vast majority of the non-English-speaking people. (52) To get to this "hard-to-reach" group, management consultant Winthrop Talbot advocated noncompulsory classes in factories. (53) He argued that such classes were simply part of the overhead for an efficient plant operation. "It is part of the care needed for maintaining the proper functioning of the human mechanisms employed for production purposes," (54) he wrote.

The *Outlook* showed the close relationship between the social control and efficiency concepts of Americanization education when it described the work of the evening schools of Rochester, New York. It termed the Rochester public school system "An Americanization

Factory," the "natural instrument for the State to use in making good Americans from the raw material that is coming into the country from abroad. . . ." (55)

The social control dimension came to the fore after World War I broke out in Europe in August of 1914. As appeals for American sympathy poured into the country from both sides in the conflict, the Americanizers saw the National Mind split on such issues as the advisability of United States military preparation, whether to favor one side or the other, and the wisdom of possible United States intervention in the conflict. Fearing that international propaganda was destroying American unity, Frances Kellor helped organize the National Americanization Day Committee in the spring of 1915. (56) This group seeded the nation with adult education materials encouraging community-wide organization of ceremonies on the Fourth of July to foster patriotism in local immigrant populations. (57) Some 150 communities responded. (58)

Here was the match applied to the vapors of fear collecting over potential internal subversion. The "Americanization Day" campaign marked the flaring forth of the extreme period of Americanization which lasted through 1916, continued at a high pitch through the years of United States involvement in World War I, slackened briefly after the war, gave a dying flash during the 1919-1920 "Big Red Scare," then dropped to a flicker in the prosperity of the 1920s, with the "return to normalcy" and the disillusionment with President Woodrow Wilson's missionary democracy. (59)

Led by Frances Kellor's National Americanization Committee which had by now absorbed most functions of her old Committee for Immigrants in America, (60) United States organizations tumbled over each other in the rush to join the Americanization bandwagon. (61) The Chamber of Commerce established an Immigration Committee in 1915. The General Federation of Women's Clubs became involved in Americanization by 1916. Church and fraternal organizations joined in. Attaching her program to the preparedness drive, Miss Kellor took the message of internal peril to the new National Security League whose members quickly embraced Americanization. The educational establishment, *soi-disant* patriotic groups, and the YMCA expanded their Americanization programs. Much to the discomfiture of many of the conservative Americanizers, even the immigrant president of the anti-immigration American Federation of Labor—Samuel Gompers—made Americanization noises. They were hardly what many of the Americanizers would recognize as their standard brand Americanism. "It is the labor movement that has been educating these people in American standards, their rights and how to maintain them," Gompers said. "The trade union movement has been teaching them that human lives and human rights are of greater importance than exploitation for private profit." (62)

America's entry into the war in April of 1917 injected an increased tone of suspicion, intolerance, and fear into the campaign to Americanize the immigrants. Activities increased on the part of such self-appointed patriotic organizations as the National Security League and the American Protective League. (63) Excesses occurred in the propaganda of the federal Committee on Public Information and in the administration of such laws as the Espionage Act and the Sedition Act. (64) Americanization became one of a series of little crusades in the One Big Crusade for Democracy—President Wilson's and America's conception of World War I.

Wartime hysteria found arguments to attack immigrants that in normal times could have been used to defend them. Samuel Hopkins Adams, concerned about sabotage possibilities, told the story of a key piece of machinery that he discovered had been tended by seven foreign workmen over a year's time. (65) There had been no security clearance for these men. There had been no sabotage, either. Instead of taking heart in the loyalty of the immigrants, he used this story to show the dangers to America in allowing aliens to serve in sensitive industrial positions. And he argued for massive Americanization efforts immediately, including the installation of company baseball diamonds on which the foreign workmen could play this American sport. (66) He did not say whether he wanted employers to compel the men to participate.

There were those who stood against the Americanization flood. As early as 1916, John Dewey publicly fought the effort to identify certain cultural characteristics as American and to Americanize for national unity around these criteria. He argued that America was a composite of races and nationalities, with no single ethnic ideal:

No matter how loudly any one proclaims his Americanism, if he assumes that any one racial strain, any one component culture, no matter how early settled it was in our territory, or how effective it has proved in its own land, is to furnish a pattern to which all other strains and cultures are to conform, he is a traitor to American nationalism. (67)

. . . the problem is not to reduce . . . [immigrants] to an anonymous and drilled homogeneity, but to see to it that all get from one another the best that each strain has to offer from its own tradition and culture. (68)

Edward A. Steiner was another early critic of the fanatical spirit of the Americanization drive. (69) Steiner indicated his own belief in the need for adult schools for the security of American institutions but opposed their forced utilization. Instead, he said the immigrants would come to realize the need to learn English to get ahead in America. Steiner blamed the fanatical tendency in Americanization on Americans' guilt feelings over their alleged laxity in educating the alien. It was just this exposed nerve that Miss Kellor and the other Americanizers kept hitting over and over in their adult education program to involve organizations in the Americanization campaign.

With the end of World War I and victory over Germany, the American crusading spirit turned against Bolshevism. United States Attorney General Mitchell Palmer led this crusade, rushing into the vacuum created by President Wilson's disabling stroke in October 1919. With one eye on expunging radical thought and the other on the White House, Palmer coupled his fight against Bolshevism with efforts to blunt end-of-the-war strikes by unions for higher wages and improved working conditions. (70) Many of the Americanizers lockstepped to this new crusade. The YMCA clambered aboard what its ubiquitous Americanizer, Peter Roberts, undoubtedly thought was the new bandwagon. Roberts called for increased support of Americanization, complaining that "The radicals have a well-organized speaker's bureau, a many-tongued press, and a fervency in attack which cannot be paralleled by any constructive and conserving agency interested in aliens." (71) John Dewey saw this two-pronged effort to suppress strikes and the spread of "Sovietism" as a "hangover of a war psychology of suspicion and fear." (72)

The Red Scare was the dying gasp of rampant Americanization. Increasingly, the totality of the Americanization concept and method came under attack. And the consensus of anti- and pro-immigration forces that undergirded the Americanization effort would soon fall apart.

Critics attacked the results of Americanization. All sides now conceded those results had been negligible. Some critics said the methods used to Americanize the immigrants were too harsh, while others condemned them as too gentle. Many questioned the assumptions of the Americanizers. Some critics asked if there really was "an American way." Others asked if anyone had the ability or the right to Americanize anyone else. Still others questioned the capacity of adult education to make Americans out of what they regarded as basically inferior types.

Enhancing this national mood of questioning were some facts that became more generally known. Although recognized by the sophisticated, it now came out in such mass-circulation periodicals as the *Saturday Evening Post* that only one-quarter of the illiterates in the United States were foreign-born or children of the foreign-born. (73) Even taking into account the number of illiterate Negroes, the majority of illiterates in the United States, then, were probably white Anglo-Saxon Protestants. This provided food for thought about the Americanizers' heavy emphasis on English and literacy as requirements for Americanism. And it became general knowledge that immigrant attendance at Americanization classes was relatively low. (74)

An important Carnegie Commission study published in 1920 attacked the emotional, unsystematic, and coercive approach to Americanization by "mushroom" citizen organizations. (75) It called for centering Americanization activity in the formal public school system and for the use there of an "educational service station" approach of informal adult education that would overcome the large drop-out problem encountered when using formal day-school approaches.

A series of articles in the *New Republic* from 1919 to 1921 blasted Americanization as "cultural tyranny" (76) by middle-class Americans over the lower class. "With his characteristic blend of hard sense and sentimentalism, the new patrician sailed forth among the imported plebs to urge it [sic] to adopt his grammar and his bathtubs, his soap and his patriotism. . . . Americanization . . . became . . . a thing to frighten children with. The very word acquired . . . a disreputable and un-American ring." (77) The magazine described the exasperation of the little party of middle-class lady Americanizers when told by one of their targets to come back when she had finished cleaning. (78) It seems her sons were in the army, her husband was at work in the munitions plant, and her daughter was out selling Liberty Bonds, so somebody had to do the cleaning. It also told of the fanatics who stoned a group of Czechs because they were wearing their national costumes when seeing sons and husbands off to fight in the United States Army. (79)

The *New Republic* branded a whole series of organizations active in Americanization as mere advocates of the economic and political status quo. (80) It convincingly backed up its charges against the YMCA and Mr. Roberts, the North American Civic League for Immigrants, the National Security League, the Loyal American League, the Veterans of Foreign Wars, United Americans, the Sons of the American Revolution, the American Legion, and the Chamber of Commerce.

There was a growing resentment by the immigrants themselves over the effects of Americanization. Sarka Hrbkova of the Czech foreign language press in the United States called Americanization "A laudable propaganda infected by ignorance." (81) Louis Adamic gave an example of one effect of posters used to further Americanization: "Don't say 'Ya'—Say 'Yes!' " "That placard," said the old man. "It was as though pasted on a wall in our home and I couldn't pull it down. My oldest boy ran away. The children could not forgive their mother and me that we were 'foreigners.' They would not let us say anything in Norwegian to them—anything intimate. They held us away. It was years before that placard wore off enough for the runaway to come back." (82)

The *New Republic*'s criticism went to the heart of the problem of Americanization education. It deplored the use of an active, transitive verb like "Americanize" to describe the process. "It implies . . . something done to somebody by someone else. . . . What it should mean, what we must make it mean, is a mutuality of action. . . ." (83)

Isaac Berkson, supervisor of schools and extension activities of the Bureau of Jewish Education and a student of John Dewey, reflected in 1920 Dewey's 1916 position in calling for cultural pluralism in the United States. (84) This would allow for a cherishing by immigrants of their Old World culture as they settled into their new lives in the American social structure. As Berkson pointed out:

The splendid loyalty that immigrants have shown toward America and their heartfelt reverence for the new Promised Land are the result of no "Americanization" program, but of living under institutions which by their very nature permitted economic advance, educational opportunities, and individual freedom in a degree unknown to them in the lands of their birth. It is the excellence of American tradition working indirectly and spontaneously which Americanizes, not the direct application of strict methods. (85)

The liberal critics of Americanization were joined by immigration restrictionists, by the racists, and by others disillusioned with democracy in the aftermath of the Versailles Peace Treaty negotiations. The latter three groups pointed to the small results of the Americanization campaign and claimed America had opted for the wrong alternative in prewar days. They now dusted off the immigration restriction arguments and again presented restriction to the public as a viable alternative to the educational campaign that they termed a failure. In *The Melting Pot Mistake*, Henry Pratt Fairchild attacked Americanization's emphasis on encouraging aliens to become citizens. (86) Fairchild, Lothrop Stoddard, and others feared this emphasis—together with the apparent failure to disabuse immigrants of such "un-American" ideas as trade-unionism and Bolshevism—merely gave these "despicable Under Men" the vote to overthrow the American Way of Life. Stoddard, an exponent of the Nordic super-race theory, used the term, the "under man," a direct translation of the German racist word for the Slavs and others to the east of Germany. (87)

The *Saturday Evening Post* in 1921 helped popularize the attack on the Americanization program, calling it a palliative, not a remedy:

In spite of the evidence on every side, sentimentalists still picture Uncle Sam as a clever chef who can take a handful of foreign scraps, a sprig of Americanism and a clove of democracy, and skillfully blend the mess into something fine and desirable. . . . Race character is as fixed a fact as race color. . . . We are fatuously strengthening the levee here and there with a few sandbags of Americanization, while we complacently watch the whole river rush through a mile-wide crevasse. . . . The trouble with our Americanization program is that a large part of our recent immigrants can never become Americans. They will always be Americanski—near-Americans with un-American ideas and ideals. (88)

Americanization had become discredited in a broad spectrum of American society. It no longer served as a viable alternative to, and thus a bulwark against, immigration restriction. In 1921, Congress passed an Emergency Quota Act with the approval of President Warren G. Harding to restrict further immigration to the United States to no more than three percent of the number of foreign-born of that nationality living in the United States in 1910. This was insufficient for many of the restrictionists. Taking its cue from President Calvin Coolidge's comment in his 1923 State of the Union Message that "America must be kept American," in May of 1924 Congress passed an even more stringent restrictionist piece of legislation, the National Origins Act. This pushed the base year back to 1890 when there were fewer southern and eastern Europeans here.

This was perhaps the harshest collective action taken toward the immigrant during this whole period. Despite its tough rhetoric about compulsion, ". . . the whole Americanization movement remained primarily a venture in persuasion. It continued to rely much more upon ideological pressure than upon the coercive power of government." (89) Meanwhile, the evening school programs fostered by the Americanization campaign took root in American society, soon developing into general adult education programs. (90) "Legislation on behalf of adult education and evening schools might not have been passed so easily had it not been for the crusading zeal of the Americanizers in sponsoring such legislation on behalf of the foreign-born. With precedent taken, the stage was set for better things to come." (91)

Dare the historian conclude that the impetus given to the growth of adult education by the Americanization program was valuable enough to offset the confusion and heartache it caused for hundreds of thousands of immigrants? A clear-cut evaluation of Americanization is, at best, difficult. It must be concluded that in the context of its time, the 1905-1925 Americanization Campaign was comparatively humane. And, most important, it held open the American door to continued immigration for a few more years than might otherwise have been possible. On the other hand, it caused severe psychological harm to many of the people it purported to help and probably damaged, rather than aided, the cause of Americanization by using rhetoric and approaches inimical to such American principles as freedom, democracy, and individual rights.

The Americanization experience clearly influenced the adult education profession in the United States. (92) Partly as the result of this experience, today's adult education criteria include the meeting of individual needs, involvement of the client in establishing objectives and evaluating programs, voluntary participation, and a whole range of such individual-oriented guidelines. Adult education in the United States has, in large part, acted as an "educational service station" (93) in the nearly 50 years since the extreme social control phase of Americanization—what Frances Kellor called "citizenship management"— ran its course. This service station concept, however, now appears to be in a period of transition, (94) and if so, it may be well for educators to reflect upon the Americanization experience at this time.

The paradigm suggested by this study of Americanization indicates that adult education by the middle class for minority groups may start altruistically enough. Soon, however, it tends to become directed toward the establishment of conformity to middle-class standards and the maintenance of the status quo in American society.

It might prove enlightening to apply this paradigm to the adult education programs now in effect or on the drawing boards to "upgrade" America's poor, primarily poor American Negroes. The Job Corps program, for example, soon reacted to middle-class criticism, with a resulting shift from the "... permissive note on which ... [it] opened ... [to] a far more disciplined atmosphere in which volunteers are increasingly impressed with standards of behavior and appearance." (95) The war on poverty has been described by humanitarians as "welfare colonialism," (96) a criticism similar to the "cultural tyranny" charges hurled earlier at the Americanizers.

While the Americanizers generally failed to achieve the compulsory programs they often espoused in the early 1900s, those who in 1971 advocated citizenship management were well on the way to requiring the involvement of the poor in their efforts. The Defense Department's program to improve the social profile of the nation and its economy as a part of national defense has led to Project 100,000. (97) This adult education program involves the drafting into the military of 100,000 men a year who would otherwise fail to qualify for military service. This compulsory Defense Department educational program was established to instill new attitudes and skills to help these men become a part of the existing society, thus to build a stable social structure. The goals of Project 100,000 may sound admirable, but the goals of the Americanizers, too, sounded good to middle-class Americans in the first quarter of this century.

Notes

1. David A. Shannon, *Twentieth Century America* (Chicago: Rand McNally and Company, 1963), pp. 67-86.
2. Richard Hofstadter, *The Age of Reform* (New York: Random House Vintage Books, 1955), p. 176.
3. John W. Higham, *Strangers in the Land* (New Brunswick, N.J.: Rutgers University Press, 1955), p. 153.
4. *Ibid.*, p. 149.
5. Hofstadter, *The Age of Reform*, p. 205.
6. *Ibid.*, p. 152.
7. Lester Ward, "Sociocracy," in Perry Miller, ed., *American Thought: Civil War to World War I* (New York: Holt, Rinehart and Winston, 1965), p. 113.
8. Robert A. Woods and Albert J. Kennedy, *The Settlement Horizon* (New York: Russell Sage Foundation, 1922), pp. 41-44.
9. John R. Commons, *Races and Immigrants in America* (New York: The Macmillan Company, 1907), p. 221.
10. Hofstadter, *The Age of Reform*, pp. 180-86.
11. United States Bureau of the Census, *Historical Statistics of the U.S.* (Washington, D.C.: Government Printing Office, 1960).
12. For a recent reappraisal of Jane Addams, see Christopher Lasch, *The New Radicalism in America, 1889-1963* (New York: Alfred A. Knopf, 1965), pp. 3-37.
13. Jane Addams, "Recent Immigration: A Field Neglected by the Scholar," *Educational Review*, XXIX (March 1905), 253 and 254.
14. See Jane Addams' autobiography, *Forty Years at Hull House* (New York: The Macmillan Company, 1935), especially Chap. XI of Volume I, pp. 231-58.
15. Jane Addams, "Autobiographical Notes Upon Twenty Years at Hull House: Echoes of the Russian Revolution," *The American Magazine*, LXX (September 1910), 644.
16. Hofstadter, *The Age of Reform*, pp. 181 and 182.
17. Higham, *Strangers in the Land*, p. 237.
18. Edward A. Ross, *Social Control* (New York: The Macmillan Company, 1901).
19. *Ibid.*, p. 178.
20. Edward A. Ross, *The Old World in the New* (New York: The Century Company, 1914), pp. 274 and 284-86.

21. *Ibid.*
22. *Ibid.*, pp. 295 and 296.
23. Charles A. Ellwood, *Sociology and Modern Social Problems* (New York: American Book Company, 1910, 1913), pp. 218-22.
24. See George M. Stephenson, *A History of American Immigration, 1820-1924* (Boston: Ginn and Company, 1926).
25. George Edward Hartmann, *The Movement to Americanize the Immigrant* (New York: Columbia University Press, 1948), pp. 64 and 65.
26. Commons, *Races and Immigrants*, p. 209.
27. *Ibid.*, p. 20.
28. Hartmann, *The Movement to Americanize*, p. 28.
29. George B. Hodge, *Association Educational Work for Men and Boys* (New York: Association Press, 1912), pp. 175 and 176.
30. *Ibid.*
31. *Ibid.*
32. *Ibid.*, p. 31.
33. Hartmann, *The Movement to Americanize*, Chap. 2, pp. 39-63.
34. Higham, *Strangers in the Land*, p. 239.
35. *Ibid.*, pp. 240 and 241.
36. See Raymond E. Callahan, *Education and the Cult of Efficiency* (Chicago: University of Chicago Press, 1962), especially pp. 19-41.
37. See Irving King, *Education for Society Efficiency* (New York: D. Appleton and Company, 1913 and 1915), for example.
38. Frances A. Kellor, "What Is Americanization," in Philip Davis, ed., *Immigration and Americanization* (Boston: Ginn and Company, 1920), pp. 625 and 626.
39. Frances A. Kellor, "Who Is Responsible for the Immigrant?" *The Outlook*, CVI (April 25, 1914), 912 and 913.
40. *Ibid.*, pp. 913 and 914.
41. *Ibid.*, p. 916.
42. Frances A. Kellor, "Americanization by Industry," *The Immigrants In America Review*, II (April 1916), 15.
43. Hartmann, *The Movement to Americanize*, pp. 88-96.
44. Kellor, "Americanization by Industry," p. 24.
45. *Ibid.*
46. Gregory Mason, "Americans First," *The Outlook*, CXIV (September 27, 1916), 193-201.
47. Hartmann, *The Movement to Americanize*, footnote, p. 29.
48. Mason, "Americans First," p. 195.
49. *Ibid.*, p. 200.
50. *Ibid.*
51. *Ibid.*, p. 201.
52. Charles H. Paull, *Americanization: A Discussion of Present Conditions with Recommendations for the Teaching of Non-Americans, A Report to the Solvay Process Co.*, 1918. Also, Charles H. Paull, "De-

velopment of Americanization Project," *Industrial Management,* LVII (March 1919), 213.

53. Winthrop Talbot, "Americanization in Industry," *Industrial Management,* LVI (December 1918), 510.

54. Winthrop Talbot, "The One Language Industrial Plant," *Industrial Management,* LVIII (October 1919), 320.

55. Gregory Mason, "An Americanization Factory," *The Outlook,* CXII (February 23, 1916), 439-41.

56. Higham, *Strangers in the Land,* p. 243.

57. Frances A. Kellor, "National Americanization Day—July 4th," *The Immigrants in America Review,* I (September 1915), 18-29.

58. Hartmann, *The Movement to Americanize,* p. 121.

59. *Ibid.,* pp. 268 and 269.

60. Higham, *Strangers in the Land,* p. 243.

61. Hartmann, *The Movement to Americanize,* p. 132; Higham, *Strangers in the Land,* pp. 243 and 244; "Americanization Work of Women's Clubs," *The Immigrants in America Review,* I (January 1916), 64; and Anthony Beck, "Promotion of Citizenship," *The Catholic World,* CIX (September 1919), 742.

62. "Americanizing Foreign Workers," *American Federationist,* XXIII (August 1916), 690.

63. Shannon, *Twentieth Century America,* pp. 179 and 180.

64. *Ibid.*

65. Samuel Hopkins Adams, *Invaded America,* Reprint from *Everybody's Magazine* (March 1918), New York, 1918, p. 2.

66. *Ibid.,* p. 14.

67. Speech before the NEA quoted by Edward A. Krug, *The Shaping of the American High School* (New York: Harper and Row, 1964), p. 425.

68. John Dewey, "Universal Service as Education," *The New Republic* (April 22 and 29, 1916), reprinted in John Dewey, *Characters and Events: Popular Essays in Social and Political Philosophy,* Joseph Ratner, ed. (New York: Henry Holt and Company, 1929), p. 467.

69. Edward A. Steiner, *Nationalizing America,* (New York: Fleming H. Revell Company, 1916).

70. Shannon, *Twentieth Century America,* pp. 182 and 201.

71. Peter Roberts, *The Problem of Americanization* (New York: The Macmillan Company, 1920), p. v.

72. John Dewey, "Freedom of Thought and Work," *The New Republic* (May 5, 1920), reprinted in John Dewey, *Characters and Events,* p. 523.

73. Forrest Crissey, "Our Country Schools," *The Saturday Evening Post,* CXCIII (April 16, 1921), 62.

74. See, for example, National Conference on Americanization in Industries, *Proceedings,* Nantucket Beach, Mass., June 22-24, 1919, p. 25.

75. Frank V. Thompson, *Schooling of the Immigrant* (New York: Harper and Brothers, 1920), pp. 239-261, 364, and 382.
76. Anzia Yezierska, "Soap and Water and the Immigrant," *The New Republic*, XVIII (February 22, 1919), 117-19.
77. M. E. Ravage, "The Immigrant's Burden," *The New Republic*, XIX (June 14, 1919), 210 and 211.
78. Edward Hale Bierstadt, "Pseudo-Americanization," *The New Republic*, XXVI (May 25, 1921), 371-73.
79. *Ibid.*
80. Edward Hale Bierstadt, "Pseudo-Americanization," *The New Republic*, XXVII (June 1, 1921), 19-23.
81. Sarka Hrbkova, " 'Bunk' In Americanization," *The Forum*, LXIII (April-May 1920), 428.
82. Louis Adamic, *A Nation of Nations* (New York: Harper and Brothers, 1944), p. 2.
83. Edward Hale Bierstadt, "Pseudo-Americanization," *The New Republic*, XXVII (June 1, 1921), 23.
84. Isaac B. Berkson, *Theories of Americanization: A Critical Study* (New York: Teachers College Bureau of Publications, 1920).
85. *Ibid.*, p. 70.
86. Henry Pratt Fairchild, *The Melting-Pot Mistake* (Boston: Little, Brown and Company, 1926), p. 196.
87. For Lothrop Stoddard's point of view, see his *Re-Forging America, the Story of Our Nationhood* (New York: Charles Scribner's Sons, 1927), especially pp. 184-93, and his *The Revolt Against Civilization, the Menace of the Under Man* (New York: Charles Scribner's Sons, 1922).
88. "Americanski," *The Saturday Evening Post*, CXCIII (May 14, 1921), 20.
89. Higham, *Strangers in the Land*, p. 259.
90. *Ibid.*, p. 260.
91. Hartmann, *The Movement to Americanize*, p. 273.
92. Morse A. Cartwright, *Ten Years of Adult Education* (New York: The Macmillan Company, 1935), p. 136.
93. Frank V. Thompson in his 1920 Carnegie Commission study had recommended the educational service station approach to adult educators in these very words. Other factors operated to encourage the service approach, including the need for adult educators to gain sufficient volume of participation to make programs self-supporting—a policy generally set by institutions for their adult education divisions.
94. Bernard J. James, "Can 'Needs' Define Educational Goals?" *Adult Education*, VII (Autumn 1956), 21 and 22.
95. Charles Bartlett, "Job Corps Program Faces Many Problems," *Capital Times*, Madison, Wisconsin, Friday, September 2, 1966, p. 34.

96. James Ridgeway, "Saul Alinsky in Smugtown," *The New Republic*, CLII (June 26, 1965), 15-17.

97. Speech before the 1967 National Adult Education Conference by Nathan Brodsky, adult education administrator with the United States Department of Defense, Bellevue-Stratford Hotel, Philadelphia, Pennsylvania, November 17, 1967.

The Americanizing of the German Immigrant: A Chapter from U. S. Social History*

Reinhard R. Doerries

ABSTRACT

While German historiography has produced a number of studies on the problem of emigration, the question of the absorption of German nationals in foreign societies has largely been neglected. Immigrants from Germany made up one of the largest contingents of the inflow to the United States throughout most of the nineteenth century. As was the case with other nationalities, they formed associations of social, economic and cultural cooperation in the New World, often designed to maintain an ethnic cohesiveness but in many cases becoming in fact vehicles of Americanization. The social structure of the German-American community is not only of interest as an ethnic microcosm; the study of the ethnic minority and its interaction with the existing American social formations also reveals a number of valuable insights into the makings of American society. The interdisciplinary approach to American social history, drawing on findings in fields such as church history, sociology, applied sociolinguistics, and organizational history shows the multi-faceted Americanization to be a natural social process.

Benjamin Franklin once voiced his concern over what he saw as a growing German influence in Pennsylvania and fearfully asked: "Why should Pennsylvania, founded by the English, become a colony of Aliens, who will shortly be so numerous as to Germanize us instead of our Anglifying them [. . .]."[1] The region of Pennsylvania, however, does appear to have been distinctly an exception in the overall German immigrant experience. The dialect known as Pennsylvania Dutch and still in use even in our time bears witness to the sturdy ethnic tradition cultivated by the early German immigrants to this area who, as research has shown, often had little or no contact with English speaking Americans until well into the 19th century. In most other heavily German settled areas, especially in the cities, even in such places as Milwaukee and St. Louis, continuous Americanization has depleted the German—American population. In fact, if one were to look at the German immigrant experience in America from the German—American side, one might indeed be strongly impressed by the argument of forced de-ethnization at the hands of eager native Americanizers.

To cite an early German voice, on October 11, 1799, an enraged group of Baltimore German Catholics bluntly approached the Propaganda Fide in Rome and wrote: "The Bishop wanted to change us all into Englishmen, rapidly and violently [. . .]. But this attempt is in vain, it is a thing impossible of achievement, for we will never consent to his destroying our vernacular German language."[2] Moved by the same concerns the Franciscan

---

* This is a revised version of a paper presented for the Bicentennial Symposia "Religious Freedom: Churches and Ethnic Communities in the American City," held in Philadelphia in December, 1975. To the friends and colleagues in Philadelphia I am indebted for valuable comments and criticism alike. In part, the lecture was made possible by financial support from the "200-Jahrfeier USA" organization in München.

[1] Leonard W. Labaree, ed., *The Papers of Benjamin Franklin,* Vol. 4 (New Haven: Yale University Press, 1961), p. 234. From "Observations Concerning the Increase of Mankind, Peopling of Countries & c.," written by Franklin in 1750 and first published in 1755.

[2] Baltimore Germans to Propaganda Fide, October 11, 1799. Scritture Riferite nei Congressi America

Father Frederick Caesarius Reuter, also of Baltimore, in the course of his bitter ethnically inspired fight with Bishop John Carroll even blurted out that he for his part was prepared to lay down his life for his German nation and for his religion: "Vitam meam aeque pro natione mea ac pro religione pono."[3] Among Protestants, at least in some quarters, the feeling appears to have been much the same. Thus, in 1790, when the dedicated founders of the German Lutheran Aid Society of Philadelphia convened to write down their organizational rules, Pastor Henry Helmuth proclaimed that "all business orally or in writing, must be transacted in the German language."[4]

Indeed, one could cite countless documents from American history, instances where German-Americans of various social background, political persuasion, and religious adherence expressed their grave concern over the way they were being or becoming Americanized, a kind of resentment or fear which incidentally can be traced among some leaders of the German ethnic community throughout the 19th and occasionally in the early 20th century. Therefore, those who would wish to pursue the obvious question of whether the Americanization process of America's (after the British) numerically most important immigrant group[5] was marked by particularly painful experiences, are faced with a mountain of primary source material carrying one overriding message, namely that the Germans, who contributed so richly to American cultural and economic life, by a series of tragic events and as a consequence of American "melting pot" pressures were unduly coerced into sacrificing their ethnic character. John Arkas Hawgood, an Englishman who took great interest in the history of German–America outdid most other authors when he entitled his still interesting study *The Tragedy of German-America*.[6]

Was the Americanizing of the German immigrant a tragic experience marked by indignities and injustices? To arrive at somewhat persuasive answers to this question, it is essential to delve back into the history and expecially the social history of German–Americans. Surely it does not suffice to tell of numbers arrived, of areas where they settled, of patriarchial or heroic ethnic leaders in religion, culture, economics or politics. It is not enough to list German builders and inventors, to describe German achievements in the farming regions, to pay hommage to some known German writers and poets, or to glorify ethnic musicians and artists. All this has been done in painstaking detail by uninspiring chroniclers and by those whom nationalist enthusiasm drove to emphasize the magnitude of the German

Centrale 3 (1791–1817). Cited here from: V. J. Fecher, *A Study of the Movement for German National Parishes in Philadelphia and Baltimore 1787–1802*, Analecta Gregoriana, Vol. 77 (Rome: Apud Aedes Universitatis Gregorianae, 1955), p. 96.

[3] *Ibid.*, p. 97.

[4] Quoted in: John G. Frank and John E. Pomfret, "The German Lutheran Aid Society of 1790," *The Pennsylvania Magazine of History and Biography*, 63 (1939), 62. Similar rules were still written into constitutions of German-American parishes even 100 years later; cf. *Constitution of St. John's Evangelical Lutheran Church, 79–81 Christopher Street, New York* (New York, 1907) (adopted 1894) and *Constitution und Kirchen-Ordnung der Deutschen Evangelisch-Lutherischen Zions-Kirche in der Stadt Utica, N. Y. Angenommen von der Gemeinde am 8. Juni 1879* (Utica, 1879).

[5] Walter F. Willcox, ed., *International Migrations*, Vol. 2 (New York, London, Paris: Gordon & Breach Science Publ., 2nd ed., 1969), pp. 384–385.

[6] John A. Hawgood, *The Tragedy of German-America* (New York, London: G. P. Putnam's Sons, 1940).

contribution to America. To be certain, in order to come to a more realistic understanding of German-America and its history, we ought to also examine those phenomena which in the past have been left aside for various reasons. In other words, the history of German–America must become part of American social history, for it was American society with its very specific "American" characteristics which received the alien German element and struggled with it for better or worse.

Not surprising, with the rapid advances made in almost all sectors of American historical and social studies, a number of valuable contributions, also to the field of German–American history, has been made by what one generally might call the New Ethnic History. Above all, it has been realized, that no ethnic group arrived on the shores of the New World by itself and that no ethnic minority entered the Americanizing process alone. We are, therefore, cognizant of the fact that each ethnic group not only was exposed to the previously existing forms of the American social structure but also that a multitude of ethnic confrontations occurred and incidentally still occur on all levels of American social, economic, intellectual, and spititual life. Thus, in the 19th century, large numbers of Germans arrived together with the Irish and, significantly, it was the close cooperation of Irish and German aid efforts which created the first large scale organized immigrant assistance at the Castle Garden depot in New York. On the other hand, Germans who settled in the Upper Midwest often bore the hardships of frontier life together with fellow immigrants from the Scandinavian countries. In the towns and cities Germans for long shared the dubious distinction of being newcomers with the Irish who for a number of reasons[7] tended to seek out the urban environment. Moreover, the influx in the latter part of the 19th century of desperate human "surplus" from Eastern and Southern Europe not only had a profound effect on the American urban structure, but it also had visible consequences for the urban survivors of previous immigration waves, such as the German-Americans.[8]

Which then are some of the specific areas for research where additional efforts and possibly new methods and approaches are urgently needed in order to achieve a more reliable picture of the acculturation process of German–Americans? First of all, it is to be hoped that emigration research will be directed to determine more exactly, possibly in some cases with the aid of quantitative methods, why large numbers of Germans left their country and what ideals and motivations they carried with them to the New World. Mack Walker with his *Germany and the Emigration 1816–1885* has pointed the way,[9] but more investigations into the background and causes of German emigration are urgently needed to cast light upon areas of partial ignorance or to clear up misunderstandings. An important case in point is our almost total disregard of the large scale persecution of Catholics in the German

---

[7] German craftsmen found it advantageous to practice their trades in the urban environment. German Catholics tended to favor the cities in order to be near church, priest, and parochial school. Countless German unskilled immigrants saw employment opportunities in the cities and lacked funds to acquire land or even to finance the move West. Generally too little research has been directed to the poverty among German immigrants. Cf. Jay P. Dolan, "Immigrants in the City. New York's Irish and German Catholics," *Church History,* 41/3, (1972), 357.

[8] As the new immigrants streamed into the poorer sections of the larger cities, earlier immigrants, such as Germans and Scandinavians tended to move farther away from these areas into suburbs and neighboring towns. The Lower East Side in New York is a particularly good example for this shift in population.

[9] Mack Walker, *Germany and the Emigration, 1816–1885* (Cambridge, Mass.: Harvard U. P., 1964).

Empire under Chancellor Bismarck. Since fathers, nuns, and lay Catholics fled Germany during this period of harassment[10] and since some of these refugees of the *Kulturkampf* became rather actively involved in the American Catholic Church,[11] it would appear to be of more than passing interest to know more about this group.

With good reason, we do, however, assume that the majority of immigrants from Germany, as from other countries, came to the New World to stay, to begin life anew. Thus, from the viewpoint of American social history, clearly more meaningful than their background and their reasons for leaving home is the complicated and many-faceted process of de-ethnization which was undergone in America, or, conversely, we must also learn more about the ways and means which the newcomers, the aliens devised to escape, at least for a time, the natural as well as the organized Americanizing forces of their new surroundings. It is this important area of research, which aside of a few almost pioneering efforts, has been rather neglected.

Is it not relevant what German–Americans did and with whom they associated after returning from their jobs at the end of a day or how they filled whatever there was of spare time or holidays? Above all, the immigrants were, in many cases, members of families, and we are painfully aware of how little serious research has been done in the past on the ethnic family. German–Americans also took part in or became members of a great number of organized activities, clubs and interest groups of every kind, generally referred to as their *Vereinswesen*. They went to sing and to drink beer together; they preached and practiced physical fitness in their *Turnvereine*; they performed amateur stage plays and read books together; they attended political meetings; they formed new lodges and joined existing ones;[12] they founded and contributed to an almost unbelievably large number of self-help type organizations, such as immigrant aid societies, mutual benefit associations and legal aid societies. They started old peoples' homes, hospitals, orphanages, homes for single girls and immigrant receiving centers. In short, countless German–Americans participated in a constant bustle of social activities and meetings within their own ethnic communities and in their towns and cities. Our knowledge of the social and economic role played by these organizations inside the immigrant ghetto and for that matter in the larger American community is still pitifully insufficient, and the widespread notion that German–Americans spent most of their leisure time imbibing beer and bellowing happy songs is but one example of the distortion born out of ignorance. In order to obtain the needed data on this ethnic microcosm, we shall have to overcome outdated prejudices, seek new avenues of research, and use unusual sources.

---

[10] *St. Raphaels-Blatt,* 1/1, 7; 1/2, 17–18; Colman J. Barry, *Geburtswehen einer Nation* (Recklinghausen and Hamburg: Paulus Verlag, 1971), pp. 24–25.

[11] Joseph Schrembs, *Contribution of the Catholic German Immigrants Towards the Development of America.* Typescript, Archives of the Catholic Central Union of America, St. Louis; Roger Aubert, "Der Aufstieg des Katholizismus in der angelsächsischen Welt. Die Vereinigten Staaten-Kanada-Australien," in Hubert Jedin, ed., *Handbuch der Kirchengeschichte* (Freiburg, Basel, Wien: Herder, 1971), p. 569; M. Francis Borgia, *He Sent Two. The Story of the Beginning of the School Sisters of St. Francis* (Milwaukee: Bruce Publ., 1965), p. 25; Michael Hynes, *History of the Diocese of Cleveland* (Cleveland: Diocese of Cleveland, 1953), p. 135; Heinz Kloss, "German-American Language Maintenance Efforts," in J. A. Fishman, V. C. Nahirny, J. E. Hofman, R. G. Hayden, *Language Loyalty in the United States* (London, The Hague, Paris: Mouton, 1966), p. 224.

[12] The latter even in the face of strong opposition from the Catholic and the Lutheran Churches.

A further major field of scholarly investigation promising to reveal most valuable insights into the fabric of ethnic life is the entire area of modern church history, a discipline very underdeveloped in Germany, but one where American historians have become increasingly productive. There is certainly no reason why non-theologically trained social scientists, including historians, should not be able to make major contributions here. All too long, for instance, immigrants from Germany have been classified indifferently with other Northern European generally Protestant ethnic groups. Only the explorative work of scholars, such as Philip Gleason and Colman Barry,[13] finally and beyond any doubt demonstrated the importance and vitality of the Catholicity of a large segment of German America. Until very recently even the name of that dedicated and belligerent Limburg merchant and guiding hand of the "St. Raphaels–Verein zum Schutze katholischer deutscher Auswanderer" Peter Paul Cahensly[14] was virtually unknown to secular historians, and standard works on German-Americans did not even bother to mention him. In fact, a number of older so-called standard works conveniently by-passed German–American Catholics altogether.[15] Whether or not one subscribes to Andrew Greeley's thesis that the immigrant experience "reinforced the faith of those who came to the New World,"[16] it certainly cannot be emphasized enough that the chapter of German–American Catholic history generally referred to derogatively as Cahenslyism represented an important effort of the German–American community to assert itself in an alien environment. In retrospect, it is clear there could be no place within the American Roman Catholic Church for a national German church, supplied with priests from Germany and, as some desired, with its own German hierarchy. Futile as the movement was, there can be no question that the study of this near-schism within the American Catholic Church reveals a vast amount of pertinent information concerning an important sector of the German ethnic community and, incidentally, about the changing role of the Catholic Church in late 19th century American society.

Among German Protestants the picture was not appreciably different. Although numerous parishes at an early point of their development had adopted English for their services,[17]

[13] Philip Gleason, *The Conservative Reformers* (Notre Dame, London: U. of Notre Dame P., 1968); Colman J. Barry, *The Catholic Church and German Americans* (Milwaukee: Bruce, 1953). Most recommendable in this direction also is Robert D. Cross, *The Emergence of Liberal Catholicism in America* (Cambridge, Mass.: Harvard U. P., 1958).

[14] Founder of the St. Raphaels–Verein and responsible for the so-called Lucerne Memorial in 1891 demanding from the Vatican the establishment of national parishes and the installation of national bishops in the U.S. The movement was of such importance that other minority groups in the U.S. such as the Polish-Americans, developed their own brand of "Cahenslyism". (Regrettably, during the Third Reich the head-office of the organization was occupied by the Nazi government and the archival holdings most probably were destroyed during the air raids on the city of Hamburg.) See P. Cahensly, *Die deutschen Auswanderer und der St. Raphaels-Verein,* (Frankfurter zeitgemäße Broschüren, 8/11) Frankfurt and Luzern: A. Foesser Nachfolger, 1887; Peter Paul Cahensly, *Der St. Raphaelsverein zum Schutze katholischer deutscher Auswanderer* (Charitas Schriften No. 5) Freiburg: Verlag des Charitasverbandes für das kathol. Deutschland, 1905.

[15] For instance the otherwise most detailed Albert B. Faust, *The German Element in the United States,* 2 vols., (New York: Steuben Society of America, rev. ed. 1927), barely mentions German-American Catholicism.

[16] Andrew M. Greeley, *The Catholic Experience* (Garden City, N. Y.: Image Books, 1969), p. 196.

[17] Maldwyn A. Jones, *American Immigration* (Chicago, London: U. of Chicago P., 6th imp., 1969), p. 77. In some instances even the early language adjustment led to schism within a parish. See for

a new language consciousness took hold toward the middle of the 19th century, and we find evidence of strong attempts to revive and to revitalize the usage of German. Lutheran ministers trained in German seminaries, such as Neuendettelsau[18] and Kropp,[19] served in the U.S., and church bodies, such as the Missoury Synod, particularly emphasized the importance of German.[20] Some of the German Protestant parishes continued the battle for language maintenance and ethnic tradition into the First World War. Certainly the evidence leaves no doubt that faith and worship played a significant part in the German ethnic community. Americanization of the immigrant church and the resistance of the churches to de-ethnization, therefore, must be considered weighty factors in any analysis of the relationship between American society and intruding alien newcomers.[21]

Intimately related to the struggle of the ethnic churches is the question of the maintenance or loss of the immigrant language. Though we have a vast body of primary sources and literature on the proclaimed cultural importance of the German vernacular for the German immigrant, the bulk of the earlier publications is only an expression of the desire to preserve the German language as a unifying factor for what the authors would have liked to have seen as a German state[22] in America. Evidently, all schemes to erect a German national unit in North America failed, – failed not only due to natural pressures of the American environment which was hardly favorably inclined toward such enclaves, but because such nationalist or nearly colonial ambitions of some Germans were based on fundamental misunderstandings of actual social and political conditions as they existed in the United States

instance Harry J. Kreider, "The English Language Schism in the Lutheran Church in New York City, 1794–1810," *The Lutheran Church Quarterly,* 21/1, Jan. 1948.

[18] Pastor Konrad Wilhelm Loehe founded the school for Lutheran missionaries in the village of Neuendettelsau with mission work among German immigrants in the U.S. in mind. Kurt Galling and others, eds., *Die Religion in Geschichte und Gegenwart,* Vol. 4 (Tuebingen: J.C.B. Mohr, 4th ed., 1960), p. 1410; A. Schmidtkonz, "Innere Mission führt uns zu der äußeren," *Lutherisches Kirchenblatt* (Reading-Philadelphia, 3/2, Jan. 9, 1886), 13; Horst Stephan, Hans Leube, *Handbuch der Kirchengeschichte für Studierende,* Part 4: *Die Neuzeit* (Tuebingen: J.C.B. Mohr, 1931), p. 315; James L. Schaaf, "Wilhelm Loehe and the Missouri Synod," *Concordia Historical Institute Quarterly,* 45/2, 1972, 53–57.

[19] Wilhelm F. Herrmann, *The Kropp Lutheran Seminary "Eben-Ezer" Germany, and Its Relations to the United Lutheran Church in America* (Master's Thesis, Luth. Theol. Sem., Philadelphia, 1938); *Minutes of the Eighteenth Convention of the General Council of the Evangelical Lutheran Church in North America* (held in Philadelphia, 1885) (Reading, Pa.: T. Wischan, 1885), pp. 55–56; D.L. Scheidt, *The Role of Linguistic Tradition in the Muhlenberg Tradition of American Lutheranism* (Dissertation, Temple U., 1963), pp. 34–37.

[20] See especially Scheidt, *op. cit.* and for the 20th century Dean W. Kohlhoff, *Missouri Synod Lutherans and the Image of Germany, 1914–1945* (Dissertation, U. of Chicago, 1973).

[21] A well researched contribution is the recently completed dissertation of Charles Shanabruch, *The Catholic Church's Role in the Americanization of Chicago's Immigrants: 1833–1928* (U. of Chicago, 1975).

[22] Cf. Ewald Schnitzer, *Der Nationalgedanke und die deutsche Auswanderung nach den Vereinigten Staaten von Amerika in der ersten Hälfte des 19. Jahrhunderts* (Dissertation, Leipzig U., 1935), pp. 20, 33, 59–105. Concerning the Braunfels settlement see Chester William, Ethel H. Geue, eds., *A New Land Beckoned: German Immigration to Texas, 1844–1847* (Waco, Texas: Texian Press, 1966); Gilbert G. Benjamin, "The Germans in Texas," Reprint from: *German American Annals,* Vol. 7, 1909, pp. 6–7.

and the territories. The German language, we now know, could be no more than the native vernacular of any immigrant group in the earlier stages of acculturation into the American social structure. Leaving aside certain creative German writing done in America, German was the natural means of communication at meetings of German ethnic groups, of German immigrant churches and the respective schools, of German ethnic newspapers, and, most of all, German was probably a major factor of cohesion in the daily life of the German, often Catholic ghetto in the American city.[23]

For the second and even later generations of German–Americans, such factors became much less vital. Church denominations among Protestants could be changed without major complications; public schools could appear more attractive than ethnic church affiliated education; upward occupational mobility as a rule required a certain facility in English;[24] and it should be emphasized that the vast majority of Germans migrated to the United States to stay, that is to become Americans. For various reasons life in the Old World had been unsatisfactory or even unbearable. The men and women who had been desperate enough to leave their native land and all human ties connected with it, as a rule could have no particular motivation to consciously retard their Americanization in order to retain the language of their forebears. For most, the continuous struggle for economic achievement had to be the overwhelming concern, and it would seem unreasonable to expect from them time and energy consuming language maintenance efforts. Finally, all too often those who have bemourned the loss of German in the United States of course were not a part of that immigrant social class which the Jewish-American poetess Emma Lazarus so fittingly called "wretched refuse."[25] In other words, as the American sociolinguist Joshua Fishman has said: "De-ethnization i. e. specifically the loss of the so-called 'mother tongue' was not, by and large, a plot of America's Anglo-populations."[26] Quite to the contrary, in America the German language became a "tote Sprache," a relic of some possible usefulness for certain cultural enterprises but one unrelated to the new life in the new land. German immigrants in the 19th century were no exception in quickly realizing that English was the *lingua franca* in America.

From the above one might well draw the hasty conclusion that Germans who came to America generally were rapidly assimilated into "Anglo"–American society in an almost picture book example as depicted in Israel Zangwill's popular play *The Melting Pot.*[27] In

---

[23] Cf. Jaroslav Pelikan, *The Riddle of Roman Catholicism* (New York, Nashville: Abingdon Press, 1959), pp. 67, 232.

[24] Stephan Thernstrom, "Immigrants and Wasps: Ethnic Differences in Occupational Mobility in Boston, 1890–1940," in S. Thernstrom, R. Sennett, eds., *Nineteenth Century Cities* (New Haven, London: Yale U. P., 3rd print., 1971), p. 130; Georg von Skal, *Das amerikanische Volk* (Berlin: Egon Fleischel,1908), p. 310.

[25] In a poem entitled "Mother of Exiles," written for a fund-raising campaign to erect the Statue of Liberty. Cf. Moses Rischin, *The Promised City* (New York, etc.: Harper Torchbook, 1970), p. 97; John Higham, *Strangers in the Land* (New York: Atheneum, 16th print., 1973), p. 23.

[26] Joshua A. Fishman, "The Third Century of Non-English Language Maintenance and Non-Anglo Ethnic Maintenance in the United States of America." I am grateful to Joshua Fishman for letting me have a copy of this keynote address presented at the 1973 TESOL convention and printed in *TESOL Quarterly*, 7/3, 1973, 221–223.

[27] On the play and the melting pot concept cf. Philip Gleason, "The Melting Pot: Symbol of Fusion or Confusion?," *American Quarterly*, 16/1, 1964, 20–46.

fact, however, older-stock Americans did not just turn German newcomers into fellow Americans; instead through a long and varied process German customs and characteristics at least in part were also integrated into American life. American society itself became changed through the constant input of large numbers of Germans as well as through the cultural and political activities of individual German immigrants. To cite a few select examples: German-Americans, not merely some brewery interests, played a conspicuous role in the long and bitter fight against temperance and prohibition. Germans in America founded a great number of self-help aid societies, notably some of the country's earliest mutual benefit insurance enterprises and most noteworthy in New York the first legal aid society which served as a model for similar organizations all across the United States. In many instances German names also were associated with socialist and real or presumed anarchist groupings.[28] It is true that Germans almost never gained control of urban political machines, and they generally have not been as important a voting block as other ethnic groups, such as the Irish, Jews or Italians. On the other hand, the German Forty-eighters, refugees of the ill-fated nationalist revolution of 1848, though numerically few, for a time became an influence of some measure in America, and their political clout, expecially through the vociferous German–American press, influenced many Germans to lend their support to Abraham Lincoln and the Republican Party. Nevertheless, as recent studies of voting behavior, such as the works of Paul Kleppner and Richard Jensen, have indicated, the German ethnic community did not fully and permanently identify with the Republican Party. Numerous practicing Christians, Catholics as well as Lutherans, often were drawn to the Democratic Party on such issues as, for instance, the public vs. private schools argument, exemplified by the Bennet Law campaign in Wisconsin or the battle over the Edwards Law in Illinois.[29]

Exceptions, such as the case of Hessian-born Illinois Governor John Peter Altgeld, who became almost an American symbol for political reform and government tolerance, or cases where Germans lent their serious support to reform groups combatting urban corruption, do not change the general impression of the German-American relative political quietude. Because many of them at the time of their arrival were somewhat less impoverished than for instance the majority of the Irish immigrants, they often continued to migrate West, away from the congestion and the competitive political environment of the Eastern metropolitan areas and are, therefore, less easily registered as a political force during the turbulent growth period of the American city. Whether indeed the Germans had brought with them from the Old World what Hermann Hagedorn in his important memoirs refers to as the "acceptance of the infallibility of authority,"[30] must remain a matter of speculation.[31] Nevertheless, their

---

[28] Robert Ernst, *Immigrant Life in New York City, 1825–1863* (New York: King's Crown Press, 1949), pp. 112–121; John J. Appel, *Immigrant Historical Societies in the United States, 1880–1950* (Dissertation, U. of Pennsylvania, 1960), p. 279. Cf. also the Haymarket affair in Chicago or the activities of Johann Most in New York.

[29] Cf. views presented in Paul Kleppner, *The Cross of Culture* (New York: Free Press, 1970); Richard Jensen, *The Winning of the Midwest* (Chicago, London: U. of Chicago P., 1971); and Frederick C. Luebke, "Politics and Missouri Synod Lutherans: A Historiographical Review," *Concordia Historical Institute Quarterly*, 45/2, 1972. See also William F. Whyte, "The Bennett Law Campaign in Wisconsin," *Wisconsin Magazine of History*, Vol. 10, 1927, 363–390.

[30] Hermann Hagedorn, *The Hyphenated Family* (New York: Macmillan, 1960), p. 227.

[31] For a more positive evaluation of German-American political conservatism see Frederick J. Turner,

over-all civic record in the United States would lead one to conclude that they were orderly participants rather than a radically innovative political people, in fact, in most cases becoming what nativists would have called "good Americans," i.e. loyal citizens in the new land they had chosen. That they had emigrated from areas of the German and the Austro–Hungarian Empires, which had little in common, that they had left the Old World at different times in history, and, most of all, that some of the German dialects almost prevented any kind of useful communication not to mention cooperation among them, added up to evident differences rather than a unified ethnic front in the New World.

Yet, inspite of all this, no other ethnic group, with the exception of the Japanese–Americans in World War II, has had its loyalty collectively and individually questioned by what can only be explained in terms of national hysteria. The sufferings of countless German–Americans in World War I have taken on an important role in the historiography of German–America. Evidence shows that Germans were maltreated and persecuted, often for no better reason than their German name or the fact that their fellow citizens knew of their German descent. Undoubtedly, much damage also was done to whatever there was of German–American institutions and culture in the United States.[32] On the other hand, the evidence of the steady process of acculturation and of a general loss of ethnic identity by the Germans in the 19th century does not appear to support the suggestion, which still plagues a number of historians today, that a strong and viable German–America was sacrificed on the altar of the American war effort. The millions of German emigrants who had left the German Empire in search for a place to live in human dignity, personal freedom and economic prosperity, and their children who often had been born in the United States, – these Germans had become Americans long before 1914. They had become part of American society, a society which they by and large had accepted, altered in some ways, used to their advantage in most cases, and one which they would defend if called upon. Their children more often than not had been educated in American public schools, and many of them worshipped in English language churches. As was the case with immigrants from other lands, they had not maintained their native language; only a small number of self-appointed would-be zealous guardians of the tradition of another nation carried on the battle for a language of another nation.[33] The absolute majority of German-Americans, however, though preserving certain social habits and cultural traits, clearly had become Americans by the late nineteenth century.[34]

"German Immigration Into the United States," *The Chicago Record Herald,* Sept. 4, 1901, 7. John Higham in "Another Look at Nativism" in his *Send These To Me* (New York: Atheneum, 1975), pp. 113–114, has some relevant comments on German occupational skill and Irish political aptitude.

[32] On the German-Americans in World War I see Frederick Luebke, *Bonds of Loyalty* (DeKalb, Ill.: Northern Illinois U. P., 1974). On specific aspects of German-American propaganda see Reinhard R. Doerries, *Washington-Berlin 1908/1917* (Duesseldorf: Schwann Verlag, 1975).

[33] Cf. especially the activities of Charles Hexamer's National German–American Alliance and of Fritz Kuhn's Bund. On the latter see Sander A. Diamond's competent investigation *The Nazi Movement in the United States, 1924–1941* (Ithaca, London: Cornell U. P., 1974).

[34] For an analysis of the local situation in Cinicinnati see G. A. Dobbert, "German–Americans between New and Old Fatherland, 1870–1914," *American Quarterly,* 19/4, 1967. – I am presently writing a larger comparative study of the acculturation of Irish-Americans and German-Americans. My own findings tend to support the research results of Guido Dobbert.

AMERICANIZATION AND THE MEXICAN IMMIGRANT, 1880-1930

by Mario T. Garcia

I

From the early period of the Southwest's economic development during the last two decades of the nineteenth century to the start of the Great Depression, approximately one million Mexican immigrants entered the United States. Pushed from their homeland by rural economic dislocation as a result of Porfirio Diaz's modernization programs and the 1910 political revolution, Mexicans crossed the border in search of jobs. The demand by expanding Eastern and Midwestern industries for new sources of raw materials had encouraged the railroad's penetration of the Southwest and opened this former Mexican territory to American investment capital and technology. Sparsely populated, Southwestern railroads, mines, smelters, ranches, and urban industries filled their labor needs by importing skilled American workers and contracting thousands of unskilled Mexican immigrants. Hardworking and cheap, Mexican labor proved indispensable to employers. At the same time the relationship between regional economic development and Mexican immigration increased cultural as well as racial tensions in the Southwest and initiated efforts to "Americanize" the Mexicans in the hope of making them more efficient and productive workers.[1]

Following the Mexican War, and indeed even before the conflict, Americans had voiced concerns about what they considered to be the Mexican's "retarding" influence on the Southwest's modernization.[2] In 1856 the Santa Barbara Gazette concluded that the native Mexican population "are habitually and universally opposed to all progress whatsoever, and that they look with decided disfavor upon every innovation which tends in the slightest degree to alter the old hereditary regime which existed under the Mexican government."[3] Several years later, as the region's economic "boom" began, other Americans expressed fears about alleged Mexican cultural liabilities. According to historian Alberto Camarillo, the "boom" strengthened negative American attitudes towards the Mexicans. "Anglos characterized the local Chicanos," Camarillo writes of Santa Barbara, "as 'an idle, indolent, sleepy set,' an 'illiterate... wasteful people,' who are also 'shiftless and indigent, little caring for work, and not given to progress.'"[4] An early El Paso historian, representing turn of the century American ethnocentric views, believed that the enterprising spirit exhibited by American merchants, miners, businessmen, and lawyers stressed the basic social and cultural differences between El Paso's older Mexican inhabitants and recent American residents. "If we are right in our surmise," Owen White wrote in 1923

> ...El Paso got the railroads with their payrolls because the Americans in the town went after the business, while the Mexicans....
> sat around following the shade from one side of the house to the other.[5]

MARIO T. GARCIA teaches History and Chicano Studies at the University of California, Santa Barbara.

The Journal of Ethnic Studies 6:2

Inspired by the entrance of the railroads, the El Paso Bureau of Information, composed of some of the town's principal American citizens, issued in 1886 a report that contained a plan for El Paso's economic development and which its writers hoped to use to attract people and capital. The report claimed, however, that progress had not always characterized El Paso due to the presence of the Mexican population:

> The population of El Paso County hitherto has not, unfortunately, been of the progressive kind. The Spanish or Mexican Indian race of whom, until the advent of the railways, four years ago, about ninety-nine hundredths of the population was composed, and of which one-half of it is still composed--has caused the county to progress scarcely a move in the great march of material wealth and improvement, beyond what it was in the days of the Spanish viceroyalty in Mexico, to which it was once subject. Up to that time (1881) this was practically a 'tierra incognita.'[6]

The Bureau believed that the migration of more Whites would remedy El Paso's economic problem. Ironically, Mexican immigrants proved to be a crucial factor in El Paso's economic growth.

Despite the Mexican's economic contributions, Americans believed that the immigrants from south of the border possessed a "pre-modern" culture. "Cultural clash," from an American perspective, involved what E. P. Thompson, Herbert Gutman and other "new labor historians" consider to be the dialectic between industrial and pre-industrial cultures.[7]

> 'Traditional social habits and customs,' J. F. C. Harrison reminds us, 'seldom fitted into the patterns of industrial life, and they had... to be discredited as hindrances to progress.' That happened regularly in the United States after 1815 as the nation absorbed and worked to transform new groups of preindustrial peoples, native whites among them. The result, however, was neither a static tension nor the mere recurrence of similar cycles, because American society itself changed as did the composition of its laboring population. But the source of the tension remained the same, and conflict often resulted....It resulted ...from the fact that the American working class was continually altered in its composition by infusions, from within and without the nation, of peasants, farmers, skilled artisans, and casual day laborers who brought into industrial society ways of work and other habits and values not associated with industrial necessities and the industrial ethos. Some shed these older ways to conform to new imperatives. Others fell victims or fled, moving from place to place. Some sought to extend and adapt older patterns of work and life to a new society. Others challenged the social system through varieties of collective associations. But for all--at different historical moments--the transition to industrial society, as E. P. Thompson has written, 'entailed

20

a severe restructuring of working habits--new disciplines, new incentives, and a new human nature upon which these incentives could bite effectively.[8]

As with other newcomers from pre-industrial cultures, Mexicans experienced economic mobility in comparison to their previous condition in Mexico; yet, they retained to a considerable degree traditional cultural habits and values formed in a predominantly agrarian nation. While further research needs to be done on the backgrounds of early Mexican immigrants, especially those from the more modernized northern states of Mexico, most Mexicans arrived in the Southwest with a greater unfamiliarity with an industrial way of life involving new forms of work patterns and discipline than did Anglo-American migrants to the region. Working principally among other Mexicans and living in segregated "barrios," Mexican cultural communities--or what Herbert Gans calls "urban villages"--sprang up and developed throughout the Southwest.[9] In some cases, these communities built upon earlier Mexican settlements. The area's proximity to Mexico, plus the constant flow of new immigrants, reinforced a distinct Mexican cultural presence north of the border. Mexican anthropologist Manuel Gamio observed in the 1920s that despite some acculturation, first-generation Mexican immigrants kept their native traditions in the form of language, folklore, food, superstitions, songs, and religious holidays which expressed both their national and rural origins.[10] As E. P. Thompson has warned "we should not assume any automatic, or over-direct, correspondence between the dynamic of economic growth and the dynamic of social or cultural life."[11] Indeed, culture continuity among Mexican immigrants aided in their adjustment to life in the United States since native customs served as "effective forms of self-assertion and self-protection."[12] Yet cultural continuity also strengthened earlier negative attitudes held by Anglos against Mexicans. More than differences between two national cultures, "cultural clash" involved distinctions based on a developing capitalist-industrial society, on the one hand, and an underdeveloped-rural society, on the other.

II

While Southwestern industries praised Mexican common labor as dependable, hardworking, and not subject to strike agitation, some employers as well as observers of Mexican labor raised doubts about the immigrants' work habits and their capacity to fully adapt to an industrial culture. The major criticism of Mexican labor compared their productivity and efficiency to those of native-born Americans and earlier European immigrants. Although his Mexican laborers worked long and hard hours, one public utility official in El Paso believed they sought any excuse not to work, especially on their religious holidays. "When a Mexican laborer wants to take a day off," claimed superintendent W. H. Watts of the Water Company,

...he can be relied on to dig up a saint or some kind of an anniversary

21

to celebrate. On St. John's day all of my Juans are out celebrating, and the Joses, Pedros, et al., get [out of] their work on St. James' and St. Peters' days. But a new anniversary was rung in on me this morning. One of my men was missing and I asked Louis Behr [sic?] what saint's day he was celebrating. Louis said the man was not celebrating any saint today, but was celebrating the anniversary of the burning of his house; that he was remaining home today to prevent fire from repeating the performance. Next they will be celebrating the anniversary of the death of some pet dog or burro. [13]

Victor Clark in his 1908 Bureau of Labor report outlined what he considered to be the significant characteristics of Mexican labor in the United States. Although certain qualities such as docility, patience, orderliness in camp, fair intelligence under competent supervision, obedience, and above all cheapness made the Mexican attractive to employers, Clark, nevertheless, expressed certain reservations. The labor inspector informed Washington that American railroad administrators in Mexico had complained that "Mexican helpers were slow and not very efficient, it requiring two or three of them to do the work of an ordinary machinist's helper in the United States." The same railroad officials considered Mexicans "to lack ambition, to be irregular in shop attendance, and to drink hard after paydays, thus losing part of their time." Clark further noted that in agricultural work north of the border "the chief complaint against the Mexicans are that they are not reliable in observing their contracts and will not work regularly." Work irregularity, later observers of Mexican labor have pointed out, also involved changes of both jobs and job locations. In addition, Judith Laird in her study of the Mexican railroad community of Argentine, Kansas, discovered that workers frequently returned to Mexico for the harvest. [14] According to Clark, irregular work habits characterized Mexicans inSouthwestern mining. Some American miners told the inspector that they refused to work with Mexicans, considering them to be careless. Dr. Walter Marritt of the sociological department of the Colorado Fuel & Iron Company explained that he believed the Mexicans to be "unadapted to the work of mining." No doubt influenced by his own racial views, Dr. Marritt viewed the Mexican as unreliable. "He is shiftless and lacks ambition," the sociologist stated.

> . . . and o..ly in time of strikes, when extra inducements are offered in the way of best rooms in the mines, generous weights, donations of liquor on the part of the pit boss, is any underground work to be gotten out of him at all; and even then he is not to be relied upon after he has a few dollars to his credit with which to buy "Dago Red," as the cheap adulterated whiskey is called.

Clark concluded that if the Mexicans developed certain traits such as thrift which would make them more regular workers and demanding of higher wages, they might lose their attractiveness to American employers. Yet Clark believed

22

that such a cultural change in the long run would add to the value of Mexican labor.[15]

Three years after Clark's report, the Dillingham Commission which investigated immigrant conditions for the U.S. Senate concurred with the labor inspector's opinions about Mexican workers. While Mexican common labor had become indispensable to Western industries such as the railroads and mining companies, the Senate investigators regarded the Mexicans as well as Southern and Eastern Europeans and the Japanese to be less productive and efficient than native-born American workers and northern European immigrants. "...it is universally agreed," the Commission emphasized,

> that the races now employed in large numbers are inferior in certain respects to the natives of the older and non-roving type and the Irish. Speaking of the two sets of races taken collectively, the differences do not lie in industry, tractability, sobriety, or in muscular strength, but rather in intelligence, experience, adaptability, teachability, progressiveness, and knowledge of English and the consequent smaller amount of supervision required.[16]

The Commission, in its comparison of Japanese and Mexican workers on Western railroads stressed the Mexican's strengths as well as weaknesses. According to its report, employers preferred Mexicans over Japanese. "They are stronger than the Japanese," the Commissioners disclosed, "and are said by most road masters to be superior in every way except in progressiveness and sobriety...." The railroads viewed Mexicans as more tractable, obedient, easily satisfied, and less likely to strike. Despite these characteristics, however, the Mexicans possessed serious liabilities. Some railroads, for example, believed that Mexicans required more supervision "because they are lazy ...." The Commission suggested that the low wages paid to Mexicans plus the fact that they rarely became foremen proved that the Mexicans had neither ambition nor much ability. "Drunkenness is the Mexicans' great weakness," the Senate committee further concluded, and "it is the universal opinion that they are in this respect the worst of all races employed in railway work. Because of it, and want of ambition, or desire to live well, they as a rule work irregularly."[17]

Not confined to men, similar criticisms arose about Mexican female labor. Clark observed that prior to 1910 few Mexican women worked in industries because husbands and fathers opposed such employment, "having a peasant prejudice to their women leaving home, and it is partly because these women lack the foundations of industrial training." Although not entirely correct, Clark also noted that due to their unfamiliarity with American "domestic arrangements," which presumably included new mechanical appliances, Mexican women did not become domestics.[18] Clark failed to realize, however, that in certain locations Americans hired Mexicans who cleaned and washed by hand. Yet even under these conditions, housewives complained about the Mexican woman's inefficiency and haphazard work. In 1919 various El Paso women

23

protested to the city council about their problems with household help. Mexican domestics, according to the American housewives, hired through the city employment bureau had proved to be inadequate despite higher wages. As Mrs. Julia Sharp put it:

> ...the bureau should give efficient help. The class of help furnished now wants to work only a few hours each day, wants two good meals and all the cast-off clothes and scrap food you have. The bureau should furnish servants who are efficient and capable. As it exists now it puts a premium on shiftlessness.[19]

Supporters of the bureau, although they insisted higher wages had to be paid by American housewives for domestic help, conceded that some form of Americanization would improve the work of the Mexican women. C. N. Idar, a Mexican American A. F. of L. organizer in El Paso, addressed the city council and spoke about the charges that concerned the character of the Mexican servants. "It is impossible to elevate the standard of efficiency and morals of the Mexican workers without the cooperation of the intelligent American woman," Idar claimed. "We should make every effort to Americanize the alien Mexicans here and the task is too large for the employment bureau." On the Mexican's inefficiency, Henry W. Walker, the director of the bureau, suggested that housewives could organize and pay a living wage and that they could contact the various Mexican social organizations and help encourage night schools to teach the Mexicans domestic science.[20]

Concern over Mexican workers' shortcomings continued into the 1920s as more Mexicans moved into urban-industrial jobs. In Los Angeles, after interviewing various industrial employers, economist Paul S. Taylor revealed varied opinions about Mexican female workers. From thirty-one questionnaires filled out by officials of different firms, in such areas as rubber production, food processing, manufacturing, meat packing, and laundering, Taylor computed that 32.5% considered the Mexican woman to be a poor worker; 21% believed that the Mexican woman born and educated in the United States represented as good a worker as any other nationality after proper training; 20.8% thought the Mexican woman no different from any other nationality; 15.4% believed the Mexican woman constituted a better worker for routine duties than other nationalities; and finally, 10.3% indicated that the Mexican woman worked better in all respects than other nationalities. Those who considered the Mexican woman an inferior worker explained that she had proved to be undependable, irregular, slow, and unintelligent. "These reasons seem to indicate," Taylor concluded, "that the Mexican woman who is looked upon as a poor worker is generally the lower class who is generally by nature inert and slow, and submerged in customs and ideas which it is very difficult to change, so that it is very difficult to place her successfull [sic] in industrial work." Moreover, the fact that 21% believed that Mexican women, when educated in the United States, became as good a worker as anyone else suggested to Taylor, "that the social heritage and backgrounds which are the possession of the average Mexican are a great handicap to the women who enter industry. For the girls who have been born and educated in the United States seem to adapt themselves more easily to work."[21]

Taylor further observed that three classes of Mexican women could be found in Los Angeles' industries. The first included "peon women" who because of their cultural drawbacks found it difficult to adapt to industrial work; although Taylor believed that after some permanency in unskilled jobs, these women "may in time become an excellent worker because of her imitative ability and her liking for routine work." Middle class Mexican women, on the other hand, as well as younger lower class women educated in the United States represented a group of more successful workers due to their greater ambition, intelligence, and above all adaptability to industrial labor. Finally, a third set involved women who because of their intelligence, education, and ambition became excellent industrial workers, but who, according to Taylor, "are so ambitious that they do not remain long in their particular work, which they consider only as a step in their progress toward more desirable positions in the business world." Unfortunately, Taylor pointed out, most Mexican women belonged to the lower classes.[22] While views such as those reported by Taylor no doubt were used by industries to justify cheap labor, they also reveal that some employers, especially in urban industries, believed recent Mexican arrivals to be ill-equipped in work habits and discipline for industrial production and, as a result, had to be closely supervised and trained.

III

In addition to questions about the Mexicans' work habits, civic officials, social reformers, educators, and writers reacted adversely to the Mexicans' lifestyle and cultural values. Racist, these views represented American beliefs that Mexican customs stood in direct contrast to the Southwest's developing urban-industrial culture. Marking no departure from previous rural practices, Mexicans in El Paso, for example, had to use the Rio Grande for bathing and recreation due to the absence of adequate sanitation facilities in the southside "barrio." Many Americans, however, considered this practice to be "immoral." "Yesterday Officer Lutterloh captured several Mexican boys," the El Paso Times reported in 1892, "who were bathing themselves in the Rio Grande and indecently exposing themselves."[23] To prevent such "indecent exposure" as well as to avoid drownings, the El Paso chief of police in the summer of 1905 prohibited swimming, bathing, or washing in the river between sunrise and sunset, "and also indecent exposure of person." Those who violated the order were subject to a fine not to exceed $100, which Chief F. J. Hall hoped would reduce the number of drownings. Yet three days later, the Times reported that

> ...the order of Chief Hall against swiming [sic] in the river is not generally understood by the Mexicans living in the lower part of the city. Yesterday afternoon about 6 o'clock some one telephoned the police headquarters that the river between the Stanton Street bridge

25

103

and the grain elevator was simply lined with men, women and children in bathing. Captain Mitchell detailed Officer Jesse Waldridge to go down to the river and arrest as many of the swimmers as he could. When the officer arrived at the river he found a great crowd of men, women and children disporting themselves in the water in various stages of undress, and ranging from a Mother Hubbard, in the case of women and a pair of trousers in the case of men, to absolute nudity.[24]

Depressed housing conditions plus rising health problems added to American distaste for the "Mexican way of life." Victor Clark in his study noted that urban Mexicans in the Southwest constructed crude shacks for their homes. "In this," Clark concluded, "as in other ways, the Mexican shows the retiring traits of the Indian and the Countryman, even after several years' experience with city life."[25] Six years later, Samuel Bryan observed the efforts of Los Angeles officials to clean up the Mexican settlement which, according to Bryan, was "moulded to a certain extent by Mexican standards...."[26] Although tenements replaced shacks in some Southwestern cities by 1920, Vera L. Sturges still believed that the Mexican would be satisfied with inferior housing. "Having few standards to begin with," Sturges wrote in The Survey, "it is not surprising that the poor Mexican immigrant is content in the tenements with one toilet and one hydrant for fifteen families, four and five of these families living in one or two rooms."[27] Poor living conditions, in turn, made Americans aware of serious health problems in the "barrios," which many attributed to the Mexican's disinterest in cleanliness. Mexican American businessman and politician Felix Martinez protested in 1910 the lack of municipal sanitation facilities in the Mexican settlement of El Paso, but at the same time blamed the Mexicans themselves. Martinez alleged that the residents of "Chihauhuita," the Mexican "barrio," would let a dead dog lie in the alleys or streets until it rotted and that they would walk around a "deposit of human filth on the sidewalk a month and never report it."[28] One year earlier on a visit to El Paso to investigate health conditions along the border, F. H. McLean, the field secretary of the Russell Sage Foundation, reported that the major blame for the high rate of tuberculosis among Mexican children lay with their mothers who, according to McLean, knew nothing about sanitation.[29]

With a growing Mexican urban population in the 1920s, "barrio" health hazards became a major issue for officials and reformers since disease or epidemics among the Mexicans could easily spread to American neighborhoods. Pearl I. Ellis in her book Americanization Through Homemaking reminded readers of the extra care they should take in teaching Mexicans proper hygiene. "The daily bath was important in prevention of skin diseases," Ellis wrote, "but Mexicans seemed apt to be lax in this respect, giving rise to the term 'dirty Mexicans.'" Ellis stressed, moreover, that in sanitation and diet, Mexicans relied on their time-honored philosophy of life: "to flow along lines of least resistance." Such thinking, Ellis reasoned, created the Mexicans' health and nutrition problems.[30] Emory Bogardus in his studies of Mexican immigrants also believed that the Mexicans' pre-industrial and pre-urban culture had much

26

to do with their impoverished and unsanitary conditions. The University of Southern California sociologist emphasized that few Mexican children drank milk due to the dietary habits their parents had transferred from Mexico. "Like others," Bogardus noted, "Mexican adults do not change their food habits easily, and hence progress is slow in improving the Mexican immigrant's diet." Bogardus further observed other Mexican beliefs and customs which he considered cultural liabilities. These included fear of doctors and hospitals because of health superstitions. "If they have an ache in their upper regions," Bogardus pointed out,

> they tie an old rag around their waist, so that the pain won't go farther down their bodies. If the pain is in the abdominal region or in the legs they think that a rag around the waist will prevent the pain going above it. Usually if they are ailing they bind up their heads for some reason.[31]

Poverty, uncleanliness, drunkenness, and crime added up, according to critics, to a set of Mexican values which could not be easily adjusted to a modern-industrial society. The Home Missions Council, an interdenominational religious organization in the 1920s, indicted the Mexicans for what the Council viewed as their "fatalistic acceptance of life." "For a right understanding of the social and economic factors as they relate to wages, work, housing, indigency and delinquency," the Council stated of the Mexicans,

> it might be well for us also to know something of the Mexican's philosophy of life. This may be described as a happy fatalism, in which all the cards are stacked in his favor....He is happy in his shack, because he has a great capacity for happiness anywhere... why should he be otherwise since God is good and the world is large.[32]

Fatalistic, Mexicans were also considered to have no idea of time, at least not in an industrial sense. Bogardus detected what he believed to be different values concerning time among unskilled Mexicans who, according to the scholar, needed constant supervision in order to work regularly. "They live so largely in the present," Bogardus write, "that time has no particular meaning to them. With them time is not commercialized as with us. Their wants are not aroused as are ours and as is natural they consequently do not drive themselves as we drive ourselves." Bogardus believed, however, that despite the differences Mexicans possessed a "greater capacity for happiness than do Americans."[33] Other commentators charged that the Mexicans' time orientation led to a definite absence of work discipline. "The Mexican peon dislikes work," Helen W. Walker noted of Southern California Mexicans,

> Work is work; joy is joy. The two are not the same. There is joy in play, in music, in color, in rest, in the dance, but not in work.

27

There is no such thing as the joy of working at difficult tasks. One does disagreeable work for money, not for joy.[34]

Walker commented that Eva Frank writing in The Nation had also encountered similar attitudes among Mexicans in their native-land. "The desire to better one's economic position," Frank stressed,

seems to lose its force in the upside-down world south of the Rio Grande. The Indian-Mexican enjoys savoring life (with rest and leisure), and the American enjoys crowding it....But they are reposeful and contented. Of course, they are happy. That is the worst of it. Until the Mexican-Indian wants money to buy things that money can buy more than he wants mastery over time, he will not labor consistently like the Americans, except by force.[35]

IV

While it is not certain what special efforts--if any--Southwestern industries made to better adapt Mexicans to an industrial culture, observers detected significant changes among Mexican workers in the United States. "The new sense of self-dependence created by migration," reputed Clark, "is said to be both a moral and an industrial stimulus to the Mexican, and does not leave him even when he returns to his own country." Clark noted that several employers in Mexico had expressed the opinion that laborers who had been in the United States constituted better workers than those who had remained. The Mexican immigrant returned, according to these employers, with increased initiative, intelligence, and efficiency. One railway manager declared that Mexicans who had worked north of the border needed less supervision in Mexico. Clark contended that after the Mexican's stay in the United States, he no longer possessed a dependent attitude toward his "patron"--his boss. Not only did he change jobs more frequently, but "He expects cash wages and offers a sort of passive resistance to many forms of industrial oppression to which he used to submit without question." In addition, Clark emphasized that the Mexican underwent a change in consumer values including a new taste for clothing and other American material goods.[36]

Besides work as a means of acculturation, the public schools represented the principal institution of Americanization utilized by both employers and reformers. In urban areas where Mexicans could obtain employment in numerous manual jobs, industrial education increasingly became a major component of the curriculum in so-called "Mexican schools." The type of training, for example, provided Mexicans by racially segregated public schools in El Paso served to complement the needs of the border city's industries and businesses for semi-skilled workers from the Mexican population. While most Mexican students left school by the fourth or fifth grades to find work to augment their family's income, the schools did little to change this condition. Rather, school officials argued that because of the need for Mexican children to work at an early age,

28

the "Mexican schools" should direct their attention to manual and domestic education that would best assist Mexicans to find jobs. On the other hand, the schools in Anglo neighborhoods presented a well-rounded curriculum with both practical and academic training.[37]

The Mexicans' educational experience in El Paso was not, of course, unique. Similar stress on vocational education existed in other Southwestern areas. J. C. Ross writing in the New Mexico Journal of Education recommended in 1911 industrial education for the Spanish-speaking population of New Mexico. Not only would this form of education provide Mexicans with a trade, but, according to Ross, would teach the "intrinsic value" of all work.[38] Ellis in her Americanization Through Homemaking emphasized that Americanization programs among the Mexicans, besides raising their standard of living and their morals, would also teach skills that would indirectly serve certain industries. Since Mexican girls, Ellis alleged, possessed a fondness for sewing and since few of them entered high school, Ellis concluded that "their ability as seamstresses must be developed in the elementary schools."[39] Kimball Young's study Mental Differences in Certain Immigrant Groups pointed out that due to the assumed inability of the Mexican child to intellectually compete with the American, reforms needed to be instituted to accommodate the curriculum of the "Mexican schools" to the type of work available when these children entered the job market. Young proposed changes that would provide Mexicans with "training for occupational efficiency; habits and attitudes as make for social cooperation," and finally "training for appreciation of the arts and sciences for satisfaction and happiness."[40]

Gilbert Gonzalez in his study of the "Mexican schools" in the Los Angeles area notes that by the early 1930s vocational training represented the core curriculum of these institutions. In El Monte, the district school superintendent not only segregated Mexican children until their thirteenth birthday, but offered them special course offerings including "woodwork, domestic science and other subjects properly arranged to help these children take their place in society." The San Bernardino School District dealt with its "Mexican problem" by establishing a segregated "barrio" school emphasizing vocational education. "It was thought," Gonzalez writes, "that this type of education would lead to habits of thrift and industry, and to ability to make necessary contacts with the industrial world."[41] Los Angeles schools besides concentrating vocational education in the east-side "Mexican schools" closely cooperated with local industries in developing an efficient vocational program for Mexicans as well as other working class children. "The interest of the businessman in the schools of Los Angeles," stressed the manager of the Industrial Department of the Chamber of Commerce in 1922,

> is naturally keen, inasmuch as he helps pay the bills of the schools. But his interest does not end there in dollars and cents. Employees of his concern are the products of the public schools and their efficiency depends in large measure upon the methods employed in the schools." (pp. 174-175)

29

As a result of efforts by Los Angeles garment manufacturers, the Chamber of Commerce, and the public schools, a cooperative trade school opened in the early 1920s which businessmen and educators hoped would meet the city's need for semi-skilled workers. According to Gonzalez, the establishment of this trade school made it possible to train future workers, a task the factories found to be impossible. In addition to providing skills, the "Mexican schools" hoped to instill an acceptance of industry's hierarchical order. As one Los Angeles teacher put it:

> Before sending boys and girls out to accept positions they must be taught that, technically expert though they may be, they must ever keep in mind that their employers carry the responsibility of the business and outline the work, and that the employees must be pliant, obedient, courteous, and willing to help the enterprise.... (p. 178)

Besides the view that both Southwestern employers and the Mexican children could best be served by manual training, the schools stressed the need to instruct the Mexicans in the ideal and ethics of American society. The schools claimed, however, that the Mexican family and culture hindered the attempt. Principal Katherine Gorbutt of the all-Mexican Aoy school in El Paso believed that the Mexican's lack of a sense of time increased school absenteeism. "In years past," she recalled, "there was the problem of getting children to school on time. Few homes had clocks and the excuse for lateness on a cloudy day would be, 'No hay sol, y el sol es mi reloj,' [There is no sun today and the sun is my clock] so one can imagine how many would be tardy during dark mornings." Yet Gorbutt did not consider the innate or cultural characteristics of the Mexicans to be all bad, although by no means equal to those of American children. "There are many things in which a Mexican excels," she stated:

> ...in his painstaking capacity for little things, in his ability to make the best of a bad bargain, and in his philosophy that is 'only worry about what cannot be helped.' The Mexicans are particularly gifted in art work and music. They make good athletes because they like to play. Aoy school has won many trophies in sports. [42]

Most American teachers shared Gorbutt's racial and cultural views and stereotypes and blamed the Mexican families for the perpetuation of ignorance and immorality. Because the schools considered Mexicans to be "culturally disadvantaged," officials developed great pride in their ability to "Americanize" the children. "It is impossible to estimate the general good that this school is doing and has done among those benighted Mexican people," the El Paso school report for 1903-1904 emphasized.

> .... Yearly there are over six hundred children who attend regularly this school. They come from the humblest homes, where in years

past, a knowledge of English and habits of cleanliness and refinement were unknown....Among the first lessons instilled into these children when they enter the school room is cleanliness. It is not an uncommon sight here to see a kind-hearted school marm standing in the lavatory room by one of these home neglected urchins, and supervising the process of bringing about conditions of personal cleanliness as he applys with vigor to rusty hands, dirty ears and neck, unkept face and head the two powerful agencies of American civilization, soap and water.[43]

In addition to cleanliness and ethics, the schools considered the teaching of English to the Mexican children as a vital ingredient in the Americanization process. Numerous educators by the 1920s voiced concerns over the Mexicans' "language problem." Not only did teachers see English as fundamental to the learning process, but they believed that as long as Spanish remained the dominant language "Mexican children would fail to become orderly participants in society."[44] Elma A. Neal, the director of elementary education in San Antonio, wrote in 1929 that "the first step in making a unified nation is to teach English to the non-English speaking portion of the population."[45] Important in developing patriotism, educators also recognized the economic importance of English. One El Paso school teacher pointed out that while Mexicans in unskilled work did not need English in "better positions he must be able to speak English," and consequently a "practical knowledge of English is very important."[46] In general, English represented a means to accomplish the goals of mass education. "Socialization of the differing social strata," Gonzalez concludes about "progressive" education,

the inculcation of correct values and behavior patterns could take place only within a common means of communication between teacher and pupil. The given, the need to harmonize society during the industrial upheaval, conditioned one task of the school to be that of teaching English to non-English speaking children. (p. 104)

V

The public school's attempt to Americanize Mexican children and to train them for particular forms of urban-industrial labor represented a logical extension of the view that perceived Mexicans to be products of a pre-industrial culture. Ironically, the Mexican's retention of traditional customs and habits proved to be an asset in their adjustment to life north of the border. However, the efforts by American institutions, such as the schools, to acculturate the Mexicans helped lay the foundation for inter-generational cultural tensions among the Mexican population and between Mexican Americans and Mexican immigrants. While much cultural change has indeed occurred among first and second generation Mexican Americans, the process of Americanization continues due to the unending movement of Mexicans--both documented and

31

undocumented--to the United States, many still arriving from rural areas or from the "urban villages" of Mexico's overpopulated cities.[47] More than a psychological phenomena, cultural and racial "clash" in the Southwest can be seen as part of the process of economic development and modernization which has rapidly transformed this section of the American "sun belt."

NOTES

[1] For patterns of Mexican immigration, see Arthur F. Carwin, "Causes of Mexican Migration to the United States: A Summary View," Perspectives in American History, vol. VII (1974), pp. 557-567; John Martinez, Mexican Emigration to the U.S. 1910-1930 (San Francisco, 1972); Lawrence Anthony Cardoso, "Mexican Emigration to the United States, 1900 to 1930," Ph.D. diss., University of Connecticut, 1974; and Mario T. Garcia, "Obreros: The Mexican Workers of El Paso, 1900-1920," Ph.D. diss., University of California, San Diego, 1975.

[2] See, for example, Richard Henry Dana, Two Years before the Mast (London, 1969); and Michael G. Webster, "Texas Manifest Destiny and the Mexican Border Conflict, 1865-1880," Ph.D. diss., Indiana University, 1972.

[3] Alberto Michael Camarillo, "The Making of a Chicano Community: A History of the Chicanos in Santa Barbara, California, 1850-1930," Ph.D.diss., University of California, Los Angeles, 1975, pp. 27-28.

[4] Ibid., p. 136.

[5] Owen White, Out of the Desert: The Historical Romance of El Paso (El Paso, 1923), p. 124.

[6] El Paso Bureau of Information, "The City and County of El Paso, Texas Containing Useful and Reliable Information Concerning the Future Great Metropolis of the Southwest Its Resources and Advantages for the Agriculturist, Artisan and Capitalist," (El Paso, 1886), p. 3. Copies of this report can be found in the Bancroft Library, Berkeley, and the Southwestern Collection, El Paso Public Library.

[7] E. P. Thompson, The Making of the English Working Class (New York, 1963); and Herbert G. Gutman, Work, Culture & Society in Industrializing America (New York, 1976).

[8] Gutman, "Work, Culture, and Society in Industrializing America, 1815-1919," in Work, Culture & Society, pp. 14-15.

[9] Herbert Gans, The Urban Villagers (New York, 1962).

[10] Manuel Gamio, Mexican Immigration to the United States (New York, 1971; first published in 1930), pp. 57-127.

[11] As quoted in Gutman, Work, Culture & Society, p. 33.

[12] Ibid.

[13]El Paso Times, March 20, 1896, p. 2; hereinafter cited as Times.

[14]Gamio, Mexican Immigration, pp. 13-56; and Judith Fincher Laird, "Argentine, Kansas: The Evolution of a Mexican-American Community: 1905-1940," Ph.D. diss., University of Kansas, 1975, pp. 159-218.

[15]Victor S. Clark, "Mexican Labor in the United States," Department of Commerce and Labor, Bureau of Labor Bulletin (No. 78, 1908) reprinted in Carlos E. Cortes, et al., ed., Mexican Labor in the United States (New York, 1974), pp. 481-499.

[16]U.S. Congress, Senate, Dillingham Commission, Immigrants in Industries. Part 25: Japanese and Other Immigrant Races in the Pacific Coast and Rocky Mountain States. Vol. III, Part I, p. 20. 61st Cong., 2nd sess., 1911, S. Doc. 633.

[17]Ibid., p. 23.

[18]Clark, "Mexican Labor," pp. 495-496.

[19]Times, Nov. 27, 1919, p. 5.

[20]Ibid., and Labor Advocate, Nov. 28, 1919, pp. 1 and 8.

[21]Paul S. Taylor, "The Success of Mexican Women in Industrial Work," unpublished paper, pp. 1-11, Paul S. Taylor Papers, Bancroft Library.

[22]Ibid.

[23]Times, June 16, 1892, p. 7.

[24]Ibid., July 26, 1905, p. 2; July 29, 1905, p. 3.

[25]Clark, "Mexican Labor," p. 510.

[26]Samuel Bryan, "Mexican Immigration in the United States," The Survey, Vol. 28 (April-Sept., 1912), p. 730.

[27]Vera L. Sturges, "Mexican Immigrants," The Survey, Vol. 46 (April-Sept., 1921), p. 470.

[28]Times, June 17, 1910, p. 8.

[29]Ibid., Nov. 24, 1900, pp. 1 and 2.

[30]As quoted in Ricardo Romo, "Mexican Workers in the City: Los Angel Angeles, 1915-1930," unpublished Ph.D. thesis, University of California, Los Angeles, 1975, pp. 196-197.

[31]Emory S. Bogardus, "The Mexican Immigrant," Sociology and Social Research, Vol. 11 (1926-27), pp. 470-488.

[32]As quoted in Gilbert G. Gonzalez, "The System of Public Education and its Function Within the Chicano Communities, 1920-1930," Ph.D. diss., University of California, Los Angeles, 1974, p. 54.

33

[33]Bogardus, "Mexican Immigrant," pp. 478 and 487. For an excellent analysis of "time" in an industrial society see E. P. Thompson, "Time, Work-Discipline and Industrial Capitalism," Past and Present, Vol. 38, no. 36 (1967), pp. 56-97.

[34]Helen W. Walker, "Mexican Immigrants and American Citizenship," Sociology and Social Research, Vol. 13 (May-June, 1929), p. 466.

[35]Ibid., p. 60.

[36]Clark, "Mexican Labor," p. 505 and pp. 517-518.

[37]Times, Sept. 8, 1908, p.8.

[38]J. C. Ross,"Industrial Education for the Spanish-Speaking People," N New Mexico Journal of Education, Vol. VII (Feb., 1911), pp. 19-21 as quoted in Gonzalez, "Public Education," pp. 115-116.

[39]As quoted in Romo, "Mexican Workers," p. 196.

[40]As quoted in Gonzalez, "Public Education," pp. 89-90.

[41]Ibid., p. 119.

[42]As quoted in Bertha Archer Schaer, Historical Sketch of Aoy School (El Paso, 1951), p. 17.

[43]Reports of the Public Schools (El Paso, 1903-1904), p. 26.

[44]Gonzalez, "Public Education," P. 99.

[45]Ibid., p. 102.

[46]Ibid., p. 103.

[47]More recent Mexican immigrants, unlike the earlier arrivals, enter the United States with a greater acquaintance with industrial culture due to Mexico's increased industrialization since 1940.

34

Americans All: World War II and the Shaping of American Identity*

Philip Gleason

Although it is four decades since the United States entered World War II, some aspects of the nation's wartime experience are still virtually unstudied. Military and diplomatic historians have labored productively for many years, but historians interested in American social and intellectual developments are just beginning to turn their attention to the wartime era. Recent general studies by Richard Polenberg and John M. Blum are especially welcome since, by drawing greater attention to the period, they should stimulate further research.[1] There is much left to be done because the war affected practically every dimension of American life. The present essay deals with one of its less obvious effects — the way in which it shaped the thinking of a whole generation on the subject of American identity.

The expression "American identity" had not yet come into use in World War II. In those days people spoke instead of American nationality or American character. All of these terms are elusive and, in many cases, simply vague. We need not enter into all the semantic complications, but a few preliminary comments are required for the discussion that follows.[2] In the first place, we should note that the underlying question in many contexts where these terms appear is, "What does it mean to be an American?"

* An earlier version of this paper was presented to a meeting of the European Association of American Studies at Amsterdam in April, 1980, and is printed in the published version of the presentations, *The American Identity, Fusion and Fragmentation,* edited by Rob Kroes (Amsterdam: Amerika Instituut, Universiteit van Amsterdam, 1980). I wish to thank Professor Richard A. Lamanna of the Department of Sociology and Anthropology at Notre Dame for comments helpful in revising this paper.

[1] John M. Blum, *V Was for Victory: Politics and American Culture during World War II* (New York, 1976); Richard Polenberg, *War and Society: The United States, 1941-1945* (Philadelphia, 1972); Richard Polenberg, *One Nation Divisible: Class, Race, and Ethnicity in the United States since 1938* (New York, 1980), esp. chaps. 1-3. (My citations are to the Penguin paperback edition of this work, which comprises volume 7 of the Pelican History of the United States [Harmondsworth and New York, 1980]). Cf. also Jim F. Heath, "Domestic American during World War II: Research Opportunities for Historians," *Journal of American History,* 58 (1971), 384-414.

[2] The following paragraphs are based on my article, "American Identity and Americanization," in *Harvard Encyclopedia of American Ethnic Groups,* ed. Stephan Thernstrom, Ann Orlov, and Oscar Handlin (Cambridge, Massachusetts, 1980), pp. 31-58. The present essay is an expansion of matters discussed in that article, esp. pp. 47-50, and makes use of some of the same evidence and formulations found there.

Although a straightforward and seemingly simple question, it raises issues of the deepest sort about the values we hold as a people, the goals we should pursue, the loyalties we may legitimately cherish, and the norms of conduct we ought to follow. These issues are not only controversial in that Americans will disagree about the appropriate answers, they are also inherently difficult in that they are subtle, complex, and resistant to perspicuous formulation. In view of these facts it is not surprising that discussions of American identity have historically been marked by a good deal of conceptual unclarity and impassioned misunderstanding.

From the earliest days of our national existence, elements of ideology and ethnicity have figured prominently in these discussions. *Ideology* here refers to the foundational values of freedom, equality, and commitment to self-government under law which served as the justification for the colonies' separation from the mother country, and on which the Founding Fathers erected the constitutional fabric. The ideological element in American identity, in other words, comprises the universalistic political and social principles for which the Republic stands, and through adherence to which individuals identify themselves with the nation. *Ethnicity,* on the other hand, refers to the more particularistic dimensions of group consciousness that have marked the American people, or portions of them, causing them to think of themselves, and to be thought of by others, as belonging to a distinctive community, set apart from others by race, religion, language, national derivation, or some combination of these and other cultural features.

A historical review of the evolution of American thinking on identity shows that ideological and ethnic elements have interacted in complex ways, and that their relative salience has varied from one epoch to another. For the revolutionary and immediate postrevolutionary generations, ideological themes predominated strongly. In the years 1830-1860, however, religion — specifically the Roman Catholicism of so many immigrants — became the focal point in controversies over what it meant to be an American. In fact, the word *Americanization* was first used to refer to immigrant assimilation in the Know-Nothing debates of the 1850's. Ethnic elements attained their greatest salience in the era that spanned the years from 1890 to the mid-1920's. Religious feeling still ran high, and by then Jews were numerous enough to play a prominent role, especially since they produced writers who helped establish the terms of discourse in respect to national identity. Israel Zangwill, who put the symbol of the Melting Pot in circulation, and Horace Kallen, who propounded the theory of cultural pluralism, were both Jews. In this era racialism was triumphant, both as scientific doctrine and as popular sentiment. Combining with the chauvinism brought on by the war, and with postwar cultural panic, racialist nativism brought about a reversal of America's century-old tradition of almost completely unrestricted immigration.

In the half-century that has passed since the climax of nativism in the 1920's there was first an ebbing and then (after the mid-1960's) a resurgence of the ethnic dimension in thinking on national identity. When ethnicity was most recessive (from about 1940 to the early 1960's) the ideological aspect of American identity was given greater emphasis than it had received since the days of the Founding Fathers. In the following pages we will explore some of the factors related to the decline of attention to the ethnic dimension after the mid-1920's, and then examine the role played by World War II in accentuating the ideological conception of American identity.

Nineteen twenty-four is the place to begin, because the passage that year of the national origins quota law ended a century of massive overseas immigration, satisfied the demands of the restrictionists, and permitted Americans hitherto alarmed about the immigrant peril to relax. As a result, the 1924 law inaugurated an era in which ethnic concerns faded from consciousness as important public issues. It is true that religious and ethnocultural feelings played a prominent role in the Al Smith campaign of 1928, but that contest proved a kind of epilogue to the era when passions of this sort loomed large in public controversy.[3]

The great depression was most decisive in pushing ethnocultural considerations into the background, but a reassessment of the concept of race contributed to this result by undercutting traditional ideas about group life. These shifting views on the nature of group life and intergroup relations become rather com-

---

[3] John Higham, *Strangers in the Land* (New York, 1975), chap. 11, describes both the passage of the national origins law and the rapid ebbing of nativist sentiment thereafter. Allan J. Lichtman, *Prejudice and the Old Politics: The Presidential Election of 1928* (Chapel Hill, North Carolina, 1979), the most recent analysis of the 1928 election, stresses the religious issue above all other ethnocultural factors.

plicated, and they demand careful analysis. The traditional view, which dominated in the late nineteenth century and reached its climax in the first two decades of the twentieth, held that inborn racial qualities determined the kind of culture a people could create. Since cultures could be ranked on a scale from lower to higher, and since race and nationality blurred together, the old racial theory jibed nicely with restrictionists' claims that the new immigrants from eastern and southern Europe were overwhelming and degrading American culture. Indeed, it gave shape through the national origins device to the kind of restriction enacted in the 1924 law. The national origins principle was not abandoned in law till the mid-sixties, but the racial theory it embodied had been discredited long before. The Second World War confirmed the shift at the level of popular thinking, but the crucial change in educated opinion came in the fifteen years before the war.

Social scientists were the first to repudiate the older racialism. Among them, the anthropologists — Franz Boas first of all — claim pride of place, not merely because they led the way in the critique of racialism, but also because the anthropological concept of culture replaced race as the key to understanding human groups. Boas had struggled for many years against the view that cultural phenomena were racially linked, but his interpretation did not attain the status of anthropological orthodoxy until the 1920's. Thereafter a sharp disjunction was posited between race as the realm of the biologically determined and culture as the domain of learned behavior, human creativity, and spiritual freedom.[4]

The incompatibility of this view with the older racialism was obvious, and by 1930 social scientists had nearly all discarded the latter, even though it required some of them to repudiate their previously published opinions.[5] Not so obvious at first were the far-reaching implications of the culture concept as an analytical and interpretive principle. Boas enlarged on some of these mat-

---

[4] It is worth noting that in Melville J. Herskovits's brief sketch of Boas's work the principal substantive chapters are headed: "Man, the Biological Organism,"; "Man, the Culture-Building Animal"; and "Man, the Creator." Cf. Herskovits, *Franz Boas* (New York, 1953). The best discussion of Boas's career and influence is George W. Stocking, Jr., *Race, Culture, and Evolution: Essays in the History of Anthropology* (New York, 1968), esp. chaps. 7-11.

[5] The social scientists' abandonment of racism in the 1920's is strikingly summed up in Stanley Coben, "The Assault on Victorianism in the Twentieth Century," *American Quarterly*, 27 (1975) 610-14. Cf. also Thomas F. Gossett, *Race: The History of an Idea in America* (New York, 1965 [orig. pub., 1963]), pp. 416-30.

ters in a 1928 volume entitled *Anthropology and Modern Life,* of which a reviewer said that it annihilated "the bases of almost all the prejudices and passions on which modern society rests."[6] But two of Boas's students were even more effective in bringing the anthropological perspective to the attention of the general reading public.

The first was Margaret Mead. Her *Coming of Age in Samoa* informed a wide readership in 1928 that adolescence was not the psychologically stressful experience in Samoa that it was in Western society because of culturally conditioned differences in family structure, attitudes toward sex, and so on. The youthful anthropologist — only twenty-three when she went to Samoa — underscored the implications of her study for Americans. Besides the general point that personality was shaped by cultural norms and institutions, she stressed the relativity of such norms and institutions, the need for tolerance and open-mindedness in evaluating human conduct, and the desirability of educating American youngsters in such a way as to enable them to choose without feelings of guilt among the many competing value systems and styles of life offered by the heterogeneous society in which they dwelt.[7]

Ruth Benedict was also a student of Franz Boas, and her book, *Patterns of Culture* (1934), reaffirmed the message of cultural relativism and the need for tolerance. Yet this work, probably the most widely read anthropological study ever written, was even more important in popularizing the view that a culture was not simply a collection of discrete institutions and traits, but an integrated complex, more or less tightly organized around some animating vision, central motif, or generalized attitude toward reality. So understood, a culture had to be viewed holistically, for none of its specific features could be adequately grasped without

---

[6] This is from Freda Kirchwey's review in *The Nation,* 127 (19 December 1928), 689.

[7] Margaret Mead, *Coming of Age in Samoa* (New York, 1928). The work is subtitled "A Psychological Study of Primitive Youth for Western Civilisation." See especially chap. 1, "Introduction"; chap. 13, "Our Educational Problems in the Light of Samoan Contrasts"; and chap. 14, "Education for Choice." In the "Preface 1973 Edition" to a reprint of the book (New York, 1973), Mead writes: "When this book was written, the very idea of culture was new to the literate world. The idea that our every thought and movement was a product not of race, not of instinct, but derived from the society within which an individual was reared, was new and unfamiliar." Stocking observes, incidentally, that "It was not Boas but his students who were largely responsible for the elaboration and development of the anthropological concept [of culture]" (Stocking, *Race, and Culture, and Evolution,* p. 231).

reference to the pattern of which they formed a part. A culture was something like an art style — it represented the collective response of a people to what Benedict called the "great arc" of human possibilities. This did not mean that all cultures were equally appealing; but appreciating the diversity of cultures helped to liberate a person from the imperatives of his own culture and provided a perspective from which to assay its dominant traits.[8]

By the eve of World War II, the culture concept was fast becoming "the foundation stone of the social sciences."[9] Even historians — a group notoriously laggard in matters methodological — saw the light by 1939, when the program chairman for their annual convention decided that "the time was ripe for a discussion of the cultural approach and for an attempt to try it out in different fields." The first group of topics treated in the published version of the sessions dealt with immigration history under the rubric "Cultural Groups." Not all the contributors drew the same inferences from the culture concept, however; one distinguished scholar even suggested that nativism might be a very positive thing from the cultural perspective, since by retarding the assimilation of immigrants it helped preserve cultural diversity.[10]

Differences in interpretation were natural enough because the anthropological concept was rather spongy in itself, and because it overlay older, more informal, senses of the word culture. In addition, sociologists had also done much work on human groups, and, as the two disciplines mutually influenced and borrowed from each other, their terminologies "half-blended in a grand con-

---

[8] Ruth Benedict, *Patterns of Culture* (Boston, 1959 [original publication, 1934]). In a preface to this "Sentry Edition" of the book, Margaret Mead comments on its influence in popularizing the anthropological notion of culture. See chaps. 2 and 3 for cultural diversity and cultural integration; chaps. 7 and 8 for applications to contemporary America and the need for tolerance.

[9] Stuart Chase, *The Proper Study of Mankind* (New York, 1948), pp. 50, 59-86, 275-76, 289-90; quotation from p. 59. The essays collected in *The Idea of Culture in the Social Sciences*, ed. Louis Schneider and Charles Bonjean (Cambridge, 1973) are extremely informative. For examples of emphasis on the culture concept in the 1930's, see Otto Klineberg, *Race Differences* (New York, 1935), part 3, "The Cultural Approach"; and Donald Young, *Research Memorandum on Minority Peoples in the Depression* (New York, no date), pp. 220-21.

[10] Caroline F. Ware, ed., *The Cultural Approach to History* (New York, 1940), p. 15 for quotation; p. 81 for R. A. Billington's comment about the "unpleasant conclusion" concerning nativism. Cf. also the difference between Carlton C. Qualey's view of "The Transitional Character of Nationality Group Culture," pp. 82-84, and the "Summary of the Discussion," by Caroline Ware and others, pp. 86-89.

fusion."[11] Since these obscurities of terminology shrouded real conceptual ambiguities, we must look more closely at what the sociologists were doing and at some of the more problematic terms that were used in the discussion of ethnic affairs.

What Franz Boas and Columbia University were to anthropology, Robert E. Park and the University of Chicago were to sociology. One authority dates the beginnings of scientific sociology in the United States from the publication of *The Polish Peasant in Europe and America,* by Park's colleague and friend, W. I. Thomas, and his Polish associate, Florian Znaniecki.[12] Personal difficulties led to Thomas's departure from Chicago about the time the book was published in 1918, but Park carried on the tradition and made racial and ethnic relations a leading specialization as sociology came of age. And although the layman often has trouble distinguishing between the work of a sociologist and an anthropologist, there was a significant difference between the Parkian approach and that of the anthropologists.

Because of their fascination with culture, anthropologists were predisposed toward an internalist approach to the study of human groups — they focused primarily on the group considered in itself, its norms, institutions, and the patterns that gave it coherence. They spoke of acculturation and cultural change, to be sure, but these matters were logically secondary, since one had to understand a culture before one could analyze its modifications. There was thus an implicit tendency toward what we might call analytical isolationism — considering each group as an isolated unit — and the characteristic work of anthropologists was carried out in remote corners of the earth, among primitive groups whose cultures could be grasped in the round.[13]

---

[11] Everett C. Hughes and Helen M. Hughes, *Where Peoples Meet* (Glencoe, Illinois, 1952), pp. 30-31. For the overlapping of the anthropological and the older humanist senses of the word culture, see Stocking, *Race, Culture, and Evolution,* pp. 69-90, 195-233.

[12] John Madge, *The Origins of Scientific Sociology* (New York, 1962), chap. 3.

[13] Melville J. Herskovits, *Acculturation* (New York, 1938), esp. pp. 22-23, 49-50, 51. Walter Goldschmidt recently began an article by stating: "The natural habitat of the cultural anthropologist is the world of native, preliterate, tribal, and peasant communities." Further on he adds that the two distinctive marks of the anthropological approach, cultural relativism (meaning the need to understand each culture in its own terms) and holism, both had "their source in that vanishing environment of ethnographic fieldwork" (Goldschmidt, "Should the Cultural Anthropologist Be Placed on the Endangered Species List?" in *New Dimensions in the Humanities and Social Sciences,* ed. Harry R. Garvin. [Lewisburg, Pennsylvania, 1977], pp. 15, 19).

Park's intellectual disposition was very different.[14] He had been a newspaperman before turning to academic life, and the metropolis was his natural metier. For him the primary fact about group life in the modern world was not that each group had its own distinctive culture, but that all groups were being thrown into contact with each other, were reacting to each other, and mutually influencing each other in all sorts of ways. Getting an intelligible grip on this melee was one of the chief tasks of social science, and to do that, one obviously needed a perspective that highlighted the processes of interaction *between* groups, rather than the peculiarities of each group considered in itself.

Park's formulation of the interaction process became famous as the "race relations cycle." It envisioned a four-stage sequence, of which the first was "competition." Here the groups involved might not even be aware of their relationship to each other, since competition was mostly a matter of economic interdependence mediated through the marketplace, the division of labor, and so on. The stage of "conflict" ensued when groups became aware of their interconnection and strove to get the better of each other by divers means, the most extreme of which was war. "Accommodation," the third stage, represented "the unstable equilibrium achieved by conflicting parties who became weary of the struggle . . . and agreed . . . to limit their claims and coexist with potential rivals." In the final stage, "assimilation," the groups in question forged more intimate links by what Park called "a process of interpenetration and fusion in which persons and groups acquire the memories and sentiments and attitudes of other persons and groups, and, by sharing their experience and history, are incorporated with them in a common cultural life."[15]

Although he spoke of "a common cultural life," Park did not

---

[14] The best treatment of Park is Fred H. Matthews, *Quest for an American Sociology: Robert E. Park and the Chicago School* (Montreal, 1977). See also the discussion of Park in Leon Bramson, *The Political Context of Sociology* (Princeton, 1961); and Robert E. L. Faris, *Chicago Sociology 1920-1932* (Chicago, 1967). Robert E. Park, *Race and Culture* (Glencoe, Illinois, 1950), collects twenty-nine of Park's papers, published from the teens to the 1940's. It also contains a very brief autobiographical note.

[15] This follows Matthews, *Quest for an American Sociology,* pp. 160-62, who refers to Park's model as "the interaction cycle, or cycle of group interaction." Park used a slightly different set of labels ("contacts, competition, accommodation and eventual assimilation") in a 1926 paper on "Our Racial Frontier on the Pacific," in which he spoke explicitly of "The Race Relations Cycle." See Park, *Race and Culture,* pp. 149-51. The sequence, competition, conflict, accommodation and assimilation as presented in Matthews is taken from chaps. 8-11, which have those titles, in Robert E. Park and Ernest W. Burgess, *Introduction to the Science of Sociology* (Chicago, 1924). For later critiques of the race relations

visualize it as requiring a high degree of cultural integration. Rather, he believed a modern society could function effectively if its constituent elements all conformed to a minimum of general norms that enabled them to get along together and cooperate in carrying out essential collective tasks.[16] He departed here from the view implicit in much anthropological work that there was something intrinsically unhealthy about a society whose cultural features were not all of a piece. This difference is quite important because it suggests that the Parkian version of "assimilation" could accommodate a greater amount of internal diversity than could the anthropological concept of culture, despite the fact that culture rather than assimilation was usually associated with the idea of tolerance for diversity. The difference noted above is also significant because it reflected a really crucial divergence between the Parkian and the anthropological approaches — viz., Park's interaction model of group relations was a dynamic one in which conflict and change were built in, whereas the view popularized by Ruth Benedict squinted toward stasis and made contact with outsiders a problematic business.[17]

This perhaps puts too fine a point on the contrast, but it was nevertheless real. And it was important, for it involved different criteria for evaluating the health of a society. Conflict, for Park, was not necessarily a morbid symptom; nor were differences in interests, goals, and values among the constituent groups making up the society. In the Benedictine perspective, however, these would be morbid symptoms, for her interpretation of culture

---

cycle, see Stanford M. Lyman, "The Race Relations Cycle of Robert E. Park," *Pacific Sociological Review*, 11 (Spring 1968), 16-22; L. Paul Metzger, "American Sociology and Black Assimilation: Conflicting Perspective," *American Journal of Sociology*, 76 (1970-71), 627-47; and Ernest A. T. Barth and Donald L. Noel, "Conceptual Frameworks for the Analysis of Race Relations: An Evaluation," *Social Forces*, 50 (March 1972), 333-48, as reprinted in Thomas F. Pettigrew, ed., *The Sociology of Race Relations; Reflection and Reform* (New York, 1980), pp. 418-22.

[16] Matthews, *Quest for an American Sociology*, pp. 167-69. See also Park's article on "Assimilation, Social" in *Encyclopedia of the Social Sciences* (New York, 1930), vol. 2, pp. 281-83, which is not included in the essays collected in *Race and Culture*, but which Matthews calls "Park's most concentrated theoretical discussion of assimilation."

[17] In an important essay contrasting "genuine" and "spurious" versions of culture, Edward Sapir in 1924 wrote that a genuine culture was "inherently harmonious, balanced, self-satisfactory," and "not a spiritual hybrid of contradictory patches." Such a culture could not tolerate the thousand "spiritual maladjustments" to be found in the spurious modern American culture. Sapir preferred the "well-rounded life of the average participant in the civilization of a typical American Indian tribe," before that culture was destroyed by contact with white civilization. Sapir, "Culture, Genuine and Spurious," *American Journal of Sociology*, 29 (1924), 410, 416. Coben, "Assault on Victorianism," pp. 607-08, discusses this article (see above note 5 for citation to Coben).

assumed internal coherence and harmony as fundamental requirements for social health. This underlying contrast was not brought clearly into the open and analyzed in the 1930's, with the result that submerged ambiguities persisted in the discussion of acculturation, assimilation, tolerance for diversity, and other matters related to ethnicity. The conceptual situation was made even more complex by semantic uncertainties associated with other terms that figured prominently in the discussion. We will look at three of these terms — *minority, ethnocentrism,* and *prejudice.*

The term *minority,* or *minority group,* entered the discussion in 1932 when Donald Young gave the title *American Minority Peoples* to a general study of group relations in the United States. He introduced the term because there was no other word that embraced strictly racial groups, those set off by "alien national cultural traits," and those (such as Asiatics) in which biological and cultural features combined. Young wanted an inclusive term, for he regarded the problems and principles of group relations as being "remarkably similar," no matter what groups were involved. In other words, he agreed with Park that interaction between groups was more significant than their inborn qualities. His minority concept caught on quickly and weakened the older racialism, not merely by providing an alternative term for racial groups, but by redirecting attention toward the *placement* of groups in the social order as a whole.[18]

Young knew he was introducing a neologism of sorts, and he justified it briefly in his preface. "To most of us," he wrote, "the word 'minority' has political connotations in that it calls to mind a political party which is not in power." Since he avoided this usage in his book, he did not think his "special application" would cause confusion.[19] But this was straining at a gnat! The real potential for confusion, and the explosive political connotations, derived from the fact that the same word had been used for years in connection with the "minorities problem" of Central Europe. This

[18] Donald Young, *American Minority Peoples* (New York, 1932), pp. xii-xiii. The classical formulation of the concept of the minority group is Louis Wirth, "The Problem of Minority Groups," in Ralph Linton, ed., *The Science of Man and the World Crisis* (New York, 1945), pp. 347-72. Cf. also Peter I. Rose, *The Subject Is Race* (New York, 1968), pp. 69-71; E. B. Reuter, "Racial Theory," *American Journal of Sociology,* 50 (May 1943), 452-61; E. F. Frazier, "Sociological Theory and Race Relations," *American Sociological Review,* 12 (June 1947), 265-71.

[19] Young, *American Minority Peoples,* pp. xiii-xiv.

Young blandly overlooked. But as his terminology entered into general circulation, the question naturally arose whether American minorities were like those of Europe, and, if so, whether they might not be dangerous, since the latter were associated with extreme nationalism and the threat of Balkanization. Nazi exploitation of minority resentments, and the Fifth Column menace, magnified the peril in the later thirties. Hence, though discussion of American minorities usually stressed the need for tolerance and mutual understanding, there was also an undercurrent of uneasiness and latent hostility.[20]

In contrast to minority, *ethnocentrism* was a concept that aroused quite unambiguous feelings. It was a bad thing, and everyone was against it! But, if not ambiguous, this was at least puzzling, since ethnocentrism was the by-product — or was it the cause? — of the tight cultural cohesion that anthropologists seemed to regard as healthy in primitive groups. Indeed, the term had been introduced in William Graham Sumner's ethnological classic, *Folkways* (1906), among a cluster of coinages (including the perennial favorites, in-group and out-group) all of which referred to the phenomenon of intense group solidarity.[21] Why, then, had the concept become so repugnant by the 1930's? The article on ethnocentrism in the *Encyclopedia of the Social Sciences* (1931) throws some light on the question.

The author, George P. Murdock, a leading anthropologist, quoted Sumner's definition of ethnocentrism as "that view of things in which our own group is the center of everything, and all others are scaled and rated with reference to it." This implied not simply approval for one's fellows, but fear, suspicion, and hostility toward outsiders and their ways. Ethnocentrism, Murdock

---

[20] The article on "Minorities, National" in the *Encyclopedia of the Social Sciences* (New York, 1933), vol. 10, pp. 518-25, deals with the European kind of minorities and does not mention American minorities. Cf. also Donald R. Taft, "Problems Arising from Minorities," in Francis J. Brown and Joseph S. Roucek, eds., *Our Racial and National Minorities* (New York, 1937), pp 18-32; Joseph S. Roucek, "Minorities — a Basis of the Refugee Problem," *The Annals*, 203 (May 1939), 1-17; Roucek, "Editorial," *Journal of Educational Sociology*, 12 (April 1939), 449-50; Stewart G. Cole, "Europe's Conflict of Cultures," in Robert M. MacIver, ed., *Group Relations and Group Antagonisms* (New York, 1944), pp. 121-56; Oscar I. Janowsky, "Ethnic and Cultural Minorities" in *ibid.*, pp. 157-70; George Britt, *The Fifth Column Is Here* (New York, 1940); and Polenberg, *One Nation Divisible*, pp. 42-45; Gunnar Myrdal, *An American Dilemma* (New York, 1962 [orig. pub. 1944]), p. 50, notes the difference between minorities in the U.S. and Europe: "The minority peoples of the United States are fighting for status within the larger society; the minorities of Europe are mainly fighting for independence from it."

[21] William Graham Sumner, *Folkways* (Boston, 1906), pp. 12ff.

declared, was a manifestation of the herd instinct; essentially irrational and primitive, it resembled the "group egotism" Wolfgang
Koehler had observed among apes. Conceding that it had survival value, Murdock stressed its negative effects in causing friction between groups, and he linked it to such contemporary
phenomena as chauvinistic nationalism, race prejudice, and
lynchings. Such fruits proved how undesirable ethnocentrism
was, and Murdock noted hopefully that education might diminish
its force and promote "toleration, catholicity and
cosmopolitanism" in its place. He concluded with just a touch of
disciplinary smugness — not to call it professional ethnocentrism — by claiming that the social sciences were particularly well-
suited to promote intergroup understanding because they
specialized in explaining cultural diversities.[22]

Well, perhaps. But these social scientists failed to address a
question that seems obvious to us. To wit: "If ethnocentrism is so
destructive, does that not discredit ethnicity itself as a legitimate
principle of group cohesion?" Admittedly, it's a lot easier for us to
ask the question today, since we have the term *ethnicity* and they
didn't. But those who commented on these matters in the thirties
were certainly acquainted with what we now call ethnicity. That
was what they usually had in mind in talking about cultural
groups, and the notion of cultural pluralism was based on the
assumption that ethnic diversity was a good thing and should be
preserved. But, to repeat, how could such diversity be a good
thing if the ethnocentrism that was central to preserving ethnic
distinctiveness was such a bad thing? Since the question was
never put in those stark terms, it was, of course, never
answered.[23] But neither was it ever made clear — and perhaps it

---

[22] *Encyclopedia of the Social Sciences* (New York, 1931), vol. 5, pp. 612-13. For Murdock's
relation to Sumner, and some differences between his approach to anthropology and that
of the Boasian school, see George P. Murdock, ed., *Studies in the Science of Society* (New
Haven, 1937), pp. xiii-xv.

[23] The issue was just below the surface in some discussions. In explaining the need to
go beyond tolerance to sharing values, Rachel Davis-DuBois warns "we must not allow
people to be so proud of their own culture that they can see no good in that of others. This
disease the sociologists call ethnocentrism. We can avoid this by putting emphasis on . . .
sharing our values so that new values will emerge which will have in them the best of those
which have gone into the merging. . . . The term 'cultural democracy' will describe this
process — a thinking, feeling and acting together, on a basis of equality." R. Davis-Dubois,
"Sharing Cultural Values," *Journal of Educational Sociology*, 12 (April 1939), 482-86. Along
the same lines, ". . . we misconceive group prejudice when we think of it as primarily a
prejudice *against* some one or more particular groups: as anti-Semitism, anti-Catholicism,
anti-Anything-in-particular. It is instead at bottom a prejudice *in favor* of 'My Own Group'

was not even recognized—that the remedies recommended for ethnocentrism (i.e., tolerance and cosmopolitanism) would inevitably work against the preservation of ethnocultural diversity because they were bound to weaken the internal solidarity of groups and blur the boundaries between them.[24] Indeed, these remedies were actually prescriptions for assimilation, scandalous as this assertion might seem to our latter-day prophets of pluralism and ethnicity.

Robert Park would not have been scandalized by such an assertion.[25] Recall that the assimilation he described envisioned groups, formerly in conflict, getting along by mutual give-and-take. Assimilation presumed enough agreement on basic matters to permit a peaceable common life, but beyond that people were free to do as they pleased. The situation was best exemplified in the great cities where all sorts of groups pursued their special interests or followed their distinctive ways. The urbane cosmopolitan might savor this spectacle of diversity. The ordinary citizen was more apt to ignore it, either from pure indifference, or from a careless attitude of live and let live. Both reactions were acceptable forms of tolerance in the Parkian system.

While Park thus prized tolerance, he was not unduly scandalized by *prejudice*. This statement strikes the modern ear as scandalous in itself, because prejudice has come to be viewed as a pathological attitude, the mark of a diseased mind. But this psychological view of prejudice was hardly adumbrated before 1939, and only established itself firmly in the next decade, with the appearance in 1950 of *The Authoritarian Personality* being the decisive landmark. In the twenties and thirties, the concept of prejudice was very much in flux. Or, more accurately, it was gradually *becoming* a technical concept besides being an everyday term of ordinary discourse. It had not yet emerged as a generalized something-in-itself that could act as an independent variable. Thus one finds no entry under "Prejudice" in the *Encyclopedia of the*

---

as against *all* others, 'pro-us' prejudice eternal, live, and waiting, ready to be focussed and intensified against *Any* Other Group." Karl N. Llewellyn, "Group Prejudice and Social Education," in R. M. MacIver, ed., *Civilization and Group Relationships* (New York, 1945), p. 13. Italics in original.

[24] This point was implicit in Billington's observation that nativists did more to make immigrants preserve their cultural heritage than disciples of the immigrant-gifts approach did. Cf. Ware, *Cultural Approach*, p. 81.

[25] The following discussion owes much to Matthews, *Quest for an American Sociology*, pp. 167-74.

Social Sciences, and the heading "Race Prejudice" yields only: "See Race Conflict."[26]

Which brings us back to Park and why it is possible to say, without slandering his memory, that he was not unduly scandalized by prejudice. Competition and conflict were built into his theory of intergroup relations. Feelings of antagonism between groups naturally accompanied these phases of the race relations cycle. Prejudice considered as a form of hostility, or a predisposition toward it, was quite intelligible within this theoretical framework. In 1924, Park suggested that prejudice might be understood as a disposition to maintain the "social distance" between groups, and that it was most apt to be called into play when change threatened to disturb the relative statuses of groups. Four years later, he distinguished between racial prejudice and racial

---

[26] I have found no historical study of the development of the concept of prejudice. John Higham's "Anti-Semitism and American Culture," in *Send These to Me* (New York, 1975), pp. 174-95, contains relevant material. Higham states that in the nineteenth century " 'Prejudice' was defined as a prepossession *for or against* anything, formed without due examination of the facts. No one supposed that it might be reified. . . . [or] that it referred distinctively to negative judgments of minorities and therefore connoted a certain kind of exclusionist mentality" (p. 176). Gordon W. Allport still used prejudice in this loose and generalized way in an article written in 1935 for a handbook of social psychology. The article dealt with "Attitudes," and, in the section headed "Prejudgment and Prejudice," Allport wrote that a preexisting attitude so strong that it "seriously distorts perception and judgment . . . [is called] a *stereotype,* a *prejudice,* or sometimes, more loosely, . . . a *logic-tight compartment.*" Allport illustrated the workings of prejudice by reference to experiments in which respondents were asked to rate the literary quality of selected passages, all of which were in fact written by the same author, although they were labeled as being the work of different authors. Prejudice was revealed by the fact that respondents consistently rated passages supposedly written by authors they admired more highly than other passages alleged to be works of lesser known writers. Other experimental results cited by Allport dealt with preferential ranking of racial and national groups, but it is clear that Allport did not regard prejudice as referring primarily to negative judgments of minorities or as connoting what Higham calls an exclusionist mentality. Cf. Gordon W. Allport, "Attitudes," in Carl A. Murchison, ed., *Handbook of Social Psychology* (New York, 1967 [orig. pub. 1935]), pp. 814-16. Myrdal, *American Dilemma,* pp. 52 n, 1141, expresses his dissatisfaction with the conceptual fuzziness of the term *prejudice.* Eugene L. Horowitz's study of " 'Race' Attitudes," undertaken as a part of the Myrdal study and published in Otto Klineberg, ed., *Characteristics of the American Negro* (New York, 1944), pp. 138-247, provides evidence of a marked shift in the understanding of prejudice around 1940. The term hardly appears at all in the body of Horowitz's study, which is a descriptive summary of numerous investigations of racial attitudes in children and other population groups. When he turns to "Suggested Hypotheses for Future Research," however, prejudice suddenly becomes the major conceptual category, although no effort whatever is made to relate the heavily psychological hypotheses concerning the origins of prejudice to the evidence adduced in the previously reviewed studies of racial attitudes. Horowitz's study also reveals, incidentally, the degree of uncertainty still prevailing around 1940 as to the content of the concept of attitude. On this general problem, see Donald Fleming, "Attitude: The History of a Concept," in *Perspectives in American History,* 1 (1967), 287-365.

antipathy—the former being a conservative, but quite rational, resistance to status-threatening change; the latter referring to the quasi-instinctive repugnance aroused by perceived differences between races, especially those connected with the sense of smell.[27]

The distinction never caught on.[28] It is true that some commentators of the thirties stressed the role of prejudice in maintaining exploitative economic relationships, which was roughly in line with Park's view that prejudice was more a rational than an irrational phenomenon.[29] But the general drift of thinking was in the opposite direction. One reason for this was the belief that prejudice sprang from ethnocentrism, and was therefore grounded in the same primitive herd instinct.[30] Ultimately more important was the fact that prejudice was increasingly claimed as a subject appropriate for psychological, rather than sociological, analysis.

Park's concept of social distance played a role here. After being operationalized by Emory S. Bogardus, who devised a way to measure it on a friendliness-hostility scale, it became an important element in the early development of attitudinal surveys.[31] Among the social psychologists, prejudice was associated from the first with "stereotyping,"[32] and other less than fully rational operations, and, because of the survey techniques employed, the focus of interest shifted from relations between groups to the attitudinal makeup of individuals. Psychoanalytical perspectives came into prominence after 1940, especially as a result of the work of the refugee scholars linked to the strongly Freudian Frankfurt School, whose outlook shaped the research that went into *The Authoritarian*

---

[27] Cf. Park, *Race and Culture*, pp. 256-60: "The Concept of Social Distance" (1924); pp. 230-43: "The Bases of Race Prejudice" (1928).

[28] Emory S. Bogardus followed the distinction slavishly in his *Immigration and Race Attitudes* (Boston, 1928), pp. 30 ff., a book dedicated to Robert Park. Eight years later, however, Donald R. Taft conflated racial antipathies with race prejudice, specifically including "Olfactory, Tactual, Gustatory, and Visual Experiences" among the "Types of Experiences Leading to Race Prejudice." See Taft, *Human Migration* (New York, 1936), p. 332.

[29] Cf. Richard Weiss, "Ethnicity and Reform: Minorities and the Ambience of the Depression Years," *Journal of American History,* 66 (December, 1979), 574-75.

[30] Everett R. Clinchy, "Prejudice and Minority Groups," in Brown and Roucek, *Our Racial and National Minorities*, pp. 538-39.

[31] Fleming, "Attitude," pp. 342 ff.; John Harding *et al.*, "Prejudice and Ethnic Relations," in G. Lindzey, ed., *Handbook of Social Psychology,* 2 vols. (Cambridge, Masachusetts, 1954), II: 1021.

[32] The concept of the stereotype was introduced in Walter Lippmann's *Public Opinion* (New York, 1922).

Personality and many other studies of prejudice in the postwar decade.[33] As a result of these developments, prejudice and discrimination came to be accounted for in terms of intolerant personality structure rather than conflicting group interests.

Besides establishing the psychoanalytical perspective, the refugee scholars reoriented the study of prejudice by giving much greater prominence to anti-Semitism. This was obviously the result of Hitlerism and the war. Perhaps the reader has wondered if we would ever get to the war. We are almost there; but first let me sum up the situation on the eve of its outbreak, adding a few descriptive generalizations about matters that cannot be discussed in detail.

The first generalization is that, despite all the conceptual ambiguities, there was growing evidence of sympathetic interest in minority groups and their place in American life.[34] The prevailing assumption in the late thirties was that national minorities were being assimilated rapidly, but that the racial split was a more stubborn matter and might even have the permanence of a caste division.[35] Most observers regarded assimilation benignly, but many were also troubled by the decline of diversity. Almost no one contemplated the indefinite perpetuation of immigrant

---

[33] Fleming, "Attitude," pp. 351 ff.; Harding, "Prejudice," p. 1021; Martin Jay, *The Dialectical Imagination. A History of the Frankfurt School and the Institute of Social Research, 1923-1950* (Boston, 1973), chap. 7. Horowitz's "Suggested Hypotheses" (see above note 26) is also relevant in this context. Arnold M. Rose, "The Causes of Prejudice," in Francis E. Merrill *et al., Social Problems* (New York, 1950), pp. 402-25, is an excellent review of the literature on the eve of the publication of *The Authoritarian Personality.*

[34] Weiss, "Ethnicity and Reform," provides evidence of sympathetic interest in minorities in the late 1930's. It is also interesting that immigration historiography reached a new level of sophistication and visibility with the publication of a cluster of outstanding works between 1938 and 1941: Ray Allen Billington, *The Protestant Crusade 1800-1860. A Study of the Origins of American Nativism* (New York, 1938); Carl Wittke, *We Who Built America. The Saga of the Immigrant* (New York, 1939); Marcus L. Hansen, *The Atlantic Migration 1607-1860* (Cambridge, Massachusetts, 1940); Hansen, *The Immigrant in American History* (Cambridge, Massachusetts, 1940); Theodore Blegen, *The Norwegian Immigration to America: The American Transition* (Northfield, Minnesota, 1940); and Oscar Handlin, *Boston's Immigrants; A Study in Acculturation* (Cambridge, Massachusetts, 1941).

[35] The prevailing view on assimilation was well presented in William C. Smith's excellent synthesis of the existing sociological and historical literature, *Americans in the Making: The Natural History of the Assimilation of Immigrants* (New York, 1939). The assumption of rapid and nearly complete assimilation of immigrants is also reflected in Ruth Benedict's curious essay, "Race Problems in America," *The Annals,* 216 (July 1941), 73-78. Myrdal, *American Dilemma,* pp. 51-53, comments on the difference in expectation about the assimilation of Negroes as contrasted to persons of immigrant stock. John Dollard's *Caste and Class in a Southern Town* (New York, 1937), gave new prominence to the concept of caste in racial matters; see also Allison Davis *et al., Deep South: A Social Anthropological Study of Caste and Class* (Chicago, 1941).

cultures without change, but forced Americanization programs were uniformly deprecated.[36] There was also a quickening of interest in second-generation immigrants, whose marginal status between two cultures was believed to entail much psychic distress. The popular Slovenian-born writer, Louis Adamic, spoke of a "psychological civil war" being waged in the souls of New Americans, and he campaigned for equality of emphasis on "Ellis Island and Plymouth Rock."[37]

Accompanying the sympathetic concern for minorities and cultural diversity, was severe disapproval of nationalism, ethnocentrism, and prejudice.[38] The grotesque but frightening rise of Nazi racism not only reinforced this disapproval, but made the whole matter more urgent because organized anti-Semitism was growing by leaps and bounds in the United States.[39] At the same time, the noisy antics of the German-American Bund, and

---

[36] A particularly authoritative statement of concern over the decline of diversity may be found in: National Resources Commission, *Problems of a Changing Population* (Washington, 1938), pp. 249-51, which reflects a strong Deweyan influence. For the other points, see for example, Brown and Roucek, *Our Racial and National Minorities*, pp. 570-72, and more generally, James H. Powell, "The Concept of Cultural Pluralism in American Social Thought, 1915-1965" (Ph. D. diss., University of Notre Dame, 1971), pp. 79 ff., esp. 106-12.

[37] Nicholas V. Montalto, "The Forgotten Dream: A History of the Intercultural Education Movement, 1924-1941" (Ph. D. diss., University of Minnesota, 1977), chap. 2, is a useful review of the concern over the second-generation problem which discusses Adamic, pp. 67-73. Adamic is also discussed in Daniel E. Weinberg, "The Foreign Language Information Service and the Foreign Born, 1918-1939: A Case Study of Cultural Assimilation Viewed as a Problem in Social Technology" (Ph. D. diss., University of Minnesota, 1973), pp. 158-62, 172-73, 177. Cf. also Weiss, "Ethnicity and Reform," pp. 579-82; and Rudolph Vecoli, "Louis Adamic and the Contemporary Search for Roots," *Ethnic Studies*, 2 (1978), 29-35. Adamic's concerns in the late 1930's are best approached through his books, *My America, 1928-1938* (New York, 1938), esp. pp. 185-259, and *From Many Lands* (New York, 1940), esp. pp. 291-301.

[38] In 1926, Carlton J. H. Hayes, the principal authority on nationalism, concluded that it was "the indivisible source of grave abuses and evils," such as a spirit of exclusiveness and narrowness; a tendency toward social uniformity; a tendency to increase the docility of the masses; an unhealthy concentration on war; jingoism; imperialism; and intolerance. If not mitigated, Hayes predicted that nationalism would be "an unqualified curse to future generations." Cf. Hayes, *Essays on Nationalism* (New York, 1926), pp. 257-60.

[39] Donald S. Strong reported in 1941 that of 119 anti-Semitic organizations in the U.S. at that time, all but five had been formed since 1933. Cited in Rose, "Causes of Prejudice," p. 416 (see note 33). Myrdal, *American Dilemma*, pp. 53, 1186 n, notes the growth of anti-Semitism in the late thirties. As a newcomer to the U.S. in 1938, Myrdal felt that anti-Semitism "probably was somewhat stronger than in Germany before the Nazi regime." The belief that anti-Semitism was growing was disputed on the basis of public opinion surveys by Otto Klineberg, "Race Prejudice and the War," *The Annals*, 223 (September 1942), 191-93. Cf. also Higham, *Send These to Me*, pp. 184-93; and Polenberg, *One Nation Divisible*, pp. 40-42.

the pro-Fascist orientation of much of the Italian-American press, raised questions about the commitment to American principles of some minority-group members.[40] Worries of this sort led to systematic efforts to promote intergroup understanding and national unity on the basis of tolerance and mutual respect. In 1937 the Progressive Education Association set up a Commission on Intercultural Education; the next year the association made "Education for Democracy" the special theme of its work, a campaign that continued into the 1940's.[41]

Motives such as these prompted the U. S. Office of Education to sponsor a series of twenty-four radio broadcasts in 1938-39 dealing with ethnic groups and their contributions to American life. Entitled "Americans All . . . Immigrants All," the series was made available on records for use by schools and civic groups. It was a prototype of much that was to come in its insistence on the themes of tolerance and diversity in the name of "the preservation of the ideals, aims, and spirit for which our democracy stands."[42]

A few months after "Americans All . . ." was aired, war erupted in Europe. It exerted a profound influence on the matters we have been discussing, and on the general question of how ethnicity and ideology figured in the national identity. The first notable effect of the war was that, by making the need for national unity more compelling, it intensified the efforts that were already under way to cut down prejudice, improve intergroup relations,

---

[40] For the Bund, see Frederick Luebke, "The Germans," in John Higham, ed., *Ethnic Leadership in America* (Baltimore, 1978), pp. 83-85; and Sander Diamond, *The Nazi Movement in the United States, 1924-1941* (Ithaca, New York, 1974). For the Italians, see John P. Diggins, *Mussolini and Fascism: The View from America* (Princeton, 1972), pp. 340-52. Diggins states that "Until the summer of 1940 there was no question that Italian-Americans in general were solidly behind Mussolini" (p. 349).

[41] Patricia A. Graham, *Progressive Education: From Arcady to Academe* (New York, 1967), pp. 81-84, 93, 105-108. Cf. also Montalto, "Forgotten Dream."

[42] Montalto, "Forgotten Dream," chap. 6, provides interesting details on the Americans All project. J. Morris Jones, *Americans All . . . Immigrants All. A Handbook for Listeners* (Washington: Federal Radio Education Committee, n.d.), and Jones, *Americans All . . . Immigrants All. A Manual* (Washington: Federal Radio Education Committee, n.d.), provide commentary and suggestions for using the recordings. For somewhat similar hortatory collections, see *The Atlantic Presents We Americans* (Boston, 1939); Alain Locke and Bernhard J. Stern, eds., *When Peoples Meet: A Study of Race and Culture Contacts* (New York, 1945 [orig. pub., 1942]); and Arnold Herrick and Herbert Askwith, eds., *This Way to Unity: For the Promotion of Good Will and Teamwork among Racial, Religious, and National Groups* (New York, 1945).

and promote greater tolerance of diversity.[43] With the very large exception of the removal of the Japanese-Americans from the West Coast, the government's record was good in this area. Despite uneasiness on the "minorities" issue, German-Americans and Italian-Americans did not become the objects of popular suspicion or official repression.[44] Internal tensions resulting from wartime population shifts, increasing Negro militance, and other social changes did cause serious concern, however, especially after outbursts of racial violence in Los Angeles and Detroit in 1943. Gunnar Myrdal's monumental *An American Dilemma,* which came out the following year, underscored the need for action, and by the end of the war no fewer than 123 national organizations were active on the race relations front.[45]

The second and most crucial result of the war was that it stimulated a great ideological reawakening.[46] It was in the context of this revival that activities in the sphere of intergroup relations took place. Myrdal's volume is revealing here, for his principal theme was the contradiction between American racial practice and "the American Creed" — the system of values which Myrdal believed Americans were genuinely committed to. He predicted

[43] From the viewpoint of intellectual content, the most substantive effort was a series of lectures sponsored at Columbia University by the Institute for Religious Studies beginning in 1942 and continuing for several years thereafter. The Columbia sociologist, Robert M. MacIver, was the leading figure in the series and the editor of volumes that it produced. These volumes, all edited by MacIver, were: *Group Relations and Group Antagonisms* (New York, 1944); *Civilization and Group Relationships* (New York, 1945); *Unity and Difference in American Life* (New York, 1947); and *Discrimination and National Welfare* (New York, 1949). MacIver's book, *The More Perfect Union: A Program for the Control of Inter-Group Discrimination in the United States* (New York, 1948), grew out of his concern with intergroup relations. Cf. also Higham, *Send These to Me,* pp. 218 ff.

[44] Cf. Everett V. Stonequist, "The Restricted Citizen," *The Annals,* 223 (September 1942), 149-56. This volume of *The Annals* is devoted to "Minority Peoples in a Nation at War." See also Polenberg, *One Nation Divisible,* pp. 59-60, 78-85.

[45] Joseph S. Roucek, "Group Discrimination and Culture Clash," in MacIver, *Civilization and Group Relationships,* pp. 39-69, is an informed discussion of wartime tensions and their implications; Robin M. Williams, Jr., *The Reduction of Intergroup Tensions: A Survey of Research on Problems of Ethnic, Racial, and Religious Group Relations* (New York, 1947), p. 7, gives the figure of 123 national organizations. For more general accounts see Neil A. Wynn, "The Impact of the Second World War on the American Negro," *Journal of Contemporary History,* 6 (May 1971), 42-54; Harvard Sitkoff, "Racial Militancy and Interracial Violence in the Second World War," *Journal of American History,* 58 (December 1971), 661-81; and Polenberg, *One Nation Divisible,* pp. 69-78.

[46] *Common Ground,* 1 (Spring 1941), 133, lists the following books as timely treatments of "America's current 'urgency' and her future": George S. Counts, *The Prospects of American Democracy* (New York, 1938); Max Lerner, *It Is Later Than You Think: The Need for a Militant Democracy* (New York, 1938); Edward L. Bernays, *Speak Up for Democracy* (New York, 1940); and John Chamberlain, *The American Stakes* (Philadelphia, 1940).

that the war would hasten the resolution of the dilemma posed by this contradiction because the ideological nature of the conflict made it increasingly glaring and intolerable.[47] He was quite right. But over and above the racial problem, what stands out in retrospect is that the monstrous contrast of nazism galvanized Americans to a new appreciation of their own ideological values. By 1940, even the detached skeptic, Carl Becker, was sufficiently aroused to vindicate "Some Generalities That Still Glitter"; and he acknowledged in doing so that Hitlerism was what threw the merits of democracy into bold relief. At about the same time, Max Lerner emphasized the importance of knowing "what we believe in, what America stands for," and the need for "a new tough-mindedness in the service of a set of fervent convictions." The respected newsman, Raymond Gram Swing, chaired a Council for Democracy organized in the fall of 1940 the purpose of which was: "To crystallize and instill in the minds of Americans the meaning, value, and workability of democracy as a dynamic, vital creed—just as Nazism, Fascism, and Communism are to their adherents." Symbolically, "Bill of Rights Day," marking the 150 anniversary of the ratification of the first ten amendments, fell on the first Sunday after Pearl Harbor and was commemorated by a radio drama written by Norman Corwin and entitled "We Hold These Truths."[48]

The ideological revival had a powerful, but somewhat paradoxical, effect on thinking about intergroup relations,

---

[47] Myrdal, *American Dilemma*, esp. chap. 45, "America Again at the Crossroads." Robert E. Park discussed the influence of the war and the ideological issue on race relations in his essay on "Race Ideologies," in William F. Ogburn, ed., *American Society in Wartime* (Chicago, 1943), pp. 165-83, reprinted in Park, *Race and Culture*, pp. 301-15., Writing to a former student after the Detroit race riot of 1943, Park said he was less concerned with stopping race riots than with stopping the fact that Negroes always lost them. Then he added: "I am in favor of winning the present war and this [racial conflict] seems to be merely one aspect of the war—war on the home front" (quoted in Matthews, *Quest for an American Sociology*, p. 189).

[48] Carl Becker, "Some Generalities That Still Glitter," *Yale Review*, 29 (June 1940), 649-67; Max Lerner quoted in Louis Adamic, "This Crisis Is an Opportunity," *Common Ground*, 1 (Autumn 1940), 73; Swing's Council for Democracy statement quoted in *ibid*, 1 (Winter 1941), 79; for Bill of Rights Day, see *New York Times Magazine*, December 14 1941; and Polenberg, *One Nation Divisible*, p. 53. Alain Locke pointed out in 1941 that "Democracy has encountered a fighting antithesis, and has awakened from considerable lethargy and decadence to a sharpened realization of its own basic values." Locke, "Pluralism and Intellectual Democracy," in Conference on Science, Philosophy and Religion in Relation to the American Way of Life, Second Symposium, *Science, Philosophy and Religion* (New York, 1942), p. 206. His point is repeated almost verbatim in Locke and Stern, *When Peoples Meet*, p. 735.

ethnocultural affairs, and national identity. The substance of its message, and its practical effect, was strongly assimilationist in tendency. That is, what was actually being urged—indeed, required—was ideological consensus as the basis for harmonious intergroup relations. Yet the message was couched in the language of pluralism and diversity, and gave rise to the confused impression that some sort of particularism either already was, or should become, the basis of the American identity. We must look into this more closely before turning to a third notable effect of the war, the stimulus it gave to explicit studies of the American character.

The statement of purposes adopted by the Common Council for American Unity illustrates several of these points. This group—the reorganized version of a society long interested in ethnic affairs—stated its first aim in these words:

> To help create among the American people the unity and mutual understanding resulting from a common citizenship, a common belief in democracy and the ideals of liberty, the placing of the common good before the interests of any group, and the acceptance, in fact as well as in law, of all citizens, whatever their national or racial origins, as equal partners in American society.[49]

The statement went on to call for appreciation of the contributions of each group, for tolerance of diversity, for the creation of an American culture "truly representative" of all the people, for an end to prejudice, and for assistance to immigrants who encountered difficulties in adjusting to American life.

Here ethnicity and pluralism of a sort are prominently featured, but it is clearly ideology—a shared commitment to certain universalistic values—that makes Americans what they are. Acceptance of all groups on an equal basis, and tolerance for diversity, are not in themselves constitutive of Americanism; rather they derive as corollaries from "a common belief in democracy and the ideals of liberty." The role of the war in sensitizing the Common Council to these matters was made explicit in the first issue of its journal, *Common Ground,* which began publication in the fall of 1940:

---

[49] The statement of purposes was carried on the inside cover of the magazine published by the Council, *Common Ground.* Weinberg, "Foreign Language Information Service" (see above note 37) traces the history of the Common Council's predecessor group from 1918 to 1939; see pp. 172-77, for the reorganization that brought the Common Council into existence.

Never has it been more important that we become intelligently
aware of the ground Americans of various strains have in common
. . . that we reawaken the old American Dream, which in its powerful emphasis on the fundamental worth and dignity of every human
being, can be a bond of unity no totalitarian attack can break.[50]

But because the American Dream was vague, or at least
multivalent, and because totalitarianism meant forced uniformity — the barbarous *Gleichschaltung* of the Nazis — it was an easy
transition to the view that diversity as such was the essence of the
American system. The transition was made almost inevitable by
the popularization of the term "cultural pluralism." Horace
Kallen coined this term in 1924, contrasting the ideal for which it
stood to assimilation or Americanization.[51] In his original formulation, cultural pluralism prescribed the indefinite perpetuation of immigrant cultures, and envisioned the United States as a
federation of ethnic nationalities rather than being a country with
a nationality of its own. While extreme and unrealistic, this was at
least fairly clear. Kallen's concept attracted almost no attention
for a number of years. By the time the expression came into
general usage in World War II, the original meaning had faded
from memory, and the notion of cultural pluralism became
hopelessly amorphous.[52] In most cases, it signified merely that the
speaker believed diversity was a good thing and always to be
prized — unless, of course, it was "divisive," for divisiveness was
somehow bad, even though pluralism was good. Yet the term also
carried with it some of the portentous freight that the culture con-

---

[50] *Common Ground*, 1 (Fall 1940), 103. The sociologist, James G. Leyburn, likewise
stressed the role of the war in bringing home a realization of the ideological nature of
American identity. Discussing ethnicity and Americanization, he stated: "What really
stirs our hearts and minds is our set of ideals and values. Often we do not realize explicitly
what these are until they are threatened. But in the present crisis we know with our inmost
being how dear to us are our American ideals of democracy, decency, and individual
freedom, our belief in free speech and in free elections and in the right to worship as we
choose, our family mores, our religious faith, our respect for certain symbols which con-
vey these ideals to our attention (the American flag, for example)" (Leyburn, "The
Problem of Ethnic and National Impact from a Sociological Point of View," in *Foreign Influences in American Life,* ed. David F. Bowers [Princeton, 1944], p. 60).

[51] On Kallen and cultural pluralism, see Powell, "The Concept of Cultural Pluralism"
(see above note 36), chap. 1; Higham, *Send These to Me,* chap. 10, "Ethnic Pluralism in
Modern American Thought"; Milton M. Gordon, *Assimilation in American Life* (New York,
1964), chap. 6; and Gleason, "American Identity and Americanization," in *Harvard Ethnic
Encyclopedia,* pp. 43-46.

[52] Higham, *Send These to Me,* pp. 220-21; Powell, "Concept of Cultural Pluralism,"
chap. 4; Weiss, "Ethnicity and Reform," pp. 578-82.

cept had accumulated in the thirties, and it seemed to be terribly important since it was often equated with democracy. Kallen himself claimed in 1943 that cultural pluralism defined "both the material and spiritual intent of the four freedoms."[53]

But the real mystification created by this kind of usage was that it effectively concealed the fact that so-called cultural pluralism was predicated upon, and made possible by, a high degree of consensus.[54] Ostensibly it repudiated assimilation; in fact it embodied assimilation because it assumed that everyone agreed about basic matters that were actually distinctive to the United States, at least in their centrality to the life of the nation, rather than being universally held by the common consent of mankind. Illustrative of such matters are: acceptance of a democratic system of government; respect for the principle of equality before the law; recognition of the dignity of the individual and the rights of minorities; willingness to uphold free speech, freedom of religion, etc., and to abide by constitutional guidelines, as interpreted by the courts, in the settlement of disputes. Kallen came close to recognizing the importance of agreement on fundamentals when he wrote in 1956 that cultural pluralism was "grounded on and consummated in the American Idea."[55] But by then the mischief was done. The popularization of the term in the preceding decade created a situation in which we have been unable ever since to talk about ethnicity and national identity without dealing in terminology that confuses the analytical task rather than clarifying it.

The third aspect of wartime influence on thinking about American identity — the boom in national character studies — stands in definite opposition to the pluralism-and-diversity motif just discussed. It is the aspect of wartime influence most explicitly related to our subject because the expression "American identity" came to be used synonymously with "American character." In contrast to the emphasis on diversity, however, national character studies stressed the presence of common traits — not to say uniformity — among Americans. Even so, we find that immigration and ethnicity figure rather prominently

---

[53] Kallen, " 'E Pluribus Unum' and the Cultures of Democracy," *Journal of Educational Sociology*, 16 (February 1943), 329-32.

[54] Higham brings this out in his brilliant essay on pluralism in *Send These to Me*, pp. 197-98, 211-13, 230.

[55] Kallen, *Cultural Pluralism and the American Idea* (Philadelphia, 1956), p. 97. Cf. Gleason, "American Identity," in *Harvard Ethnic Encyclopedia*, p. 50.

in these studies. What makes the development of American character studies even more interesting is the fact that our friends the cultural anthropologists pioneered in making the kind of scientific investigations that were said to redeem the study of national character from crude racialism and to elevate it above the level of mere belle-lettristic speculation.

This all came about, as Margaret Mead later explained, when she and other social scientists like Ruth Benedict and Erik Erikson were called upon by agencies of the government to apply their skills to such questions as how civilian morale might be maintained, or what kind of propaganda was most likely to influence the enemy.[56] To answer these questions, the social scientists turned to the techniques of the culture-and-personality school of anthropologists, who combined psychological assumptions and ethnographic observation in trying to identify the "basic personality structure" impressed on individuals by the norms of the group to which they belonged. "By the end of the war," Mead wrote, "the term 'national character' was being applied to studies that used anthropological methods from the field of culture and personality, psychiatric models from psychoanalysis, statistical analysis of attitude tests, and experimental models of small-group process."[57]

Mead's *Coming of Age in Samoa* had been one of the earliest culture-and-personality studies; in the 1942 volume, *And Keep Your Powder Dry,* she contributed the first of the new national character studies. Despite her claims to the contrary, there was little that was scientific about the book, a loose and rambling af-

---

[56] The literature on national character is very large, but two essays by Margaret Mead are especially useful in pinning down the connection with wartime needs. See Mead, "The Study of National Character," in Daniel Lerner and Harold D. Lasswell, ed., *The Policy Sciences* (Stanford, 1951), pp. 79-85; and Mead, "National Character and the Science of Anthropology," in Seymour M. Lipset and Leo Lowenthal, eds., *Culture and Social Character* (Glencoe, Illinois, 1961), pp. 15-26. Thomas L. Hartshorne, *The Distorted Image: Changing Conceptions of the American Character since Turner* (Cleveland, 1968), chaps. 6-7, sets the new approach to national character studies in context. Revaluations of the late 1960's, when the concept had lost most of its attractiveness, may be found in E. Adamson Hoebel, "Anthropological Perspectives on National Character," *The Annals,* 370 (March 1967), 1-7; Daniel Bell, "National Character Revisited: A Proposal for Renegotiating the Concept," in Edward Norbeck *et al.,* eds., *The Study of Personality* (New York, 1968), pp. 103-20; and David E. Stannard, "American Historians and the Idea of National Character," *American Quarterly,* 23 (1971), 202-20.

[57] Mead in Lipset and Lowenthal, *Culture and Social Character,* p. 18. Cf. also Margaret Mead and Rhoda Metraux, eds., *The Study of Culture at a Distance* (Chicago, 1953); and Morroe Berger, " 'Understanding National Character' — and War," *Commentary,* 11 (1951), 375-86.

fair written in a style of impressionistic omniscience and intended as a contribution to the war effort. Yet the assertion that an American character really did exist carried much weight coming from an anthropologist intimately acquainted with half a dozen exotic cultures. Aside from her emphasis on parent-child relationships, there was nothing terribly novel about the Americans she described—moralistic, ambivalent about aggressiveness, oriented toward the future, and inclined to interpret success or failure as an index of personal merit. A certain ideological interest attaches to her statement that postwar planning would have to eliminate those "social behaviors which automatically preclude the building of a democratic world" and her (unsuccessful) effort to show that such a commitment did not violate the principle that cultural differences were all to be tolerated.[58] But what is more pertinent here is that Mead singles out an aspect of immigrant assimilation as having paradigmatic significance for understanding the American character.

References to immigration recur frequently throughout the book, and its most striking interpretive metaphor is developed in chapter three, "We Are All Third Generation." Mead's point was not so much that many Americans actually were the grandchildren of immigrants, but that nearly all had the kind of "character structure" that resulted from growing up in a family of second-generation parents and third-generation children. She described the outlook produced by this familial setting in these words:

> Father is to be outdistanced and outmoded, but not because he is a strong representative of another culture . . . [and] not because he is a weak and ineffectual attempt to imitate a new culture; he did very well in his way, but he is out of date. He, like us, was moving forwards, moving away from something symbolized by his own ancestors, moving towards something symbolized by other people's ancestors. . . . [We need not rebel against Father. We merely need to pass him.] And to pass him it is only necessary to keep on going and to see that one buys a new model every year. Only if one slackens, loses one's interest in the race towards success, does one slip back.[59]

---

[58] Margaret Mead, *And Keep Your Power Dry* (New York, 1942), pp. 239 ff., comprises Mead's unsuccessful effort to reconcile cultural relativism with a commitment to the imperatives of democratic ideology. She resorted to the analogy of "disease," arguing that postwar reconstruction should treat institutions that breed fascism as "dangerous viruses," while the individuals infected by these institutions should be regarded as "carriers of fatal social diseases" (p. 245). Quotation in text from p. 255.

[59] *Ibid.*, pp. 52-53.

Mead's colleague in national character work, Geoffrey Gorer, pushed the analysis back a generation further. His book, *The American People* (1948), begins with a chapter entitled "Europe and the Rejected Father," depicting the problem of the first-generation immigrant who must abandon much of his past in order to become an American. The immigrant, alas, cannot transform himself completely; the Old World still clings to him, and he becomes an object of scorn to his American-born offspring, who reject their father as role model and authority figure. "It is this break of continuity between the immigrants of the first generation and their children of the second generation which is . . . of major importance in the development of the modern American character," Gorer announced. He then proceeded to elaborate this insight along Freudian lines in explaining Americans' lack of respect for authority, the marginal family role of fathers as compared to mothers, and so on.[60]

For Mead and Gorer, then, the "ethnic" — that is, the immigrant or person of immigrant derivation — is a prototypically American figure, *not* because of any distinctiveness of cultural heritage, but for exactly the opposite reason, namely, because he exhibits in extreme degree the "character structure" produced by the *American* experience of change, mobility, and loss of contact with the past. This interpretation differed drastically from what the celebration of diversity and cultural pluralism might lead one to anticipate about the American character, but it accorded nicely with the interpretation offered by Oscar Handlin in *The Uprooted*, a work that shaped an entire generation's understanding of the immigrant experience. Published in 1951 when interest in the American character was near its zenith, the book began with the assertion that "the immigrants *were* American history," and the central metaphor of uprootedness was easily transferable to Americans generally. After all, Handlin explained, the "experience of displacement" was the crucial thing; having undergone it, the immigrants "were on the way toward being Americans almost before they stepped off the boat."[61]

Handlin did not fail to note that migration meant liberation and that uprootedness called forth new creative energies, but the tone of the book was elegiac: it was the immigrant's alienation that impressed itself upon the reader. Within a few years, people

---

[60] Geoffrey Gorer, *The American People* (New York, 1948), p. 26.

[61] Oscar Handlin, *The Uprooted* (Boston, 1951), pp. 3, 305.

would be talking about this sort of thing in terms of identity problems and identity crises. Indeed, these terms have become so indispensable that it is almost a shock to note their absence from Handlin's conceptual armamentarium. But identity in this sense derives primarily from the work of Erik Erikson, and he was just beginning to put the term in circulation. His book, *Childhood and Society,* published only a year before *The Uprooted,* marks its real introduction. It is also a landmark in American character studies since the chapter entitled, "Reflections on the American Identity," was the first major publication to equate American character and American identity.[62]

Erikson did not give immigration the same prominence as Mead or Gorer, but he mentioned it, and what he says is interesting: "We begin to conceptualize matters of identity at the very time in history when they become a problem. For we do so in a country which attempts to make a super-identity out of all the identities imported by its constituent immigrants." In an autobiographical account published twenty years later, Erikson, an immigrant himself, quoted this passage and added that the terms identity and identity crisis seemed to grow out of "the experience of emigration, immigration, and Americanization." Identity problems, he said, "were in the mental baggage of generations of new Americans, who left their motherlands and fatherlands behind to merge their ancestral identities in the common one of the self-made man."[63]

All this put the ethnics right in the middle of things as far as understanding the American character was concerned. It also suggested, however, that they might be particularly prone to the characteristic defects of Americans. Uprooted as they were, alienated, unsure of their identities, were the ethnics also more anxious about status than other Americans? Were they more obsessively conformist? More rigid in their thinking? More intolerant? More ethnocentric?

This was potentially a matter for grave concern, since these

---

[62] Erik H. Erikson, *Childhood and Society* (New York, 1950), pp. 244-83. Erikson used American identity in the sense of American character in "Ego Development and Historical Change," *Psychoanalytic Study of the Child,* 2 (1946), 359-96,, but that technical journal had a very limited readership. Robert Coles, *Erik H. Erikson* (Boston, 1970), is an informative biography which provides extensive commentary on Erikson's writings.

[63] Erikson, *Childhood and Society,* p. 242; Erikson, " 'Identity Crisis' in Autobiographic Perspective," in *Life History and the Historical Moment* (New York, 1975), p. 43. Cf. also Erikson, "Identity and Uprootedness in Our Time," in *Insight and Responsibility* (New York, 1964), pp. 83-107.

qualities of mind and disposition marked "the authoritarian personality." And here we return momentarily to the study of prejudice. Recall that it was beginning to turn toward psychology in the later 1930's, and soon became strongly psychoanalytical under the influence of refugee scholars from Europe. But with the key group—the Frankfurt School—psychology was closely interwoven with the critique of modern society, since their so-called dialectical method represented a fusion of Marxist and Freudian elements. This was the orientation within which the study of anti-Semitism was undertaken that resulted in the publication in 1950 of *The Authoritarian Personality*. Given this background, it is understandable that prejudice is implicitly interpreted there, not simply as a psychological disorder, but as a highly ideological kind of disorder produced by the stresses of an advanced capitalist society. Frustrated by the contradictions of bourgeois civilization, and seeking to "escape from freedom," the typical prejudiced individual was naturally disposed to authoritarianism—in short, he was a potential fascist and the degree of his susceptibility could be measured on the famous F-scale.[64]

No sooner had this diagnosis been offered than the eruption of McCarthyism seemed to confirm it. Here was a political movement exhibiting semihysterical rigidities in thinking and a total incapacity to tolerate ambiguities. It was clearly fascist in tendency, according to the best qualified observers, and demanded explanation in terms of social psychology. Analysis of this kind was soon forthcoming, and was authoritatively summed up in the volume edited by Daniel Bell under the title, *The New American Right* (1955). And who do we find singled out here as the population group most susceptible to the status anxieties and resent-

---

[64] Cf. Jay, *Dialectical Imagination,* pp. 217-218 and chap. 7 *passim,* esp. pp. 226-34. Max Horkheimer and Samuel H. Flowerman, "Foreword to Studies in Prejudice," in T. W. Adorno *et al., The Authoritarian Personality* (New York, 1950), pp. v-vii, provides some background information on the anti-Semitism project. Theodor W. Adorno, "Scientific Experiences of a European Scholar in America," *Perspectives in American History,* 2 (1968), 355-65, is a commentary by the principal investigator. Fleming, "Attitude" (see note 26), pp. 352-57, discusses *The Authoritarian Personality* within the context of attitudinal surveys. Referring to the "Aesopian" terminology developed by the Frankfurt group while in America at a time when "Marx and Marxism could not be mentioned," Henry Pachter notes that "they used Hegel or 'German idealism' as code words. They said alienation when they meant capitalism, reason when they meant revolution, and *Eros* when they meant proletariat. . . . When the success story of the word *alienation* in America is written the contribution of the Institute people will receive its due acknowledgment" (Pachter, "On Being an Exile," in Robert Boyers, ed., *The Legacy of the German Refugee Intellectuals* [New York, 1972], p. 36).

ments mobilized by McCarthy? Ethnics, of course. The point was made by several of the contributors, most notably by Richard Hofstadter, whose concept of "pseudoconservatism" was taken straight from *The Authoritarian Personality,* and who likewise referred to Margaret Mead's "we-are-all-third-generation" view of the American character.[65]

A decade later, Hofstadter qualified much of his analysis, noting that some of his remarks about immigrant authoritarianism were "gratuitously speculative," and regretting in general his "excessive emphasis" on "the clinical side of the problem."[66] By that time interest in the American character had fallen off sharply, while ethnicity and the American ideology stood on the verge of the seismic transvaluation that would occur in the midst of the Vietnam war, whose effects on thinking about American identity were just the opposite of those of World War II. In the cultural crisis brought on by Vietnam, the racial upheaval, the counterculture, women's liberation, and Watergate, the ideological dimension of the American identity was severely discredited and ethnicity assumed greater positive salience than it had ever had before. But that is another story. What is now in order is a reflective look back at the epoch we have just sketched.

To summarize, then, the argument advanced in this essay is that World War II shaped the self-understanding of Americans, not only with respect to the nation's role in world affairs but also in regard to what we now call the American identity. Following upon a period in which ethnic factors had receded from prominence in discussions of national identity, the war gave unprecedented salience to the ideological dimension. For a whole generation, the question "What does it mean to be an American?" was answered primarily by reference to "the values America stands for": democracy, freedom, equality, respect for individual dignity, and so on. Since these values were abstract and univer-

---

[65] Richard Hofstadter, "The Pseudo-Conservative Revolt," in Daniel Bell, ed., *The Radical Right* (Garden City, New York, 1964), pp. 75-95. (*The Radical Right* is an expanded and updated version of *The New American Right,* originally published in 1955.) For references to ethnics by other contributors, see *Radical Right,* pp. 129, 216-17, 319. At about the same time, Samuel Lubell offered an ethnic explanation for isolationism. See Lubell, *The Future of American Politics* (New York, 1952), p. 132.

[66] Hofstadter's second and third thoughts are found in *Radical Right,* pp. 97-103; and Hofstadter, *The Paranoid Style in American Politics* (New York, 1965), pp. 56 n., 66-92.

sal, American identity could not be linked exclusively with any single ethnic derivation. Persons of any race, color, religion, or national background could be, or become, Americans. Hence, "Americans all . . . Immigrants all!" Historically, however, particularistic ethnic loyalties ("racial," religious, nationality, etc.) had been obscurely, but intimately, interwoven with the commitment to universalistic political and social principles as ingredients in the citizen's sense of Americanness — and this was true of those comprising "old American stock" just as much as it was for the more recently arrived Americans. The war-related emphasis on ideology should therefore be understood as the accentuation of one element — albeit a crucially important one — in a preexisting mix of beliefs, attachments, and loyalties.

Prewar developments, both social and intellectual, reshaped the context within which wartime thinking on national identity took place. Our understanding of these complex shifts is dim, however, because they have been so little studied by historians. The key developments, in my view, were: the discrediting of racialism, both intellectually and morally; the growth of the social sciences and the increasing attention given to group life and group relations by anthropologists and sociologists; the emergence of the culture concept as the most influential analytical perspective employed in the human sciences; the sketching out by Robert Park of a contrasting conflict theory of assimilation; the growing recognition that the problems of minorities, and intergroup relations generally, constituted serious social issues; and the closely related beliefs that ethnocentrism and prejudice exacerbated these problems, while the promotion of tolerance for diversity would mitigate them.

Given the relative newness of social-scientific study of human relations, and the elusive nature of the phenomena being studied, it is not surprising that the terms of discourse were sometimes vague and that latent tensions existed among the concepts employed. Special difficulties surrounded the culture concept and the relation in which it was thought to stand with respect to other important concepts. Thus, though the words were often used interchangeably, *acculturation* and *assimilation* derived from different disciplinary approaches and reflected different kinds of assumptions. When Everett and Helen Hughes spoke of the terminologies of anthropology and sociology having "half-blended in a grand confusion," *acculturation* and *assimilation* figured foremost among the examples they gave.[67]

Besides the uncertainty as to whether these two widely employed terms meant the same thing — or, if not, wherein they differed — there was also a problem built into the relationships that were thought to exist between the concepts of culture, tolerance for diversity, and ethnocentrism. In most discussions, tolerance for diversity was positively linked with the culture concept, while ethnocentrism was looked upon as the exact opposite of the cultural understanding preached by the exponents of the Boas-Mead-Benedict viewpoint. These relationships, however, are not logically entailed in the concepts themselves. As Robert Redfield wrote in criticism of the doctrine of cultural relativity: "It cannot be proved, from the proposition that [cultural] values are relative, that we ought to respect all systems of values. We might just as well hate them all."[68] And, in fact, tolerance for diversity comes close to being flatly inconsistent with the cultural concept as such if we understand it as referring to a self-contained, cohesive ensemble of values and norms that operates holistically in guiding people's lives. Shocking as it may seem, it is ethnocentrism rather than tolerance that is implicit in the cultural concept considered in itself. Robert Park was therefore correct in observing that "When we speak of culture . . . we think of a small, familiar, ethnocentric group."[69]

If the conventional wisdom on these matters was so illogical, the question naturally arises as to how it ever got established. A general and a more particular explanation can be suggested. The general explanation is that the proponents of the cultural concept were themselves sophisticated cosmopolitans; their personal values and outlook transcended the relatively narrow boundaries of any single culture. This enabled them to appreciate the good things to be found in the ways of life of the peoples they studied as anthropologists, and disposed them to urge their fellow citizens still locked within the ethnocentric confines of their own traditional culture to be more broad-minded and tolerant. Considered in this light, it is not dealing in paradox to say that tolerance of diversity is a function of assimilation, since it comes easiest to

---

[67] Hughes and Hughes, *Where Peoples Meet,* pp. 30-31.

[68] Robert Redfield, *The Primitive World and Its Transformations* (Ithaca, New York, 1953), p. 147.

[69] Park, *Race and Culture,* p. 18.

those who have detached themselves somewhat from a specific familial, local, or ethnic tradition, and have learned to get along with others whose background differs from their own.

But something besides cosmopolitanism was involved. A more particular motive impelling the Boasian anthropologists to leap from the empirical observation that cultural diversity existed to the ethical imperative that it should be tolerated, or even prized, derived from the fact that they were alienated from, and critical of, their own culture, which they regarded as notably repressive and intolerant. Mead, Benedict, and other leading disciples of Boas formed their views in the 1920's, and were inevitably affected by the prevailing disaffection from American civilization felt by the intellectuals of the day. Edward Sapir openly avowed his preference for the "genuine" culture of American Indians over the "spurious" civilization of modern America; Margaret Mead contrasted the emotionally crippling effects of the Puritanical American family to the freer and healthier sexual codes and child-rearing patterns of the South Pacific; and the implications of Ruth Benedict's admiring report on the calm and noncompetitive communalism of Zuñi culture were equally clear.[70] In affirming that cultural diversity should teach Americans tolerance, these writers were really saying that other cultures were preferable in some respects and that modifications of American culture in those directions were desirable.

Ethnocentrism very likely came to be thought of as opposed to the cultural approach because chauvinistic nationalism was one of the features of American life in the 1920's that intellectuals found most repugnant. The relativistic tolerance of diversity preached by the anthropologists was clearly opposed to nativist prejudice, or to ethnocentrism understood in that sense, with the result that the built-in relationship between ethnocentrism and the close cultural cohesion prized by Benedict was lost to view.

The concept of assimilation was also affected by the intellectuals' reaction against chauvinism, but the situation in this case was much more complicated. Understood as the belief that many different elements would voluntarily fuse into one American people, assimilation was an ideal as old and honorable as the national

---

[70] Coben, "Assault on Victorianism" (see note 5 above), pp. 605-08; F. H. Matthews, "The Revolt against Americanism: Cultural Pluralism and Cultural Relativism as an Ideology of Liberation," *Canadian Review of American Studies*, 1 (Spring 1970), 4-31, esp. 16 ff. See above notes 17, 7, and 8, for citations to the works of Sapir, Mead, and Benedict.

motto, *e pluribus unum*. The term acquired negative connotations of intolerance in the twenties, however, through association with fanatical drives for "Hundred Percent Americanization." Besides these usages, sociologists employed it as a neutral scientific term: in Park and Burgess's famous *Introduction to the Science of Sociology* assimilation designated the final stage in a natural process of social interaction discoverable anywhere in the world, not just in the United States. And Park later sketched out—but did not develop systematically—a version of assimilation that left much room for diversity within the framework of agreement on fundamentals. As a practical reality, assimilation made a "great leap forward" after the immigration restriction law of 1924 drastically cut back the influx of immigrants.[71] The advance of assimilation was regarded benignly, on the whole, since it reduced the likelihood of intergroup friction and enabled minority group members to participate more fully in American life. But there were also regretful murmurs about the decline of diversity entailed by assimilation. All of these crosscurrents (in addition to its uncertain relation to acculturation) made assimilation a somewhat problematic term by the eve of World War II.

Discussions of ethnicity, intergroup relations, and national identity were thus complex and burdened with submerged confusions when the war came along. It clarified some matters (by making democratic values the touchstone of American identity), but made others more baffling than ever (by formulating the demand for unity in terms of pluralism). The treatment in part two of this article, despite being exploratory and incomplete, raises more issues than can be systematically analyzed here. I will therefore close, not with a conclusion, but with some retrospective observations.

First, it should be noted that the practical effect of wartime experience was assimilative in the sense that it enhanced national unity and a common sense of national belongingness. Commenting in 1952 on the war as an integrating force in American life, Robin Williams pointed out that its impact "galvanized into concerted action a wide range of previously discordant segments of the society." He added that service in the armed forces, no matter how unpleasant at the time, constituted for millions of young men and women a common experience "which in the end left a new

---

[71] Higham, *Send These to Me,* pp. 211-12, speaks of the "great leap forward" in assimilation.

residue of shared values and traditions." And two more recent investigators have stressed the effects of the war in broadening the horizons and hastening the assimilation of second- and third-generation immigrants in the Pittsburgh area.[72]

More directly relevant to our interest, of course, was the great ideological reawakening of the wartime years which simultaneously: (1) promoted national unity on the basis of value consensus; (2) exalted toleration and respect for cultural differences as the means of attaining intergroup harmony; and (3) stimulated curiosity about the way in which the American social and cultural environment shaped persons of all derivations toward a common national type.

One aspect of the ideological revival not mentioned earlier that deserves notice is the remarkable contrast it affords to the situation in the 1920's in respect to the attitudes held by intellectuals concerning American culture. In the twenties intellectuals were alienated. Americanizations had assumed forms hateful to liberals like Horace Kallen; anthropologists like Sapir, Mead, and Benedict were repelled by the shallowness and discontinuity of American civilization. In World War II, however, intellectuals (including Kallen, Mead, and Benedict) rallied to the nation. Simple patriotism in a time of danger was no doubt a factor; but in the battle against nazism, America stood for universalistic values dear to the intellectual community. As Carl Becker explained, the rational and humane values that democracy affirmed were "older and more universal than democracy" itself, to say nothing of their being older than the American nation.[73] Yet the United States based itself on these values, and in the war it was their foremost champion. Since intellectuals are the ones who articulate a people's understanding of itself, their identification with the national cause goes far toward accounting for the generally positive and strongly ideological interpretation of national identity that established itself during the wartime era.

But the very generality and abstractness of American values meant that they were subject to divergent interpretations which gave rise to divisive conflicts over whose was the correct understanding of true Americanism. An ironic instance was reported in a 1944 symposium entitled "Approaches to National

---

[72] Robin M. Williams, Jr., *American Society; A Sociological Interpretation* (New York, 1952), p. 527; Howard F. Stein and Robert F. Hill, *The Ethnic Imperative* (University Park, Pennsylvania, 1977), pp. 35-36, 82 ff.; and Polenberg, *One Nation Divisible,* pp. 46-54, 57.

[73] Becker, "Some Generalities" (see above at note 48), pp. 666-67.

Unity." The symposium was the fifth sponsored by a group called "The Conference on Science, Philosophy and Religion in their Relation to the American Way of Life," which had been formed in 1940; after its second meeting, "certain philosophical humanists, positivists, and naturalists" withdrew because they were offended by the religious pronouncements of various participants in the original group. Hence there was by 1943 a rival "Conference on the Scientific Spirit and the Democratic Faith," whose members regarded as dangerously undemocratic the views of some of their erstwhile collaborators in the search for unity.[74]

Of the same sort, but more serious and long-lasting, were the issues of loyalty and un-Americanism that reached a climax in the McCarthy era. The nature of the cold war contest with communism, both on the world scene and as a potential source of internal subversion, heightened the ideological dimension, but the wartime stress on commitment to American values made it inevitable that fissures in national unity would open up along ideological, rather than ethnic, fault lines. Hence the national loyalty of Catholics was not called into question, despite the sharp controversies that broke out in the late forties between Catholics and Protestants, Jews, and secular liberals. On the contrary, it was because national identity was defined in ideological, rather than ethnic, terms that "to be an Irish Catholic became *prima facie* evidence of loyalty. Harvard men were to be checked; Fordham men would do the checking."[75]

There were thus very definite limits to the toleration of diversity in the ideological sphere. In the broader area of intergroup relations, however, tolerance was the touchstone, and to the degree that it was formulated in terms of cultural pluralism it became almost impossible to determine what the limits of tolerance were, if there were any, or, in many cases, even to determine what was being talked about. In battling against totalitarian enemies, it was understandable, as John Higham has written, that Americans should exalt the principle of diversity. But he goes to say: "The astonishing fact about the emphatic endorsement of cultural pluralism in the postwar years was not its

---

[74] See Ordway Tead, "Survey and Critique of the Conference on Science, Philosophy and Religion," in *Approaches to National Unity; Fifth Symposium,* ed. Lyman Bryson *et al.* (New York, 1945), pp. 783-92. Cf. the proceedings of the first conference held by the secessionist group, entitled *The Scientific Spirit and the Democratic Faith* (New York, 1944).

[75] Nathan Glazer and Daniel P. Moynihan, *Beyond the Melting Pot* (Cambridge, Massachusetts, 1963), p. 271.

occurrence but rather a general unwillingness or inability to assess critically its relation to the apparently contrary imperative of national integration." As diversity was hailed, even while divisiveness was deplored, the "traditions of pluralism and assimilation blurred into a rosy haze."[76]

To make matters worse, a group of political scientists who analyzed American society in terms of interest groups and cross-cutting pressures became known as "pluralists."[77] The relationship of this perspective to that of cultural pluralism was never clarified and possibly not even adverted to at the time. But the growing tendency to speak of pluralism without the modifier "cultural" made the term even more generalized and abstract, as did usages such as "pluralistic," and "pluralistically." Then there is the fact that cultural pluralism itself can be appealed to by persons who have significantly different goals in mind. What might be called a cosmopolitan version of cultural pluralism appeals to persons relatively detached from any specific ethnic tradition as a general vision of a society made up of diverse groups, all interacting harmoniously without losing their distinctiveness. But cultural pluralism can equally well stand for a highly particularistic vision when appealed to by persons who care little about the overall design of American society, but are passionately determined to preserve their (often quite "ethnocentric") group traditions.[78]

In short, cultural pluralism in all its ambiguities and complexities is the crucial legacy of World War II in respect to American identity. The frequency with which it is invoked today testifies to its continuing relevance to our present efforts to define what it means to be an American. A great deal more study is needed to clarify the circumstances of its popularization in the wartime era and the vicissitudes of its conceptual evolution since then.

---

[76] Higham, *Send These to Me*, pp. 220-21.

[77] *Ibid.*, pp. 225-27.

[78] The distinction between these two versions of pluralism has never been developed systematically, but see *ibid.*, pp. 197-99, 228-29; and David A. Hollinger, "Ethnic Diversity, Cosmopolitanism and the Emergence of the American Liberal Intelligentsia," *American Quarterly*, 27 (1975), 133-51, esp. 142.

AMERICANIZATION AT THE
FACTORY GATE

GERD KORMAN

IN THE decade of World War I the militant wing of the Americanization movement tried to impose its solutions for national vigor and harmony upon welfare and safety programs designed to make industrial relations less exploitive and wasteful. Convinced that the teaching of English and civics was essential for the nation's welfare, militant Americanizers used the war in Europe to launch a campaign for disciplining the loyalties and languages of America's immigrant. This crusade brought them to factories employing large numbers of newcomers. They tried to make existing welfare and safety programs instruments of their crusade and sought to institute practices designed to make immigrant workers learn English and civics. Though they failed to make welfare and safety programs an integral part of the Americanization movement, militant Americanizers helped shape the educational programs large employers of labor were developing for their workers.

BEGINNINGS OF THE MOVEMENT

The twentieth-century origins of the Americanization movement reached back to the 1880's and 1890's when fear about the future composition of America's population and her economic life gripped many native Americans and "old" immigrants.[1] By the 1900's, many influential elements had joined the clamor for legislation that would restrict immigration from southern and eastern Europe. Among them were New Englanders spinning out racist arguments, and eugenicists perverting the science of human genetics to fit their preconceptions about immigrants not of "Anglo-Saxon" or "Teutonic" stock.[2] Numerous attempts were made to pass variations of the literacy test. In 1907 Congress established the Immigration Commission. Under the chairmanship of Vermont's Senator William P. Dillingham, the Commission labored for three years in order to demonstrate that the nation had to adopt effective restrictive legislation to keep out southern and eastern Europeans.[3]

The growing clamor for restricting

The setting for this article is the decade of World War I, when a substantial group of disciplinarians strove to modernize American society. The study examines the interplay between the Americanization movement and developing welfare and safety programs, and evaluates the effects which Americanizers had on these programs.
Gerd Korman is assistant professor at the New York State School of Industrial and Labor Relations, Cornell University. This article is part of a book scheduled for publication later this year. — EDITOR

[1] Merle E. Curti, *The Roots of American Loyalty* (New York: Columbia University Press, 1946), pp. 74, 184–187; John Higham, *Strangers in the Land: Patterns of American Nativism, 1860–1925* (New Brunswick, N.J.: Rutgers University Press, 1955), pp. 1–182.
[2] *Ibid.*, pp. 131–157; see also Oscar Handlin, *Race and Nationality in American Life* (New York: Doubleday, 1957), pp. 57–73.
[3] *Ibid.*, p. 79.

396

immigration around the turn of the century reflected misgivings in many quarters of America about the workings of the long-cherished melting pot inherited from an agricultural economy.[4] Something was wrong with the entire absorption process, for obviously the nation could no longer create the "American" idealized by St. Jean de Crévecoeur. Faith in a laissez-faire absorption process had been shaken, and many felt it necessary to affect conditions that heretofore had been left to the safekeeping of natural laws supposed to be operative in American society.[5] In short, those who had lost faith felt it essential to replace an approach symbolized by the melting pot with one that a future generation could symbolize by the pressure cooker.

Conscious participation in the absorption process was possible in a number of areas other than immigration legislation. In the nineteenth century, the public school was usually looked upon as the lubricant for greasing the melting-pot machinery. School officials, however, did little to meet the needs of the first or second generation student; they assumed that somehow education for native Americans was sufficient for all. Toward the end of the century a number of cities in the East and Midwest began to provide evening classes in the English language and in citizenship, but these were usually

of a temporary nature.[6] Nevertheless, a beginning had been made in expanding the facilities of public school education. In the years to come, all those interested in Americanization continued to look to the schools as one of the most important agencies for teaching English and civics.

The decades of the 1890's and 1900's saw participation in the absorption process gain momentum. The impetus came from social settlement workers, militant nationalists in patriotic societies, and from "public spirited" businessmen in New England. These three groups injected their particular viewpoints into the Americanization movement and competed with each other for leadership.

The settlement workers had not lost faith in the beneficent operation of the melting pot. Instead of breaking with the melting-pot tradition they modified it to mean cultural pluralism. They felt that love and understanding were needed as catalysts in order to make the absorption process operate smoothly. The militant nationalists attempted to change the newcomer into a "good" and "loyal" American by making him conform to their loosely defined ideals and values. Businessmen in New England, fearful for the well-being of their economic order, reluctant to advocate immigration restriction because of their use of immigrant labor, turned to local communities in order to prevent radicals from making serious inroads among immigrant workers. Three years after the founding of the I.W.W., businessmen in New England organized the North American Civic League which sought to improve the protection, dis-

---

[4] "In the crucible of the frontier," wrote Frederick Jackson Turner in 1893, "the immigrants were Americanized, liberated, and fused into a mixed race, English in neither nationality nor characteristics. The process has gone on from the early days to our own." Turner, "The Significance of the Frontier in American History," in George B. Taylor, ed., *The Turner Thesis Concerning the Role of the Frontier in American History* (Boston: Heath, 1949), p. 11.

[5] Higham, *Strangers in the Land*, pp. 21, 23, 106–124; Curti, *Roots of American Loyalty*, pp. 70–71, 183–187, 215–222, 238.

[6] *Ibid.*, pp. 189–190; Arthur M. Schlesinger, *The Rise of the City* (New York: Macmillan, 1933), p. 66; *Wisconsin Journal of Education*, vol. 10, October 1880, p. 432; Higham, *Strangers in the Land*, pp. 235–236; *Milwaukee Sentinel*, March 8, 1893; *Milwaukee Germania Abendpost*, Oct. 8, 1897.

tribution, and education of immigrants. The League initially stressed language education and civics but, after the upheavals at Lawrence, Massachusetts, and Paterson, New Jersey, its emphasis shifted to a program of industrial spying, strike breaking, and undercutting recruitment drives by organized labor and radical groups.[7]

Few of those concerned with the immigrants' problems or America's problems with the immigrants would have denied that teaching English to immigrants was an important aspect in effecting the absorption process. Militant nationalists and the League insisted that the teaching of English was an essential element in order to Americanize newcomers. Social settlement workers viewed language programs as desirable tools for helping the alien adjust to his urban and industrial surroundings. Private immigrant groups, concerned with the protection and distribution of countrymen just arriving, often included educational programs that stressed the teaching of English.[8]

All of these groups agitated for an expansion of public school facilities, and by 1914 had made some progress in this direction. The federal Bureau of Naturalization and Immigration made the public schools the focal point of its own Americanization program.[9] Local communities expanded school facilities for educating immigrants. In Milwaukee after 1910, for example, evening classes in the public school were supplemented by night classes in social centers under the jurisdiction of an extension division of the city's school board. In February 1914, three such centers offered language classes to assist immigrants to become naturalized Americans. In the same year, the board began similar programs in ten schools located in immigrant neighborhoods.[10] This work in Milwaukee was similar to activities going on in New York and Chicago.[11]

To enthusiastic proponents of Americanization, however, the nation's schools by themselves could not cope with the problem. They claimed that the teaching of English and civics by most states and municipalities fell far short of the need. They charged that legislators and school officials had little understanding of the problems and functions of adult education. Texts were carelessly selected from among books that in themselves were usually poorly prepared for teaching English to adult foreigners. The time and place of evening school classes was too often determined by factors other than the need of immigrant workers to indicate serious concern and interest in the problem. Specialization in the super-

[7]Higham, *Strangers in the Land*, pp. 121–122, 236, 240, 250–254; Curti, *Roots of American Loyalty*, p. 238; Edward George Hartman, *The Movement to Americanize the Immigrant* (New York: Columbia University Press, 1948), pp. 31–36, 38–63, 88–90; *United States Census, 1910*, vol. 2, p. 853; National Convention of the Socialist Party, *Proceedings, 1908:* pp. 313–314, *1910*, pp. 20, 307, *1912*, pp. 237–242; Ira Kipnis, *The American Socialist Movement, 1897–1912* (New York: Columbia University Press, 1952), pp. 272–274. During the war, the Committee on Public Information "most consistently applied" the view of the social settlement workers. Higham, *Strangers in the Land*, p. 252.

[8]*Ibid.*, p. 236; Hartman, *Movement to Americanize the Immigrant*, pp. 25–36.

[9]Richard M. Campbell, commissioner of the Bureau of Naturalization and Immigration to Peter Roberts, Washington, Jan. 11, 20, 1916, Case File, 27671/614, National Archives; H. H. Wheaton, "Survey of Adult Immigrant Education," *Immigrants in America Review*, vol. 1, June 1915, pp. 51–53.

[10]*Milwaukee Leader*, Feb. 3, 1914; broadside issued by the Social Center Publicity Department of the Milwaukee Board of Education, in the newspaper scrapbook of the Board; Wisconsin State Council of Defense, Minutes of Meetings, May 25, 1917, Mss., Box 3, Series 76/1/10, Wisconsin Archives, WSHS.

[11]Higham, *Strangers in the Land*, pp. 235–236.

vision of public evening education for immigrants was still a novelty practiced by only Rochester and Cleveland; in New York, Boston, Philadelphia, Providence, Buffalo, Chicago, and Detroit the night programs were supervised and taught by administrators and teachers of day school programs. These men, it was charged, had too many daytime responsibilities to give the night programs the attention they deserved.[12]

Beset with these difficulties, and knowing that attendance in public schools was voluntary, some private groups advocating Americanization sought to institute English-language classes in factories. This aspect of the Americanization movement consisted of two phases. The first phase, begun under the auspices of the YMCA and interacting with the industrial safety campaign, was not a part of the movement's militant wing. The second phase got under way in 1915, and this drive was an integral part of the Americanization crusade.

The remainder of this article traces these two phases in a variety of settings in order to show in detail the different, but often interacting, ways by which reformers of industrial relations and Americanizers tried to reach the immigrant.

EARLY PROGRAMS AND THE YMCA

The first phase was started by Peter Roberts, a Welshman who had spent some years among immigrants in Pennsylvania's coal fields. In 1907, as the new head of the industrial department of the national council of the YMCA, he launched the "Y's" program for immigrant workers. The geographic focus of his drive was in an area which Roberts called the "immigrant zone"; that industrial region bounded on the west by the Mississippi and on the south by the Potomac and Ohio rivers. By 1915, the "Y" had about 500 branches operating in this region with 300 of them engaged in educational work for immigrants. The program had recruited about 1900 language instructors from various walks of life: men who lived in "Y" homes; Bible-class members; employees of industrial plants; a few professional men; students in colleges, universities, and seminaries; businessmen; and public servants. These instructors were provided with material Roberts had worked out for teaching English to immigrant workers and with literature selected by the "Y" from such organizations as the Sons of the American Revolution, the National Temperance League, and the National Safety Council.[13]

In establishing English-language classes for factory employees, the YMCA operated under a number of handicaps. In the first place, many workers considered the "Y" a tool of employers. Second, many immigrants were Catholic while the "Y" was a Protestant organization. Roberts strove to overcome this difficulty by eliminating proselytizing, but numerous employers continued to feel that their Catholic workers were reluctant to participate in "Y" activities.[14] Third, the

[12]Peter Roberts to Raymond Crist, deputy commissioner of the United States Bureau of Naturalization and Immigration, New York, Jan. 6, 1916; Roberts to Campbell, Jan. 17, 1916, Case File 27671/614, National Archives; H. H. Wheaton, "Survey of Adult Immigrant Education," pp. 51–53.

[13]Edith T. Bremer, "Development of Private Social Work with the Foreign-born," *Annals of the American Academy of Political and Social Science*, vol. 262, March 1949, p. 140; Peter Roberts, "The YMCA Teaching Foreign-Speaking Men," *Immigrants in America Review*, vol. 1, June 1915, pp. 18–19, 21; William M. Leiserson, *Adjusting Industry and Immigrant* (New York: Harper, 1924), pp. 121–122.

[14]National Conference on Americanization, *Proceedings, 1918*, pp. 20–23; Peter Roberts, *The*

"Y" included sermons on temperance and patriotism. These practices probably alienated some immigrants. Temperance propaganda could not have sat well with immigrants who traditionally drank wine and beer. Lectures accompanied by patriotic songs about the blessings of America's political and economic opportunities often suffered by the comparisons immigrants made with the realities of their situation. One Italian workman, for example, listened to the song "America" and asked his instructor to explain to him the meaning of the words "sweet land of liberty." At the end of the explanation, the workman simply said, "Teacher, the song is making a mistake."[15]

In spite of the handicaps, the "Y" was more successful than other private groups in establishing and participating in English-language classes in industry. Roberts had the advantage of working for an organization that had the endorsement of powerful employers. Toward the end of the century, an increasing number of companies permitted noon-day factory meetings to be held by "Y" representatives. Roberts' own enthusiasm and ability helped to convince employers of the importance of his program. He knew how to adjust his work to developments occurring within the industrial world. His emphasis on the practical was amenable to the needs of large corporations. With the proper adjustments, his introductory lessons could be made to fit welfare and safety programs of individual companies. Roberts' language-teaching technique

frowned on irrelevent content and abstract teaching methods. He divided his curriculum into three interrelated parts — introductory, intermediate, and advanced. The intermediate and advanced courses focused on reading lessons in history, geography, and civics; the advanced course of thirty-five lessons was devoted almost entirely to the latter subject as preparatory work for naturalization and good citizenship. The most significant course was the introductory one of thirty lessons, since few immigrants actually went beyond this stage. This course stressed the practical and necessary: the first ten lessons were devoted to common phrases used at home; the next ten to teaching words related to factory employment; the last ten stressed words pertinent to buying, selling, traveling, and trading. The lessons were to be taught by acting out words and sentences.[16] One "Y" worker all but undressed himself in order to teach English equivalents for various pieces of clothing.[17]

The purpose of these introductory lessons, according to Roberts, was one of social service. He spoke of "coming Americans" and tended to stay away from the label "Americanization." He did not belong to the militant nationalists but, like many other social settlement workers, he felt that the "new immigrant" could become a dangerous problem if left to himself. He was convinced that men like himself had to go to the immigrant's home and place of work if newcomers were to be exposed to what he considered healthy American influences. "Shun the foreigner, leave him to himself, let him alone in dirt and disease," said Roberts in 1915, "and unseen by an appreciative

---

New Immigration (New York: Macmillan, 1912), p. 320. See also, Howard K. Beale, "Teaching English to Foreigners," and "Y.M.C.A. English Class," undergraduate themes done in 1918 and 1920, Beale Mss. I am indebted to the late Mr. Beale for permitting me to see these.

[15]Society for Italian Immigrants, *Annual Report, 1913*, pp. 11–12.

[16]Peter Roberts, "Y.M.C.A. Teaching Foreign-Speaking Men," pp. 20–21; Peter Roberts, *The Problem of Americanization* (New York: Macmillan, 1920), pp. 97–107.

[17]Beale, "Teaching English to Foreigners."

eye he will simply drift. We would do the same."[18]

Among the companies which introduced the Roberts' method were the International Harvester Company, the United States Steel Corporation, and the Ford Motor Company. Each of these industrial firms incorporated the "Y" 's program for immigrant workers with their welfare and safety efforts and integrated it with their attempts to discipline their employees.

The Roberts' method was introduced at International Harvester in 1910. The Chicago "Y" presented the Roberts' method to a welfare committee composed of production personnel, welfare workers, and industrial safety workers. The "Y" stressed the fact that the lessons were practical and included material that gave the "foreigners the first necessary English required in getting a job and taking hold."[19] The program was favorably received by some of the superintendents who immediately viewed it in terms of the activities already taking place in the company. They believed that the Roberts' method would "be a real aid to the efficiency of the safeguarding against injury and lastly, although by no means least, in the improved relations of the men to the community."[20] The then chief social secretary for the company and secretary of the welfare board also endorsed the Roberts' method. She argued that English classes could maximize the immigrant worker's potential in the company and made it plain that she considered this

another area in a welfare program directed at improving the efficiency of the company's work force.[21]

In 1911 English-language education began at the Weber Works of International Harvester. "An important line in the interest of welfare work has been undertaken recently," explained the *Harvester World*, "...and is now tried out...and, so far with signal success."[22] The "Y" was conducting night classes "for the benefit of 'coming Americans' among the Greeks and Lithuanians." These classes were attended by men and women who sought to prepare themselves for naturalization. Officials of the company claimed it was most gratifying to them to see that class attendance had not wavered in spite of the fact that the "Y" began to charge a nominal fee after the first ten free lessons.[23]

EARLY PROGRAMS AND MANAGEMENT

The "Y" 's jurisdiction over these classes did not last long. By January 1912, they had been placed under the control of the superintendent of the Weber Works. He had worked out a course "... on the line of a series of lessons dealing with the work of the plant."[24] This meant that the lessons at the Weber Works and, by March 1912, at two other Harvester plants in Chicago stressed shop discipline, welfare work, and safety. It was the aim of the company, said one of its spokesmen, that the "embryo American, and employee of the works should at one and the same time learn to speak English correctly and also have impressed upon him the rules he should follow while in and around the works." The

[18]Roberts, "Y.M.C.A. Teaching Foreign-Speaking Men," pp. 20–21. Roberts, *New Immigration*, pp. viii, 306–307. By 1920 he wrote a book entitled *The Problem of Americanization*, but its theme was opposition to militancy and coercion. *Ibid., passim.*

[19]*Harvester World*, vol. 2, December 1910, p. 29.

[20]*Ibid.*, vol. 2, September 1911, p. 28. See also *ibid.*, vol. 5, March 1914, p. 30.

[21]*Ibid.*, vol. 3, January 1912, p. 32.

[22]*Loc. cit.*

[23]*Loc. cit.*

[24]*Loc. cit.* See also *ibid.*, vol. 3, March 1912, p. 31.

immigrant was expected to learn how to "think and talk intelligently about all the important operations in the works, in his own department as well as in other departments." Immigrants were to become "good American citizens and good employees."[25]

Two lessons of the company's special English-language curriculum stressed discipline, welfare, and safety work in particular. The first lesson entitled "General" was devoted exclusively to matters of discipline.

> I hear the whistle. I must hurry.
> I hear the five minute whistle.
> It is time to go into the shop.
> I take my check from the gate board and hang it on the department board.
> I change my clothes and get ready to work.
> The starting whistle blows.
> I eat my lunch.
> It is forbidden to eat until then.
> The whistle blows at five minutes of starting time.
> I get ready to go to work.
> I work until the whistle blows to quit.
> I leave my place nice and clean.
> I put all my clothes in my locker.
> I go home.[26]

Lesson One was followed by a series of others devoted to various parts of a plant and to specific tools. Like the first one, they dealt with the familiar in line with the Roberts' method.[27] One of them com-

bined elements of the welfare and safety program under way at the company.

> The Employee Benefit Association is composed of the employees of the International Harvester Company.
> When you are sick or hurt report to your timekeeper and the doctor at once.
> If you get sick at home send word at once to your timekeeper or your foreman.
> You are paid one half of your regular daily earnings for every day you are sick after one week.
> While you are sick do not leave the city without first seeing the doctor and telling him about it.
> The doctor takes care of all accidents that happen in the works.
> You should call on the doctor when you are able; do not wait for him to call on you.
> When the door of the doctor's office is closed, knock and wait for him to say, 'come in,' before you open the door.
> Do not try to take slivers out of the hand or cinders out of the eye for yourself or another, but go directly to the doctor's office.
> When you are hurt in the works, you will be paid one half wages for all the time you are disabled, provided you report the accident at once to your timekeeper and the doctor.
> No benefits will be paid if you are hurt while scuffling or fooling.
> No benefits will be paid if you are hurt or get sick as a result of having been drinking.[28]

The United States Steel Corporation adopted the Roberts' method in a man-

---

[25]*Ibid.*, p. 30. See also *ibid.*, vol. 3, January 1912, p. 32.

[26]*Ibid.*, vol. 3, March 1912, p. 31.

[27]For other uses of the familiar in teaching English to foreigners, see for example: Lillian P. Clark, *Federal Textbook on Citizenship Training* (Washington: United States Department of Labor, 1924), *passim;* Issac Price, *The Direct Method of Teaching English to Foreigners* (New York: Noble and Noble, 1909), *passim;* Sarah R. O'Brien, *English to Foreigners* (New York: Houghton Mifflin, 1909), *passim;* William E.

Chancellor, *Reading and Language Lessons for Every School* (New York: American Book Company, 1904), *passim.*

[28]*Harvester World*, vol. 3, March 1912, p. 31.

ner similar to the one used at International Harvester. In 1908 U.S. Steel launched its safety program. A committee of safety was established to provide a clearing house for safety and general welfare information for the many subsidiaries in the corporate organization.[29] After 1910 the committee published a bulletin entirely devoted to matters of safety, welfare, and sanitation.[30] Before World War I, the bulletin did not explicitly refer to Americanization but it did present examples of lesson plans being used in English-language classes. The lessons were based on the Roberts' method; Roberts himself had worked closely with U.S. Steel in the initial stages of the language program. These lessons were entirely devoted to safety matters.[31]

The Ford Motor Company had also introduced this type of language education for immigrants. At Ford, however, the beginnings occurred around the time when militant Americanizers called for education in civics and the rapid naturalization of immigrants.[32] These features of Ford's program for immigrants were thus associated with the militant Americanizers, but in fact the language program, as it existed at International Har-

vester and at the United States Steel Corporation, was tied much more closely to safety and welfare work than it was to civics and naturalization.[33] By 1914 Ford had one of the nation's most elaborate welfare programs, similar in many ways to the program at International Harvester, except that at Ford welfare work was directly tied to hiring and firing practices, and to wage increases.[34] The safety campaign had come to Detroit later than it had to some other industrial areas, but it had arrived before 1914; indeed, when militant Americanizers launched their language campaign in Detroit in 1915, employers used safety committees as one of the means for propagandizing the language drive.[35] Safety men had concerned themselves with the immigrant before English-language education was begun.[36] Robert Shaw, safety engineer for the company in 1917, claimed that they had felt that instruction in the English language would help them in their activities and had urged the use of such education. Before Ford established its English School in May 1914, the company had issued a safety bulletin in forty-two different languages. "We had the problem of...different nationalities and the first thing we decided was that we would use only the English language. Every sign, every danger sign or construction notice," claimed Shaw, "was put into English and the first thing we did was to start an English school. It has solved the bad

---

[29]United States Steel Corporation, Committee of Safety, *Bulletin*, October 1910, n.p.

[30]*Ibid.*, October 1910 to December 1925.

[31]Roberts, *Problems of Americanization*, p. 99; United States Steel Corporation, Committee of Safety, *Bulletin*, November 1913, p. 8.

[32]*Immigrants in American Review*, vol. 1, September 1915, p. 6; Hartman, *Movement to Americanize the Immigrant*, p. 129. The Committee for Immigrants in America had been instrumental in beginning Detroit's drive. Esther E. Lape, "The English First Movement in Detroit," *Immigrants in America Review*, vol. 1, September 1915, pp. 46–50; Allan Nevins and Frank Ernest Hill, *Ford: the times, the man, the company* (New York: Scribner, 1954), vol. 1, pp. 532–545, 557; vol. 2, 340–341; John R. Lee, "So-called Profit Sharing System in the Ford Plant," *Annals of the American Academy of Political and Social Science*, vol. 65, May 1916, pp. 297–310; Higham, *Strangers in the Land*, p. 248.

[33]Nevins and Hill, *Ford*, vol. 1, pp. 532–545.

[34]*Ibid.*: vol. 1, pp. 513–515, 551–554, 556, vol. 2, pp. 332–340.

[35]Lape, "The English First Movement in Detroit," p. 46.

[36]Nevins and Hill, *Ford*, vol. 1, pp. 520–522; Robert H. Shaw, safety engineer, Ford Motor Company, in National Safety Council, *Proceedings, 1916*, p. 225. See also, *ibid., 1917*, p. 795, for comments of W. Ernest William, safety engineer of the Packard Motor Company.

problem in regard to our safety work."[37] Language education included lessons similar to those at U.S. Steel and at International Harvester. Safety, shop discipline, and other aspects of company welfare programs, including material stressing Ford's benevolence, were all subjects built into language lessons.[38] This similarity reflected the influence of Peter Roberts. He trained volunteer teachers in the use of his methods and designed lesson plans to meet the needs of the Ford organization.[39]

Thus the first phase of language education for immigrants in factories emerged from an industrial context. The classes were not introduced either because of fear of the immigrants effect on America or for making his adjustment to America less disturbing. The classes grew out of the same demands that had resulted in welfare and safety activities and were an integral part of these programs. The classes concerned themselves primarily with only one sphere of the immigrant's surroundings: factory life. YMCA workers at International Harvester and U.S. Steel encountered situations demanding that they work within the framework set by the production personnel. Instructors recruited by the YMCA may often have entered English-language classes with the noblest of ambitions and a genuine urge to teach the immigrant basic language skills. They were not interested in, if not outrightly hostile to, the content of an English-language curriculum that an industrial

organization wanted taught. To them the classes represented a device to help the immigrant cope with America, and the interests of an industrial organization were simply too narrow to satisfy them. It required stubbornness and resourcefulness on the part of such a "Y" worker to overcome the pressure of companies. In Chicago at a "Y" class of Illinois Steel, a subsidiary of U.S. Steel, it took all the ingenuity of an instructor to convince foremen visiting his class that the company's "shop" lessons were of little use or interest to the men and women seeking to learn English for general use.[40]

THE WAR YEARS

The war in Europe gave Americanizers the opportunity to give their movement a sense of urgency. The wrangle over the rights of neutrals began in the first year of war and made American participation in the conflict a possibility. When, in May 1915, a German submarine brought death to over a hundred Americans by sinking the *Lusitania*, cries for the nation's entry into war against Germany were heard in many quarters of the land.[41] Americanization now became synonymous with national interest and with national defense. The opportunity was at hand to mount a campaign for disciplining loyalties and languages; in short, for disciplining American nationalism. And this opportunity came at a time when the spread of welfare work and other practices for systematizing human relations in factories gained momentum, thus creating a condition in industry seemingly conducive to militant Americanizers.

One of the most influential persons in

[37]*Ibid.*, *1917*, p. 236.

[38]Nevins and Hill, *Ford*, vol. 1, p. 557.

[39]Henry Ford to Detroit YMCA, Detroit, Dec. 2, 1914 in *The Association Among 59 Nationalities* in File 27671/614, Records of Immigration and Naturalization Service, National Archives. For the "Y"'s brief account of Roberts' work at Detroit, see *loc. cit.* Nevins identifies Peter Roberts only as "a Dr. Roberts." Nevins and Hill, *Ford*, vol. 1, p. 557.

[40]Beale, "A YMCA English Class" and "Teaching English to Foreigners."

[41]Carl Wittke, *The German-Language Press in America* (Lexington: University of Kentucky Press, 1957), pp. 252–254.

the Americanization crusade was Frances Kellor. She injected into Americanization a zeal for making the nation's economy and body-politic function more efficiently. Miss Kellor began her public service career as a lawyer turned "social worker." In 1904, she published an analysis of employment offices in New York City, paying particular attention to immigrants and to the chaotic manner in which labor was distributed. In the next few years, she worked for municipal and state agencies investigating the many social problems confronting the urban communities. She soon became an authority on urban immigrants and immigrant legislation. By 1906, she had already become influential in shaping Theodore Roosevelt's views on matters of immigration.[42]

In the midst of her activities as a public servant for the New York Commission on Immigration, Miss Kellor obtained the support of two wealthy New Yorkers, Frank Trumbull and Felix Warburg, for Americanization work. In 1909 they established a branch of New England's North American Civic League, but from its founding the New York group's basic approach to Americanization differed from that of the parent body. The New Yorkers had a genuine interest in changing general environmental conditions throughout the nation. Between 1912 and 1914, the differences between the parent body and the New Yorkers increased. The activities of the I.W.W. at Lawrence, Paterson, and elsewhere in the Northeast heightened the fear of the League about the effects of radical foreign-language organizers among immigrants. Subsequently, the League turned to spying and

other tactics in order to block strikes and union activity among the foreign-born. At the same time Miss Kellor became an enthusiastic worker for the Progressive party; she served as the head of its research and publicity department. Early in 1914, the New York branch of the League broke with the parent body and established the Committee for Immigrants in America. Miss Kellor became vice-chairman and its guiding light. In 1915, she became editor of *Immigrants in America Review,* a journal published by the committee and devoted to Americanization. Miss Kellor now had an organization and a journal through which she could hope to marshall national opinion. In this effort she had the support of a number of well-known intellectuals committed to Roosevelt's New Nationalism; Herbert Croly, Walter Lippmann, and Felix Frankfurter served on the advisory board of *Immigrants in America Review.*[43]

The absence of a clearing house for centralizing Americanization activities gave the Kellor group the opportunity for filling the void. With the help of the United States Bureau of Education, the committee created, staffed, and financed the Division of Immigrant Education within the Bureau. This division became the federal agency through which the committee obtained official endorsement for much of its propaganda.[44] In May of 1915 the United States Bureau of Naturalization and Immigration held a mass celebration of naturalization ceremonies in Philadelphia; President Wilson graced the occasion and chose it for his "Too

---

[42]Higham, *Strangers in the Land,* pp. 239–241; Frances Kellor, *Out of Work: A Study of Employment Agencies, Their Treatment of the Unemployed, and Their Influence upon Homes and Business* (New York: Putnam, 1904), *passim.*

[43]Hartman, *Movement to Americanize the Immigrant,* pp. 56–63, 91–97; *Immigrants in America Review,* vol. 1, March 1915, p. 102.

[44]*Ibid.,* vol. 1, September 1915, pp. 3–4, 15, 30–32; Hartman, *Movement to Americanize the Immigrant,* pp. 97–100, 112–114.

Proud to Fight" speech.[45] Between the Philadelphia celebration and July 4 the committee made Independence Day, 1915, the occasion for mass celebrations of naturalization in 100 American cities. The success of the Independence Day campaign helped the committee become established as the nation's organization leading the crusade for Americanization.[46]

Until 1915, Miss Kellor was a nationalist of the Croly-Roosevelt persuasion. She was an energetic advocate for systematizing industrial production, distribution, and factory personnel. She looked toward the day when America's population would be more or less homogeneous in its loyalties to the state, and when the country's economy would be so regulated that conflict between labor and capital would be reduced to a minimum. She preached, as John Higham has noted, social welfare and national discipline.[47]

The official statement of purpose issued by the committee reflected these views. It considered Amercianization a domestic immigration policy, which dealt with the following problems: the reduction of unemployment; the elimination of discriminatory state and municipal legislation; the improvement of the immigrants' standard of living; the distribution of alien workers according to the needs of the economy and the abilities of the immigrants; the protection of immigrants, particularly their savings; finally, the improvement of educational facilities for newcomers, including opportunities for industrial training.[48] Two parts of the *Review* also focused attention on

these problems. "The Record of Progress" pointed to activities in the area of unemployment, legislation, and education. The book review section listed and discussed books pertinent for an understanding of the problem raised by the formal policy statement. These included books concerned with industrial service work.[49]

MILITANT NATIONALISM

With the first issue of *Immigrants in America Review*, in March 1915, however, it was plain that the militant nationalist in Miss Kellor was coming to the fore. The need now, she said, was the "conscious effort to forge the people of this country into an American race that will stand together for America in time of peace and war." By September she sounded frightened about the potentialities of un-Americanized immigrants. "Because of our lack of patriotism, efficiency, and consideration we have failed to inspire our better conditioned immigrants and their sons with a love for this country which supplants that of other countries." This failure was a serious weakness, for immigrants and often their children had deep attachments for the mother country. It was "more widespread than we know," she claimed, and warned that "in case of war we would have in this country if not actual traitors, a division of forces such as would make a victory precarious in any prolonged warfare." In January 1916, she cried that America faced a crisis. The big problem was not "whether we need a larger army and navy, but whether we shall have a United America back of that army and navy, and whether America, with her

[45]*Ibid.*, pp. 107–111; *Immigrants in America Review*, vol. 1, September 1915, pp. 303–332.

[46]*Loc. cit.*; Hartman, *Movement to Americanize the Immigrant*, pp. 112–124.

[47]Higham, *Strangers in the Land*, p. 239.

[48]*Immigrants in America Review*, vol. 1, March 1915, pp. 3–15, 17–86.

[49]*Ibid.*: vol. 1, March 1915, pp. 90–94, June 1915, pp. 76, 87, 94, September 1915, pp. 98, 108; vol. 2, June 1916, pp. 110–111.

many races and divided allegiances will survive as a great nation."[50]

Miss Kellor's militancy and one-sided approach to Americanization evoked sharp criticism in some quarters, and in January 1916, she responded by printing an article written by Horace Kallen, a social psychologist, who had been developing his concepts of cultural pluralism since the early years of the century.[51] Kallen's piece was a careful statement on the evolution and meaning of such American ideals as liberty, union, and democracy. He attacked militants like Miss Kellor because they engaged in "vicious abstractionism," a term Kallen borrowed from William James. Even T.R., maintained Kallen, would hardly consent to a marriage between his son and a Negress in the interest of New Nationalism. The whole issue of double loyalties, maintained Kallen, had got out of hand because of people who did not distinguish between treason and differences in values and beliefs. He charged that those obsessed with this issue were distorting the meaning of American democracy. "In essence democracy involves not the elimination of differences but the perfection and conservation of differences. It aims through union, not at uniformity but at variety."[52]

The editor had, however, moved too far towards militant nationalism to take heed of Kallen's comments. By 1916, the militant nationalists rather than the so-cial settlement workers were giving Americanization its main direction. In that year, Miss Kellor published her book, *Straight America* in which she espoused an "America First" position on the question of Americanization.[53] This was the viewpoint that she attempted to spread among the nation's employers.

Throughout 1915, Miss Kellor considered the place of industry in Americanization work. In the spring she called on the nation's chambers of commerce to add "industrial assimilation of the immigrant workmen" to their programs in the hope that the chambers of commerce could assist in changing the alien's feeling that he was an "outsider, on a different footing from the American workmen." She called for a program of civics and English and measures providing for equality of opportunity to newcomers. This emphasis soon changed. After the successful July 4 celebrations, she stepped up her campaign to recruit local chambers of commerce, trade associations, and industrial plants. On the inside cover of the *Immigrants in America Review*, published after the Fourth, she addressed "businessmen" for the first time as a group who ought to join the crusade. Miss Kellor argued that Americanization would increase the efficiency of immigrant employees, prevent accidents, and help "businessmen" understand the needs of immigrants. It would "eliminate industrial misunderstanding and...maintain our American standard of living."

During the winter, Miss Kellor and three other leading members of the Committee for Immigrants in America took their campaign into the organizational structure of the United States Chamber of Commerce. The Chamber established an Immigration Committee with Frank Trumbull, chairman, William F. Mor-

[50]*Ibid.:* vol. 1, March 1915, p. 15, September 1915, pp. 3, 4–5, January 1916, p. 3.

[51]Kallen told the author in 1962 that he began to develop his ideas about cultural pluralism just after the turn of the century. Kallen was then studying philosophy under William James at Harvard. See also Kallen's *Culture and Democracy in the United States* (New York: Boni and Liveright, 1924).

[52]Kallen, "The Meaning of Americanism," *Immigrants in America Review*, vol. 1, January 1916, pp. 12–19.

[53]Higham, *Strangers in the Land*, pp. 242–244.

gan, treasurer, and with Miss Kellor, assistant to the chairman. The Immigration Committee became an effective organ for the Kellor group, although this was not at first generally known.[54] The Deputy Commissioner of the Bureau of Naturalization and Immigration had not recognized the linkage until he was told about it by the Chamber's Immigration Committee.[55]

The Immigration Committee of the Chamber tuned in on the industrial service movement that was gaining momentum in these years. "The nationwide Americanization movement," the committee explained to members of the Chamber of Commerce, "is part of the present day trend toward humanizing industry. It aims to take what is commonly called welfare work out of paternalism and make it a part of legitimate business organizations everywhere.... There is no agreement among American employers now as to the extent and manner of its organization or where it really belongs. There are no recognized standards. What we need is to extend scientific methods to the human phase of industrial organizations and give welfare work a more definite place and recognized standards. ..."[56]

By linking Americanization to the "trend toward humanizing industry,"

Miss Kellor's group demonstrated an appreciation of the strategic role that autocratic industrial organizations could play in the crusade, and at the same time accepted one of the fundamental underpinnings of that "humanizing trend." Miss Kellor applauded the actions of Detroit employers, who were among the first to use their coercive power to make immigrants attend English-language and civics classes in the public schools or factories. In 1915 she praised the Packard Motor Company for making attendance a condition of promotion. Indeed, by 1916 she was prepared to argue that such coercion was perhaps one of the few ways to force immigrants into educational programs advocated by Americanizers.[57] And, as she supported this use of power so too did she accept one of the basic assumptions behind the "humanizing trend." In January 1916, she gave this explanation of the significance of Americanization for industry:

It will mean first of all industrial peace. So long as our industrial communities are made up of large groups of un-Americanized immigrants, without the English language, without understanding American conditions, too helpless to bring their grievances to the attention of their employers, too ignorant to force them in legitimate ways if they were not offered, able to understand only the radical agitators addressing them in their own languages — [sic] just so long will the industrial history of America be blotted out by Calumets, Ludlows, Lawrences, and Wheatlands. The road to American citizenship, to the English language, and an understanding of American social and political ideals is the road to industrial peace. Even now in peace, our country is honeycombed with industrial strife, disorder and disputes involving the destruction of life and property.[58]

[54]*Immigrants in America Review:* vol. 1, June 1915, pp. 2, 9, September 1915, p. 2, January 1916, p. 86; Hartman, *Movement to Americanize the Immigrant,* pp. 113–132.

[55]Richard M. Campbell, commissioner of the Bureau of Naturalization and Immigration to Eliot H. Goodwin, secretary, United States Chamber of Commerce, August 18, 1917, Sept. 8, 1917, Frances A. Kellor to Campbell, Sept. 5, 1917, Bureau of Naturalization and Immigration, Case File, 27671/1832, National Archives.

[56]*Report of the Committee on Immigration of the Chamber of Commerce of the United States of America, Fifth Annual Meeting, 1917,* p. 2, in Bureau of Naturalization and Immigration, Case File, 27671/1832, National Archives.

[57]*Immigrants in America Review:* vol. 1, September 1915, p. 16, January 1916, p. 6.

[58]*Ibid.,* p. 4.

In the years from 1916 to 1918, Miss Kellor and her supporters intensified their campaign to convince employers that Americanization was part of the "humanizing" efforts being carried on by industrial organizations. In March 1917, the Committee for Immigrants in America created still another committee. This was the Committee on Industrial Engineering staffed by numerous experts recruited from universities and industry. The group published its own bulletin which concerned itself with industrial service work. These were subjects that the *Immigrants in America Review*, now defunct, had always stressed. At the same time, the Immigration Committee of the Chamber of Commerce continued its own publicity drive, and at the end of 1917 claimed marked success in establishing factory classes for immigrants. In the spring of 1918, as America entered its second year of war, the Kellor group centralized much of its work by operating through federal agencies. It expanded the facilities of the Bureau of Education. It enlisted the support of the Department of Interior and was able to convince the National Council of Defense, a war-time agency, to accept its Americanization program.[59]

MANAGEMENT RESPONSE

Industry responded to Miss Kellor's campaign on its own terms. Among the

safety inspectors, the budding employment managers and the visiting nurses, and other men and women in the forefront of safety and welfare work Miss Kellor's views made slow headway. Before 1915, the link between safety and Americanization was rarely discussed in the conferences of the National Safety Council, but in subsequent years discussion of the linkage increased as militant Americanizers tried to persuade the Council to use its educational bulletins for safety and health to compel immigrants to learn English. Dr. J. W. Schereschewsky of the United States Public Health Service objected to translations of such bulletins into foreign languages. Speaking in the fall of 1917 he said: "When we consider educational measures among workers, we ought not to give them the opportunity for perpetuating their native speech, but make them understand that now is the time for them to become true American citizens and learn to speak the language of this country."[60]

W. S. Tenor of the American Wire and Steel Company in Cleveland supported Schereschewsky's position on language because of conditions in his company. He had published, he said, safety literature in various languages, but on one occasion this led to a strike because "we omitted a certain language." This omission, he claimed, led to national animosities as the excluded group was ridiculed by other language groups. They said "why did the company not think of putting your language in the book" and insisted that the excluded group had no right to national aspirations. For that and other reasons, said Tenor, "it is best to confine work to

[59]*Ibid.*, vol. 1–2, *passim;* Frank P. Walsh of the United Mine Workers saw clearly the relationship between Kellor's Americanization drive and the efforts to humanize the industry. He also sharply attacked Kellor's group for not including unions in its campaign. *United Mine Workers Journal*, vol. 25, Feb. 3, 1916, p. 7; United States Chamber of Commerce, Immigration Committee, *Bulletin*, Feb. 15, 1917, March 1, 1917, April 15, 1917, June 15, 1917, Dec. 15, 1917, Jan. 2, 1918, Bureau of Naturalization and Immigration, Case File 27671/1832, National Archives; Hartman, *Movement to Americanize the Immigrant*, pp. 165–166, 187–205.

[60]National Safety Council, *Proceedings, 1917*, p. 235. For an example of establishing a linkage between Safety and Americanization before 1915, see *ibid., 1912*, pp. 13–15.

English and we have pretty well abandoned the idea of using any other languages."[61]

J. B. Douglas, of the United Gas Improvement Company in Philadelphia, chairman of a meeting of the Public Utilities Section of the Council, expressed his cautious support of Americanization. He referred in particular to a ruling of the Pennsylvania Department of Labor and Industry requiring foremen engaged in hazardous work to speak and understand the language of their workers. "While this ruling may be termed progressive, I am in doubt as to how it will work out in practice." "It does point, however," said Douglas, "to the importance of employees being able to speak English and I firmly believe that just as soon as labor conditions will permit all progressive employers will give the 'Americanization' of their employees the attention it undoubtedly deserves."[62]

There were others who pleaded for using safety and health literature as teaching devices for Americanization. Charles B. Milner of the Hammermill Paper Company of Erie, Pennsylvania, urged that special cards, printed in the immigrant's languages, be tacked to bulletin boards; these cards should tell immigrants to have English bulletins translated for them.[63] Charles A. Prosser, director of the United States Board of Vocational Education, agreed that safety bulletins could "be made a very practical drill in English."[64] The most outspoken advocate of militancy was undoubtedly J. R. de la Torre Bueno. He was a naturalized citizen, and editor of the house organ of the General Chemical Company, a firm that had twenty plants in the United States and Canada.[65] He assumed that foreign languages perpetuated national allegiances. In 1918 he maintained that foreigners be taught English and insisted that the nation "must do away with foreign languages" and that "the foreign language press. . .ought to be suppressed." To de la Torre Bueno such measures were fundamental prerequisites for a successful Americanization program.[66]

The staff of the Council and the majority of its members did not greet these views with enthusiasm. The Council was designing symbols to mark danger spots in factories. The alternatives for the types of symbols to be used by employers and state agencies were numerous and the factors involved in choosing symbols complex. Special committees were assigned to the task of testing and picking the most satisfactory symbols and between 1915 and 1917 they made their reports to the general membership of the Council.[67] One of the questions inherent in the choice of any symbol was whether or not it conveyed its meaning to foreign-born workers. As late as 1917 no definite choices had been made, but the committee in that year clearly favored signs with captions translated for the benefit of immigrants. The chairman of the special committee stressed the need for translations. He asked his listeners to imagine themselves as workers in Poland and then confronted them with a sign carrying only a caption in Polish. The point was obvious.[68]

The Council also translated its safety bulletins. In 1916, a number of member firms asked the Council to help them translate safety literature or at least to provide them with names of competent

---

[61]*Ibid., 1917*, pp. 235–236.
[62]*Ibid., 1917*, pp. 484–485.
[63]*Ibid., 1918*, pp. 563–564.
[64]*Ibid., 1918*, p. 296.

[65]*Ibid., 1918*, p. 409.
[66]*Ibid., 1918*, pp. 417–418.
[67]*Ibid., 1917*, pp. 25–37.
[68]*Ibid., 1917*, p. 37.

translators.[69] William H. Cameron, the general manager of the Council, told the firms that the Council hesitated to translate bulletins for three reasons: it was too expensive; it was too complicated to provide bulletins for all of the different language groups in industry; and finally, the officers of the Council were "more or less in sympathy with the Americanizers."[70] However, pressure for translations from Council members prevented the Council from following militant Americanizers. In 1917, the editor of the organization's annual proceedings informed members that "if any one wants translations into any of a dozen languages they can secure this service through General Manager Cameron."[71]

The Council did make some efforts in developing English-language lesson plans for immigrant workers. In 1915, a special education committee asked Peter Roberts to work out special lessons devoted to safety. In the following year the Council had available for its members English-language lesson plans on such subjects as boilers, "Health and Safety," and "Safety First and Sober Always. ..."[72] These lessons were similar to the ones Roberts had worked out for individual firms.

SOME INDIVIDUAL RESPONSES

Although the Council failed to support Americanization enthusiastically, its participating firms did not close their gates to Americanizers. Astute safety and welfare workers related their activities to the acculturation process. In 1916, Arthur H. Young, a former safety inspector who had recently become employment manager at

Illinois Steel, indicated where he stood on Americanization. He had just explained to Council members that his employment applications asked for the following information: the employee's place and date of birth and race, the place of birth and race of his parents, the number of years he had lived in the United States, naturalization status, marital status, number of offspring, the place of residence of his family, and the state of his literacy in English and in a foreign language. "I will frankly say," Young commented about these questions, "that the answers to some of...[them] are of far more interest to Uncle Sam than plant executives. ..."[73] At the same time, however, Young described the relation of his own work to the acculturation process. "America," he explained, "is the melting pot she is because each industrial plant, each social settlement, and each civic center in her broad expanse, is in itself a melting pot, and the employment chief is like unto a chef, in charge of the mixture at the particular plant ...he refines a product of American manhood. ...The melting pot is there and the executive who neglects a proper supervision of its activities neglects a profitable and patriotic service."[74]

Two visiting nurses employed by different companies described in some detail how they viewed their work with immigrants. One was Florence S. Wright who was employed by the Clark Thread Company in Newark, New Jersey. She said nothing about Americanization as such, but she did claim to be highly influential in changing the home life of an immigrant worker and in spreading the good will of the company.

I find the Italian family taking boarders. ...The father has his chest examined, is

---

[69]*Ibid., 1916*, pp. 125–126, 365–366. B. B. Folger, chairman of the Safety Committee of the Manufacturers Association of Ludlow, Massachusetts, was among this group. *Loc. cit.*

[70]*Ibid., 1916*, p. 131.

[71]*Ibid., 1917*, p. 234.

[72]*Ibid., 1916*, pp. 53–54.

[73]*Ibid., 1916*, p. 522.

[74]*Ibid., 1916*, p. 526.

found to be an incipient tuberculosis case, and after a period of rest and education is given outdoor work suited to his strength. The mother is taught to buy and cook. The children are sent to an open air school. It takes time but in the end the boarders are no longer there, the father is well and doing suitable work, the children are going to school, and the mother is making a home of which the family and the nurse is proud. . . . I have increased my Italian vocabulary and have six firm friends. Needless to say, the unseen employer who sent me also has six loyal friends, although he may never know of their existence.[75]

Miss Nester C. Edwards worked for the Kimberly-Clark Company in Neenah, Wisconsin, and was instrumental in placing nurses in various companies in the state and elsewhere. To her, the visiting nurse, if properly instructed for factory work, functioned as a factory social worker. She felt that it made little difference whether the original training was for nursing or social work. Successful social work in factories depended largely on only two prerequisites: the individual had first to have "the capacity and ability to take hold and get next to the individual," and needed to know the power foremen could wield. You can "never bring to the plant that healthy diffusion you want," she said, "unless you are working with the foremen's force. These are the forces to be reckoned with, your superintendent and your general management."[76]

She was in sympathy with the Americanization movement but pleaded that industrial interests and national interests should not be confused. English-language classes had no place in the factory, she argued, for the simple reason, that language education was not the function of

industry but the responsibility of the public school and private organizations such as the YMCA.[77] The class was an unwanted stepchild in the factory, Miss Edwards argued in the fall of 1917. "At the close of the day the group was assigned to the attic, or basement, or often crowded into the president's or board of director's office."[78]

Miss Edwards charged employers with the responsibility of using their power in three ways to make workers learn English outside of the factory. First, give an increase in pay to every man who acquired a speaking knowledge of English. Second, do not promote a man until he had learned the required amount of English. Third, she said, make "it plain at the time of hiring that men and women are employed on the grounds that they will attend the night school for a required time." These methods she felt lay within the province of employer activity and were at the same time a "Safety First Measure." In order to make the pressure as effective as possible she counselled that employment secretaries or service workers keep a check on immigrants who needed to attend night school.[79]

It was Young, manager in 1918 of industrial relations at International Harvester, who expressed the views of those operating within the industrial framework. He insisted that immigrant workers receive special attention from employers and their service workers, not in the spirit of militant Americanization but in the spirit of the safety movement. Immigrants, he explained, "are transplanted

---

[75]*Ibid., 1916*, pp. 545–553. The quotation may be found in *ibid., 1916*, pp. 548–549 where it is presented in the third person singular.

[76]*Ibid., 1917*, pp. 333–334.

[77]*Ibid., 1917*, pp. 424–425.

[78]*Ibid., 1917*, p. 424.

[79]*Ibid., 1917*, pp. 424–425. The use of economic power to affect the styles of life outside the workshop was not, of course, limited to immigrants. A frank statement about its use in "holding...colored labor" can be found in *ibid., 1917*, pp. 1294–1295.

suddenly into the center of a very busy industrial plant from farms or street car work, or from excavation work on the streets where the hazards are entirely similar." "If we pass them through an employment office and put them on a job without instructions only natural results may be expected." Thus it was important that immigrants were interviewed in their own language, and when unable to speak or read English, to be instructed in their own language; his department had a Polish interpreter, who translated important speeches to Polish workers during wartime ceremonies. "Americanization of our foreigners, the teaching of English to them and then a higher education," said Young, "there again the educational director and the employment man must work hand in hand. Lessons can be gotten up in English on safety problems and they can be inculcated in the man's mind and part of the regular curriculum of the school."[80]

OTHER COMPANY PROGRAMS

A number of large industrial organizations participated in the Americanization movement, but always on their terms and within the framework of safety and welfare programs which they had developed earlier. At the Ford School, established initially as a result of the safety movement, the first thing the immigrant learned to say was, "I am an American"; pageants dramatizing this verbal conversion had newcomers dressed in the clothing of the old world enter onto stage and then leave the stage dressed in "American" clothing.[81] By the end of 1916, Ford had about 2,700 immigrants receiving language instruction from some 160 volunteer teachers using Roberts' method. The immigrant student was expected to attend classes for six to eight months before or after his work shift. At the end of his course of 72 lessons, a printed diploma qualified him for his first naturalization papers without further examination by federal authorities.[82]

The expansion and functioning of the school was, however, determined by the needs of the entire work force and by the firm's economic requirements. At the end of 1916, the school added mathematics, psychology, and public speaking to the curriculum. These courses were attended by about three hundred native-born workers. In the same year, the company established the Henry Ford Trade School and this institution increasingly outweighted the language school in importance in the company's educational scheme. When industrial considerations came into conflict with those of the Americanizers, the industrial ones triumphed. In 1917, during the war, the allotment of rooms for English classes was cut from 22 to 3, and after that English-language education was continued on a limited scale, with some 500 students and 30 instructors.[83]

When the United States Steel Corporation and a number of its subsidiaries joined the Americanization crusade, it was clear that Americanization work was but an adjunct of programs already in operation.[84] As the Americanization crusade mounted in intensity, U.S. Steel's

---

[80]*Ibid.*, *1918*, pp. 785–787. Cf. with the comment Young made in 1916 when he was supervisor of labor and safety at the Illinois Steel Company. *Ibid.*, *1916*, pp. 518–520. For examples of the activities of the Polish translator, see *Harvester World*, vol. 10, July 1918, p. 16. For comments of safety men who shared Young's views, see National Safety Council, *Proceedings: 1916*, pp. 138, 627–628, *1918*, pp. 528, 577.

[81]Higham, *Strangers in the Land*, p. 248.
[82]Nevins and Hill, *Ford*, vol. 1, p. 557.
[83]*Ibid.*, vol. 2, pp. 340–341.
[84]Americanization in the steel industry is discussed in a different context by David Brody in his *Steelworkers in America* (Cambridge, Mass.: Harvard University Press, 1960), pp. 189–192.

Bureau of Safety, Sanitation, and Welfare incorporated aspects of the crusade in its publication, but treated Americanization as something apart from safety and welfare activity. In 1916, the Bureau commented on its welfare work and noted that the Corporation's English-language education taught foreign labor "the principles of clean, wholesome living" and good citizenship.[85] In 1917, immigrant education was entirely ignored, but in 1918 the Bureau devoted a special section of its bulletin to Americanization. In the issue of 1918, however, the Bureau also discussed movies used in safety work. One of these, a film made in 1912, was oriented entirely towards the immigrant but it was not discussed in the Americanization section. The Bureau described the film, about an "ignorant Hungarian peasant...stupid and uneducated" who became a forward looking, industrious workman at a plant in Gary, Indiana because of U.S. Steel's safety and welfare program, as part of its safety education.[86]

In the special section of the 1918 publication, the education and Americanization of the "foreign-born workers" had become a "national problem of vital importance." It was necessary to have a "hundred percent America." The Bureau of Safety, Sanitation, and Welfare insisted that "we must help the foreign-born laborer improve the opportunities afforded to him for education and training, so that, through knowledge of the language and familiarity with the standards of living in this country his condition will be improved."[87] Now, in the midst of the Americanization crusade, the Bureau had for the moment accepted concerns outside the industrial framework. The help

to be given a foreign-born worker would, according to the Bureau, "awaken in him a respect for and love for American ideals which...[would] develop strong loyalty towards his adopted country. ..."[88]

Subsidiary companies of the Corporation implemented Americanization work in different ways.[89] Shop-language and safety-language classes were supplemented by encouraging workers to attend YMCA and public school classes. Americanization posters took their place beside safety posters. Naturalization was stressed. In one community, for example, the Americanization work of a U.S. Steel subsidiary strongly supported efforts for enabling workers to obtain naturalization papers by providing space and financial assistance to the local public schools and private groups interested in English-language lessons and civic programs. The American Bridge Company made English language lessons part of its educational program that included mathematics, mechanics, and drawing, and supplemented language instructions with "a series of pictorial charts with descriptive texts giving a sketch of, the name, use, etc. of the various tools and other objects in and around the plant." The lessons were taught by employees. The company expected English-language classes to improve the skill and "mental alertness" of the firm's immigrant workers.

The Illinois Steel Company, whose comprehensive safety program was in operation by 1913, also injected English-language classes for foreigners into its general educational program. In 1918, the company claimed that it offered the following courses: "Machine shop, Me-

[85]United States Steel Corporation, Committee of Safety, *Bulletin*, December 1916, pp. 52–53.

[86]*Ibid.*, December 1918, pp. 5–6.

[87]*Ibid.*, p. 95.

[88]*Loc. cit.*

[89]The discussion of Americanization activities at U.S. Steel subsidiaries is based on *ibid.*, pp. 95–103. See also National Safety Council, *Proceedings: 1916*, pp. 1009–1010, *1917*, pp. 237–238, 1206.

chanical drawing, Electricity, English for foreigners, Shop Mathematics, Mathematics, Woodshop, [high school] English, Forge, Bookkeeping, Stenography, Chemistry, Eighth Grade." The English-language classes were run by the YMCA and, although attendance was voluntary, the instructor was required to file a form with the company indicating by number which worker was absent. Foremen would check personally on the work of the teacher as well as on the workers' attendance, and also attempted to orient the lessons of an instructor to actual operations in the company.[90]

The Amercian Steel and Wire Company followed similar practices but arranged for more elaborate Americanization activities at some of its plants. Two committees were created that showed a striking similarity to those characteristic of the safety organization. At the Waukegan Works of the company, a general Americanization committee was established consisting of the superintendent, the "employment man," the safety engineer, four Finns, three Austrians, three Swedes, three Lithuanians, two Armenians, two Poles, one Dane, and one German. This group arranged for three Americanization parades and four mass meetings and organized a thirty-eight piece band. Another committee was established consisting of the departmental foreman and representatives from each nationality in the department. These groups were to meet periodically and "keep in close touch with all men needing instruction in English"; they were "to help to get out their citizen papers"; they were to try "to get them to join the evening school." Provision for English-language classes at a public school were arranged through the committees of the company.

The organ of the International Harvester Company reflected the entry of Americanization into an industrial organization that had not joined the crusade at its inception. In November of 1914, two months after the outbreak of war in Europe, an editorial statement on the inside cover of the *Harvester World* stated the company's position about the conflict. The firm fully endorsed Wilson's policy of neutrality and stressed that one of the reasons for doing so was its many international connections. The editorial took pains to remind foreign-born employees that they were American citizens, but recognized explicitly that it was only natural for an immigrant to favor his country of origin. Nevertheless, the firm stressed that "this country and this company has only one interest in the present struggle; an early termination of hostilities."[91] Between November 1914 and the eve of America's entry into battle, little was said about the war or Americanization. Only once in this period did the house organ indicate that there was concern about Americanization. The exception, however, was not without significance, for it was in the safety and welfare section of the journal and referred to activities at the Weber Works, a plant that had begun English-language classes in 1912.

In May 1916, the foremen's club at the Weber Works decided to assist employees of foreign nationality to become citizens. On the suggestion of the plant superintendent, the Club established a special committee to make a survey of those who had not made applications for first papers, and to check on the progress of those in the process of obtaining first and

[90] Interview with Howard K. Beale, 1956. The late Howard Beale was a "Y" instructor at the Illinois Steel Company in Chicago in 1918.

[91] *Harvester World*, vol. 5, November 1914, inside front cover.

second papers.[92] In order to facilitate filing procedures for naturalization, the committee arranged with the clerk of the Superior Court of Cook County to meet the applicant group in a body at a time and place so arranged as to prevent loss of wages. All this was done in the name of the community and country. "Although the [foremen's] club feels that... the work may be slow," said *Harvester World*, "yet it feels that it is demanded by the best interest of the city and the nation."[93]

Following this report, there was no further reference to Americanization activity until February 1917, but then news of Americanization work came often. During the war, other works besides the Weber plant sought to increase the number of citizens among their employees and "do their bit" for teaching immigrants English. The Keystone Works announced with great pride to readers of *Harvester World* that all but two of the Works' immigrants had become naturalized or had taken out their first papers.[94] Keystone had also established an English-language class in one of the offices to which immigrants came two evenings a week for one-and-a-half hours. Following classes, a mock naturalization court was conducted in the hope that applicants for citizenship could gain some experience with naturalization proceedings. According to a spokesman of Keystone, the following dialogue was typical of exchanges between the "judge" and the "applicant."

Teacher: Who was the first president of the United States?

Alien: George da Wash.

Teacher: Who is president now?

Alien: Mr. da Wils.

Teacher: Could you be president?

Alien: Excuse me please, I got pretty good job on the Keystone.[95]

By the summer of 1918, classes for English and citizenship had become characteristic of numerous branches of the International Harvester Company. This was particularly so in the Chicago area. Some of the factories there conducted classes themselves during two noon hours of the work week. At other units, the classes were handled by the YMCA. In St. Paul, the company had teachers come to the factory for twenty minutes during the noon hour.[96] The use of YMCA personnel in 1918 was explained by the *Harvester World*. It had been found that "when the YMCA conducted these classes the results were better than when English courses were part of the regular shop schools."[97] Special campaigns for naturalization similar to those begun by the Weber Works were now also conducted by other installations of the company. The Deering Works, for example, used the questionnaire method for determining the number of citizens among its workers and used its club-house facilities for issuing first papers.[98]

News about Americanization was usually printed in the safety and welfare section of the *Harvester World* and was often accompanied by pictures of employees surrounded with a maze of flags. A two-page spread showed special ceremonies using the various patriotic symbols. The journal printed pictures of work rooms bedecked with flags and

[92]*Ibid.*, vol. 7, May 1916, p. 30.
[93]*Loc. cit.*
[94]F. F. Trigg, "Keystone Works—100 Percent American," in *ibid.*, vol. 9, June 1918, p. 8.

[95]*Ibid.*, pp. 8-9.
[96]*Ibid.*, vol. 9, July 1918, p. 13; A. E. Conrath, International Harvester Company, St. Paul, Minnesota, in National Safety Council, *Proceedings, 1918*, pp. 582-583.
[97]*Harvester World*, vol. 9, July 1918, p. 13.
[98]*Loc. cit.*

often noted that most of the employees who had done the decorating were of foreign birth. Liberty-bond drives were publicized by reporting how this or that plant had gone "over the top" of its goal. The campaign of Herbert Hoover to conserve food was announced by a full-page spread that included a facsimile of the conservation pledge that was being distributed by the government. The *Harvester World* also reproduced pictures of plant honor boards dedicated to men in military service, and printed news about employees sending Christmas packages to the front.[99]

All these news items about war activity in the plants were in keeping with tactics found useful by house organ editors in attracting readers in the work force. The editor of the *Harvester World*, as well as editors of other company house organs, was trying to personalize the war effort as much as possible in order to inject another common denominator into the work force. By 1918, Americanization and other war activities had been linked together and formed "100% Americanism." House organ editors assumed that a worker's enthusiastic participation in "100% Americanism" would aid in producing harmonious relations within the shop and would stimulate production.[100]

The *Harvester World*, as did other company organs, also printed editorials and super-patriotic speeches in its campaign for "100% Americanism." An editorial in August 1918, for example, concerned itself with nominations of candidates seeking re-election to Congress. The journal insisted that only those men should be nominated who were loyal and patriotic. "If a weak or a bad man sits in the next Congress—a stupid man, a mere self seeker, or a shifty sneaking pacifist—" said the journal, "the blame will be on his district."[101] This political appeal may have been motivated in part by the fact that the controversial socialist, Victor Berger, was then seeking re-election from the Fifth Congressional District in Milwaukee, a city in which the International Harvester Company had an important plant.

It was from this plant, where English-language classes and naturalization exercises were not in operation, that the journal received a bombastic appeal for "100% Americanism." In September 1918, the *Harvester World* printed the speech to Milwaukee workers in which Paul Schryer, the superintendent, appealed to the plant's employees to go "over the top" in the fourth liberty-bond drive.[102]

To dramatize the appeal, Schryer's talk was preceded by flag-raising ceremonies, and the superintendent then built his address around the flag and the men at the front fighting in defense of the nation. He inferred that many in his work force had sided with the Central Powers before America had joined the conflict. "As I told the boys here last night...it is immaterial now as to who started the war. We are not going to take any time talking about that, but I am sure of one thing," shouted Schryer, "and that is, who is going to finish the war. There is but one answer — *America*." He pounded out the theme of the need for 100% participation in the bond drive. "I will be very much disappointed if I cannot call up our Chicago office...and re-

<hr>

[99]*Ibid.:* vol. 8, September 1917, pp. 5–7, 17, October 1917, pp. 12–13, 16, vol. 9, February, 1918, pp. 9, 11, March 1918, p. 10, July 1918, pp. 16–17.

[100]For a frank discussion by house organ editors of the methods they used, see "The Employee's Publication," round-table discussion in National Safety Council, *Proceedings, 1918*, pp. 409–430. See also *ibid.*, pp. 345–346.

[101]*Harvester World*, vol. 9, August 1918, p. 3.
[102]*Ibid.*, vol. 9, October 1918, p. 10.

port that Milwaukee Works' employees are not simply loyal but are absolutely 100 percent loyal." In closing his appeal, he reiterated part of a statement that he had made at the beginning. One employee recalled many years later that German and Hungarian workmen huddled in corners after the superintendent said this: "If there is one man in this organization who would hesitate to contribute to alleviate or lessen the suffering of... [the men at the front] I would advise him to go somewhere out on the prairie away from the gaze of civilization and drain the yellow blood out of his heart."[103]

For the *Harvester World*, the printing of Schryer's appeal marked the high point of its 100% Americanism. Following the end of hostilities, the journal reported on the continuation of Americanization classes in the various works of the company.[104] While the years of 1919 and 1920 brought a fresh impetus to such activities, the journal's tone changed rather drastically. In 1919, *Harvester World* printed and applauded statements about Americanization that criticized the aim and premise of 100% Americanism and editorially questioned the merits of militancy. It gave much publicity to its industrial council plan that, according to the house organ, would provide the "machinery for solving differences between management and labor and also give workers a share in the planning and execution of matters in their immediate interest."[105] International Harvester had

also embarked on a program that resulted in an industrial relations department and a broadening of existing industrial service work, and had joined the Inter-Racial Council of Frances Kellor.[106]

CONCLUSION

Harvester World's change in posture reflected changes in Miss Kellor's viewpoints and activities. With the end of the war, she had returned to non-governmental agencies in her efforts to link Americanization to "harmonizing efforts." The return of peace rapidly brought to an end the war-time agencies engaged in Americanization, and also saw the Bureau of Education withdraw from the field.[107] The only federal agency remaining in Americanization work was the Bureau of Naturalization and Immigration, and this Bureau was interested only in conducting work for immigrants through the public schools.[108] Her new organization became the Inter-Racial Council, a direct descendant of the Committee of Immigrants in America that had also disbanded with the end of the conflict.

The new group, founded in late November 1918, soon represented hundreds of industrial corporations with Miss Kellor serving as the chief executive officer. Until the depression of 1921 ended the Council's life, the group was preoccupied with the spector of Bolshevism and with the related problem of gaining a tighter grip on the industrial loyalties of immigrant workers;[109] this problem had been

---

[103]The writer had asked the employee, over 65 years old, what he remembered about the days of World War I. The first thing that came to his mind was Schryer's talk. Interview with A. F. Leidel, 1956.

[104]*Harvester World:* vol. 10, July 1919, pp. 8, 11, October 1919, p. 9, vol. 11, April 1920, p. 11.

[105]*Ibid.*, vol. 10, March 1919, p. 10; Cyrus McCormick, Jr., "Cooperation and Industrial Progress," address to the National Safety Council, *Proceedings, 1919*, pp. 40–50. This address was

reprinted in *Harvester World.* See also *ibid.*, vol. 10, August 1919, pp. 1–2.

[106]Cyrus McCormick, Jr., "The Advantages of a Superintendent of Labor," in *ibid.*, vol. 9, April 1918, p. 4; *ibid.*, inside front cover; *ibid.*, vol. 11, December 1920, p. 24; Hartman, *Movement to Americanize the Immigrant*, p. 220, n. 7.

[107]*Ibid.*, pp. 228–234.

[108]*Ibid.*, pp. 236–237.

[109]*Ibid.*, pp. 220–225; Higham, *Strangers in the Land*, p. 257.

accentuated by the Steel Strike of 1919. Miss Kellor's work became fully integrated with managerial efforts to systematize human relations in factories in the interests of industrial stability and harmony. She dropped the shrill tones of militant nationalism and turned to techniques of veiled coercion in order to convince immigrants not to act against the interests of their employers. Among her methods was the utilization of the immigrant press for achieving her ends diplomatically. She gained control of the American Association of Foreign Language Newspapers and was able to flood the immigrant press with "patriotic articles, admonitions against emigration to Europe, and anti-radical propaganda."[110]

It is "essential to develop in the foreign-language press a friendly interest in American affairs," she told the convention of the National Association of Manufacturers in 1920, "an attitude that is pro-American." "I believe it to be one of the best antidotes to Bolshevism, that when any thing good is being done in industry, the story of it should be told in the foreign-language press, so that these men get something besides attacks on capital. . . . We think it is one of the most practical ways of reaching these people and getting them interested in Americanism."[111] Frances Kellor, once a New Nationalist progressive, then a militant Americanizer, had now become a spokesman for the industrial relations of welfare capitalism, promoted through the power of corporations to impose "educational" programs on workers.

[110]*Ibid.*, pp. 257–258.

[111]Quoted in Hartman, *Movement to Americanize the Immigrant*, pp. 222–223.

LIBERAL PROGRESSIVES AND "NEW IMMIGRANTS": THE IMMIGRANTS' PROTECTIVE LEAGUE OF CHICAGO, 1908-1919

RIVKA LISSAK

At the turn of the century many native Americans regarded the so-called "new immigration" from eastern and southern Europe that began in the 1880s as the principal cause of their country's social, economic, and political problems. They attributed the situation to the differences in character, culture, and traditions between the "new immigrants" and native Americans. They were especially worried about these "new immigrants'" tendency to segregate themselves in ethnic-cultural enclaves, believing that this affected the newcomers' chances of becoming assimilated into American society. Native Americans responded to this situation in two main ways. In 1894 the New England "aristocracy" established the immigration Restriction League, which campaigned for the restriction of immigration. Within a decade other groups among the urban upper middle class began to sponsor voluntary and governmental agencies to cope with the so-called "immigrant situation." The Immigrants' Protective League, established in Chicago in 1908, was one of these agencies.[1]

Although efforts to work out a solution to the "immigrant situation" were not confined to Progressives, the latter played a leading role in shaping the policy of the voluntary and governmental agencies that dealt with this problem. While the Immigrants' Protective League adopted many programs similar to those of other voluntary and governmental agencies, it did not concern itself with the assimilation of the immigrant. Its leaders were convinced that the League differed from these agencies both in its basic objectives and in its attitude towards immigrants and their leaders.[2]

---

1 Barbara M. Solomon, *Ancestors and Immigrants: A Changing New England Tradition* (Cambridge, Mass., 1956); Edward E. Hartmann, *The Movement to Americanize the Immigrant* (New York, 1948), pp. 38–39, 50–57, 97; John Higham, *Strangers in the Land: Patterns of American Nativism, 1860–1925* (New Jersey, 1955), pp. 240–241; Reymond A. Mohl, "The International Institutes and Immigrant Education, 1910–1940," paper presented at the Duquesne University History Forum, 19 October 1978; New York State Department of Labor, *First Annual Report of the Bureau of Industries and Immigration, 1911* (Albany, New York 1912).

2 Hartmann, *The Movement to Americanize the Immigrant*, pp. 44–47, 61–63, 71–72, 88, 90–104, 111–128, 158; "The National Conference on Immigration and

League leaders explained these differences in approach as reflections of differences in ideology. They shared the Progressive consensus as to the general problems confronted by American society: the need to destroy the political machines, to extend the functions of government, and to strengthen its control by the people. They believed that these objectives could be attained within the framework of constitutional government and capitalism. However, the League leaders represented a liberal trend in the Progressive movement. The uniqueness of the liberal wing lay in its emphasis on a more socio-humanitarian conception of democracy, which meant taking into account the needs of *all* components of society: ensuring better opportunities for under-privileged groups through welfare and labor legislation, and adhering to liberal and democratic principles by accepting all nationalities and creeds without discrimination, with respect and tolerance. League leaders believed that these principles provided a sound basis for solving the immigrant problem and for establishing the immigrants' roles as equals in American society.[3]

This article examines the role the League's leaders wished to perform in the adjustment of "new immigrants" to the socio-economic and political system; their relations with the immigrant leadership; and their perception of the place the new immigrants should occupy in American society.

The League did not differ essentially from other voluntary organizations, Progressives included, in assigning a passive role to the new immigrants as such in American society. The differences, which should not be underes-timated, were in methods and attitudes rather than in goals. Liberal Progres-sives shared the native American consensus that the representatives of the host society should guide the immigrants' adjustment, though for different reasons. They rejected the right of the immigrant lower level leadership—the lower middle class small businessmen—to cultural brokerage and leader-ship. Liberal Progressives were willing, on the other hand, to cooperate with the emerging immigrant upper level leadership—middle class professionals and businessmen—upon the assumption that they shared a common value system and Progressive ideology. This approach reflected an elitist conception of

Americanization," *Immigrants in America Review* 2 (April 1916), 42–43; Grace Abbot, *The Immigrant and the Community* (New York, 1917), pp. 221–298; Immigrants Protective League, *Annual Reports, 1909–1917* (hereafter IPL).

3 Richard Hofstadter, *The Age of Reform: From Bryan to F.D.R.* (New York, 1955); Samuel P. Hays, *The Response of Industrialism; 1885–1914* (Chicago, 1957); Robert H. Wiebe, *The Search for Order, 1877–1920* (New York, 1967); Samuel P. Hays, "The Politics of Reform in Municipal Government in the Progressive Era," *Pacific Northwest Quarterly* 55 (October 1964), 157–169; Harold U. Faulkner, *The Quest for Social Justice, 1898–1914* (New York, 1931); Allen F. Davis, *Spearheads for Reform: The Social Settlements and the Progressive Movement, 1890–1914* (New York, 1967); Irwin Yellowitz, *Labor and the Pro-gressive Movement in New York State, 1897–1915* (Ithaca, New York, 1965).

the role of the so-called "better element" in American society, and the desire to reunify a segmented American society around the concept of a deferential society.[4]

The idea of establishing an Immigrants' Protective League in Chicago to protect new arrivals from exploitation and fraud, and to help them during their early years in the country, originated in the Hull House circle. The League's methods and programs were formulated during its early years both as an outgrowth of encounters with the immigrants' problems and as a reflection of the leaders' conception of American society and the immigrants' role within it.

Jane Addams raised the problem of the exploitation of "new immigrants" as early as December 1904:

> From the time they first make the acquaintance of the steamship agent in their own village, at least until a grandchild is born on the new soil, the immigrants are subjected to various processes of exploitation from purely commercial and self-seeking interests. It begins with the representatives of the trans-Atantic lines and their allies.... The exploitation continues under the employment agency ... the politician ... the petty lawyer ... the liquor dealers ... the lodging-house keepers and the landlords. It is a long, dreary road and the immigrant is successfully exploited at each turn.

However, she proposed no actual plan to cope with the problem. A concrete program to deal with immigrant problems was developed during this period by the staff of the Womens' Trade Union League of Chicago. In the course of dealing with the problems of female immigrants as industrial workers, this group became aware that newcomers were often subjected to personal exploitation and harassment during and after the voyage to America. Since the Womens' Trade Union League was not in a position to deal with this type of exploitation, Sophonisba P. Breckinridge, a Hull House resident, suggested that a volunteer organization be formed to cope with this and other types of exploitation of newcomers. Jane Addams assumed the responsibility of bringing about the realization of this idea. Making good use of her connections with Chicago's civic-minded elements, she aroused interest in the

---

4   "The cultural broker plays a crucial role in the definition and interpretation of immigrant and American cultures, as well as in promoting or discouraging a sense of ethnic solidarity." See Colin E. De'Ath and Peter Padbury, "Brokers and the Social Ecology of Minority Groups," in George L. Hicks and Philip E. Leis, eds., *Ethnic Encounters* (Belmont, California, 1977), pp. 181–200; Josef J. Barton, "Eastern and Southern Europeans, " in John Higham, ed., *Ethnic Leadership in America* (Baltimore, 1978), pp. 150–175. These studies deal with the terms cultural brokerage, and lower and upper level leadership.

project among a group of Progressives. The organization of the Immigrants'
Protective League followed in the spring of 1908.[5]

The Hull House circle continued to play an influencial role in the League.
Jane Addams served as second vice president, while the Board of Trustees
included several Hull House residents. One of these, Grace Abbott, a student
at the University of Chicago, was appointed director, and another, Sophonisba
P. Breckinridge, secretary. While Jane Addams's views on how new immigrants should fit into American society influenced the new organizations'
ideology, Grace Abbott and S.P. Breckinridge were largely responsible for
shaping and directing the activities of the Immigrants' Protective League.

Highly influential as well during the formative years were the first two
presidents of the League, Judge Julian W. Mack and Alexander A. Mc-
Cormick. A second generation German Jew, Mack became deeply involved
in social problems both through his judicial work and as a board member of
the Associated Hebrew Charities. McCormick was a journalist and a Progressive politician. Two members of the Executive Committee, Professors Ernst
Freund and George H. Mead of the University of Chicago, also contributed
significantly to the formulation of policy. Freund, who was on the faculty
of the University of Chicago School of Law, served as chairman of the
League's legislative committee, and was involved in drafting Progressive bills
presented before the Illinois legislature. G.H. Mead, an eminent philosopher
and social theorist, served as the League's first vice president and was also
chairman of the City Club of Chicago's committee on education. More conservative than the rest of the executive committee was the League's treasurer,
Charles L. Hutchinson, a prominent banker and leading figure in various
banking and civic organizations.[6]

5   Jane Addams, "Recent Immigration, A Field Neglected by the Scholar," *Educa-
    tional Review* 29 (March 1905), 247–249; IPL, *First Annual Report* (1909/10),
    4, 8; "Eleven years of Community Service," January 1920, p. 2, Box 60, Supple-
    ment II, IPL Records," University of Illinois; Edith Abbot, "Grace Abbot and
    Hull House: 1908–1921," *Social Service Review* 24 (1950), 374–376; Robert L.
    Buroker, "From Voluntary Association to Welfare State: The Illinois Immigrants
    Protective League, 1908–1926," *Journal of American History* 58 (December 1971),
    644–647; Henry B. Leonard, "The Immigrants Protective League of Chicago 1908–
    1921," *Journal of the Illinois State Historical Society* 56 (Autumn 1973), 272–273.
6   "Eleven Years of Community Service," pp. 9–10; Abbot, "Grace Abbot and Hull
    House," 374–376; Jane Addams, *Twenty Years of Hull House* (New York, 1910),
    p. 222; Buroker, "Voluntary Association," 273–274; Robert M. Barry, "A Man
    and a City: George Herbert Mead in Chicago," in Michael Novac, ed., *American
    Philosophy and the Future* (New York, 1968), pp. 173–174; Oscar Kraines, *The
    World and Ideas of Ernest Freund* (Alabama, 1974), pp. 1–60; 137–146; "In
    Memoriam—Illinois Merchants Trust Company," Charles L. Hutchinson Papers,
    Chicago Historical Society, hereafter CHS; "In Memoriam—The Caxton Club,"
    Charles L. Hutchinson Papers, CHS; *Book of Chicagoans* (Chicago, 1905), pp.

In general, the League's executive committee included more professional than business oriented members—unlike the executive committees of the majority of the city's civic organizations—being composed largely of lawyers, professors, settlement workers, and wives of philanthropic businessmen rather than of the upper middle class business elite. The members of the executive committee resembled the typical Chicago Progressive in being of white, Anglo-Saxon, Protestant, origin and not Chicago-born, though some "old immigrants," chiefly German Jews, were also represented. The League's board of trustees also differed markedly from those of other civic organizations in its ethnic composition, particularly in giving representation at all to "new immigrants," who made up about 40 percent of the board. And no less important, unlike other voluntary agencies, the League's staff was wholly composed of foreign-born social workers.[7]

Although the League was a "Progressive agency" in the sense that most of its leaders belonged to the Chicago Progressive elite, only about 25 percent of this elite was to be found on the membership list of the League. Among those were many of the city's famous Progressive leaders. They supported the League and procured for it the cooperation of the important civic clubs and organizations on issues related to the "immigration situation." Nevertheless, most of the burden rested with the League itself.

As defined in its charter, the League's objectives were:

> To apply the civic, social and philanthropic resources of the city to the needs of the foreigners in Chicago, to protect them from exploitation, to cooperate with federal, state and local authorities and with similar organizations in other localities, and to protect the rights of asylum in all proper cases.[8]

An examination of these objectives and of the activities developed by the League reveals that the League perceived itself as a civic-minded and humanitarian organization of enlightened citizens dedicated to helping newcomers to adjust to their environment and to become good American citizens. This was to be achieved by welcoming them on arrival to Chicago with friendship and sympathy, protecting them from exploitation and fraud, and

---

306, 357, 469; Frederick C. Jahar, *The Urban Establishment: Upper Strata in Boston, New York, Charleston, Chicago, Los Angeles* (Chicago, 1982), pp. 482–492; Harry Barnard, *The Forging of an American Jew: The Life and Times of Judge Julian W. Mack* (New York, 1974).

7   IPL, *First Annual Report* (1909/10), 40–43; IPL, *Fifth Annual Report* (1914), 18–28; IPL, *Seventh Annual Report* (1916), 21–29; Buroker, "Voluntary Association," 647–649; S.J. Diner, *A City and its Universities* (Chapel Hill, 1980), pp. 187–190.

8   IPL, *Ninth Annual Report* (1917), 2.

extending to them different kinds of personal services, thus showing them the "better side of America." By "adjustment," a term the League leaders preferred to "assimilation," they meant helping immigrants to function successfully within the American socio-economic and political systems and adapting American institutions to their needs. By helping newcomers to adjust to their new environment the League conceived giving direction and advice on employment, medical care, loan associations, and charity organizations. Unlike other American agencies the League proclaimed its objection to forced Americanization. The League made no attempt to force immigrants to give up their languages, customs, or culture. Learning English and acquiring knowledge of the country's laws, history, and system of government were viewed as instruments for better functioning in daily life. By also adapting American institutions to immigrants' needs, Liberal Progressives saw themselves as taking into consideration both the heterogeneous composition and the working class origin of the newcomers. League leaders prided themselves on their welfare program, on their foreign-born staff, and on the representation of immigrants on their board, viewing these as successful examples of such adaptation. Moreover, they prided themselves on their altruism, believing that their efforts on behalf of the immigrants, unlike those of some of the sectarian agencies, immigrant businessmen and ward bosses, were disinterested, since they were not tied to any material or political gain for themselves.[9]

In spite of its good intentions, the League failed to attract "new immigrants" to use its clearing-house services in any meaningful numbers. Out of about 400,000 immigrants arriving in Chicago during the years 1909–1919, only 25,000 or about 5 percent, took advantage of the League's services at its Bureau of Information and Social Service.[10] Among the circumstances that contributed to this failure were a limited budget totally dependent on contributions; the "new immigrants'" pattern of behavior toward American institutions during the critical years of initial adjustment; and, above all, the fact that the League's structural conception of division of functions between governmental and voluntary agencies under its auspices and its conception of the kinds of services that needed to be rendered to newcomers did not in

9   IPL, *First Annual Report* (1909/10), 5; IPL, *Fourth Annual Report* (1913), 3; IPL, *Sixth Annual Report* (1915), 3; IPL, *Eighth Annual Report* (1917), 3; Sophonisba P. Breckinridge, *New Homes for Old* (New York, 1921), pp. 123–230, 243–276, 280–286, 298–304; Ethel Bird, "Informal Discussion on the Value of the Foreign Language Worker," in the *National Conference of Social Work Proceedings* (1019), p. 746.

10 "Eleven Years of Community Services," pp. 6–7; Lewis W. Hill, *The People of Chicago Census Data on Foreign Born Stock and Race, 1837–1970* (Chicago: Report of the Department of Development and Planning, 1976). The League welcomed, according to its own statistics, some 80,000 immigrants at the Dearborn Railroad Station during the years 1909 to 1914.

practice answer the latters' needs, and were not adapted to their cultural norms.

Despite the relative ineffectuality of the League's services, it is worthwhile to concentrate on the League as a mirror of Liberal Progressive natures and intentions.

League leaders were well aware of the fact that in their effort to establish a system of services for newcomers they were not entering a vacuum. In fact, the immigrants' needs were already taken care of by relatives and friends, immigrant businessmen, employment agents, bankers, immigrant mutual benefit societies, religious institutions (chiefly Catholic and Jewish), ward bosses, and their precinct captains.

A careful analysis of the laws initiated by the League against exploitation and fraud, and the administrative system established by the League to help newcomers, prove the existence of additional primary objectives besides protecting newcomers and meeting their needs. One ulterior objective was to eliminate the network of private business services which immigrant small businessmen established for newcomers, the employment agencies of the padrones, the commissary system for room and board in the construction and railroad camps run by bosses, and the immigrant banks whose major function was to transmit money to the families of immigrants in Europe. Another ulterior objective was to create alternative welfare services to those established in immigrant neighborhoods by ward bosses, which distributed jobs and relief. In short, the League wished to transfer all the services given to newcomers to governmental and upper middle class agencies, and thus to put an end to the economic dependence of "new immigrants" on the small businessmen of their own groups, and on the political machines. The League fought against the influence and political control of immigrant small businessmen on the so-called "immigrant vote," and to eliminate their role as mediators between immigrants and the American socio-economic and political system, and as interpreters of American institutions.

The desire of the League's leaders to destroy these small businessmen was based on the assumption that an alliance existed between "new immigrant" small businessmen and ward bosses to manipulate the "immigrant vote" for their selfish interests. According to this assumption the padrones, the bosses and the bankers took advantage of the economic dependence of "new immigrants" on their services, and terrorized them, forcing them to give their votes in exchange for jobs and other services. These businessmen in turn sold these votes to ward bosses in exchange for personal financial and business benefits and political positions. They acted as mediators between immigrants and the party machines and thus gave corrupt politicians their political power. And above all, the League's leaders were alarmed that these corrupt businessmen were interpreting American democracy to the "new immigrants." Their role as cultural brokers precluded any chances of close contacts between "new immigrants" and the "better element" in American society. By perpetuating the immigrants' segregation beyond the reasonable period the League leaders believed newcomers needed for their adjustment, immigrant businessmen were establishing disciplined interest groups and securing their own political base as spokesmen of the immigrant blocs.

The League's leaders set out to release immigrants from the hold of these scoundrels, bringing the right notions of American democracy to the "new immigrants," and to gain the support of "the better element" in their efforts to eliminate the corrupt party machines and their allies, and to establish American politics on a sound basis, making America a better place to live in for both immigrants and native born.

The primary objective of the League was to create an alternative system of services to those given by immigrant businessmen and ward bosses. This included, as stated in the League's charter, a network of governmental and upper middle class voluntary agencies, with the League serving as a clearing house, rendering direct services only when not available from other agencies.

The bills for the amendment of the Employment Agency Law and for the reorganization of the State Free Employment Offices, introduced by the League before the Illinois General Assembly between 1909 and 1915, were intended to transfer the major function of the private employment agencies, namely, the distribution of unskilled labor, especially railroad and construction workers, to the State Employment Offices. Chicago did have private employment agencies which belonged to native Americans and "old immigrants." But because the unskilled immigrants from eastern and southern Europe did not speak English or preferred to be handled by their own countrymen, this kind of labor was either dealt with directly by "new immigrant" agents, or indirectly by American agencies using immigrant interpreters (or "bosses") who were paid by the employment agencies to accompany their countrymen to labor camps. Thus "new immigrant" agents and bosses—mostly Italians and Slavs—played a considerable role in the unskilled labor market. The League campaigned for the establishment of a Chicago branch of the Federal Bureau of Information, later called the Bureau of Distribution, concerned with interstate distribution of labor. It was instrumental in the opening of a City Employment Bureau, and was involved, between 1912 and 1917, in the efforts to enact a law for the abolishment of private banks in Illinois. The law included clauses which prohibited the transmitting of immigrants' savings abroad through immigrant banks, and abolished small private banks in immigrant neighborhoods altogether. The League supported the City Civil Service Law, which would transfer the distribution of municipal unskilled and temporary jobs to the Civil Service Commission, as a means of depriving ward bosses of their control. In its legislative efforts the League cooperated with upper middle class civic clubs and other Progressive organizations.[11]

Other instances of the League's strategy in fighting the exploitation of immigrants by private and ward agencies are revealing. The League's leaders negotiated with railroad corporations in an attempt to persuade them to regulate and even to take over the commissary system run by immigrant bosses in labor camps. The League's Bureau of Information and Social Service, in its capacity as a clearing house, directed clients to upper middle-class charitable organizations along with its recommendations to use city and state charitable institutions.[12]

The League sought to assume a leading role in the adjustment of new immigrants by becoming a clearing house for services to the newcomers. The League hoped to achieve this role by taking over control of newcomers on arrival to Chicago and by chanelling their distribution to agencies, according to their needs. A bureau was opened at the Dearborn Railroad Station to welcome newcomers and to direct them to use the League's headquarters for all their needs.[13]

The League gave several explanations to justify its effort to transfer the care of newcomers to governmental and upper middle class voluntary agencies under its direction. The League leaders maintained that it was the responsibility of city, state and federal government to help underprivileged groups. Surely, therefore, it was government's responsibility to protect its future citizens and help them during their first years in their new home. It was also the responsibility of disinterested, civic-minded citizens, namely the "better element," to contribute to the protection and advancement of their fellow citizens. Furthermore, the League believed that government control of services to immigrants, supplemented by voluntary agencies, would both improve the

---

11 IPL, *First Annual Report* (1909/10), 27–28; IPL, *Fourth Annual Report* (1913), 16–20; IPL, *Fifth Annual Report* (1914), 15–16; IPL, *Sixth Annual Report* (1915), 10–30; IPL, *Eighth Annual Report* (1917), 14–16; Abbot, "Grace Abbott and Hull House," pp. 384–385; Edith Abbott, "Grace Abbott, A Sister's Memories," *Social Service Review* 13 (September 1939), 359–374; Grace Abbott, "The Chicago Employment Agency and the Immigrant Workers," *American Journal of Sociology* 24 (November 1908), 289–305; William Dillingham, *Reports of the Immigration Commission* (Washington 1911), 37, 324; Edward Beekner, *A History of Labor Legislation* (Chicago 1929), pp. 398–418; Joseph B. Kingsbury, "The Merit System in Chicago from 1895–1915," *Public Personnel Studies* 13 (November 1925), 306–311, 4 (February 1926), 54–65, 4 (May 1926), 154–165, 4 (June 1926), 178–184; see note 18.

12 IPL, *Fourth Annual Report* (1913), 17, 21–22; IPL, *Fifth Annual Report* (1914), 16–17; IPL, *Sixth Annual Report* (1915), 20–21; IPL, *Seventh Annual Report* (1916), 18.

13 Abbot, "Sisters' Memories," pp. 365–367; Buroker, "Voluntary Association," pp. 643–660.

quality of the services rendered, and put an end to exploitation and fraud. And above all, only government agencies had the authority and resources needed to handle a comprehensive system of services to meet the "new immigrants'" various needs, and furnish honest, efficient, professional and disinterested services.[14]

Yet the alternatives the League was able to offer its clients to replace the services of the padrones, bosses, bankers, and ward agencies proved to be inadequate. The State Employment Offices did not deal with construction and railroad jobs, the major occupation available for unskilled immigrants. Contrary to its original intentions, the League drafted a bill in cooperation with the City Club of Chicago which included no provision for securing jobs for unskilled. The League dropped its position following a letter from David Ross, secretary of the Office of Commissioners of Labor of the State of Illinois, to the City Club, explaining that if the state employment agencies were to deal with railroad employment, the kind "new immigrants" needed, an increase in budget would be necessary to pay contractors for seasonal work and to hire interpreters and foremen. These expenses would require an increase in state expenditures and more taxes. The local Bureau of Distribution in Chicago suggested interstate jobs for unskilled in agriculture. Immigrants, however, showed little interest in these jobs, which were poorly paid. Furthermore, the Postal Savings Banks in immigrant neighborhoods, being substations, were not permitted to issue foreign money orders because they lacked the necessary knowledge in foreign exchange and postal technicalities. Moreover, the clerks in the State Employment Offices and the Postal Savings Banks did not speak foreign languages. And above all, these governmental agencies did not offer the other services furnished by padrones and bankers such as forwarding mail, writing letters for the illiterate, cashing checks, and acting as legal advisers and interpreters. Immigrant businessmen even furnished lodging and board at moderate cost and assisted in the management of their clients' property. These businesses were responsive to immigrants' needs in ways that American institutions were incapable of.[15]

14 IPL, *Seventh Annual Report* (1916), 19.
15 Beckner, *History of Labor*, pp. 398–418; City Club of Chicago, "Report of the Sub-Committee on Employment Agencies, 1908/09," vol. 3, City Club Records, CHS; City Club of Chicago, "Minutes of the Meeting of the Committee on Labor Conditions," 2 February 1909, vol. 3, City Club Records, CHS; David Ross, Secretary of the Office of the Commissioners of Labor, "Illinois Bureau of Labor Statistics to the Committee on Labor Conditions," 16 February 1911, vol. 5, City Club Records, CHS; City Club of Chicago, "Report of the Committee on Labor Conditions on the Facilities in Chicago for Furnishing Employment," 13 April 1911, vol. 5, City Club Records, CHS; *The City Club Bulletin* (Chicago), 4 (5 July 1911), 159–160; City Club of Chicago, "Minutes of the Meeting of the Committee on Labor Conditions," 8 April 1915, vol. 10, City Club Records, CHS; IPL,

The League's leaders were aware of the fact that the government agencies were not yet accustomed or adapted to provide such services, nor were the legislators and public officials convinced that these services were governmental responsibility. The League was, however, persistent in its belief that eventually government would have no choice but to respond to the newcomers' needs. The League never considered organizing such services on a permanent basis, although it ran a women's employment agency on an experimental basis for a year in 1909, and an emergency employment service on a limited scale during the two-year depression of 1914–1916. Thus immigrants' needs were sacrified, in the short run, to a long-term solution. The voluntary organizations, to whom the League directed its clients, did not meet the League's expectations. League leaders greatly criticized the methods used by these agencies and their attitudes towards their clients. The major criticism dealt with their lack of understanding of immigrants and their needs. Yet, in spite of the deficiencies of the agencies selected by the League, it preferred their services to those rendered by immigrant businessmen and ward bosses. They maintained that the voluntary organizations were at least directed by honest and disinterested volunteers, and employed efficient and professional social workers.[16]

Progressives attached great importance to disinterestedness and administrative efficiency. Honesty and personal ethics were given high priority. Yet moral ethics alone do not account for the persistence of the League's leaders in seeking to transfer the services for newcomers to agencies unable to perform their task. The League had another reason to explain its rejection of immigrant small businessmen, namely, the economic exploitation of their countrymen.

The League based its desire for depriving private employment agencies of their control of the distribution of unskilled labor on the grounds that these agencies were "interested only in the collection of fees, and not in so distributing labor as to serve the larger interest of the community." They were accused of charging fees varying from $1 to $14 dollars per man, when the registration fee fixed by an Illinois statute recommended $2; for charging employees for full train fare, when transportation was in fact free or available at reduced rates; for getting fees for jobs that did not exist; and many other kinds of fraud. As early as 1897, investigations held in Chicago by Liberal Progressives and federal authorities resulted in accusations that immigrant-owned employment agencies, especially Italian padrones dealing with railroad

---

Seventh Annual Report (1917), 15–16; New York State, *Report of the Commission of Immigration*, 1909, p. 27; Breckinridge, *New Homes for Old*, pp. 85–116; Dillingham, *Immigration Commission*, 37, 209–350; *The Jewish Courier*, 25 December 1911; *Forward*, 2 February 1919, 16 March 1919.
16 Jane Addams, *Democracy and Social Ethics* (Cambridge, Mass., 1902), pp. 13–70.

laborers, exploited their own countrymen. In a statement to the *Chicago Evening Post* in November 1897, Jane Addams and Graham Taylor, head residents of the two most famous settlement houses in Chicago, claimed that 90 percent of the Italian laborers (constituting the major unskilled labor force in Chicago) were under the "absolute control of padrones," in a state of "slavery," and "under terror of being blacklisted by the padrone." Padrones and bosses were also accused of supplying gang workers at construction camps with room and board of inferior quality at high prices.[17]

During 1913, as a consequence of the Chicago banking panic of 1912, the League staff surveyed the immigrant banking situation in the city, investigating 127 of the 200 immigrant banks the League located in the Chicago area. The investigators found most of the immigrant bankers to be "irresponsible and unreliable persons," noting that even those who were honest were inexperienced and unacquainted with banking procedures. They used the depositors' money in their own businesses, and, lacking the proper facilities, they conducted their banking business in grocery stores, drug stores, saloons, barber shops, and real estate offices. Since these banks were unincorporated and not subject to any regulation, their assets and liabilities were part of their owners' personal property and in case of failures, the depositors were not given any preference in the distribution of the bankers' property. Immigrant bankers were also accused of delaying or even failing to transmit money sent to immigrants' families abroad.[18]

17 Abbot, "Chicago Employment Agency," pp. 289–305; *The Evening Post (Chicago)*, 8 November 1897; Florence Kelley, "The Italians of Chicago, A Social and Economic Study," in the *9th Special Report of the Commissioner of Labor, United States Bureau of Labor* (Washington, 1897); "Italians in Chicago," *Bulletin of the Department of Labor, United States Bureau of Labor* 2 (1897), 691–727; Dillingham, *Immigration Commission*, 18, 331–343; Illinois Bureau of Labor Statistics, *Tenth Annual Report of the Free Employment Offices for the year ending September 30, 1908* (Springfield, 1909), pp. 76–84; Illinois Bureau of Labor Statistics, *Thirteenth Annual Report of the Free Employment Offices for the year ending September 30, 1911* (Springfield), 1912, pp. 91–111; Illinois Bureau of Labor Statistics, *Fourteenth Annual Report of the Free Employment Offices for the year ending September 30, 1912* (Springfield, 1913), pp. 100–121; City of Chicago, *Report of the Mayor's Commission on Unemployment* (Chicago, March 1914), pp. 48–75.

18 City of Chicago, *Journal of the Proceedings of the City Council of Chicago for the Council Year 1911/12* (Chicago, 1912), pp. 408–409, 690, 1477; City of Chicago, *Journal of the Proceedings of the City Council of Chicago for the Council year 1912/13* (Chicago, 1913), pp. 1811, 2036, 3367–3372; City of Chicago, *Journal of the Proceedings of the City Council of Chicago for the Council year 1914/15* (Chicago, 1915), pp. 182, 466, 486; City of Chicago, *Journal of the Proceedings of the City Council of Chicago for the year 1915/16* (Chicago, 1916), p. 1609; City of Chicago, *Journal of the Proceedings of the City Council of Chicago for the Council year 1916/17* (Chicago, 1917), pp. 2202–2207, 2810, 4402;

The preoccupation of native Americans in general, and Liberal Progressives in particular, with the "exploitation and fraud" of immigrants by their countrymen, can hardly be explained by the actual circumstances. The numerous investigations conducted on federal and state levels, and the large amount of literature published on the exploitation of immigrants by immigrant businessmen treated exploitation and fraud as a new phenomenon, which became possible because of the unscrupulousness of the "new immigrant" businessmen and because of the helplessness and ignorance of the unskilled "new immigrant" masses. This however was not strictly true.

If one distinguishes between facts and interpretations in contemporary studies, and takes into account the findings of recent studies, it turns out that the focus on "new immigrant" businessmen in this context was disproportionate. First, the system of labor distribution and immigrant banking established in the United States before the arrival of the "new immigration" was more or less unchanged since the 1880s, and had already exhibited its exploitative features. The only difference since then was in the composition of the labor force, reflecting the predominance of immigrants from southern and eastern Europe. Secondly, "new immigrant" businessmen were investigated far more rigorously than native American employers, because their exploitation seemed direct and open, while the exploitation by the American employer was indirect and latent. Native Americans and "old immigrants" were, however, at least equally responsible for the exploitation of newcomers. Thirdly, the relationship between immigrant businessmen and unskilled immigrants was misinterpreted by native Americans. In spite of some objectionable aspects, the padrones and bankers filled important functions, and were generally respected by the unskilled masses. Moreover, as the following facts reveal, the accusations of exploitation served as a cover for the League's

City of Chicago, *Journal of the Proceedings of the City Council of Chicago for the Council year 1917/18* (Chicago, 1918), pp. 272–273, 1164–1165; State of Illinois, *Journal of the House of Representatives of the 50th General Assembly, for the year 1917* (Springfield, 1917), pp. 85, 147, 198, 228–229, 247, 302–303, 636, 846, 916, 952, 1148; State of Illinois, *Journal of the Senate of the 50th General Assembly for the year 1917* (Springfield, 1917), pp. 430, 438, 531–532, 655, 798–799, 828–830, 842–843, 876–883, 897–901, 918, 920–921, 1237, 1295, 1304–1307, 1326–1329; State of Illinois, *Laws of the State of Illinois enacted by the 50th General Assembly, 1917* (Springfield, 1917), pp. 206–215; Jaher, *The Urban Establishment*, pp. 472–573; Joel A. Tarr, "J.R. Walsh of Chicago: A Case Study in Banking and Politics, 1881–1905," *Business History Review* 40 (1966), 451–466; R.G. Thomas, "Bank Failures in Chicago before 1925," *Illinois State Historical Society Journal* 28 (October 1935), 188–203; Frank C. James, *The Growth of the Chicago Banks* (New York, 1938), II, 824–866, 909–923; Frances Nurray Huston, *Financing an Empire: History of Banking in Illinois* (Chicago, 1926), I, 201, 208, 453, 551–587.

efforts to destroy the economic dependence of "new immigrants" on immigrant businessmen and ward bosses.

The major source of misunderstanding between unskilled immigrants and their padrones seems to have been the fact that there were no fixed rules on agency fees, railroad fares, etc. The workers did not understand that these were determined by the law of supply and demand, and by varying policies on the part of agents and railroads. As a result, immigrant laborers were often confused, and held the agents and bosses responsible for these continuous changes. Evidence gathered from public investigations in New York, Chicago and other cities, proved that the average fee for jobs that lasted a few months was three to five dollars. When the fee amounted to $10 to $14, they usually included railroad fares, which were $4 east and $6 west of the Missouri River. Moreover, Progressive critics of the system usually ignored the expenditures involved in this kind of business, such as interpreters, advertisements, office rent, etc. According to the testimony of Mr. Clapp of Clapp, Norstrom and Riley, a large agency, the expenditure for placing 15,000 laborers amounted to $7,200 a year. The expenditures of the State Free Employment Offices in Chicago, which handled 10,000 to 15,000 people a year, ranged between $8,000 to $10,000 during the years 1908–1912. A $2 fee scarcely met the agent's expenses. The failure of some voluntary societies to run free employment agencies indicated that both laborers and American employers preferred the services provided by private employment agencies, when given the choice. In spite of their deficiencies, private agencies were more efficient. But above all, the free employment agencies found it impossible to meet the expenses involved in the labor distribution business.[19]

19 John Koren, "The Padrone System and Padrone Banks," in *Bulletin of the Department of Labor* 2 (1897), 113–129; Frank J. Sheridan, "Italian, Slavic and Hungarian Unskilled Immigrant Laborers in the United States," *Bulletin of the Bureau of Labor, United States Bureau of Labor* 72 (1907), 403–486; Rudolph J. Vecoli, "Chicago's Italians Prior to World War I: A Study of their Social and Economic Adjustment" (unpublished Ph.D. dissertation, University of Wisconsin, 1962), pp. 235–278; Humbert S. Nelli, *The Italians in Chicago, 1880–1930* (New York, 1970), pp. 55–87; Edwin Fenton, *Immigrants and Unions: A Case Study: Italians and American Labor, 1870–1920* (New York, 1975), pp. 71–135; Robert F. Harney, "The Padrone and the Immigrant," *Canadian Review of American Studies* 5 (1974), 101–118; John S. Macdonald and Leatrice O. Macdonald, "Chain Migration, Ethnic Neighborhood Formation and Social Networks," *Milbank Memorial Fund Quarterly* 42 (January 1964), 82–97; Sharlene Herse-Biber, "The Ethnic Ghetto as Private Welfare," *Italian Americana* 3 (1976), 45–54; Victor Greene, "Becoming Americans: The Role of Ethnic Leaders—Swedes, Poles, Italians, Jews," in Melvin G. Helli and Peter d'A. Jones, eds., *The Ethnic Frontier: Essays in the History of Group Surcical in Chicago and Midwest* (Chicago, 1977), pp. 158–161; Breckinridge, *New Homes for Old*, pp. 118, 193; Charles B. Phipard, "The Philanthropist-Padrone, what is being done to raise the standard through competition

The situation was complicated, as recent studies about the relationship between the Italian padrones and Italian unskilled laborers have shown. Furthermore, the pattern of relationships and norms of behavior of one society cannot be interpreted in terms of those of another. If complaints are an indication of exploitation, the average of 1,000 complaints a year per 200,000 to 300,000 jobs comes to less than half a percent. Padrones and bosses were not as diabolical, nor Italian laborers as helpless and naive, as they were portrayed by Liberal Progressives. Some, no doubt, were unscrupulous, and many took advantage of the dependence of their countrymen in different ways. In that, however, they were no different from native American and "old immigrant" employers, contractors, and employment agents. Unlike the swindlers of diverse origins who appeared in immigrant colonies during periods of depression, collected fees for promised jobs, and disappeared, most padrones and bosses in Chicago were permanent residents of their immigrant communities. They lived there with their families, relatives, and friends who had come from the same villages in Italy, in relatively small, closely knit colonies. They would not have been able to survive community criticism and social ostracism, had they been engaged in continuous, large scale exploitation of their neighbors. The few who did run away after taking advantage of their countrymen's confidence in them prove that exploitation and fraud were not accepted or tolerated norms in Italian enclaves.[20]

State and federal commissions investigated the exploitative aspects of the

and example," *Survey* 12 (7 May 1904), 470–472; "Table of Complaints and Services for the year 1915," Folder 53, IPL Papers, University of Illinois; Robert F. Harney, "The Padrone System and Sojourners in the Canadian North, 1855–1920," in George E. Pozzetta, ed., *Pane e lavoro: The Italian American Working Class, Proceedings of the 11th Annual Conference of the American Italian Historical Association, 1978* (Toronto, 1980); Jane Addams, *Twenty Years at Hull House,* p. 207; Abraham Bisno, *Abraham Bisno: Union Pioneer* (Madison, Wisconsin, 1967), pp. 144–145; Earl R. Beckner, *History of Labor Legislation in Illinois,* pp. 153–155.

20 Frances A. Kellor, *Out of Work: A Study of Employment Agencies, their Treatment of the Unemployed, and their Influence upon Homes and Business* (New York, 1904); *Report of the Commission of Immigration of the State of New York,* 5 April 1909 (Albany, 1909); *Reports of the Industrial Commission on Immigration and on Education* (Washington, 1901), vol. XV; *Final Report of the Industrial Commission* (Washington, 1902), vol. XIX; Lillian D. Wald and Frances A. Kellor, "The Construction Camps of the People," *Survey* 23 (1 January 1910), 449–465; Frances A. Kellor, "Who is Responsible for the Immigrant," *Outlook* 106 (25 April 1914), 912–917; Koren, "The Padrone System and Padrone Banks," 113–129; Sheridan, "Italian, Slavs and Hungarian Unskilled," 403–486; Dillingham, *Reports of the Immigration Commission,* 42 vols.; Charlotte Erickson, *American Industry and the European Immigrants, 1860–1885* (Cambridge, Mass., 1957), pp. 70–93, 99–105. See note 24.

padrones and commissary system. But no commission even investigated the rates charged by American railroad corporations and contractors for room and board. Railroad corporations and American contractors charged $18 to $20 a month for room and board, which included three full meals a day. The monthly expenses for room and board, under the so-called "exploitative commissary system," was only $7, enabling Italian laborers to save an extra $11, and in all about $30 a month, for their families. Besides preferring their own Italian kitchen, Italian workers hoped to save more money by cooking for themselves. An Italian government study of camp conditions comparing camp food with food available in local villages in Italy, stated that the food eaten by Italian laborers in America was more abundant, varied, and rich. These facts put the accusations against the commissary system in a different light. Investigators were preoccupied with the rates and unnutritious food sold to immigrant workers by commissary bosses. They never raised the question of how families could have been expected to survive on the $15 to $17 a month left out of their total $35, had they used the alternative offered by American corporations and contractors.[21]

The League presented little evidence of complaints of fraud or bank failure against immigrant banks, and the English press in Chicago, controlled by Progressives, which gave a great deal of publicity to the private banking situation, mentioned only few "new immigrant" bankers. On the other hand, an American financial expert was of the opinion that "compared with the tens of millions of dollars entrusted to [immigrant bankers] the percentage that fails to reach its destination is infinitesimal." It seems that the involvement of the so-called "immigrant banks" in Chicago in the "bank crisis" in Illinois was negligible. Nevertheless, in its report for 1917, the League noted with great satisfaction that a private banking law had just been enacted by the General Assembly, and that "the private banking situation improved... many of the smaller banks which were such a source of exploitation to the immigrant have gone out of existence, and some of the

21 Grace Abbot, *The Immigrant and the Community*, pp. 26–54, 291–192; Abbott, "Employment Agency," pp. 289–305; Nelli, *Italians in Chicago*, pp. 55–67; Koren, "The Padrone System and Padrone Banks," pp. 113–129; Sheridan, "Italian, Slavs, and Hungarian Unskilled," pp. 403–486; IPL, *Fourth Annual Report* (1913), 17; Dillingham, *Reports of the Immigration Commission*, 18, 331–343; 37, 179–195; Wald and Kellor, "The Construction Camps of the People," pp. 449–469; Gino C. Speranza, "Handicaps in America," *Survey* 23 (10 January 1910), 465–472; Kellor, "Who is Responsible for the Immigrant," pp. 912–917; Luciano J. Iorizzo, "The Padrone and Immigrant Distribution," in Silvano M. Tomasi and Madeline H. Engel, eds., *The Italian Experience in the United States* (New York, 1917), pp. 52–58; Humbert S. Nelli, "The Padrone System: An Exchange of Letters," *Labor History* 17 (1976), 406–412.

larger private ones in immigrant neighborhoods have become state banks." [22]

What really bothered native Americans was less the exploitation and fraud suffered by helpless immigrants, than the role played by padrones, bosses and bankers in influencing the process of Americanization of immigrant laborers. While native Americans were preoccupied with Americanizing the immigrants, Liberal Progressives were primarily interested in transferring the functions performed by immigrant businessmen and ward bosses to government and voluntary agencies, as part of their social welfare and political reform programs. Their purpose was to eliminate the political influence of these businessmen on unskilled workers and their role in shaping the immigrants' notions of citizenship. As Jane Addams stated:

> The greatest evil of the system, and the one most to be feared by Americans, is the political influence of the padrones. In this direction they are a tremendous power. [23]

At stake was the political role played by these immigrant entrepreneurs in selling the votes of immigrant workers to ward bosses. Because they profited from their mediatory and broker role, these entrepreneurs were viewed by the Liberal Progressives as interested in perpetuating the immigrant's dependence on them through segregation. The imposition of honest and efficient dealing on the existing system by means of regulation would not in itself remedy the evil. The role of these businessmen had to be eliminated to allow other political views to be voiced, even though, as far as the immigrants' well-being went, the formers' services were better adapted to their countrymen's needs and mentality. This suggests that the Liberal Progressives' campaign for transferring employment distribution and banking services for immigrants to government agencies was motivated not only by their notion of government responsibility towards underprivileged groups and the desire to secure honesty, efficiency and professionalism, but also by their political reform program and by their desire to shape immigrants' adjustment to the American socio-economic and political system. [24]

22 IPL, *Fourth Annual Report* (1913), 17–20; IPL, *Sixth Annual Report* (1915), 10–12; IPL, *Eighth Annual Report* (1917), 8; IPL, *Ninth Annual Report* (1917), 19–20; Abbot, *The Immigrant and the Community*, pp. 81–94; Luciano John Iorizzo, "Italian Immigration and the Impact of the Padrone System" (Ph.D. Dissertation, University of Syracuse, 1966), pp. 100–160; Charles F. Speare, "What America Pays Europe for Immigrant Labor," *North American Review* 187 (January 1908), 106–116.

23 *The Evening Post* (Chicago), 9 November 1897; Addams, *Democracy and Social Ethics*, pp. 221–277; Abbott, *The Immigrant and the Community*, pp. 256, 264.

24 IPL, *Fourth Annual Report* (1913), 17; Vecoli, " "Chicago's Italians," 314–315, 319–338.

The other component in the "exploitation and fraud thesis" was the help-lessness and ignorance of the "new immigrant" masses. This was a favorite theme in Liberal Progressive writings. In spite of their being unquestionably less prejudiced and more sympathetic towards the "new immigrant" masses than other Progressives, the Liberal Progressive perception of immigrant helplessness reflected a belief in the newcomers' backwardness. Its underlying assumption was that these people were a bewildered mass, unable to care for themselves. Being helpless and without appropriate leadership, they needed the guidance of disinterested and well-intentioned leaders.[25]

Liberal Progressives wanted to assume for themselves, as the "better ele-ment" of the host society, the role of cultural brokerage and leadership. As President Mack noted in addressing this subject:

> He [the immigrant] arrives here bewildered, unacquainted with our language habits and customs, and a ready prey for the scoundrel. His entire future loyalty and patriotism to the country that is going to be his home may be seriously affected by his first contact with its men and women. Not merely as a matter of humanity towards the brother and sister in need, but as a matter of duty to ourselves and our own children is it important that the newcomers receive the best possible impression of those who are to be their fellow-citizens.[26]

The combination of these elements, the helplessness of newcomers, their exploitation by their own kind, the urgent need, for the sake of American society, to ensure that immigrants got the right notions as to the nature of their new country, and the role of the "better element" as representatives of the host society, constituted the main components of the League's Liberal Progressive ideology.

"Exploitation and fraud" was neither a new phenomenon nor were busi-nessmen from eastern and southern Europe more unscrupulous than American and "old immigrant" businessmen. Furthermore, "new immigrants" were not helpless so much as unacquainted with the new environment. Since both themes continued to be dealt with by native Americans in this unbalanced manner well into the twentieth century, even after many of the objectional features of the system had been reformed and "new immigrants" became better acquainted with the American environment, there must be an additional explanation besides prejudice and/or humanitarism for this preoccupation.

25 Jane Addams, "The Subjective Necessity for Social Settlements," in Jane Addams *et al., Philanthropy and Social Progress* (Boston, 1893), pp. 4–5, 16; Addams, *Democracy and Social Ethics,* pp. 221–278; Jane Addams, "The Chicago Settle-ments and Social Unrest," *Charities and the Commons* 20 (2 May 1908), 155–166.
26 IPL, *First Annual Report* (1909/10), 5.

The "exploitation and fraud thesis" in its relation to "new immigrants," was one of the responses of native Americans to the change in the ethnic composition of the immigration flowing into the country from the 1880s on, and to what they conceived to be its implications. Three different groups, pursuing different goals, developed this thesis: restrictionists, voluntary organizations dealing with immigrants, and Liberal Progressives.

Liberal Progressives had two issues in mind. First, by criticising the unscrupulousness of immigrant businessmen and pointing out the helplessness of the immigrant masses, they sought to persuade the American public and its representatives of the need to regulate private business and create a public welfare system. Second, and not less important, was the Liberal Progressive dilemma of how to justify the passive role assigned to new immigrants in their adjustment to American society, and how to justify the fact that their unbalanced attack against "new immigrant" small business had direct relation to the leadership and brokerage role of these businessmen in immigrant communities. They actually stood in the way of Liberal Progressives' claim for leadership, and control of immigrants as part of their claim for a leading role as the "better element" in American society.

These immigrant businessmen constituted the non-religious leadership which emerged in "new immigrant" colonies after the 1880s. The businessmen, padrones, bankers, grocery and saloon owners had arrived a few years earlier. They had started at the bottom of the socio-economic ladder and had succeeded in establishing themselves economically. Being better acquainted with the American environment, they were in a position to take advantage of the new opportunities created by the mass immigration from eastern and southern Europe. They performed an important and useful function for both American employers and the masses of unskilled workers. Being the owners of the few meeting places where newcomers could gather, these businessmen, of the same ethnic and social background as the newcomers they served, gave, in addition, information, advice, and personal help. They manipulated the resources of both parties' political machines to take care of their countrymen's needs. For the same purpose they initiated local self-help societies, the mutual benefit societies, to care for the health and other insurance needs of "new immigrants." It was only natural that they become presidents, secretaries and treasurers of these societies, and act as brokers between the ward boss and the members of ethnic groups who were unable to speak English. These very businessmen often got party and city jobs, because they were the naturally selected and recognized leaders of their communities. Some, it is true, took advantage of their positions for personal gain. Their moral standards and motivation had, however, nothing to do with the fact that they helped their countrymen to get jobs, relief and other kinds of help, and served as the representatives of their groups' interests. They performed an important role in the adjustment of their countrymen to the realities of the American working class environment.[27]

Settlement workers, who played a leading role in the League, were the first to draw attention to the social welfare functions performed by party machines, and to the alliance between ward bosses and immigrant business-men. They misinterpreted, however, both the relationship between newcomers and their padrones and the real motives behind the so-called "immigrant vote," although they admitted that both functioned quite effectively in furnishing jobs and relief to immigrants. The chief criticism by Liberal Progressives was directed at the source of the money and at the low ethical standards and dubious motivations of the people in these roles.[28]

Since the political machine was believed to control the "immigrant vote" through the immigrant lower level leadership, political reform leaders sought to manipulate the "immigrant vote." There were two ways to do this. One was through cooperation with immigrant leaders and recognition of their role, and the other was through elimination of the source of their influence and power. Imbued with Anglo-Saxon protestant ethics, Liberal Progressives considered motivations and intentions to be the ultimate criterion of a good deed. Therefore they must have found it hard to cooperate with what they saw as immoral leadership. The crux of the issue, however, was power and leadership, and the right to represent immigrant group interests. In their disguised and perhaps only half-conscious struggle for power against the indigenous immigrant brokers, they aimed to destroy their immigrant competitors.

27   Barton, "Eastern and Southern Europeans," pp. 150–175; Greene, "Becoming American," pp. 158–165; Breckinridge, *New Homes for Old*, pp. 108, 118, 124–229; Addams, *Democracy and Social Ethics*, pp. 231–233, 235, 248–250; Peter Roberts, *The New Immigration* (New York, 1912), pp. 63–77, 109–116; Nelli, *Italians in Chicago*, p. 63; Vecoli, "Chicago's Italians," pp. 259–261; Hesse-Bibber, "The Ethnic Ghetto as Private Welfare," pp. 9–14; MacDonald, "Chain Migration," pp. 82–93; Perry Duis, "The Saloon in a Changing Chicago," *Chicago History* 4 (1975/6), 219–220.

28   Addams, *Democracy and Social Ethics*, pp. 221–277; Ray S. Baker, "Hull House and the Ward Boss," *Outlook* 57 (28 March 1898), 769–771; Anne Firor Scott, "Saint Jane and the Ward Boss," *American Heritage* 12 (December 1960), 12–17, 94–99; Allen F. Davis, "Jane Addams vs. the Ward Boss," *Journal of the Illinois State Historical Society* 53 (Autumn 1960), 247–265; Jane Addams, "Why the Ward Boss Rules," *Outlook* 58 (2 April 1898), 879–882; Sonya Forthal, "Relief and Friendly Service by Political Precinct Leaders," *Social Service Review* 7 (December 1933), 616–618; Edward C. Banfield and James Q. Wilson, *City Politics* (Cambridge, Mass., 1966), pp. 115–121; Michael Johnston, *Political Corruption and Public Policy in America* (Monterey, California, 1982), pp. 36–57; Harold F. Gosnell, *Machine Politics, Chicago Model* (Chicago, 1937), pp. 69–125; Addams, *Democracy and Social Ethics*, pp. 221–277; Elmer E. Cornwell, Jr., "Bosses, Machines and Ethnic Groups," *Annals* 353 (May 1964), 27–37.

Liberal Progressives sought for a liberal-democratic rationalization and justification for their desire to replace the generally recognized leaders, and to assume their brokerage and leadership positions in immigrant communities. They rejected the notion, popular among native Americans, that as descendants of the founding fathers they had inherited the right to shape and control the country's character and destiny. They criticized this approach as undemocratic: "We cannot go on in this country and simply assume that the descendants of the same people are going to continue as a matter of course in control." The two underlying assumptions of the "exploitation and fraud" thesis—the unscrupulousness of immigrant leaders, and the helplessness of the immigrant masses—gave liberal Progressives their justification to denounce these immigrant leaders, and the rationalization that immigrant masses needed their help. They justified their undermining role by the accusation that this leadership had lost its right to lead by betraying its constituency, by its low moral standards, and by its pursuit of selfish material and political interests. It became the humanitarian, moral and civic duty of the "better element" to rescue helpless immigrants from their exploiters—to release them from their dependence on unworthy leaders, and to give them and America a chance for a better future.

The "exploitation and fraud" thesis was still only one component in the comprehensive Progressive conception of leadership, shared by Liberal Progressives. They conceived that influence and leadership in a democracy was to be determined by free competition, and "the best" should win. Those who wished to lead "have got to deserve the control if they are going to have it . . . no race should predominate except in so far as it has virtue and ability." Thus, the "better element" did not only feel it was its civic, moral and humanitarian responsibility to take upon themselves a leading role; they believed they deserved, by merit and virtue, the exclusive right and privilege of leadership.[29]

This approach was articulated in the Progressive concept of "merit and virtue." This conception they defined by class, culture and the necessities of survival; but in such a way as to make even the best-intentioned Liberal Progressives rivals of "new immigrants" in their struggle to survive in America. The conception of "merit and virtue" represented an elitist view of leadership colored by the moralistic background of this upper middle class, mostly Anglo-Saxon and Protestant. By "merit," Progressives meant that eligibility for public service—voluntary, administrative and elective—should be conditioned by proof of personal competence. This could be proved by success in business, by a distinguished career in the professions, or by a

---

29   IPL, Seventh Annual Report (1916), 26; Emily K. Abel, "The Educational Thought of Samuel Barnett," *Social Service Review* 31 (December 1978), 596–628.

combination of intellectual competency and personal qualities of character. These did not prevail among the lower classes because of the financial resources required for this kind of business or professional career, and because of the price of socialization and the education it involved. The most capable and ambitious newcomers needed about twenty to thirty years to achieve a middle-class status and to internalize its value system, while the majority had little chance for such mobility. Furthermore, "virtue" was interpreted as the pursuit of altruistic objectives for the common good of the whole society, in contrast to a narrow class or group vision of society and a desire for personal material or political gains. This attitude was influenced by the Protestant tradition and ethic of service. These criteria confined public service to the members of the middle class. Only the well-to-do could, during their service of the public, rely on family and/or business sources of income and thus be less dependent on the public treasury for their livelihood. They could afford, the reasoning went, not to pursue personal, narrow class or material gains, because they did not have to struggle for subsistence.[30]

The middle class was conceived by Progressives as the equilibrium force, the counterbalance between the upper class which had command of financial power, and the lower classes which had the mass of the vote. Being well-to-do, and occupying a middle position in the class structure, the members of the middle class could be, Progressives believed, less easily corrupted by graft and motivated by big business interests. Being in a position to consider the interests and needs of all components of society in a disinterested way, they represented the middle way in politics. This perception of the social and political function of the urban middle class reflected an adaptation of the Anglo-Saxon and American traditional view of the middle class as the backbone of society. This conception of the middle class role further strengthened the class orientation of Progressives. It also reflected the fact that Progressives and Liberal Progressives being molded in small-town and country communities, continued to think of themselves as middle class, namely "the

---

30 Emily K. Abel, "Middle-Class Culture for the Urban Poors,"; Paul C. Violas, Progressive Social Philosophy: Charles H. Cooley and Edward A. Ross," in Clarence J. Karier *et al.*, *Roots of Crisis: American Education in the Twentieth Century* (Chicago, 1955), pp. 40–65; Paul C. Violas, "Jane Addams and the New Liberalism," *ibid.*, pp. 81–83; Clarence J. Karier, "Liberal Ideology and the Quest for Orderly Change," *ibid.*, pp. 84–107; Hays, "The Politics of Reform," 157–169; Addams, "Subjective Necessity for Social Settlements," pp. 1–27; Dorothy G. Becker, "Social Welfare Leaders as Spokesmen for the Poor," *Social Casework* 49 (February 1968), 82–89; Davis, *Spearheads for Reform*, pp. 33–39; James Weinstein, *The Corporate Ideal in the Liberal State, 1900–1918* (Boston, 1968), pp. 16, 21.

people", and view American society as a middle class society. Both, however, were in need of redefinition at that time.[31]

The underlying assumption Progressives took for granted was the existence of a wide foundation of common interest and common welfare in American society, best interpreted and represented by the middle class. This assumption denied the eligibility of the lower classes for public service and leadership and also the legitimacy of immigrants for group representation. The members of the lower classes were ill-equipped for leadership. They lacked the middle-class value system which enabled its members to look beyond their personal, narrow and selfish interests to the good of the whole society. That Liberal Progressives denied immigrant groups legitimate right to political interest group representation is implicit in the criticism by Liberal Progressives of the ethics of Union leaders, although they recognized their right to represent the socio-economic needs of workers in industrial relations. But speaking on leadership in the broader sense, the lower classes, and "new immigrants" among them, were expected to have confidence in the altruistic nature and disinterested position in the social structure of the representatives of the so-called middle class, to protect them from exploitation and to care for their needs. They were, however, invited to cooperate "on equal terms." This represented the traditional American concept of deferential society.[32]

The Progressive concept of deferential society under the leadership of the middle class was also evident in the policy of another Progressive agency in Chicago, which Liberal Progressives strongly supported—the Chicago Municipal Voters' League. A sampling of the candidates for aldermen recommended by the Chicago Municipal Voters' League, an upper middle class civic organization, during the years 1896–1925, embodied the Progressive concept of class, virtue and merit. The favored candidate was a member of the middle class. The MVL supported middle class candidates in "new immigrant" neighborhoods as well. It even contributed money to the election campaigns of its recommended candidates.[33]

31 Abel, "Middle-Class Culture," pp. 611, 614–616; J.R. Pole, "Historians and the Problem of Early American Democracy," *American Historical Review* 67 (April 1962), 626–646.

32 Abel, "Middle Class Culture for the Urban Poor," pp. 615–616; Jane Addams, "The Settlement as a Factor in the Labor Movement," in Jane Addams *et al.*, *Hull House Maps and Papers* (Boston, 1895), pp. 183–206; Jane Addams, "Trade Unions and Public Duty," *American Journal of Sociology* 2 (January 1899), 488–462; Weinstein, *The Corporate Ideal in the Liberal State 1900–1918*, pp. 18–21; Jane Addams, "The Present Crisis in Trade-Union Morals," *North American Review* 179 (August 1904), 178–193; Addams, *Democracy and Social Ethics*, pp. 137–177.

33 Joan B. Miller, "The Politics of Municipal Reform in Chicago during the Progressive Era: The Municipal Voters' League as a Test Case, 1896–1920" (unpublished Masters Dissertation, Roosevelt University, 1966), pp. 23–30; Lists of aldermen, in

Similarly, the League, supported by the same Chicago upper middle class constituency, totally rejected immigrant leaders of lower and lower middle class, as leaders representing personal or narrow group interests. On the other hand, the League invited "new immigrants," middle class people, mostly professionals, to serve as members of its board of trustees. These professional and businessmen established federated fraternal organizations and welfare agencies and constituted the upper-level leadership of immigrant groups. The Leagues leaders assumed that by the time these leaders achieved middle-class status, they would be already better acquainted with American institutions and inculcated with the middle-class value system and point of view, thus being able to look beyond their personal and group interests to see the good of the whole. They were accepted by Liberal Progressives upon the underlying assumption that they shared the Progressive ideology, and that they accepted their secondary position in this relationship.[34]

League leaders belonged to the upper middle class of an emerging urban society. As members of this elite, they had a vested interest in ensuring the stability of the social and economic order, and their leading role in society, although their cultural moralistic upbringing made it impossible for them to admit this, even to themselves. Immigration, or the "immigrant situation," along with the closely connected industrialism and urbanism, were three forces that endangered stability. League leaders undertook to deal with the "immigrant situation," in order to dissolve this source of tension and danger to the new order along Progressive lines and humanitarian and Liberal principles.[35]

As to the broader implication of the Liberal Progressive ideology on the

the *Journals of the Proceedings of the City Council of Chicago* for the years 1896–1925; Chicago Municipal Voters' League. "Official Records of Aldermen for the years 1896–1925," Municipal Voters' League Papers, hereafter MVL, CHS; Municipal voters' League, "Minutes of the Executive Committee," 20 February 1905, 27 February 1908, 25 February 1910, MVL Papers.

34 IPL, lists of members of the Board of Trustees, 1909/10–1918; For biographies of the new immigrant members of the Board of Trustees: A.N. Marquis, *The Book of Chicagoans* (1st edn. 1905; 2nd edn. 1911; 3rd edn. 1917); *The Chicago City Directory* for the years 1908–1920; Francis Boleck, ed., *Who is Who in Polish America* (New York, 1943); David Droba, ed., *Czeck and Slovak Leaders in Metropolitan Areas* (Chicago, 1931); Barton, "Eastern and Southern Europeans," pp. 150–175.

35 Hays, "The Politics of Reforms," pp. 157–169; Diner, *A City and its Universities,* pp. 187–207; Jahar, *The Urban Establishment,* pp. 472–552; Miller, "The Politics of Municipal Reform in Chicago during the Progressive Era: The Municipal Voters' League as a Test Case, 1896–1920," pp. 23–30; Sidney I. Roberts, "Chicago Civic Profiles: The Businessman as Reformer," *Men and Events, Union League Club Bulletin* 3 (September-October, 1957), 22–24, 31–32; Buroker, "Voluntary Association," pp. 649–652; Weinstein, *The Corporate Ideal,* pp. 3, 7.

role of immigrants in American society, the conclusion to be drawn from the examination of the League's activities and rhetoric, and its rejection of the lower level leadership, is that Liberal Progressives assigned a passive role to new immigrants as such in American society. New immigrants had special needs but did not consist of distinct interest groups. Liberal Progressives thought in terms of the common public interest and not of a system of "balance of interests," or pluralism. They recognized the special needs of immigrant individuals, and their right to form voluntary associations to pursue their needs. They opposed, however, group representation in politics, rejecting ethnic or class origin as narrow interests.

This emphasis on the public interest as opposed to class and ethnic interests, and the middle class as the disinterested and true representative of the public interest, was a fundamental component of the Liberal Progressives' vision of American society, as a unified organism whose different parts cooperate in harmony led of course by the "better element." Identifying the crisis of American society as a problem of segmentation and social disorganization caused by urbanization, industrialization and immigration, Liberal Progressives sought to reconstruct the fragmented social organism through cooperation between the fragmented parts of society upon the principle of mutual dependence and common interest, through breaking down class and ethnic barriers, and social reform under an enlightened leadership.[36]

Liberal Progressives envisioned a harmonized, holistic society that would unify the members of American society, natives and newcomers, upon an individual base. This implied the notion of assimilation of newcomers into American society.

36 Johnston, *Political Corruption and Public Policy*, pp. 51–52; Jane Addams, "The Subjective Necessity for Social Settlements," pp. 1–26; Banfield and Wilson, *City Politics*, pp. 127–140; Daniel J. Elazar, *American Federalism: A View from the States* (New York, 1972), pp. 96–99; Harry P. Kraus, *The Settlement House Movement in New York City, 1886–1914* (New York, 1980), pp. 1–45; Barry, "A Man and a City," pp. 173–192; Weinstein, *The Corporate Ideal*, pp. 3, 7.

Myth and Reality: The Pattern of Relationship between the Hull House Circle and the "New Immigrants" on Chicago's West Side, 1890–1919

RIVKA LISSAK

THE SETTLEMENT HOUSE MOVEMENT was established at the end of the nineteenth century in the slums of America's cities by groups of men and women drawn from the middle and upper classes. They chose to live among the working class, undertook systematic studies of the social problems encountered and sought to carry out the proposed solutions. They saw the solution of the problems of the working class as an integral part of a comprehensive reform program affecting all spheres of life. They soon discovered, however, that the working class consisted mostly of immigrants, and that the newest amongst them, who came from eastern and southern Europe, had to adjust to a new environment and country, apart from their problems as industrial workers. Since the settlement workers considered improving the lot of the working class as vital to the reconstruction of American society, their views on the "new immigrants" and that group's adjustment to the American environment shaped settlement attitudes towards the working class. These concerns determined the methods they used and the programs they urged upon the different levels of government.

Differences of opinion existed within the Settlement House movement on such issues as the attitude towards the immigrants and their cultures, the ways in dealing with their problems, and the role they were to play in American society. The two main attitudes were formulated by Robert A. Woods of South End House in Boston and by Jane Addams of Hull House in Chicago.

Robert A. Woods was an active member of the Immigration Restriction League, which was involved in racist propaganda against "new immigrants." His own settlement devoted much of its time and energy in studying the immigrant situation, and its publications contributed to the strengthening of the negative image of the "new immigrant" groups. Woods and his colleagues adopted rigid standards towards the qualities of immigrant groups. Although they explained these qualities in terms of social and cultural backwardness rather than in terms of heredity and race inferiority, they were of the opinion that the process of remolding and re-educating "new immigrants" according to the Anglo-Saxon model had been very slow, and was becoming impossible because of the great numbers of immigrants coming into the country. Woods complained that certain settlement houses "become more or less assimilated to standards of the immigrant group or groups about it . . . . Occasional residents take on the more showy personal qualities of certain European types, adopt less rigid standards with respect to personal relations than those of our own country, and incline toward an internationalism based on indiscriminate mixture of peoples."[1]

American historians have formulated two different approaches towards Jane Addams and her attitude towards the "new immigrants" and their role in American society. One group praised her as unique in her sympathy for the immigrants. She was, they argue, among the few who succeeded in transcending her upper class biases towards the "new immigrants." They emphasize her special relationship with them, her sympathetic formulation of the immigrant problem and proposed solutions to their difficulties, and her courage in defending them. She belonged, they say, to a small group of Americans who accepted the immigrants as their equals, respected their cultures and defended their right to preserve and foster their ethnic traditions. They disagree, however, on whether she adopted a cosmopolitan or a cultural pluralist conception of American society.[2] The second group of historians uncovered prejudice and a sense of superiority in her writings on "new immigrants." They reject the idea that she had a pluralist conception of American society and hold that her views conformed wit the current notions of Americanization and assimilation.[3]

Among her contemporaries, Jane Addams' settlement work was considered unique. She was chosen in various magazine polls as the most popular woman in the United States. One of the reasons for her popularity was her devotion to the "new immigrants'" cause, as it was envisioned in the public eye. Jane Addams was looked upon as an American Saint, a Joan of Arc. Her contemporaries pointed at her as the representative of the whole movement in shaping its liberal and humanitarian attitude towards "new immigrants," and her creation, Hull House, as the model institution where immigrants were understood and helped to adjust to American society and where their cultural contributions were appreciated and even encouraged.[4]

However, those who honored her belonged to the upper and middle classes. What was her image among the "new immigrants" in Hull House's neighborhood, and what were the actual relations between Hull House and the colonies of "new immigrants" on Chicago's West Side? What was their response to her suggestions on how to deal with their economic, social, political and cultural problems of adjustment, and what was the policy of Hull House towards the immigrants' cultures? Briefly, what was the reality behind the myth and ideology that were created around this most influential woman?

Historians have based their approaches mainly on the Jane Addams writings, occasionally using Hull House Bulletins and Year Books. This study of Jane Addams probes beyond her writings to the immigrant sources, making use of data in the Hull House Bulletins and Year Books largely overlooked by other historians, in a search for the actual relationship between Hull House as a social center and the colonies of Russian-Jews, Italians and Greeks on Chicago's West Side.

Hull House, one of the first settlement houses in the United States, was established in September 1889 in an immigrant neighborhood on Chicago's West Side by Jane Addams and Ellen G. Starr, two upper class women. When it first opened its doors as a social and cultural center, the neighborhood was in a state of transformation. Its old residents, native-born Americans, Irish and Germans, were being replaced by new residents, "new immigrants," mainly Italians, Russian-Jews and Greeks.[5]

During the first decade of its existence, those who participated in Hull House activities were principally native-born Americans and "old immigrants"—Irish and Germans—who were English speaking and belonged to the upper level of the working class and the lower middle class. Many of them had already moved out of the neighborhood and while the younger children stopped participating in Hull House activities, a number of the older children and adults continued to visit Hull House. "New immigrants" formed a small minority of the Hull House clientele in those days, although they comprised a considerable part of the neighborhood's population. The Italian and Russian-Jewish groups were as large as the Irish and the native-born Americans. Yet, the number of Italians who visited Hull House was negligible; significantly, they belonged to the small Italian intelligentsia. Greeks did not attend Hull House at all, and only small numbers of German-Jews and Russian-Jews participated in Hull House activities. Towards the turn of the century, however, the number of Russian-Jews participating in Hull House activities rose until they became the largest ethnic group at Hull House by 1906/07. This was evident by the number of Russian-Jewish children at the boys' club, the dramatic clubs, and the college extension courses, as well as by the youth clubs' statistics. Immigrant sources confirm this evidence. That year marked the turning point in the ethnic composition of Hull House; from then on "new immigrants" became the majority. The number of Italians grew steadily, and Greeks began to visit Hull House at that time too, while the number of Russian-Jews began to decrease around 1908. By the second decade of the century, Italians replaced the Jews as the largest ethnic group. In the twenties, Hull House was an "Italian Institution" in the sense that the majority of its participants were Italian.[6]

An analysis of the curve of the graph of "new immigrant" participation in Hull House activities and its composition reveals a significant difference in the pattern of relationship between Hull House and its Russian-Jewish, Italian and Greek neighbors.

Jewish immigrants from Eastern Europe began to flow into Chicago from the 1870s on. A Jewish ghetto was gradually established on Chicago's West Side, whose population in the immediate neighborhood of Hull House amounted to about six thousand at the beginning of the twentieth century and grew to more than fourteen thousand by 1914.[7]

Jewish adults rarely visited Hull House. They organized typically immigrant institutions: Orthodox congregations, fraternal orders, landsmanshaftn, and literary, radical and Zionist societies. Within these institutions they developed an active Jewish social, cultural and ideological life. In addition, welfare institutions, two Yiddish theatres and Hebrew and Yiddish newspapers provided an outlet for their social and cultural needs.[8] The younger generation started participating in Hull House activities around the middle of the nineties. Their number grew to a few hundred at the turn of the century when they comprised about a third of Hull House club membership, becoming the largest ethnic group. In 1906/07 they numbered about a thousand, but their proportion decreased afterwards to one-fourth, and it continued to dwindle until they became a small minority during the second decade.[9] Hull House did not encourage the Russian-Jewish youngsters to preserve or cultivate their Jewish culture in separate Jewish clubs. Since the Jewish group preferred educational and cultural programs, they chose those clubs which emphasized such programs. Within a short time, Jews became a majority in the debating and literary clubs. Hull House did not initiate Jewish programs during its first fifteen years. Only on two occasions, in 1906 and 1913, did Hull House sponsor Jewish cultural events. No real effort was ever made in Hull House to encourage programs with Jewish cultural content.[10]

Hull House's influence among the Jewish younger generation on the West Side remained minimal. Jewish members of the Settlement formed a small proportion of their generation. More importantly, those who did attend Hull House had no influence in the Jewish ghetto. The majority of Jewish youngsters preferred to establish independent political and social clubs and societies of two kinds: the Jewish East European and the American types. Young people whose personality was molded in Eastern Europe preferred societies of Jewish ethnic composition and content, such as the Hebrew Literary Society established in 1893 and the Chicago Zionist Society organized in 1895. The Jewish Workingmans' Educational Club, established in 1887 and the Lassale Political Club, organized a few years later, were social and intellectual centers which attracted East European Jewish radicals just as the two former were social and intellectual centers for Jewish Maskilim (lay Jewish scholars) and Zionists of East European origin. There were, however, Jewish youngsters who were influenced by the Americanization process and were not attracted to the East European types of societies. Many also rejected American institutions like Hull House, accusing them of a patronizing attitude. In 1894, for example, they established the Self Educational Club which was Jewish in its ethnic composition but modelled after Hull House. This club concentrated on teaching English and American history to young Jewish immigrants and provided social and cultural programs of the American type. The Jewish youngsters who went to Hull House were also influenced by the Americanization process. Some of them even alienated themselves from Judaism and turned towards American institutions with their mixed ethnic composition and American ethos. Others were attracted to Hull House because of its better facilities for educational and cultural programs.[11]

A group of Jewish Maskilim and Zionists came to the conclusion that these various alternatives met neither the needs of the American-Jewish generation growing up in Chicago, nor the needs of the Jewish group as an ethnic entity. The search for a suitable sociocultural framework resulted in the establishment of the Chicago Hebrew Institute (a Jewish community center) at the end of 1903 by Zionist initiative supported by the orthodox leadership and the Russian-Jewish community as a whole. The purpose of this Institute was to furnish the American-Jewish younger generation with a social and cultural center to preserve and foster Jewish culture and identity along with American identity. In other words, to develop and cultivate an American-Jewish ethnic and cultural identity. The Chicago Hebrew Institute (CHI) struggled for survival during the first years of existence because it lacked financial resources. The Institute began to prosper from 1907 on, only after purchasing its new quarters on Blue Island Avenue—not far from Hull House—with German-Jewish support. The year the Institute moved to its new quarters coincided with the period the Jewish group at Hull House reached its peak and began to decrease afterwards. As the Institute grew in number, so did the percentage of Jews decrease at Hull House. The Institute's weekly visitors increased from 11,368 in 1910 to 16,363 in 1912, while Hull House visitors, Jewish and non-Jewish, amounted to 9,000 a week.[12]

Young Jews went to Hull House in considerable numbers as long as no Jewish social center existed which was able to meet their needs as Americans, and compete with the Settlement's facilities and educational and cultural opportunities. After the establishment of such a Jewish Institute, the Jewish youngsters who continued to participate in Hull House activities were those whose Americanization and/or alienation from Judaism predominated.

The Chicago Hebrew Institute was modelled after Hull House in many of its features. It was, however, not established as a social center alongside Hull House, but as a substitute as far as the American-Jewish youth was concerned. The Institute offered the Jewish young generation sports, social, dramatic and literary clubs, art and craft classes, a playground, and courses in humanities and in social, political and natural sciences. It sponsored concerts, lectures, art exhibitions and other cultural programs, and opened some social welfare services.[13] The Jewish immigrants received instruction in English and civics; and the Institute also opened a Naturalization Advisory Bureau, an elementary and secondary evening school, and a trade school to help immigrants overcome handicaps in adjusting to the American environment. The Institute stressed educating new immigrants in good citizenship by teaching them American ideas and traditions and celebrating national holidays.[14]

The uniqueness of the Institute, however, lay in its emphasis on teaching Jewish values, culture and traditions and developing a Jewish ethnic-national identity. This was achieved by conducting a modern synagogue whose prayer languages were Hebrew and English, by celebrating all Jewish religious and national holidays, by lecturing on Jewish topics, sponsoring concerts of Jewish music, organizing exhibitions of Jewish art and Jewish artists, and encouraging dramatic clubs to perform Jewish plays in Hebrew, Yiddish and English. In October 1917, the Institute initiated the Hebrew Oratorio Society whose purpose was "to cultivate, develop and produce Jewish music in all its branches, extending from ancient to modern times." The Institute was determined to revive Jewish education by opening a Sabbath and Hebrew School in which progressive teaching methods were used. The Sabbath School taught religion and the Hebrew School taught the Hebrew language, Jewish history and Judaism. In the report of the Institute for the year 1913/14, the typical pupil of the Hebrew School was described as "a most desirable type of the Jewish-American body. Conscious of the great past of his nation, of the glorious contribution of his people to civilization, he makes a proud Jew, and a good American citizen."[15] The halls and rooms of the Institute became the meeting place of various Russian-Jewish societies and organizations, conferences, mass meetings and other events. Many of the West Side literary, dramatic and social clubs, relief societies, landsmanshaftn and Socialist and Zionist groups met regularly at the Institute, and it became the community center of the East European Jews of the West Side.[16] The fact that a considerable portion of American-Jewish youth preferred the Chicago Hebrew Institute over Hull House proved that they found in the Institute a more suitable synthesis between the Americanization process, and a growing ethnic consciousness and identity, which was strengthened by anti-Semitism, intolerance towards the Jews in Chicago, and the establishment of the Zionist movement.

The pogroms in Russia, the rise of anti-Semitism in Chicago and elsewhere combined with the yearning for a sense of belonging in an American society from which they were alienated, and the news of Theodor Herzl's new gospel of modern Zionism fostered Jewish awareness and a sense of national-ethnic identity among Russian-Jewish immigrants and even in the younger generation on the West Side. The strengthened sense of Jewish identity was expressed in mass meetings held in the ghetto during the Dreyfus affair and the Russian pogroms, and when the news of Herzl's death reached Chicago. The Jews on the West Side were the victims of many anti-Semitic incidents: attacks on synagogues, on Jewish families in their homes, and on Jewish peddlers on the streets, as well as discrimination in educational institutions and jobs.

The younger generation responded by establishing defense societies such as the Self Defense League. Students at the University of Chicago and graduates of the Jewish Training School (established on the West Side by Reform Jews to Americanize Russian-Jewish children), formed societies to study Judaism. Other groups of Jewish youngsters joined the Order of the Knights of Zion—the Chicago Zionist organization. About a third of the active members of the Order were born or/and educated in the United States.[17] The Zionist Movement on the West Side spurred a religious awakening and an educational revival. Many young people who had drifted away from Judaism were won back and began to take an interest in Jewish subjects. The educational revival sponsored by Zionists in the ghetto, through remolding the curriculum of Jewish educational institutes and replacing the old type teachers with more qualified ones, culminated in the establishment of the Jewish Board of Education in 1912. The influence of Zionists on the curriculum of the Sabbath and Hebrew Schools on the West Side during the first decade of the twentieth century should not be underestimated, nor the effect of their ideas considering the fact that about two-thirds of the nine thousand Jewish children between the ages of six and fourteen received some Jewish education at the beginning of the century. Due to the efforts of Zionists, the Chicago Board of Education voted in April 1912, for the introduction of Hebrew and Yiddish into public high schools in Jewish neighborhoods. Another achievement was the naming of a public school after Herzl. An attempt to name a street after him failed, however. One of the strongest expressions of Jewish ethnic-national feelings was the mobilization of West Side Jewry's financial resources for the project "Bread for Palestine" sponsored by Zionists after the outbreak of World War I. Ethnic-national feelings among the Jewish younger generation were expressed by joining Zionist youth movements. During World War I, the three Zionist youth movements—Young Maccabees, Young Judea and Hamizrahi—numbered about two thousand boys and girls.[18] The growing prestige of Zionism in Chicago in those days can be ascertained through the attitude of public non-Jewish authorities towards the Knights of Zion. As early as 1904, the Mayor of Chicago sent his Public Prosecutor to represent him at the Zionist Annual Convention. In 1915, the Governor of Illinois addressed the Zionist Annual Convention.[19]

While ethnic-national consciousness and identity began to play a major role among "new immigrant" groups in Chicago and in America around the outbreak of World War I, this process was anticipated in the Jewish ghetto on Chicago's West Side about a decade earlier.

Contrary to Jane Addams' view of immigrant leadership as being helpless and in need of guidance and leadership from Hull House, the Russian-Jewish community on the West Side did have able leaders. These leaders created real Jewish communal life, established welfare and cultural institutions and proved their leadership qualities by dealing effectively with the problems of civic rights, anti-Semitism, and immigration restriction. They neither requested nor received guidance or patronage from Hull House or any other source. Jewish leaders, however, cooperated with Hull House on several occasions: the "Averbuch Affair" and the "Radowitz Affair" in 1908, and the "Beilis Affair" in 1913. Averbuch, a Russian-Jew was shot to death by Chicago's Police Chief in 1908. The police's statement on the case justified the killing, accusing Averbuch of being an anarchist who came to the home of the Chief of Police to assassinate him as part of an anarchist conspiracy. The affair was widely discussed in the American press and resulted in public hysteria against immigrants in general, and East European Jews in particular. Jane Addams described Hull House's role in the "Averbuch Affair" in terms of "coming to the rescue" of helpless foreigners who came to Hull House "in the moment of their perplexity and distress." However, an examination of the data gives quite a different version of the role played by Hull House and the Russian-Jewish leaders during this affair. The Jewish leaders were neither helpless nor perplexed. When considering the attitude of the American public and officials towards immigrants, they preferred to play a behind the scenes role, asking Jane Addams only to do the lobbying for them. They acted along the same lines in the "Beilis Affair." Beilis was a Russian-Jew put on trial by the old imperial Russian government in 1913 on the false accusation of blood libel. The Russian-Jewish community of Chicago cooperated with the German-Jewish community and Chicago liberals on this issue. Its leaders initiated mass protest meetings against the Beilis trial and lobbied among Illinois congressmen in order to get the United States to protest to the Russian Government. In the Radowitz Affair, Russian-Jewish leaders played a secondary role since Radowitz was not Jewish and the affair had a wider American implication. In 1908, the Russian Government demanded from the United States the arrest and extradition of Radowitz, a Lithuanian carpenter, on the pretence that he was wanted for murder. The extradition of Radowitz, who was a revolutionary and a political refugee, on such a pretence, was a dangerous precedent which could be used not only against Jewish revolutionaries, but also against Jewish army and conscription deserters. Judge Julian W. Mack in Chicago called a conference which was attended by the Russian-Jewish leaders in order to organize public opinion and lobby against the extradition of Radowitz. Hull House fulfilled only a limited role in the daily life of the Jewish community. Jane Addams and Hull House found sympathy in Jewish circles because of the support they gave the Jewish community in its struggle against anti-Semitism and for equal civic rights. The Jews, however, showed no inclination to give Hull House any foothold in the education of their youth, or in meeting their social, educational, cultural and welfare needs. Hull House had a closer relationship with the Jewish marginal elements, the assimilationists and the radicals. The former participated in Hull House activities, and left the Jewish ghetto as soon as they could afford to. The radicals maintained good relations with Hull House. Abraham Bisno and Sidney Hillman cooperated with Hull House on certain issues involving industrial struggles. Peter Sisman enlisted Hull House in the struggle against the extradition of political refugees to Russia. The only Jewish radical who really became closely connected with Hull House was Philip Davis, who left the Jewish Labor movement to become a settlement worker. Jewish radicals, however, were independently organized and visited Hull House only occasionally.[20]

The attitude of the Russian-Jewish community towards Hull House was determined by the long history of Jewish segregation, self-esteem, independent character, ability and desire to reconstruct its communal life in a form it was accustomed to, possessing a long tradition of minority self-rule. Conversely, Jane Addams' conception of the Jews as a religion and her failure to recognize the importance of the Yiddish language and culture as a unifying factor and an expression of a Jewish ethnic identity made it impossible for her to understand the mentality of the Russian-Jewish community. She was sympathetic towards Jewish suffering, but she never expressed any appreciation for Jewish culture and Jewish nationalism (Zionism), as she did towards Italian and Greek culture and nationalism. She failed to understand the strong desire of Jews to remain a community.[21]

Italian immigration from southern Italy began to flow into Chicago in the 1870s, and during the next decade the "Italian Colony" in the Nineteenth Ward was established. The colony in the immediate neighborhood of Hull House included more than five thousand people at the beginning of the century and increased to twenty-seven thousand by 1914.[22]

Italian adults in the neighborhood were mostly peasants from south Italy. In 1910, 75 percent of them were church members in the four Italian Catholic churches of the colony. They were extremely family-oriented and organized in mutual benefit societies for insurance and social purposes, according to the villages of their origin. A survey made by the Chicago Department of Public Welfare in 1911 listed 110 such societies while the secretary of the Unione Siciliana (the federation of Sicilian mutual benefit societies) estimated their number to be 160. Most of the Italian adults in the neighborhood were devoted to their village societies and showed no inclination to come in contact with people outside of their village, particularly non-Italians. Nevertheless, a small group of middle class, educated Italians would visit the Hull House receptions organized from time to time for Italians. Under the influence of Alessandro Mastro-Valerio, an Italian journalist who became a Hull House resident, these Italians began to conduct monthly meetings of their Italian literary, dramatic and national societies at Hull House. Hull House efforts to hold an Italian mothers' club met with many difficulties. In 1925 the club numbered only 45 women. Italian women had little social life of their own.[23]

The proportion of Italian youngsters in the Hull House clubs during 1907/08 did not exceed 25 percent. Unlike the Jews, the Italian youngsters tended to segregate into ethnic clubs. Most of them were boys, but gradually girls grew in number among the Italian groups in Hull House. The number of Italian children participating in Hull House activities soon began to rise, and during the second decade of the twentieth century, they formed a majority.[24] The increase in membership of the Italian clubs at Hull House was the outcome of their adjustment to the American environment. Italian parents were hostile and suspicious towards what they thought to be a Protestant mission. The children, however, soon learned to distinguish between a social center and a mission as they came more closely in contact with the American milieu. The Italian church near Hull House, the Guardian Angel, established an Italian settlement called the "Madonna Center" to attract the younger generation. Those devoted to the church went there, but the more Americanized children, and those attracted to Hull House's better facilities preferred Hull House in growing numbers.[25]

Sixty-two percent of the Italian children who joined the Hull House boys' club in 1907/08 were public and high school pupils, many of whom came from lower middle class origins, and only a minority were working youngsters (semi-skilled workers). The rank and file of Italian youth who were unskilled or semi-skilled workers, characterized by a high percentage of juvenile delinquency, rarely visited Hull House. The typical Hull House Italian member was far from being the average Italian youngster in the Italian colony. According to a sample prepared by the United States Immigration Commission in 1908, the percentage of all Italian children in the Chicago public schools was lower by about 20 percent than those Italian children who were in the Hull House boys' club, and only 22 percent of Italian children studied at high schools in Chicago in comparison with 31 percent among the Hull House Italian club membership. Moreover, the occupational structure of the Italian boys' club was not typical of Italians in Chicago or other parts of the United States.[26]

The cultural policy formed by Hull House during the 1890s adapted itself to the needs of its club membership, Americans, Irish, Germans and Jews who were eager for education and culture. Hull House programs were designed, therefore, to bring the accomplishments of civilization to the poor. This included concerts of classical music, art exhibitions, public lectures in English on a great variety of topics and college extension courses in history, literature and natural, social and political sciences taught by university graduate volunteers. Hull House clubs, which were modelled after middle class clubs, devoted their programs to political, social and cultural discussions along with social evenings.[27]

These programs were unsuitable to the Italian youngsters in the neighborhood who came from peasant families of Southern Italy. Being of peasant origins and unskilled families, the economic and social opportunities of the average Italian children were quite limited. Illiterate and living below the poverty line—the average yearly income of an Italian family in Chicago in 1908 was $504 while the average yearly income of an immigrant family was $683 (the minimum needed was $850)—Italian parents were unable to see the long range advantage of education for their children; and believing they should contribute their share to the family's income, the parents took the children out of school at an early age. The average education of Italian youngsters was the sixth grade. Exhausted after a long tiring day of work in unskilled jobs, lacking any motivation for education and no interest in culture, Italian boys moved around, organized in street corner gangs looking for adventure and fun. The girls, on the other hand, were kept at home, exploited in sewing and cigar or artificial flower making for long tedious hours, and preoccupied in the household raising the family's children.[28]

Hull House changed its cultural policy in order to adjust its programs to the changing neighborhood, shifting the emphasis from educational and cultural programs to sports, dancing, playing and crafts. The first indication of Hull House's awareness of this situation can be traced to November 1900, when a Labor Museum was opened at Hull House. More significant changes took place during the first decade of the twentieth century: in 1902 Hull House had thirty-two educational courses and nine manual and craft courses. In 1905, the proportion was nine to twenty-three. Another compromise with reality was the introduction of billiards, bowling and other games available in the West Side public halls, and a brass instrument band was formed for popular music.[29] The rank and file of Italian youth, however, visited Hull House only occasionally and Hull House remained a social center primarily for the Italian "better element."

The major factors that contributed to this situation were the educational aims of Hull House and the kind of club directors who worked with the club members. These were not adapted to the needs and experience of the average Italian boy who was unskilled and a member of a street corner gang.[30] The educational goals of Hull House were formulated in accordance with the nature and aims of Hull House, and the conceptions of the Settlement House movement; social settlements aimed at bridging the gap between classes and uniting American society into an integral organism along democratic and humanitarian concepts. This, they claimed, could be achieved by bringing into close daily contact, upper and middle class Americans with the working class, and by economically and culturally elevating the lower classes. Educationally this meant raising the socioeconomic status of the children of the working class by developing their personal qualifications through education, drama and art and creating in them ambition and motivation to improve their lives through adaptation of American middle class values along with social standards, and norms of behavior—the so-called American way of life. Instilling this consciousness in immigrant children meant breaking off ethnic-cultural barriers and creating an integrated society.[31]

The educational aims and patterns of socialization of Hull House contradicted those of the Italian group. In contrast to the American middle class oriented society, Italians still preserved their old social structure of a "peer group society," which shaped the personality of its members on entirely different conceptual lines. While the American middle class family was "child centered," the Italian peasant family was "adult oriented." The Italian child was educated to be "person oriented," while American middle class children were raised to be "object oriented." In Italian families the emphasis was on conformity and loyalty to the "peer

group'' and not on the development of the individual personality, and the
ambition to excellence. Any deviation from a ''peer group'' behavior resulted in a loss of status and alienation within the peer group. Adaptation
of Hull House values and norms of behavior resulted in the weakening of
attachments to the ethnic groups and assimilation into American mainstream society. An average Italian boy, with only six years of education,
working since he was twelve or fourteen years of age in unskilled or
semi-skilled jobs, within a peer group pattern of socialization, who had
very limited economic and social opportunities, was unable to absorb
Hull House values, nor adapt its norms of behavior. Although there was a
decisive effort on the part of the directors of Hull House to destroy the
''peer group'' structure of behavior of the Italian children, it succeeded
only in a minority of cases.[32]

The club directors were supportive of Hull House educational aims,
and the concepts of the Settlement House movement. Fifty-seven percent
of the Hull House staff were upper and middle class women, just as a considerable portion of settlement workers were women. Living in a male-
oriented conservative society, this was almost the only outlet for the talent
and energy of college-educated young women. Giving meaning and purpose to the lives of these women was the ''subjective'' aim of settlements. The male-oriented Italian youngster found it beneath his dignity to
be directed by women. When Hull House residents recognized this problem, they nominated male directors to the boys' club. The main problem
still remained unsolved. The average Italian boy found it difficult to
communicate with upper class white Anglo-Saxon Protestants, university
graduates or middle class German or Irish intellectuals who volunteered at
Hull House. The sociocultural gap was almost unbridgeable. Italian directors had a better chance and capability to communicate with Italian
children. Of the 382 men and women on the Hull House staff between
1889–1929, only 3 percent were Italian, although Italians comprised the
largest group among the House's clientele since the second decade of the
twentieth century, and most of the Italian directors were engaged in work-
shops and sports. They were not considered fit to transmit American
norms and values to working class children nor could they contribute to
class mingling.[33]

The new cultural policy of Hull House which was aimed to fit the needs
of Italian children still remained unsuitable to the average Italian boy.
Hull House daily rules were influenced by its middle class norms: children up to sixteen years of age were allowed to use its facilities only up to

five o'clock in the evening, making it impossible for working boys under this age to attend Hull House. Hull House introduced billiards, bowling and other games, but children under sixteen years of age were not permitted to use these facilities. After seven hours of work, Italian children showed little interest in craft shops, separated dancing groups for boys and girls, educational games or parliamentary laws or club procedure. They wanted to have fun and good times. Italian girls fitted better into Hull House's conception of girls.[34]

Around 1920, more Italian working youngsters began spending their time at Hull House, using its sports facilities and playroom, while others rented rooms for their independent clubs, taking advantage of the sports facilities. Unfortunately, Hull House had no influence over these youngsters, and they participated in Hull House programs only occasionally. The West Side Sportsmen's Club serves as an example of the lack of influence which Hull House residents had on these Italian youngsters. From 1920 the club began to rent rooms and use Hull House's sports facilities. The president of the club, William Gargano, a former poolroom owner, could hardly be considered a favorable type of club president. Robert A. Cairo, the club's director, was for many years a member of the boys' club, and was also a resident of Hull House. He was, however, not considered trustworthy by all of the Hull House leaders. The club conducted its activities independently, and Hull House residents had no idea what was the real business of the club. They were shocked when, in 1931, the police informed them that the club was connected with some of the worst Italian gangsters in Chicago, and that forty-six of the ninety-two members had police records.[35]

Jane Addams and Hull House residents succeeded in creating a good understanding and close relationship with the leadership of the small Italian intelligentsia. They also formed cordial relations with Italian socialist leaders, though not without some friction from time to time because of Jane Addams' compromising attitude on some social issues. However, the relationship with the leadership of the largest Italian group in the neighborhood, the Italian peasants of Southern Italy, remained distant and sometimes hostile for many years.

Hull House's contact with the Italian intelligentsia was through Mastro-Valerio. The youngsters tended to segregate into ethnic clubs where the Italian culture was fostered, within the Hull House club system. The adults, however, preferred their independent clubs, renting rooms and halls at Hull House for their monthly meetings. The clubs and societies of this group also used the facilities of Hull House for their national events and evenings in memory of Garibaldi and Mazzini and cooperated with Hull House in its political campaigns and efforts to adjust Italians to the American environment. Italian socialists and some of the Italian unions used Hull House facilities from time to time. However, Hull House was not their regular meeting place. Jane Addams was bitterly attacked a few times by the Italian socialist newspaper, *La Parola dei Socialisti*. She was criticized on 21 January 1911 for her refusal to permit Italian garment workers to continue using Hull House hall for their meetings because she did not approve of the policy of the union which was on strike. On 10 January 1914, the newspaper blamed Jane Addams for pretending to be liberal and progressive. "Where has your liberal spirit gone?" This accusation was made because of Hull House's refusal to permit the Giordano Bruno Club, after its expulsion from Hull House, to hold a meeting there in memory of their anticlerical hero, Giordano Bruno.[36]

The Italian pastors of the neighboring church considered Hull House a threat to the Catholicism of Italian children and established the "Madonna Center," a Catholic settlement, as a substitute for Hull House, to keep the children away from the influence of Hull House. This settlement was financed by German-American Catholics and most of its 115 workers were German-American Catholic volunteers. Edmund Dunne, the pastor of the Guardian Angel Church, accused Jane Addams and Hull House of being anticlerical and anarchist. This antagonism became evident in the 1890s in educational and political matters. The pastor was interested in opening a new parochial school in the Nineteenth Ward while Jane Addams and Hull House campaigned for an additional public school. During the elections in the 1890s, Pastor Dunne supported John Powers, the ward boss, against the Hull House candidate who was supported by the small Italian intelligentsia and the Italian press. The Italians in the neighborhood followed the advice of their pastor and other leaders and voted for John Powers, thus increasing tensions with Hull House. The attacks on the pastor and the local church in *La Tribuna*, an Italian newspaper edited by Mastro-Valerio, a Hull House resident, the fact that an anticlerical club, the Giordano Bruno Club, met regularly at Hull House, and the campaign Mastro-Valerio and his group conducted for naming the new public school after Garibaldi, the enemy of the Catholic church, resulted in bitter attacks on Jane Addams and Hull House in *The New World*, the Chicago Catholic newspaper. There were years of tension before the neighboring church and Hull House came to terms.[37]

The relationship with the nonreligious Italian leadership was just as difficult. These people controlled the Italian Mutual Aid societies, especially the Unione Siciliana, the padrone system, and some of the Italian unions, and cooperated with the ward boss. Hull House residents accused them of exploiting their countrymen and wielding their power for economic and political advantages. Moreover, the total rejection of Italian personal and moral judgment in choosing their leaders, evident in Jane Addams' writings and Hull House's residents' attitude towards those leaders, did not contribute to the improvement of Hull House relations with its Italian neighbors. In analyzing the circumstances which enabled "boss rule" in the Nineteenth Ward, Jane Addams identified the major cause as the stage of ethical and moral development of the Italian constituency. "In certain stages of moral evolution a man is incapable of action unless the result will benefit himself or some of his acquaintances, and it is a long step in moral progress to set the good of the many before the interest of the few, and to be concerned for the welfare of a community without hope of an individual return. . . . What headway can the notion of civic purity, of honesty of administration make?" The antagonism between the Italian leaders and Hull House was also due to their contradictory interests. The Italian leaders were interested in continued segregation of the Italian community within its own organizations because therein was the source of their power. Hull House residents were interested in breaking the barriers of ethnicity and integrating Italians into the American environment by taking over the leadership. In 1895, Jane Addams invited Italian leaders to give their approval to the establishment of an Italian Welfare Institution to be sponsored by Hull House and its friends. Italian leaders were unwilling to cooperate, and only a few attended the meeting. Another initiative, to ask all the societies and organizations to join in a neighborhood council established by Hull House in 1910 under the direction of Grace Abbott, a Hull House resident and director of the Immigrants' Protective League, failed too. Anthony Sorrentino, an Italian immigrant who grew up in the neighborhood and was involved in its reconstruction through the West Side Area Project in the early 1930s, blamed West Side settlements for trying to improve the condition of the neighborhood "without its residents and local leaders being actively involved."[38]

Gradually, Hull House did succeed in attracting some Italian adults to the Settlement by renting Hull House's rooms and facilities at lower prices. Twenty-six different kinds of Italian societies out of about two hundred held their meetings at Hull House in 1921. This "success" was achieved only after Hull House became reconciled with its neutralized position as a center with no influence. As such, Hull House succeeded at last in becoming "recognized" as a neighborhood institution. Thomas Holland, a Hull House resident in the early 1920s, wrote: "I do not think that Hull House ever had much impact on the community life . . .. It was evident in 1923 that the place was becoming an empty shell."[39]

The Italian community was divided along sociocultural lines. The unifying factor, an Italian ethnic consciousness and identity, was missing since the peasants were still in the prenational stage. Hull House failed with the Italian community because it cooperated with the intelligentsia in its effort to win the leadership of the community rather than with the indigenous leadership, using national and cultural slogans along with progressive norms which were alien to the Italian peasants' background. Jane Addams' sympathy towards Italian culture and nationality attracted the educated element only. It did not speak to the Italian peasants.[40]

Greek immigration into Chicago started in the early 1890s. A Greek colony was established in the streets neighboring Hull House, growing from 500 in 1904 to 11,500 in 1920. The beginning of the ties between Jane Addams and the Greek community can be traced to 1903 when a group of Greeks were invited to Hull House by Miss Barrow, from Boston, for the performance of a Greek play before an American audience, a project she initiated all over the country. Only gradually did Greeks start to visit Hull House. During the 1910s, they became the second largest ethnic group at Hull House, after the Italians, although the difference in size was considerable.[41]

The Greek community was well integrated owing to its strong religious-national-cultural consciousness. As early as 1897, the Holy Trinity, a Greek-Orthodox church, was built and a priest was brought from Greece. The Greeks' communal life was concentrated around the Church and their mutual benefit societies established along village of origin lines. Gradually literary, dramatic and national societies were established. Greek adults did not participate in activities sponsored by Hull House. Lack of rooms and other facilities for their meetings, however, convinced the leaders of the Greek community to accept Hull House's invitation to use its rooms and other facilities for their community social and cultural meetings. Greek women were allowed to join a Greek womens' club, initiated by Hull House, yet few women participated, and it never met regularly. Greek children did participate in some of Hull House's activities, mainly sports, music and crafts. However, when they reached the age of fourteen, they joined Greek independent clubs which met at Hull House, using its facilities. The Greek clubs developed typical Greek social-cultural programs. They also used Hull House sports facilities and won the cup in many sport contests for Hull House. The gradual increase in membership of Greek children at Hull House was due to the special relationship created between Jane Addams and the Greek leadership. The priest and the other leaders of the Greek community removed their objection to the participation of their youth in some of Hull House's activities after they made sure it would not endanger the educational goals of the Greek community.[42]

The pattern of relationship between Hull House and the Greek community was entirely different from that of the Russian-Jews and Italians. After the great success in performing an ancient Greek play at Hull House in 1903, some more Greek plays were performed by Greek dramatic clubs, giving them an opportunity to show the Greek culture to Americans. A Greek-American meeting initiated by Greek leaders for the purpose of continuing the dialogue on the Greek civilization with Americans contributed to the growing mutual respect between Hull House residents and the small Greek community. During the first decade Hull House residents succeeded in gaining the confidence and close cooperation of the Greeks. This relationship resulted in a concentration of Greek community social life at Hull House, establishing in fact, a self-contained Greek community center within Hull House. They conducted their social, educational, cultural and national activities at Hull House: a Greek evening school, mutual aid societies, social and dramatic clubs, the Greek Olympic Athletic Club and a branch of the Pan-Hellenic Union and other national organizations. Greeks celebrated their national holidays at Hull House and held their social and communal meetings there. They even trained their volunteers for the Balkan War in 1912 at Hull House. The majority of Greek societies—twenty-one—met there in 1929.[43]

In 1907, the Greek newspaper, *The Star*, called Jane Addams "one of the best friends of Greek people of Chicago," and Dr. Soter, who attended Hull House in the 1910s, described the Settlement later in *The Greek Press*, as the community center of the Greek neighborhood and Jane Addams as the "sweetest physiognomy, the saintliest woman I have ever known." This relationship, however, was achieved by her giving up any effort to interfere in, or influence Greek activities at Hull House. Jane Addams, the pacifist, even shut her eyes to the military training and militant nationalism of her Greek friends.[44] In all likelihood, the special relationship with the Greeks was due to the lesson that Jane Addams learned from her failures with the Jews and Italians, as well as to the unique character of the Greek community, together with her special affection towards Greek culture.

The Greek community differed from the Jewish and the Italian communities. Unlike the Italian, it was well integrated owing to its strong religious-national-cultural consciousness and identity, and its middle class educated leadership was able to communicate with Hull House residents. The sympathy of Hull House residents towards Greek culture and the Greek struggle against Turkish atrocities on the one hand, and the reconciliation with the reality of ethnicity, on the other hand, created the background for mutual respect and cooperation. Contrary to the Italians' slow mobility, the Greeks' rapid economic advancement made them less suspicious and more willing to cooperate—on their own terms—with American institutions. Unlike the Jews, the smallness of the Greek community made it impossible for them to mobilize the financial resources needed for the building of a community center of its own, after the building of a church and a parochial school exhausted their resources. Hull House solved their problems, without interfering in their affairs.[45]

Although "new immigrants" comprised a considerable portion of Hull House's neighborhood population, ten to fifteen years had to pass before this could be reflected in Hull House membership. This was rooted in the nature of the institute, its staff, and the Settlement movement as well as in the pace of immigrant adjustment to the American environment. Hull House was influential among a small segment of immigrant youngsters who were fascinated by the American way of life and preferred individual mobility and integration to ethnic group life and identity. The majority remained attached to their ethnic group: the Jewish youth went to Hull House only as long as there was no Jewish social center which was able to meet their needs as American-Jews; the Greek children participated in Hull House activities selectively also; and the average Italian youngster gradually learned to take advantage of Hull House facilities without being influenced by its spirit. The intention of Hull House residents to become the center of influence in the communal life of the neighborhood through cooperation with those in the immigrant communities who were willing to cooperate, did not materialize. However, Hull House fulfilled some functions in the immigrant communities, though mainly maintaining a close relationship with its marginal elements. The desire of the immigrant groups to preserve their ethnic entity and identity was stronger than the influences of the American environment. Jane Addams and Hull House residents needed time to understand the "new immigrant" communities and to recognize and reconcile this understanding with the reality of ethnic identity. The Settlement workers failed to understand Jewish ethnicity and Italian background and needs. However, they learned the lesson and succeeded in creating a relationship of mutual respect with the Greeks.

NOTES

1. Robert A. Woods, ed., *Americans in Process* (Boston, 1902); idem, ed., *The City Wilderness* (New York, 1893); idem, *The Neighborhood In Nation Building* (Boston, 1923); Barbara M. Solomon, *Ancestors and Immigrants, A Changing New England Tradition* (New York, 1956), pp. 63, 70, 77–78, 136, 141–143; Robert A. Woods and Albert J. Kennedy, *The Settlement Horizon* (New York, 1922), p. 331.

2. John Higham, *Strangers in the Land: Patterns of American Nativism, 1860–1925* (New York, 1955); Mark Krug, *The Melting of the Ethnics, Education of the Immigrants* (Bloomington, Ill., 1976); Alvin Kogut, "The Settlements and Ethnicity: 1890–1914," *Social Work*, 17 (May 1972): 22–31; George C. White, "Social Settlements and Immigrant Neighbors, 1886–1914," *Social Service Review*, 33 (1959): 55–66.

3. Paul McBride, *Cultural Clash* (San Francisco, 1975); Robert A. Carlson, *The Quest for Conformity: Americanization through Education* (New York, 1975); Paul C. Violas, "Jane Addams and the New Liberalism," in *Roots of Crisis, American Education in the Twentieth Century*, Clarence J. Karier et al., (Chicago, 1955), pp. 66–83; Daniel Levine, *Varieties of Reform Thought* (New York, 1964), pp. 10–32.

4. Allen F. Davis, *American Heroine, The Life and Legend of Jane Addams* (New York, 1973), pp. 203–207.

5. Agnes S. Holbrook, "Maps, Notes and Comments," in *Hull House Maps and Papers*, ed. Jane Addams (Boston, 1895), pp. 3–26.

6. Jane Addams *Twenty Years at Hull House* (New York, 1910), pp. 179–183, 342; Jane Addams, "Objective Value of a Social Settlement," in *Philanthropy and Social Progress*, Jane Addams et al., (Boston, 1893), pp. 36–37; "Hull House Outline Sketch," in *Hull House Maps and Papers*, ed. Jane Addams (Boston, 1895), pp. 216–218; Florence Kelley, "Hull House," *New England Magazine*, 18 (July 1898): 560–561; Alice Miller, "Hull House," *The Charities Review*, 1 (February 1892): 170–171; Alzina P. Stevens, "Life in a Settlement-Hull House Chicago," *Self Culture*, 9 (March 1899): 49–50; "Hull House A Social Settlement," 1 March 1892, Hull House Papers, University of Illinois (hereafter cited as H.H. Papers); *Hull House Bulletins*, Club Lists, 1896–1905/06; *Hull House Year Books*, Club Lists, 1906/07–1921, H.H. Papers; Hull House Women's Club, 1902/03, 1903/04, 1905/06, 1906/,07, 1909/10, 1925/26, Louise DeKoven Bowen Papers, Chicago Historical Society. The estimates of Hull House membership according to ethnic groups are based on a comparison between views expressed by comtemporaries directly connected with Hull House and the neighborhood, and an analysis of the numbers accumulated from Hull House Bulletins and Year Books. The analysis is based on the assumption of the existence of a certain correlation between the ethnic composition of club membership and club committees.

Women's Club:

Year	% of Americans		% of Irish		% of Germans and German-Jews		% of Russian-Jews	
	Members	Committee Members	Members	Committee Members	Members	Committee Members	Members	Committee Members
1896	--	60	--	40	--	--	--	--
1902/03	64	--	20	--	13	--	--	--
1906/07	68	71	13	14	14	14	1	--
1909/10	55	67	14	10	14	19	3	--
1925/26	46	--	19	--	16	--	--	--

Lists of Hull House youth clubs' committee members give the following picture:

Year	% of Anglo-Saxons[a]	% of Irish	% of Germans	% of Russian-Jews	% of Italians[a]	% of Others (Slavs mainly)
1896	44	13.5	17	13.5	2	10
1897	33	19.5	13	24.5	2	8
1899	26	5	15	29.5	13	11.5
1902	30	13	18	32	--	7
1903/04	44	22	8	18	5	3
1905/06	36	9	7	29	17	2
1906/07	11	31	8	28	22	--
1910	20	23	6	20	31	--

NOTE: No lists are given after 1910. No Greeks were included in these lists.

[a]Anglo-Saxons refer to native-born or immigrants of Anglo-Saxon origin

Ethnic composition of the Boys' Club 1907/08

	%	Number
Russian-Jews	41	668
Italians	24	382
Irish	12	202
Anglo-Saxons	9	147
Germans	5	81
Polish	2	22
Greeks	1	15
Others	6	101
	100	1618

Dramatic Association (Junior)

	Total	% of Russian-Jews
1900	26	8
1906	14	18
1916	17	4
1921	27	4

7. Edith Abbott, *The Tenements of Chicago, 1908–1935* (Chicago, 1936), pp. 85–92; Philip Davis, "General Aspects of the Population of Chicago," in *The Russian Jew in the United States*, ed. Charles S. Bernheimer (Philadelphia, 1905), p. 58.

8. Philip P. Bregstone, *Chicago and Its Jews, A Cultural History* (Chicago, 1933), pp.

51–54; Mrs. Benjamin Davis, "Religious Activity," in *The Russian Jew*, ed. Bern-heimer, p. 174; Davis, "General Aspects," ibid, p. 58; I.K. Friedman, "Amusements and Social Life," ibid, pp. 252–254; Minnie F. Low, "Philanthropy," ibid, p. 92; Morris A. Gutstein, *Profiles of Freedom* (Chicago, 1967), pp. 105–124; Bernard Horwich, *My First Eighty Years* (Chicago, 1939), pp. 145–152; Hyman L. Meites, *History of the Jews of Chicago* (Chicago, 1924), pp. 176, 657–676; Seymour J. Pomerenz, "Aspects of Chicago Russian Jewish Life, 1893–1915," in *The Chicago Pinkas*, ed. Simon Rawidowicz (Chicago, 1952), pp. 117, 126–129; Charles Zublin, "The Chicago Ghetto," in *Hull House Maps and Papers*, ed. Jane Addams (Boston, 1895), p. 108; *Jewish Courier*, 4 April 1910, Reel 35; 24 October 1910, Reel 32; The Jewish newspapers, The Foreign Language Press Survey, 1942, Chicago Public Library (hereafter cited as FLPS). Jewish newspapers used in this article are from this survey, Reels 31–41.

9. "Hull House A Social Settlement," 15 January 1895, H.H. Papers; *Hull House Bulletins*, 1896–1905/06, Club Lists; *Hull House Year Books*, 1906/07–1916, Club Lists; Hull House Boys' Club, 1907/08, Juvenile Protective Association Papers, University of Illinois, (hereafter cited as JPA); "Hull House Players, List of members for the years 1898–1924," H.H. Papers; Interview with Alex Elson, 23 August 1977; Interview with Moshe Ghitzes, 11 September 1977; Interview with Nat. M. Kahn, November 1977; Interview with Rabbi Morris A. Gutstein, 22 August 1977; Interview with Thomas W. Holland, 5 August 1978.

Year	Number of Hull House visitors per week	Optimal Number and % of Jewish visitors per week[a]	% of Jewish Officials on Club Committees	
1896	2000	540 (27)	(1899)	31
1906/07	9000	1400 (16.5)		23
1913	9000	1300 (14.5)	(1910)	22

[a] Based on the number of clubs and courses visited by Jews multiplied by 40, the optimal number of members for courses and clubs at Hull House.

Bregstone, *Chicago and its Jews*, pp. 17–18; Philip Davis, "Educational Influences," in *The Russian Jew*, ed. Bernheimer, pp. 214, 217; Francis Hacket, "Hull House—A Souvenir," in *Eighty Years at Hull House*, Allen F. Davis and Mary L. McCree (Chicago, 1969), p. 72; "Hull House Outline Sketch," pp. 224–225; Low, "Philanthropy," pp. 87–89; Meites, *History of the Jews*, pp. 184–185, 391–392; Miller, "Hull House," p. 169; Hannah G. Solomon, *Fabric of My Life* (New York, 1946), pp. 93–96; Louis Wirth, *The Ghetto: A Study in Isolation* (Chicago, 1928), p. 188; Victor S. Yarros, "Hull House Unique Melting Pot Experiment," *Evening Post* (New York), 2 December 1916, Newspaper clippings, Jane Addams Papers, Swarthmore College Peace Collection (hereafter cited as SCPC).

10. Davis, "Educational Influences," p. 217; *Hull House Year Book*, 1906/07, p. 38; 1913, p. 8; 1921, pp. 37–39; Interview with Alex Elson, 23 August 1977; Interview with Benny Goodman's sister, 11 September 1977.

11. Bregstone, *Chicago and its Jews*, pp. 8–9, 13–15, 115–116; Davis, "Educational Influences," pp. 211–212; Davis, "Religious Activity," pp. 177–181; Morris A. Gutstein, *Priceless Heritage, The Epic Growth of Nineteenth Century Chicago Jewry* (New York, 1953), pp. 403–409; Gutstein, *Profiles of Freedom*, pp. 140–144; Meites, *History of the Jews*, passim; *Reform Advocate*, 11 November 1893; 4 May 1901; Reel 35; *Courier*, 22 November 1907; 2 May 1909; 7 April 1910; 9 October 1912; 31 January 1913, Reel 35, FLPS.

12. Bregstone, *Chicago and its Jews*, *passim*; Horwich, *Eighty Years*, *passim*; Nathan D. Kaplan, "*Zionism*," *The Sentinel: 100 Years of Chicago Jewish Life* (Chicago, 1948), pp. 39, 50; Anita L. Lebeson, "Zionism Comes to Chicago," in *Early History of Zionism in America*, Isidore S. Meyer (New York, 1958), p. 177; Meites, *History of the Jews*, pp. 216–226, 243; Max Shulman, "The First American Disciples," *Theodor Herzl Memorial, New Palestine* (New York, 1929), p. 223; Zvi Scharfstein, *History of Jewish Education* (Jerusalem, 1970), 3: 55; *The American Hebrew*, 21 April 1899, p. 841; *Courier*, 13 October 1907, Reel 32, FLPS; *Chicago Hebrew Institute Messenger*, November 1909, Reel 31, 37, FLPS; *Chicago Hebrew Institute Observer*, December 1911, Reel 31, FLPS; *Reform Advocate*, 13 February 1926, Reel 34, FLPS; Chicago Hebrew Institute, Minutes of the Meeting of the Board of Directors, 1907/08, Chicago Hebrew Institute Papers, Chicago Historical Society (hereafter cited as CHI Papers); CHI, Minutes of the Meeting of the Board of Directors, 19 January 1910, CHI Papers; *Hull House Year Book*, 1910, p. 6; 1913, pp. 6–7; Dr. E.A. Fischkin to Julius Rosenwald, 11 March 1908, Julius Rosenwald Papers, Box 18, University of Chicago; Interview with Lusil Pintozzi, 29 August 1977.

13. *CHI Messenger*, November 1909, Reels 31, 35, 36, FLPS; *CHI Observer*, November 1912, Reels 31, 34, 36, FLPS; *CHI Observer*, December 1913, Reel 31, FLPS; *CHI Observer*, May 1914, p. 14, CHI Papers; February 1915, p. 18; April 1915, pp. 6–8; May 1915, pp. 57, 61–63; March 1916, pp. 3–6; April 1917, p. 2; May 1917, pp. 15, 98; June–July 1917, pp. 6–7; November 1917, pp. 20–21; December–January 1917/18, p. 2; May 1918, p. 59; December–January 1918/19, pp. 2, 20; December 1919, p. 48; *Courier*, 10 October 1909, Reel 31; 15 October 1913, Reel 31; 15 April 1918, Reel 34, FLPS; *Reform Advocate*, 13 February 1926, Reel 34, FLPS.

14. CHI, Minutes of the Meeting of The Board of Directors, 1907/08, Box 1, CHI Papers; *CHI Messenger*, November 1909, Reel 31; *CHI Observer*, December 1911, Reel 31, 36, FLPS; December 1913, p. 18; December 1915, pp. 28–29; May 1917, pp. 8–15; *CHI General Directors Report*, 1921, pp. 4–14, CHI Papers; *Courier*, 6 November 1911, Reel 37; 16 July 1915, Reel 31, FLPS.

15. Bregstone, *Chicago and its Jews*, pp. 234, 291; Horwich, *Eighty Years*, pp. 274–275; *CHI Messenger*, November 1909, Reels 31, 33, FLPS; *CHI Observer*, December 1911, Reel 31, FLPS; September 1914, pp. 5–8; May 1914, pp. 14–15; January 1915, p. 18; March 1916, p. 15; September 1916, pp. 3–6; November 1916, pp. 27–28; April 1917, p. 2; December–January 1917/1918, p. 2; December–January 1918/1919, pp. 2, 21; December 1919, pp. 47–48; *Courier*, 13 October 1907, Reel 32; 13 October 1908, Reel 38; 16 October 1908, Reel 35; 8 December 1911, Reel 35; 9 March 1915, Reel 31; 6 March 1916, Reel 35; 10 July 1917, Reel 35; 10 November 1920, Reel 35, FLPS; CHI, Hebrew Oratorio Society, October 1917, Julius Rosenwald Papers, Box 6.

16. Meites, *History of the Jews*, p. 226; *CHI Observer*, December 1914, Reel 33, FLPS; *Courier*, 31 October 1907, Reel 39; 2 January 1914, Reel 39; 5 February 1915, Reel 33; 18 September 1916, Reel 39; 21 September 1916, Reel 32, FLPS; *Forward*, 6 March 1919, Reel 33, FLPS.

17. Bregstone, *Chicago and its Jews*, pp. 88, 94–100, 137–138; Marnin Feinstein, *American Zionism, 1884–1904* (New York, 1965), p. 30; Horwich, *Eighty Years*, pp. 122–125, 130, 135; Jacob R. Marcus, "European Bibliographical Items on Chicago," in *The Chicago Pinkas*, ed. Rawidowicz, pp. 178–179; Meites, *History of the Jews*, pp. 167–168, 195, 197, 203–205, 244–249, 290, 408; *Record Herald* (Chicago), 22 November 1905, Reel 32, FLPS; *Reform Advocate*, 20 May 1905, Reel 36, FLPS; *Chicago Chronicle*, 20 November 1905, Reel 32, 27, FLPS; *Illinois Staats Zeitung*, 19 April 1901, Reel 37, FLPS; *Courier*, 20 June 1906, Reel 32, FLPS; *Hameliz*, 32 (7 March 1886): 502.

18. Bregstone, *Chicago and its Jews*, *passim*; Davis, "Educational Activities," pp. 211–220; Feinstein, *American Zionism*, pp. 214–238; Harold Korey, "The History of Jewish Education in Chicago," (M.A. thesis, University of Chicago, 1942), pp. 80–81, 99–100, 104, 126–127; Meites, *History of the Jews*, *passim*; Chayim M. Rothblatt, "Chicago Hebrew Press," in *The Chicago Pinkas*, ed. Rawidowicz, pp. MD, MH, ND; Shulman, "American Disciples," pp. 223–224; *Courier*, 2 May, 7 June 1912, Reel 31, FLPS; 5 March, 24 September 1916, Reel 39, FLPS; 19 May 1918, Reel 39, FLPS; 28 August 1919, Reel 39, FLPS; *Hayahudi*, 31 (1910), p. 15; *The Maccabean*, 3 (June 1902): 342; 4 (January 1905): 55; *The Sentinel*, 19 March 1915, Reel 36, FLPS; *CHI Observer*, May 1914, p. 22; May 1916, pp. 70–71; October 1916, p. 16; May 1917, p. 78; September 1917, p. 9; May 1919, p. 58.

19. *The Maccabean*, 6 (February 1904): 98; *CHI Observer*, January 1916, p. 15.

20. Jane Addams, "The Chicago Settlements and Social Unrest," *Charities and the Commons*, 20 (2 May 1908): 155–167; Addams, *Twenty Years*, pp. 403–416; Abraham Bisno, *Abraham Bisno, Union Pioneer* (Madison, Wis., 1967), pp. 98–99, 119–120, 171–172; Bregstone, *Chicago and its Jews*, *passim*; Davis, *Eighty Years*, p. 107; Davis, "Religious Activity," pp. 172–175; Philip Davis, *And Crown Thy Goods* (New York, 1952), pp. 48, 65, 82–120; Horwich, *Eighty Years*, *passim*; Matthew Josephson, *Sidney Hillman, Statesman of American Labor* (Garden City, New York, 1952), pp. 42–57; Low, "Philanthropy," p. 94; Meites, *History of the Jews, passim*; Pomrenze, "Aspects of Russian Jewish Life," p. 127; *The American* (Chicago), 6 November 1910, newspaper clippings, Addams Papers, SCPC; *Chicago Post*, 2 May 1908, *ibid*; *Chicago Tribune*, 19 May 1903; 3 May 1908; 12, 21 December 1908; 30 October 1910, *ibid*; *Courier*, 20 June 1910, Reel 38; 29 October 1920, Reel 33, FLPS; *Evening Post* (Chicago), 4, 5, 25 November, December 1910, newspaper clippings, Addams Papers, SCPC; *Forward*, 3 August 1920, Reel 33, FLPS; *L'Italia*, 28 September 1915, Reel 30; *La Parola Dei Socialisti*, 21 January 1911, Reel 30, The Italian newspapers, FLPS. Italian newspapers used in this article are from this source, Reels 30, 31; *New York Times*, 6 November 1910, newspaper clippings, Addams paper, SCPC; *Record Herald* (Chicago), 19 May 1903; 28 November 1910, *ibid*; Clarence Darrow to Jane Addams, 11 September 1901, Addams Papers, SCPC; John O. Bentall, State Secretary of the Socialist Party of Chicago to Jane Addams, 17 December 1908, Addams Papers, SCPC; Sidney Hillman to Jane Addams, 22 December 1915, H.H. Papers.

21. Addams, *Twenty Years*, pp. 232, 256–258, 426, 436–437; Jane Addams, *Newer Ideals of Peace* (New York, 1907), p. 70; Jane Addams, "Recent Immigration, A Field Neglected By The Scholar," *Education Review*, 29 (March 1905): 245–263; Davis, "Religious Activity," p. 250; Zublin, "The Chicago Ghetto," pp. 101–111; Interview with Rabbi E. Mushkin, August 1977.

22. Humbert S. Nelli, *Italians in Chicago, 1880–1930* (New York, 1970), pp. 34–37; see n. 5.

23. Addams, *Twenty Years*, pp. 103, 209, 232, 350, 358–359; Addams "Objective Value," pp. 35, 37,, 44–47; Sophonisba P. Breckinridge, *New Homes for Old* (New York, 1921), pp. 218, 241, 246, 239; Edmund M. Dunne, "Memoirs of 'Zi Pre'" *The Ecclesiatical Review*, 59 (August 1913): 192–203; "The Italian and the Settlement," *Survey*, 30 (April 1913): 58–59; Robert E. Park and Herbert A. Miller, *Old World Traits Transplanted* (Chicago, 1925), pp. 152, 158; Nelli, *Italians in Chicago, passim*; Kate G. Prindiville, "Italy in Chicago," *Catholic World*, 76 (July 1903): 452–461; Giovanni E. Schiavo, *The Italians in Chicago* (Chicago, 1928), pp. 6, 55–57, 68–70; Rudolph J. Vecoli, "Contadini in Chicago: A Critique of the Uprooted," *Journal of American History* 15 (1964): 406–408, 414; William F. Whyte, *Street Corner Society, The Social Structure of an Italian Slum* (Chicago, 1943), p. 99; Woods and Kennedy, *Settlement*

Horizon, p. 191; "Hull House Program," p. 2, 1892, Box 1, Series 13a, Addams Papers, SCPC; "Hull House A Social Settlement," 15 January 1895, H.H. Papers; Hull House Relief Account, 1891–1894, H.H. Papers; *Hull House Bulletin*, no. 6 (1896), p. 7, no. 7 (1896), p. 8; no. 1 (1897), p. 9; no. 5 (1897), p. 7; no. 1 (1901), p. 7; no. 2 (1903/04), p. 14; *Hull House Year Book*, 1913, p. 41; 1916, p. 46; 1929, pp. 26–27, Hull House Summer Record, 1907, 1908, JPA; *Chicago Tribune*, 19 May 1890, newspaper clippings, H.H. Papers; *L' Italia*, 24 August 1895, Reel 30, FLPS; G. Orrico, letter, *La Parola*, 19 July 1913, Reel 30, FLPS; Interview with Nicolette Mallone, 17 August 1977; Interview with G. De Filippis, 17 August 1977; Interview with Florence Scala, 2 August 1977; Interview with Pasqualino Scala, 4 September 1977.

24. Jane Addams, *Second Twenty Years at Hull House* (New York, 1930), p. 397; Addams, "Objective Values," pp. 36–37; Lilian A. Brandt, "Transplanted Birthright, The Development of the Second Generation of the Italians in an American Environment," *Charities*, 12 (1904): 496; Herbert J. Gans, *The Urban Villagers, Group and Class in the Life of Italian Americans* (Glencoe, New York, 1962), p. 158; John Landesco, "The Life History of a Member of the '42 Gang,'" *Journal of Criminal Law and Criminology*, 24 (March 1933): 969; Nelli, *Italians in Chicago*, p. 92; Anthony Sorrentino, *Organizing Against Crime* (New York, 1977), pp. 46–49; *Evening Post*, 2 December 1916, newspaper clippings, Addams Papers, SCPC; "Hull House A Social Settlement," 1 March 1892, 15 January 1895, H.H. Papers; *Hull House Bulletin*, no. 1 (1896); no. 5 (1896), p. 7; no. 8, (1897), p. 7; no. 1 (1898), p. 9; no. 4–5 (1898), p. 8; no. 6 (1898), p. 8; no. 7 (1898), p. 6; no. 8–9 (1899), p. 7; no. 4 (1901), p. 15; no. 2 (1903–4), pp. 14–17; no. 1 (1905/06), pp. 11, 14, 15; *Hull House Year Book*, 1906/07, pp. 21–28, 41–43; 1910, pp. 20, 25–29, 31, 44; 1913, pp. 17–22, 28–32, 41–42; 1916, pp. 17, 26–29, 33–37, 39; 1921, pp. 35–39; Hull House Boys' Club, 1907/08, JPA; Hull House Summer Record, 1907/08, JPA; Hull House Players Membership List, 1898–1941, H.H. Papers; Interview with M. Ghitzes, 11 September 1977; Interview with M. Gamboni, 14 September 1977; Interview with G. De Filippis, 17 August 1977; Interview with A. Sorrentino, 2 August 1977; Thomas W. Holland to author, 5 August 1978; E.G. Starr to M. Blaisdell, 18 May 1890, Starr Papers, S. Smith Collection, Smith College; *Chicago Tribune*, 19 May 1890, newspaper clippings, Addams Papers, SCPC; *L'Italia*, 4–5 May 1895, Reel 30, 9 April 1904, Reel 31, FLPS.

25. Addams, *Second Twenty Years*, p. 397; Addams, *Twenty Years*, pp. 235–236; Mary A. Amberg, *Madonna Center* (Chicago, 1976), pp. 39, 40–46, 67–82, 100–103; Paul J. Campisi, "Ethnic Family Patterns: The Italian Family in the United States," *American Journal of Sociology*, 53 (May 1948): 447–449; Dunne, "Memoirs," pp. 201–203; Gans, *Urban Villagers*, *passim*; Francis A.J. Ianni, "The Italo-American Teen-Ager," *Annals*, 338 (November 1961): 73–74; Nelli, *Italians in Chicago, passim*; Prindiville, "Italy in Chicago," pp. 452–461; Schiavo, *Italians in Chicago*, p. 75; Sorrentino, *Organizing Against Crime*, pp. 82, 90–92; Rudolph J. Vecoli, "Prelates and Peasants: Italian Immigrants and the Catholic Church," *Journal of Social History*, 2 (Spring 1969): 228–233; John P. Walsh, "The Catholic Church in Chicago and the Problems of Urban Society, 1893–1915," (Ph.D. diss., University of Chicago, 1948) pp. 36–37; *Hull House Year Book*, 1921, pp. 25–26; *L'Italia*, 24–25 August 1895, Reel 30; 2 May 1903, Reel 31; 11 March 1911, Reel 31; *La Tribuna*, 14 January 1905, Reel 30, FLPS; *New World*, 16 November 1910; 22 March 1913; 29 November 1913; 8 October 1915; 22 October 1915; 30 November 1917, Catholic Diocese of Chicago Library; Interview with G. De Filippis, 17 August 1977; Interview with Pasqualino Scala, 4 September 1977; Interview with A. Sorrentino, 2 August 1977.

26. Addams, *Twenty Years*, pp. 106–125, 198–207, 250–254, 323–328; Edith Abbott and Sophonisba P. Breckinridge, *Truancy and Non-Attendance in the Chicago Schools* (Chicago, 1917), pp. 121–129; Sophonisba P. Breckinridge and Edith Abbott, *The Delinquent Child and the Home* (New York, 1918), pp. 72–75, 81–82, 130–138, 150–153; William L. Bodine, "Compulsory Education in Chicago," in *The Child in the City*, Sophonisba P. Breckinridge (Chicago, 1912), p. 155, 264; Gertrude H. Britton, "An Intensive Study of the Census of Truancy," 1906, H.H. Papers; John D'Alesandro, "Occupational Trends of Italians in New York City," in *The Italians*, Francesco Cordasco and Eugene Bucchioni (Clifton, N.J., 1974), pp. 425–426; United States, Immigration Commission, *Reports*, 26 (1911): 308–311, 313–314, 318; 27 (1911): 144–146, 149; 30 (1911): 566; Gans, *Urban Villagers*, pp. 24–25; Edward P. Hutchinson, *Immigrants and Their Children, 1850–1950* (New York, 1956), p. 174; John Landesco, "Crime and the Failure of Institutions in The Chicago Immigrant Areas," *Journal of the American Institute of Criminal Law and Criminology*, 23 (July–August 1932): 241–243; Anne E. Nicholes, "From School to Work in Chicago," *Charities and the Commons*, 16 (12 May 1906): 231, 233–234; Frederick M. Thrasher, *The Gang* (Chicago, 1927), pp. 8–37, 67; *Hull House Year Book*, 1929, p. 31; Hull House Boys' Club, 1907/08, JPA.

27. Addams, *Twenty Years*, pp. 154–230, 373–378, 383–389, 395, 428–440; Addams, "Objective Value," pp. 22, 38–44; Helen Horwitz, *Culture and the City, Cultural Philanthropy in Chicago from 1880s to 1917* (Lexington, Ky., 1976), pp. 126–142.

28. United States, Immigration Commission, *Reports*, 26 (1911):318; 27 (1911):149; 30 (1911) 566; Abbott and Breckinridge, *Truancy*, pp. 121, 129; Addams, *Twenty Years*, pp. 106–107; Breckinridge and Abbott, *The Delinquent Child*, pp. 75, 81–82, 131; Dunne, "Memoirs," pp. 193–196, 199; Landesco, "Crime and the Failure of Institutions in Chicago," pp. 240–244; Nicholes, "From School to Work," pp. 233–234; Nelli, *Italians in Chicago*, pp. 55–72.

29. "Hull House, A Social Settlement," 1892, H.H. Papers; *Hull House Bullentin*, no. 1 (1896); no. 1 (1902), pp. 10–11; no. 1 (1905/06), pp. 11–14; *Hull House Year Book*, 1906/1907, pp. 8–9, 11–12, 21–26, 35, 37; 1910, pp. 8–13, 21–22, 25–26; 1913, pp. 6–14, 42; 1916, pp. 6–20, 42; Hull House Trade School, 1913, Addams Papers, SCPC; Gertrude H. Britton, "The Boy Problem in the Nineteenth Ward," November 1920, Chicago, H.H. Papers; *Weekly Times* (Denver, Colorado), 24 August 1898, newspaper clippings, Addams Papers, SCPC; *New York Evening Telegram*, 3 March 1910, newspaper clippings, Addams Papers, SCPC; "First Report of a Labor Museum at Hull House," 1901/02, H.H. Papers.

Year	Educational Courses	Art, Workshop & Craft Courses
1892	26	7
1902	32	9
1905	9	23
1906/07	9	21
1910	11	18
1913	8	19[a]
1916	6	15[a]

[a]Hull House Trade School Included

Year	Debating Clubs	Social Clubs
1896	13	1
1902	6	6
1905/06	5	10
1906/07	5	7
1910	2	8

30. Sorrentino, *Organizing Against Crime*, pp. 46–47; Gans, *Urban Villagers*, pp. 37–38; Landesco, "Crime and the Failure of Institutions in Chicago," pp. 241–247; William F. Whyte, "Social Organization in the Slums," *American Sociological Review*, 8 (February 1943): 38; Interview with A. Sorrentino, 2 August 1977.

31. Jane Addams, "The Subjective Necessity for Social Settlements," in *Philanthropy and Social Progress*, Jane Addams et al. (Boston, 1893), pp. 1–27; Addams, *Twenty Years*, pp. 41–42, 113–128, 452–453; Allen F. Davis, *Spearheads for Reform, The Social Settlements and the Progressive Movement*, 1890–1914 (New York, 1967), pp. 3–26; Davis, *American Heroine*, pp. 53–66.

32. Addams, *Twenty Years*, pp. 281–296, 323–341; Breckinridge, *New Homes*, p. 238; Camprisi, "Ethnic Patterns," p. 447; Davis, *Crown Thy Good*, pp. 95, 108; Davis, *Spearheads for Reform*, pp. 60–83, 170–193; Gans, *Urban Villagers, passim*; Florence Kelley, "The Settlements: Their Lost Opportunity," *Charities and the Commons*, 16 (7 April 1906): 79–82; Kelley, "Hull House," p. 565; Moryal Knox, "Social Settlements and its Critics," *Survey*, 22 (8 August 1914): 486–487; Whyte, *Street Corner Society*, pp. 98–107; Woods and Kennedy, *Settlement Horizon*, pp. 74, 137–274.

33. Addams, "Subjective Necessity," pp. 1–17; Grace Abbott, *The Immigrant and the Community* (New York, 1917), p. 195; Gans, *Urban Villagers*, pp. 272–277; Francis Hackett, "Hull House—A Souvenir," (1 June 1925): 275–280; David G. Loth, *Swope of General Electric* (New York, 1958); Whyte, *Street Corner Society*, pp. 44, 98–107; Residents lists, 1889–1929, H.H. Papers; *Hull House Bullentin*, no. 1 (1905/06), p. 15; *Hull House Year Book*, 1906/07, pp. 5–13, 41–42; 1910, pp. 5, 8–14, 21; 1913, pp. 5, 8–14, 18; 1916, pp. 5, 8–11, 28, 36, 41–42.

34. Addams, *Twenty Years*, p. 147; Brandt, "Transplanted Birthright," p. 497; Gans, *Urban Villagers*, pp. 65–70; Landesco, "Member of the '42 Gang,'" pp. 970–998; Sorrentino, *Organizing Against Crime*, p. 130; Thrasher, *The Gang*, pp. 83–101; Woods and Kennedy, *Settlement Horizon*, p. 75; Louise DeKoven Bowen to Mary R. Smith, 9 January 1932, Addams Papers, SCPC; *Hull House Bulletin*, no. 1 (1896); no. 1 (1902), pp. 13–14; no. 1 (1905/06), pp. 11, 18–19; *Hull House Year Book*, 1906/07, p. 21; 1910, pp. 20, 44–47; 1929, p. 31; Interview with Nicolette Mallone, 17 August 1977; Interview with Florence Scala, 2 August 1977; Interview with Libonnati 23 August, 1977; Interview with A. Sorrentino, 2 August 1977.

35. Gans, *Urban Villagers*, pp. 133, 153–156; Landesco, "Member of the '42 Gang,'" p. 969; John Landesco, *Organized Crime in Chicago* (Chicago, 1929), pp. 126–127, 180, 196, 200–201; *Hull House Year Book*, 1921, p. 9; 1929, p. 11–12; Robert A. Cairo to Jane Addams, 21 December 1931, Addams Papers, SCPC; Louise DeKoven Bowen to Jane Addams, 8 January 1932, Addams Papers, SCPC; Louise DeKoven Bowen to Mary R. Smith, 9 January 1932, Addams Papers, SCPC; Louise DeKoven Bowen to Mary R. Smith, 14 January 1932, Addams Papers, SCPC; Interview with Libonnati, 23 August 1977; William J. Granata to Jane Addams, 11 January 1932, Addams Papers, SCPC.

36. Abbott and Breckinridge, *Truancy*, p. 277; Addams, "Objective Value," p. 37; Addams, *Twenty Years*, pp. 231–233, 256–258; Breckinridge, *New Homes*, pp. 189, 217; Nelli, *Italians in Chicago, passim*; Vecoli, "Contadini in Chicago," pp. 405–409, 412–414; Vecoli, "Prelates and Peasants," p. 231; *L'Italia*, 23 March 1889, Reel 30; 25 January 1890, Reel 30; 13 February, 14 May, 29 October 1892, Reel 30; 8 January, 16 September 1893, Reel 30; 16-17 February 1895, Reel 31; 24-25 August 1895, Reel 30; 25 November 1899, Reel 30; 24 May 1902, Reel 30; 23 May 1903, Reel 31; 26 September 1903, Reel 30; 10 December 1904, Reel 30; 12, 19 December 1908, Reel 30; 10 June 1911, Reel 31; 3 May 1914, Reel 30; 28 September 1915, Reel 30; *La Parola*, 17 January 1908, Reel 30; 12 April, 24 May, 19 July, 6, 27 September 1913, Reel 30; 30 January 1915, Reel 30; *Record Herald* (Chicago), 1 March 1908, Reel 30; *La Tribuna*, 11, 18, 20 June 1904, Reel 30; 15 July 1906, Reel 31; 13 August 1907, Reel 30; *L'Avanti*, 5 December 1918, Reel 30; 1 March 1919, Reel 30, FLPS; *Hull House Bulletin*, no. 4 (1901), p. 15; no. 1 (1902), pp. 2, 15; no 2 (1902), p. 2; no. 2 (1903/04), pp. 11–14; no. 1 (1905/06), pp. 2, 15, 23; *Hull House Year Book*, 1906/07, p. 49.

37. Addams, "Objective Value," p. 49; Amberg, *Madonna Center*, pp. 40–46, 83; Ray S. Baker, "Hull House and the Ward Boss," *Outlook* 57 (28 March 1898):770; Davis, *Spearheads*, pp. 153, 161–162; Anne F. Scott, "Saint Jane and the Ward Boss," *American Heritage*, 12 (December 1916): 96; Vecoli, "Prelates and Peasants," pp. 258–259; Florence Kelley to Henry Lloyd, 26 September 1898, Henry Lloyd Papers, Wisconsin State Historical Society; Thomas W. Holland to author, 5 August 1978; *Hull House Year Book*, 1906/07, pp. 28–29; *La Tribuna*, 11, 25 June, 2 July, 20 August 1904, Reel 30; 9 September 1906, Reel 30; *New World*, 30 April 1904; 29 November 1906; 29 February 1908; 7 March 1908; 14 March 1908; 15 March 1913; 27 February 1914; 6 March 1914, Catholic Diocese of Chicago Library; *La Parola*, 5 March 1908, Reel 31; 10 January 1914, Reel 31; *Record Herald*, 1 March 1908, Reel 30, FLPS.

38. Abbott, *The Immigrant and the Community*, pp. 83–95; Grace Abbott, "The Chicago Employment Agency and the Immigrant Worker," *American Journal of Sociology*, 14 (November 1908): 289-305; Edith Abbott "Grace Abbott, A Sisters' Memories," *Social Service Review*, 13 (September 1939): 359, 367–369; Jane Addams, "Ethical Survivals in Municipal Corruption," *International Journal of Ethics*, 3 (April 1898): 273–291; Breckinridge, *New Homes*, p. 276; Dunne, "Memoirs," pp. 200–201; Nelli, *Italians in Chicago*, pp. 62–63, 79–80, 105; Humbert S. Nelli, "The Italian Padrone System in the United States," *Labor History*, 5 (Spring 1964): 153–167; Sorrentino, *Organizing Against Crime*, p. 74; Vecoli, "Contadini in Chicago," pp. 412–414; *Hull House Year Book*, 1910, p. 10; *Inter Ocean* (Chicago), 11 February 1895, newspaper clippings, Addams Papers, SCPC; *L'Italia*, 15–17 February, 24–25 August 1895, Reel 30; *La Parola*, 19 July 1913, Reel 30; *La Tribuna*, 11 February 1895, newspaper clippings, H.H. Papers; *Annual Reports of the Immigrants Protective League*, 1909–1917, Immigrants Protective League Papers, University of Illinois.

39. Nelli, *Italians in Chicago*, p. 173; *Hull House Bulletin*, no. 1 (1905/06), pp. 3–4; *Hull House Year Book*, 1906/07, p. 37; 1910, pp. 25, 32; 1921, pp. 12–13, 34; 1929, pp. 13, 15–16; Thomas W. Holland to Allen F. Davis, 5 June 1975; Thomas W. Holland to author, 5 August 1978.

40. Addams, "Why the Ward Boss Rule," pp. 879–882; Baker, "Hull House and the Ward Boss," pp. 769–771; Allen F. Davis, "Jane Addams vs. The Ward Boss," *Journal of the Illinois State Historical Society*, 53 (Autumn 1960): 247–265; Nelli, *Italians in Chicago*, pp. 16–20, 22, 73, 98–100, 170–181, 250; Scott, "Saint Jane and the Ward Boss," pp. 94–99; Vecoli, "Contandini in Chicago," pp. 405–406, 408–409, 412–413; Vecoli, "Prelates and Peasants," p. 231' *Chicago Record*, 26 January 1898, newspaper

clippings, Addams Papers, SCPC; *Chicago Tribune*, 8 March 1898, Addams Papers, SCPC; *Evening Post* (Chicago), 7 March 1898, Addams Papers, SCPC; *Inter Ocean* (Chicago), 6 March 1898, Addams Papers, SCPC; *Times Herald*, 6, 29 March 1898, Addams Papers, SCPC.

41. Addams, *Twenty Years*, pp. 388–389; Edith C. Barrows, "The Greek Play at Hull House" *Commons*, 9 (January 1904): 6–10; Thomas Burgess, *Greeks in America* (New York, 1970), p. 124; Clinton Hall, "The Greek Play," *Charities*, 12 (February 1904): 125; George A. Kourvetaris, *First and Second Generation Greeks in Chicago* (Athens, 1971), pp. 49–50; *The Greek Press*, 25 November 1964, H.H. Papers; City of Chicago, The Board of Education, *Proceedings*, (1904/05), pp. 97, 101–108; *Hull House Year Book*, 1906/07, p. 36; 1916, pp. 33, 42.

42. Grace Abbott, "Study of Greeks in Chicago," *American Journal of Sociology*, 15 (November 1909): 386–387, 392; Kourvetaris, *First and Second Generation*, pp. 51–53, 67–69, 72–77, 81–84, 95; George J. Rakas, "Recollections of Jane Addams," August 1972, Box 10, Series 4, Addams Papers, SCPC; *Hull House Year Book*, 1910, pp. 23, 24–25, 51; 1913, pp. 23, 26–27, 41; 1916, pp. 12–14, 23, 26–27, 31–33, 37, 42; 1921, pp. 9–10, 24; 1929, p. 27; Hull House Boys' Club, 1907/08, JPA; Dr. S.D. Soter to author, 24 July 1979; Mrs. J.A. Britton to Miss Longan, 23 August 1919, Addams Papers, SCPC; Interview with Alex Elson, 23 August 1977; Thomas W. Holland to author, 5 August 1978; *Loxias*, 27 January 1909; 7, 21 November 1914, The Greek Newspapers, FLPS. Greek newspapers used in this article are from this source, Reels 23–28; *Saloniki*, 17 January, 5 September, 5 December 1914, Reel 23; 18 September, 9 October 1915, Reel 23; 22 January, 5 February, 4 March, 8 April 1916, Reel 23; 31 March, Reel 23; 19 May 1917, Reel 26; 22 November 1919, Reel 23; *The Star*, 15 March, 29 November 1907, Reel 23; *Chicago Tribune*, 9 April 1939, Greek Community Folder, West Side Historical Society Papers, University of Illinois; *The Greek Press*, 25 November 1964, H.H. Papers.

43. Addams, *Twenty Years*, pp. 256–257, 388–389; Barrows, "Greek Play," pp. 6–10; Burgess, *Greeks in America*, pp. 123–126; Kourvetaris, *First and Second Generation*, pp. 64–66; Steiner, *On the Trail*, pp. 286–287, 291; *Chicago Tribune*, 9 April 1939; *The Greek Press*, 25 November 1964; *Hull House Bulletin*, no. 1 (1905–06), p. 23; *Hull House Year Book*, 1906/07, pp. 36, 37, 48; 1910, pp. 23, 24, 29, 51; 1913, pp. 25, 30–31, 39; 1916, p. 14; 1921, pp. 11–13, 34; 1929, pp. 12–16; *Loxias*, 2 November 1912, Reel 23; 1, 21 November 1914, Reel 23; 14 April 1915, Reel 26; *Saloniki*, 29 November 1913, Reel 23; 17 April 1915, Reel 26; 8 April 1916, Reel 23; *The Star*, 24 November, 1 December 1905, Reel 23; 30 March, 29 June, 6 July, 19 October 1906, Reel 23; 25 January, 25 October, 22 November 1907, Reel 23; 2 July 1909, Reel 26.

44. *The Star*, 25 October 1907, Reel 23; *The Greek Press*, 25 November 1964, H.H. Papers.

45. Abbott, "Study of Greeks in Chicago," pp. 386–387; Burgess, *Greeks in America*, pp. 123–125; Kourvetaris, *First and Second Generation*, pp. 49–53, 58, 64–69, 72–77, 81–82, 84, 95; Steiner, *On the Trail*, pp. 286–287; *Chicago Tribune*, 9 April 1939, West Side Historical Society Papers; *The Greek Press*, 25 November 1964, H.H. Papers.

Up to 15,000 immigrants per day landed at Ellis Island. In this photo taken shortly before World War I, immigrants wearing numbered tags ride ferry across New York Harbor.

The Federal Government and the Americanization Movement, 1915-24

JOHN F. McCLYMER

Americanization may well be the least studied major social movement in American history. This crusade aimed at nothing less than cramming the assimilation experience, normally the product of generations of living in America, into a short-term indoctrination in "the American way." The extent of the movement is difficult to exaggerate. More than thirty states, in the years surrounding World War I, passed laws establishing Americanization programs; hundreds of chambers of commerce organized English and civics classes in thousands of factories; more than three thousand school boards initiated Americanization classes; unions, especially the United Mine Workers, encouraged members to learn English and take out citizenship papers; philanthropic organizations, such as the Young Men's and Young Women's Christian Associations and numerous settlement houses, began Americanization programs in hundreds of communities; and, of course, patriotic organizations— from the Daughters and Sons of the American Revolution to the newly formed American Legion—entered the field. Under their combined impact, naturalization proceedings became

© 1978 by John F. McClymer

The author is assistant professor of history at Assumption College.

public events, the Fourth of July became Americanization Day, employers vowed not to promote their unnaturalized employees, and, in Iowa at least, it was against the law to speak a foreign language.

The few scholarly studies of this broad-gaged movement that have appeared have focused on the efforts of private organizations — the National Americanization Committee and the Foreign Language Information Service in particular.[1] Federal Americanization efforts have been largely ignored, the connections of private, state, and federal agencies unexplored. It is not easy to account for this almost complete lack of attention to the federal role. Perhaps the absence of congressional and presidential action has led to an assumption that the federal role was minor. If that has been the case, even the most cursory examination of the Americanization records of the Bureaus of Naturalization and Education will suffice to demonstrate that the federal efforts were, if anything, even more extensive than those of state, local, and private agencies.[2]

Whatever the reason, Americanization is too important a movement to ignore any longer, for it has much to tell us about ethnicity and assimilation,[3] about nativism and immigration

restriction, about the domestic impact of World War I, about the genesis of the notorious Red Scare, and about the emergence in America of a style of politics based upon accusations of disloyalty.

World War I marked a turning point in the history of ethnic relations in the United States, and Americanization was one of the major manifestations of the change. Prior to the war, continuous large-scale immigration had been a constant factor in the nation's development and ranked with urbanization and industrialization as one of the forces transforming American society. The war put a temporary end to European emigration, and Congress, first with a literacy requirement in 1917 and then with a series of restriction acts climaxed by the Johnson-Reed Act of 1924, voted to make that temporary suspension permanent. A social revolution had begun, albeit negatively. One of the most significant terms in the American equation had been canceled out.

Beyond the fact that the war years marked a drastic reduction in the number of immigrants lay an equally important but more subtle change in the attitudes of native Americans toward immigrants and ethnic groups. Like immigration itself, nativism had been a constant in American history and, like the annual immigration totals, had waxed and waned for more than a century.[4] From 1914 on, the danger of war and then the war itself transformed this "normal" quotient of distrust natives felt for aliens into a suspiciousness that resembled paranoia. Older Americans experienced a growing and, for some, an hysterical fear that immigrants were unassimilable. The United States, many believed, was threatened with Balkaniza-

[1] Edward Hartmann, *The Movement to Americanize the Immigrant* (New York, 1948), is an uncritical account of the N.A.C. John Higham, *Strangers in the Land: Patterns of American Nativism, 1865-1925* (New Brunswick, N.J., 1955) includes an account of the movement; it is partially based upon Hartmann but is far superior. Daniel Erwin Weinberg has attempted, but not very persuasively, to refute Higham's assumption that Americanizers were nativists in *The Foreign Language Information Service and the Foreign Born: A Case Study of Cultural Assimilation Viewed as a Problem in Social Technology* (Ph.D. dissertation, Univ. of Minnesota, 1973). The programs of the Y.W.C.A.'s International Institutes are described in Raymond Mohl and Neil Batten, "Ethnic Adjustment in the Industrial City: The International Institute of Gary, 1919-1940," *International Migration Review* 6 (Winter 1972):361-376. An incisive study of Americanization in a single city is A. Gerd Korman, *Industrialization, Immigrants and Americanizers: The View From Milwaukee, 1866-1921* (Madison, 1967).

[2] The records of the Bureaus of Naturalization and Education are in Records of the Immigration and Naturalization Service, Record Group 85, and Records of the Office of Education, Record Group 12, National Archives (hereinafter cited as RG____, NA). Korman used the Naturalization records that related to his study of Milwaukee. No other account of the movement has utilized either collection. See Joseph B. Howerton, "Some Sources of Federal Documentation of Minority Groups in Chicago," paper given at the Conference on the National Archives and Urban Research, June 1970.

[3] The sociological literature on ethnicity scarcely recognizes that the Americanization movement ever existed. Milton Gordon, *Assimilation in American Life: The Role of Race,*

Religion, and National Origins (New York, 1964), briefly adverts to the movement but only as a backdrop to a discussion of cultural pluralism. The studies collected in Nathan Glazer and Daniel P. Moynihan, eds., *Ethnicity: Theory and Experience* (Cambridge, Mass., 1975), share, for the most part, the working assumption that ethnicity is a *new* phenomenon. Historians must bear much of the responsibility for this lack of historical awareness.

[4] The standard accounts of nativism in America are Ray Allen Billington, *The Protestant Crusade, 1800-1860: A Study of the Origins of American Nativism* (New York, 1938), and Higham, *Strangers in the Land.* As the subtitle of Higham's classic account indicates, nativism in America had settled into several stereotypical forms: anti-Catholicism, racism, and anti-radicalism. Higham argues that nativism became most virulent during periods of national self-doubt; e.g., during economic downturns. The return of confidence led to a kind of benign neglect of the issue. Interestingly, there does not appear to be any correlation between rising immigration totals and increased nativism.

The streets adjoining the office in New York City where the Labor Department admitted new Americans to full citizenship were filled with entrepreneurs anxious to offer their services—for a fee.

tion as ethnic groups banded together in ghetto neighborhoods isolated from what cultural monopolists called "American life." Even worse, to those troubled, was the prospect that immigrants would retain their Old World political loyalties. These permanent aliens might then, as spies and saboteurs, undermine the American war effort from within.

Some of this fear was no doubt inevitable, for nativism ran deep in American political culture.

But some of it also derived from the political rhetoric of 1916 and 1917. Theodore Roosevelt peppered his quest for the Republican nomination with denunciations of "hyphenated" Americans (e.g., German-Americans). And he was the first major political figure to campaign for "100% Americanism." Roosevelt, however, did not have the issue to himself for long. At Woodrow Wilson's dictation, the 1916 Democratic platform condemned ethnic "conspiracies" to influence American foreign policy. By early 1917 the most implausible claims were given a serious hearing. Sen. Lee Overman (D−N.C.), for example, warned the American people of a hundred thousand spies in their midst.[5] Members of the Immigration Restric-

[5] See "Colonel Roosevelt's New Crusade," *Literary Digest*

Franklin Knight Lane, President Wilson's choice to head the Department of the Interior, sought to increase his agency's role in acculturating the immigrant.

tion League, and those who shared their creed of Anglo-conformity, lost no time in pressing home their opportunity.[6] Besides restricting immigration, the war years also facilitated the efforts of those who sought to assimilate the immigrant by forcefeeding him huge portions of patriotic pabulum; i.e., the efforts of the Americanizers.

The first requirement for an understanding of Americanization is a reliable inventory of the groups, agencies, and organizations that participated in the movement. This in itself is a herculean task. The National Americanization Committee tried to coordinate all the manifold Americanization programs in the country and compiled a roster of interested parties which, as of June 1918, contained well over one hundred entries. And even this "list of lists"[7] was incomplete. It is better to begin with the federal agencies most closely involved: the Bureau of Naturalization in the Department of Labor, the Bureau of Education in the Department of the Interior, the Committee on Public Information (Creel Committee), and the Council of National Defense. Such a starting point has several advantages. It will partially fill in the major gaps in our knowledge of the movement. It will permit us to focus on the arena in which the various interests struggling to assume direction of the movement fought it out. Perhaps most significant, a focus on the federal effort will allow us to exploit and describe extraordinarily rich records of the Bureaus of Naturalization and Education.

While more than thirty states enacted Americanization measures and hundreds of cities followed suit, the federal agencies operated in what amounted to a legislative vacuum. Further, as will be seen, the executive branch failed to give needed direction to those bureaus and departments interested in the subject. Instead of resulting in federal inactivity, however, the absence of legislative or executive guidance presented bureaucrats, politicians, and interested third parties with a variety of opportunities to create policy at the subcabinet level. Particularly bitter rivals in the resulting infighting were Raymond A. Crist, deputy commissioner of naturalization from 1915 to 1919,[8] supported by his superior, Commissioner Richard Campbell, and, in the Bureau of Education, Commissioner P. P. Claxton, who could rely on the backing of his superior, Secretary of the Interior Franklin K. Lane.

---

52 (June 3, 1916): 1618; "Democratic Campaign Issues," ibid. 53 (July 1, 1916):4; "To Make Us Spy-Proof and Bomb Proof," ibid. 54 (Mar. 10, 1917):610. Overman based his estimate on "creditable reports from secret-service men" passed on to him by the Justice Department. See also Theodore Roosevelt, *America for Americans* (n.p., 1916) for a fuller account of his crusade for "100% Americanism."

⁶ See Barbara Miller Solomon, *Ancestors and Immigrants: A Changing New England Tradition* (Chicago, 1956). The phrase "Anglo-conformity" comes from Gordon, *Assimilation in American Life*.

⁷ Frances A. Kellor to [Commissioner of Education] P. P. Claxton, June 24, 1918, enclosing "List of Lists Found in the Office," box 106, RG 12, NA.

⁸ Crist had the following titles: deputy commissioner of naturalization, 1915-19; director of citizenship, 1919-21; chief naturalization officer, 1921-23; and commissioner of naturalization, 1923-25. See National Archives and Records Service, "Report on Series Identification Sheets for Department of Labor [,] Immigration and Naturalization Service — Americanization Section," in "Immigration and Naturalization (Access. 192)," p. 2.

Crist and others in the Bureau of Naturalization saw Americanization primarily as a matter of naturalizing the unnaturalized, and they moved quickly to stake out the field. By 1916 they had put together a citizenship textbook that was distributed free of charge to aliens attending Americanization courses.[9] At the same time they sought to persuade school boards to begin such courses and aliens to attend them.[10]

This foray into the schools may have seemed a logical extension of the Naturalization Service to Crist and Commissioner Campbell, but it was a clear case of trespass to the Bureau of Education, which moved swiftly to defend its administrative territory. About a week before the July 10, 1916, Americanization conference, which Naturalization held to compile its citizenship textbook, the Bureau of Education sponsored an Americanization conference of its own. Both conferences were for educators working with the foreign born, and the two can thus be looked upon as the beginning of the public phase of the rivalry between the bureaus. Education easily won the first round for while Naturalization managed to get President Woodrow Wilson to deliver a welcoming address, Education attracted more educators by scheduling its conference to meet in conjunction with the annual convention of the National Education Association.[11]

Out of the Bureau of Education's conference came a "Committee of One Hundred" consisting of, according to Commissioner Claxton, "educators, businessmen, editors, representa-

George Creel, chairman of the Committee on Public Information, worked to Americanize the immigrants, as part of a larger effort to propagandize Americans into supporting a war that caused deep misgivings.

tives of patriotic societies and labor organizations in those states and cities in which there are large numbers of foreigners." This committee was Education's first attempt to coordinate and control the entire movement and Claxton apparently wished to use it to coopt the Bureau of Naturalization. This, at least, would appear to have been his motive in inviting Commissioner Campbell to join the committee. Campbell found the offer "interesting" and while he claimed his official duties prevented him from accepting, he did want his bureau represented. In particular, he wanted someone from Naturalization on the executive committee.[12]

Up to this point it appeared possible that the two agencies might coordinate their efforts, especially when Claxton agreed to name a repre-

[9] See file E420-D, RG 85, NA. Crist had the job of compiling the textbook. He farmed out its writing to various individuals. For an example of how this worked, see [Commissioner of Naturalization] Richard Campbell to J. M. Berkey [Director of Special Schools, Pittsburgh], June 15, 1916: "your suggestions . . . are so complete and so well arranged that they will be used practically in the form submitted." Berkey wrote lessons 1-8. The textbook also reprinted previously published material. See Williams S. McDowell to Crist, July 5, 1916, giving permission to reprint pages 1-30 of McDowell's booklet *The Constitution As It Is.*

[10] Files E16132 and 27671/495, RG 85, NA. A sample of every tenth letter sent to the bureau by aliens in response to its circular letter from 1915 through 1919 shows that respondents declined the bureau's invitation by a consistent three to one margin.

[11] See file 27671/1974, ibid., and *Proceedings* of the First Citizenship Convention (Washington, 1917) in file E420-E, ibid. Presiding Officer Crist noted, "This morning we represent a small, a very small, gathering." Ibid., p. 8. Neither bureau invited the other to send a representative to its conference.

[12] Claxton to Campbell, Aug. 26, 1916, Campbell to Claxton, Aug. 30, 1916, file 27671/1974, ibid.

sentative of Campbell's choosing to both the general and executive committees. Even Raymond Crist, usually suspicious, was optimistic. He thought the Committee of One Hundred's activities "can only tend to support and strengthen the work now being carried on by the Bureau of Naturalization with the public school authorities." [13] But it is important to note the reason for Crist's optimism. He thought Naturalization would be able to use the Committee of One Hundred to promote its own programs and lost no time in requesting Claxton to make sure that publicity sent out by the committee "contain a specific reference to this work which the public schools and this Bureau are carrying on, so that the support which the Bureau feels you are ready to lend will be manifested in such a practical way." Claxton refused. He claimed the conference had not authorized that type of publicity and it did not "seem advisable to deviate from the kind of publicity" the conferees had requested. Commissioner Campbell rejoined the correspondence at this point to expostulate that "such publicity . . . will not be mentioning something that the public schools are not already actively engaged in — their cooperation with this bureau." [14] That, although Claxton did not say so,[15] was the whole point. Neither bureau would consider working with the other save in terms of cooptation, and their brief attempt to coordinate fizzled in this argument over publicity.

Thereafter Education would sedulously ignore Naturalization's program whenever possible; it would, for example, omit it from the lists it sent to schools of agencies working with the foreign born. When forced to recognize its rival's existence, the bureau would concede Naturalization could, as Interior Secretary Lane put it, "do much in the way of giving definite instruction in matters of citizenship to those who have applied for citizenship papers." But it reserved to itself "the larger task of educating all aliens in the use of the English language, in the history and resources of the country, in our industrial requirements, in our manners and customs and in our civic, social and political ideals." [16] For its part, Naturalization kept a wary eye on its rival and encouraged the chief naturalization examiners [C.N.E.s] in the field to report on Education's every move in their districts.[17]

Such bureaucratic jealousies are neither unusual nor even very interesting, except to the participants. Only the coming of the war made the Americanization movement a potential empire worthy of a jealous ruler. Because of the war too, Education and Naturalization would have to face other rivals, though most of these were not serious. The Treasury Department, for example, established an office to persuade the foreign born to buy Liberty bonds. The War and Navy departments set up special programs for the large numbers of non-English-speaking recruits.

More threatening, both to aliens and to other federal agencies, were the activities of the Department of Justice, which defined Americanization as the prevention of espionage and sabotage. The best-known examples of this approach were the Palmer raids of 1920, but the department had been active throughout the war years as well.[18] Justice, of course, had no interest in directing public school programs, but it sought Congressional authorization to deal with the question of the alien's "hyphenated" loyalties, and Congress passed the Espionage Act of 1917 and the Sedition Act of 1918 while failing to pass legislation pushed by Education and Naturalization. The Espionage and Sedi-

[16] Franklin K. Lane to B. F. Welty, May 15, 1918, box 106, RG 12, NA. Congressman Welty had introduced an alien registration bill that would have given the Bureau of Naturalization jurisdiction over immigrant education. Lane, on the other hand, supported the Smith-Bankhead bill which would have given Education jurisdiction. For the failure of these and other Americanization measures, see below.

[17] See, for example, the Feb. 25, 1919, report from Chicago C.N.E. W. H. Wagner to the bureau recording his understanding of Education's plans based on an Education-sponsored conference on Americanization he attended; file E1780, RG 85, NA.

[18] The standard general account is William Preston, Jr., *Aliens and Dissenters: Federal Suppression of Radicals, 1903-1933* (Cambridge, Mass., 1963). For the war years, see H. C. Peterson and Gilbert Fite, *Opponents of War, 1917-1918* (Seattle, 1957). See also Zechariah Chafee, Jr., *Free Speech in the United States* (Cambridge, Mass., 1941), for the classic discussion of the constitutional issues involved. Justice, in addition to its own Bureau of Investigation, employed the volunteer services of the 250,000-member National Security League.

[13] Claxton to Campbell, Sept. 19, 1916, Acting Commissioner [Crist] to Seattle C.N.E. John Speed Smith, Sept. 21, 1916, ibid.

[14] Crist to Claxton, Sept. 25, 1916, Claxton to Crist, Oct. 7, 1916, Campbell to Claxton, Oct. 16, 1916, ibid.

[15] There is no record in either the Naturalization or Education files of any reply to Campbell. Negotiations, it appears, broke off at this point and no representative of Naturalization to the Committee of One Hundred was appointed, as a 1917 roster of the committee in file 1974, RG 85, makes plain.

tion Acts were, as Zachariah Chafee has pointed out,[19] draconian measures and fell with particular severity on recent immigrants.[20] Fortunately, deportation, Justice's favorite means of dealing with alleged alien radicals, required the cooperation of the Department of Labor. In 1920, Assistant Secretary of Labor Louis F. Post made a determined and largely successful effort to end the "deportations delirium" growing out of the Palmer raids.[21] Here was one case, at least, where interdepartmental rivalry proved conducive to the public good.

In addition to increasing the activities of established agencies, the war led to the creation of many new ones, two of which proved important in federal Americanization efforts. One was George Creel's Committee on Public Information, established by executive order.[22] It saw the inculcation of patriotism as its special province. It also, as the official propaganda agency of the government, perceived a responsibility to watch over and domesticate the foreign-language press.[23] It is not surprising that Creel early set up a Division of Work With the Foreign Born and embarked upon his own version of Americanization even though President Wilson's order contained nothing explicit on the subject.

The other new agency was the Council of National Defense, charged by Congress with coordinating the war effort. When first Congress and then the executive branch failed to place any one agency in charge of Americanization, it fell to the council to try to adjudicate the conflicting claims of the disputants.

All of this was obviously a recipe for acrimony, not to say chaos, and a measure of both did result. The absence of congressional and executive leadership left agencies free to set up their own programs, which were limited only by their need for funds and the success of their competitors. That lack of leadership creates problems for the historian accustomed to employing either a presidential or a congressional synthesis in analyzing federal policy. Here our focus is necessarily on the bureaucracy and its relationships with public and private interests. We will continue to emphasize the Bureaus of Education and Naturalization which managed to remain the federal agencies most involved in Americanization and will, in the remainder of this article, sketch the networks of alliances each tried to create both inside and outside government and attempt a preliminary assessment of the success each had in imposing its leadership on the thousands of Americanization programs conducted on the state and local levels.

Without question the Bureau of Education was far more successful at winning allies than its chief rival, but it was so dependent upon one ally, the National Americanization Committee, that it is more accurate to say that Education became a subsidiary of the N.A.C. The reason for this was simple. Congress appropriated no funds for the bureau's Americanization work and so the N.A.C. financed it until it became illegal for federal agencies to use private funds; that is, until the end of fiscal year 1919. According to N.A.C. Chairman Frank Trumbull, this subsidy, from April 1914 to June 1919, amounted to exactly $85,247.80. He added, "It is not too much to say that we think it [the subsidy] has been largely responsible for the Americanization work undertaken under Secretary Lane's direction." [24]

Also known as the Committee for Immigrants in America,[25] the National Americanization Committee was a business group that viewed Americanization largely in terms of fitting immigrant labor into American industry.[26] The top leadership of the N.A.C. overlapped almost completely with the Immigration Committee, formed in 1917, of the United States Chamber of Commerce.[27] According to Trumbull, the

[19] Chafee, Free Speech, pp. 56, 57-58, 362.

[20] The title of Preston's Aliens and Dissenters makes this point.

[21] See Louis F. Post, The Deportations Delirium of 1920 (Chicago, 1923). See also Sundry File re: Alledged [sic] disloyalty, files 16/359, 167/603, 167/642, and 167/174, in General Records of the Department of Labor, RG 174, NA.

[22] See George Creel, How We Advertised America (New York, 1920). See also James R. Mock and Cedric Lawson, Words That Won the War: The Story of the Committee on Public Information, 1917-1919 (Princeton, 1930).

[23] Creel, How We Advertised, pp. 113, 114, 162; Mock and Lawson, Words That Won the War, pp. 68-70, 73ff, 216-229.

[24] Frank Trumbull to Claxton, Apr. 1, 1919, box 106, RG 12, NA. This letter was actually the final "résumé" of N.A.C. activities.

[25] See National Americanization Committee, "Contributions Received During Fiscal Year October, 1916–September, 1917," and "Contributions From October 1, 1917, to March 31, 1918," ibid. For membership lists, see Hartmann, Movement to Americanize the Immigrant, pp. 38-39n, 220-221n.

[26] See John F. McClymer, "Scientific Nativism: Style Versus Substance in Progressive Schemes for Assimilation," paper given at the Organization of American Historians Annual Meeting, April 1976.

[27] Frank Trumbull was chairman of the N.A.C., the Chamber's Immigration Committee, and the Committee for Im-

chairman of both, the N.A.C. "largely financed the work of the Immigration Committee of the Chamber of Commerce of the U.S.A."[28] So while it is true that scores of local chambers of commerce, unaffiliated with the United States Chamber, sponsored Americanization drives in their communities, and that some employers, most notably Henry Ford, did likewise, the fact is clear that the N.A.C. was the authoritative voice of business on the Americanization question.

Because it paid the piper, the N.A.C. called the tune. Its formal agreement with the Bureau of Education did stipulate that "policies will be determined by the Commissioner of Education under the direction of the Secretary of the Interior who can alone be responsible for them. All important policies will, before their adoption, be discussed with the duly authorized representatives of the National Americanization Committee."[29] This left the bureau technically free to disregard N.A.C. recommendations, but legal guarantees meant little in practice. When, for example, his Division of Immigrant Education needed two additional typewriters, the commissioner of education had to go, hat in hand, to the N.A.C.[30] Similarly, when the N.A.C. objected to Division Director H. H. Wheaton communicating directly with foreign-language groups, preferring that such matters pass through the hands of its own staff, the commissioner immediately concurred.[31]

Such examples of abject dependence — there were many more — pale in significance when compared to N.A.C. initiative in establishing policy. N.A.C. Vice-Chairman Frances Kellor, for example, drew up the plans for the War Work Extension of the Division of Immigrant Education and was placed in charge of its work with the title of special advisor to the commissioner

of education. The extension, which was the bureau's most important wartime program, was so completely her creation that she could write to Commissioner Claxton, "I am willing to undertake its financing until such time as government funds can be secured for this work." She meant, of course, that the N.A.C. would put up the money.[32] The National Americanization Committee was no mere lobbying group — it had the Bureau of Education in its hip pocket.

From this relationship the Bureau of Education gained the wherewithal to stake out a claim in the field of Americanization without congressional or executive authorization. Put another way, the bureau bought time to lobby for the Smith-Bankhead and Kenyon bills which would have granted it both money and legal standing for its Americanization efforts. Time, however, was not on the bureau's side. Those bills failed and, at the end of fiscal year 1919, the bureau's subsidy from the N.A.C. came under congressional ban.

As the senior partner, the National Americanization Committee stood to gain much more from its sponsorship of the Division of Immigrant Education. The subsidy meant, among other advantages, that the N.A.C. could rely on the support of the commissioner of education and the secretary of the interior in its lobbying activities. It used this favorable position very effectively, for example, with the Council of National Defense. According to a confidential report of the council, "the matter of the alien and his relation to the war activities of the United States was first acted upon officially" when the council approved Interior Secretary Lane's motion that an advisory commission prepare recommendations on the matter. This commission then "called into conference representatives of the National Americanization Committee and its affiliated organizations" to help prepare a "War Policy for Aliens."[33]

The policy proposed by the N.A.C. was sweeping indeed. It called on the Council of National Defense to appoint a committee on Americanization and urge its state councils to

migrants. William Fellowes Morgan was treasurer of all three. Frances A. Kellor was assistant to the chairman of the Chamber's committee, vice-chairman of the Committee for Immigrants, a member of the Executive Committee, and later vice-chairman of the N.A.C. George A. Cullen, vice-chairman of the Chamber's committee, was also secretary of the Committee for Immigrants. See file 27671/1832, RG 85, NA.

[28] Trumbull to Claxton, Apr. 1, 1919, box 106, RG 12, NA.

[29] "Memorandum of Understanding Between the Secretary of the Interior and the National Americanization Committee for the Extension of the Work of the Division of Immigrant Education in the Bureau of Education," May 2, 1918, box 106, RG 12, NA.

[30] Claxton to Kellor, Mar. 20, 1918, ibid.

[31] Kellor to Claxton, June 14, 19, 1918, Claxton to Kellor, June 22, 1918, ibid.

[32] Claxton to Lane, Apr. 16, 1918, ibid. Enclosed with this letter were seven exhibits setting forth Miss Kellor's plans. They include her letter to Claxton, Apr. 10, 1918, offering to finance the work. The "Memorandum of Understanding" cited above grew out of this proposal.

[33] W. E. Gifford [director, Council of National Defense] to Claxton, Jan. 24, 1918, and "Memorandum on the Alien Situation in the United States," n.d., p. 1, ibid.

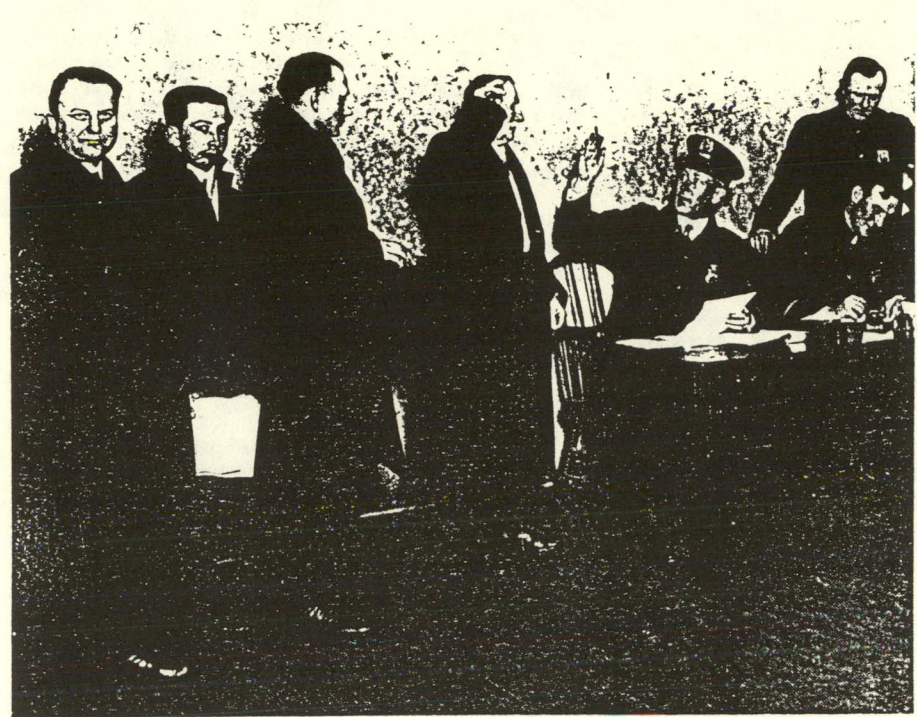

More than thirty thousand enemy aliens, who became the objects of Americanization, were registered in New York City alone.

do likewise. It recommended laws to require landlords to register the names of their alien tenants semiannually; require immigrants to declare their intention of learning English and applying for citizenship on pain of deportation; create a federal bureau to regulate private employment agencies; and fund the Division of Immigrant Education. In addition, the N.A.C. urged the council to regulate housing and working conditions, establish standards of industrial safety and public health, prohibit the soliciting of labor from war industries, and create a priority board for the allocation of labor. Finally, the council was to set up an Americanization program that would study and tighten citizenship requirements, secure the cooperation of ethnic societies in a war policy for aliens, and hold English and civics classes for interned enemy aliens.[34] The advisory commission con-

solidated most of these recommendations into a call for a special committee of "experts on immigration and alien conditions" which would coordinate federal Americanization efforts, formulate "a sound national policy," and prepare "recommendations for legislative actions."[35]

Even in this milder, more vague, form, the N.A.C.'s war policy seemed "unwise" to the council, which held that it should not "take any special or extraordinary action apart from the normal and customary functions now exercised with reference to aliens by authorized agencies." The council voted to refer the report to the Bureau of Education and the Department of Labor, which housed the Bureau of Naturalization, with the advice that "the alien question should continue to be handled along broad educational lines as heretofore, and that the

---

[34] "Memorandum to the Advisory Commission of the Council of National Defense Concerning a War Policy for Aliens," Oct. 31, 1917, p. 38. Quoted in Hartmann, *Movement to Americanize the Immigrant*, pp. 171-172.

[35] "Memorandum on the Alien Situation," p. 5, box 106, RG 12, NA.

direction of effort should be toward expediting normal processes." [36]

Following this rejection, the N.A.C.'s war policy would have been a dead letter had it not been for its connections with the Bureau of Education. For, in keeping with its general view of Americanization as an educational matter, the council did, on December 13, 1917, endorse "the efforts of the United States Bureau of Education . . . and request the cooperation of the State Councils of Defense and committees of public safety, [in] developing this educational policy." [37] When the bureau subsequently submitted a proposal for the cooperation of state councils, the council routinely approved it. In so doing, it approved a number of N.A.C. recommendations it had previously rejected.[38] Other N.A.C. proposals were incorporated into the duties of the bureau's War Work Extension. The extension, as noted above, was strictly an N.A.C. operation with the N.A.C. providing the plans, the funds, the staff, and even the headquarters.[39]

By war's end, N.A.C. Chairman Frank Trumbull could report that fourteen of the committee's twenty-one policy recommendations had been wholly or partially implemented; he did not find it necessary to recall that the Council of National Defense had once rejected them all.[40] Clearly the businessmen in the N.A.C. could regard their $85,000 investment in the Bureau of Education as money well spent.

Few private interest groups have been able to metamorphose themselves into federal agencies as the N.A.C. did when it effectively became the War Work Extension of the Bureau of Education. And in its new official capacity it struck out boldly to monopolize the Americanization movement throughout the country. This put it in direct competition with at least two other federal agencies, the Creel Committee and the Bureau of Naturalization.

Creel claimed his committee "avoided the professional 'Americanizers', and steered clear of the accepted forms of 'Americanization'"; this was, at the least, an overstatement. Frank Trumbull reported that his staff spent four months surveying ethnic and Americanization organizations for the Creel Committee. Creel turned to the N.A.C. because he wanted his committee to work with ethic groups "from the *inside*." His idea was to form "loyal" ethnic associations and for this he needed a survey of the existing organizations of the foreign born. According to Trumbull, the survey extended to some fifty thousand national, state, and local agencies. There is, unfortunately, no way to check this extraordinary figure. We do know that the N.A.C. survey turned up only a handful of associations which existed "primarily to work for America and only secondarily for its native land." From this small list of safe immigrants Creel set up more than a dozen ethnic associations, including the American Friends of German Democracy and the American-Hungarian Loyalty League.[41]

In charge of the Americanization survey was Frances Kellor who, at the same time, was drawing up plans for the War Work Extension that she subsequently directed. At Secretary Lane's suggestion, Education Commissioner Claxton talked to Creel about Miss Kellor's plans. Claxton reported, "He says Miss Kellor is admirably fitted for this work, but that she is liable to undertake more than can be done well." [42] All of this hardly squares with Creel's postwar claim that he "avoided the professional 'Americanizers.'" On the other hand, it does indicate the N.A.C.'s considerable skill at bureaucratic maneuvering. It would be needed because the War Work Extension's operations overlapped with the Creel Committee's in at least three main areas: propaganda in the foreign-language press, sponsorship of safe

[36] Gifford to Claxton, Jan. 24, 1918, ibid.

[37] "Memorandum on the Alien Situation," p. 2, ibid. Hartmann incorrectly claims that the council endorsed the N.A.C. program; *Movement to Americanize the Immigrant*, pp. 188-189.

[38] Henry M. Robinson [assistant chief, State Councils Section, Council of National Defense] to Claxton, Feb. 12, 1918, box 106, RG 12, NA. For the parallels between the N.A.C. and Bureau of Education proposals, compare "Memorandum to the Advisory Commission" and Council of National Defense, Bulletin no. 86, *Americanization of Aliens*, Feb. 12, 1918, ibid.

[39] See Claxton to Lane, Apr. 16, 1918, and "Memorandum of Understanding," ibid. The extension was housed at N.A.C. headquarters in New York City.

[40] Trumbull to Claxton, Dec. 5, 1918; "Summary Report of the National Americanization Committee Confirming in Particular Its Relation to the United States Bureau of Education, Recommendations Made to the Council of National Defense . . . and Action Taken Thereon," ibid.

[41] Creel, *How We Advertised*, pp. 184, 187-192; Trumbull to Claxton, Apr. 1, 1919, box 106, RG 12, NA. Howard C. Hill, "The Americanization Movement," *The American Journal of Sociology* 24, no. 6 (May 1919): 614-615. See also Mock and Lawson, *Words That Won the War*, pp. 216-229.

[42] Claxton to Lane, Apr. 16, 1918, box 106, RG 12, NA.

racial groups within ethnic communities, and organization of patriotic pageantry for the foreign born.

To head off potential disputes, the commissioner of education, the chairman of the Committee on Public Information, and the chief of the States Councils Section of the Council of National Defense adopted a "Memorandum of Understanding" which N.A.C. Chairman Trumbull claimed, recognized that "the Americanization work shall be headed up in the Bureau of Education." [43] The memorandum was not quite that explicit; it was a full description of the scope of the War Work Extension's activities with the acknowledgement that "the Committee on Public Information and the Council of National Defense are also interested in certain phases of this work." To avoid "loss of time, money or energy by overlapping or through lack of harmony in their work," the three officials agreed to submit "projects pertaining to the foreign-born population . . . in writing to the other parties to this understanding." They further agreed "for the present at least" to hold weekly conferences.[44]

Whether the understanding would have held up over the course of a long war can be doubted, but the memorandum seems to have been generally in effect during the six months between its signing and the Armistice. In part this was due to an honest desire of the Bureau of Education, which regarded it as a significant victory, to abide by it.[45] More important, probably, was the fact that the extension's programs had barely grown beyond the pilot stage when the war ended. Its campaign to create loyal "racial" associations never extended beyond New York City. If it had, however, trouble might have been unavoidable since the Creel Committee was busily plowing the same field, and the Kellor group, despite its pro-business orientation,

showed a surprising willingness to enlist Zionists, and even "social revolutionists." [46]

Even more potential for competition lay in the extension's interest in the foreign-language press. Creel clearly tried to monopolize federal publicity and propaganda and, while he never quite succeeded, his committee's Division of Work With the Foreign Born inundated the ethnic press with patriotic copy. Creel estimated that some six hundred newspapers, with a combined circulation of over five million, "turned over their news and advertising columns" to the committee.[47] Yet the War Work Extension issued its own press releases, employed its own translators, and made its own bargains with the foreign-language press.[48] Potential competition became actual after the war. By then the N.A.C. had severed its ties with the Bureau of Education and reconstituted itself as the Inter-Racial Council.[49] The Division of Work With the Foreign Born, meanwhile, survived the demise of the Creel Committee, first as a subsidiary of the American Red Cross and then as the Foreign Language Information Service.[50]

It is admittedly somewhat hazardous to surmise that the War Work Extension and the Division of Work With the Foreign Born would have crossed swords had the war not ended by comparing the activities of their postwar successors. But the differences are at least suggestive. The Inter-Racial Council moved directly to control the foreign-language press by purchasing the American Association of Foreign Language Newspapers.[51] The association supplied news stories and advertising to the ethnic press, and the business-dominated council intended to use it as part of a grand campaign against radicalism, particularly labor radicalism. Vice-Chairman Frances Kellor made this plain when

---

[43] Trumbull to Henry S. Pritchett [of the Carnegie Corporation], May 2, 1918, ibid. Trumbull also claimed that Kellor negotiated this understanding.

[44] "Memorandum of Understanding Between the Commissioner of Education, the Chairman of the Committee on Public Information and the Chief of the States Councils Section of the Council of National Defense," n.d. [May 1918], ibid.

[45] See Claxton to Kellor, June 6, 1918, ibid.: "It is my purpose that we shall carry out both in letter and in spirit the agreement with the Committee on Public Information and the States Division of the Council of National Defense not to encroach on their field."

[46] See "List of Persons Invited to Conference of June 20th, 1918. The Large Russian Committee," ibid. One member of the seven-member "Smaller Russian Committee" was Sergey Ingerman, described as the "Leader of the Russian Social Democrats Mensheviki."

[47] Mock and Lawson, *Words That Won the War*, p. 92; Creel, *How We Advertised*, p. 162.

[48] See, for examples, Kellor to Claxton, May 16, 1918, Kellor to J. Personine [editor, *Il Cittadino*], July 16, 1918, and Claxton to Steven Hattala [editor, *Ameriki Magyar Nepazavas*], June 10, 1918, box 106, RG 12, NA.

[49] Trumbull to Claxton, Apr. 1, 1919, ibid.

[50] See Weinberg, *Foreign Language Information Service*, pp. 21-22, 107-115.

[51] See *The Survey* 41 (Mar. 22, 1919):909.

she promised the National Association of Manufacturers that "we can make" the foreign-language press "pro-American if we go about it the right way." The "right way" was for the N.A.M. to use the advertising facilities of the association as "a means of controlling the foreign-language press and shaping its influence along the lines of a better Americanism and in opposition to Bolshevism." The N.A.M. endorsed her proposal.[52] Meanwhile, the Foreign Language Information Service abjured seeking control of the editorial policies of the foreign-language press and instead tried to serve as liaison between it and federal agencies.[53] This represented a major change from its role as government propagandist when it was still part of the Creel Committee, and a power struggle would have been inevitable if the War Work Extension had had time to develop the sort of program it later launched as the Inter-Racial Council.

An early peace then made possible the relative amity and modicum of cooperation that characterized relations among the Bureau of Education, the Council of National Defense, and the Committee on Public Information; peace, that is, and the adroit maneuvering of the N.A.C. which found ways of influencing, to a greater or lesser degree, the policies of all three agencies. As noted above, however, open warfare had broken out as early as 1916 between the Bureaus of Education and Naturalization over the direction of Americanization efforts in the nation's public schools.

It might seem from the foregoing that the deck was stacked in favor of the Education-N.A.C. alliance. N.A.C. control of the Chamber of Commerce's Americanization Committee guaranteed its authority to speak for the business community. The Council of National Defense, however indirectly, had adopted much of its Americanization program and it had worked out an understanding with the Creel Committee. The Bureau of Naturalization, in contrast, had been distinctly remiss in forging bureaucratic alliances. It did not even contact the

Committee on Public Information until October 1918 when it thought to use the committee's "Four Minute Men" to promote its public school programs.[54] Its relations with the Council of National Defense were more tenuous still. When the national council sent out a list of "Americanization Agencies Now in the Field" to the state councils, the Bureau of Naturalization was not even mentioned. The council did list the Bureau of Immigration, also in the Department of Labor, but with the notation that it referred "matters pertaining to immigrant education to the United States Bureau of Education."[55] No more plaintive evidence of bureaucratic isolation can be imagined. Naturalization lost the struggle for bureaucratic support by default. While its rival was busy negotiating memorandums of understanding, it could not get itself mentioned in government press releases. It did try to gain support in the business community by ardently seeking the endorsement of the United States Chamber of Commerce. This was a hopeless quest since, as noted above, the chamber's Immigration Committee was financed by the National Americanization Committee, and the N.A.C., of course, was promoting the work of the Bureau of Education. Naturalization refused to resign itself to the situation. Instead it attempted to bypass the chamber's Immigration Committee and deal directly with its general secretary. At one point Commissioner Campbell wrote that "the Bureau has recently been advised that this committee [the N.A.C.] is not the mouthpiece of the Chamber of Commerce . . . although until that time it had been led to believe such was the case." If Campbell had, in fact, believed this, he was certainly disabused when he learned that his letter had been turned over to Frances Kellor to answer. Campbell, though, did not give up easily and he again wrote to the general secretary. This time he claimed that the bureau's communications with local chambers of com-

[52] Kellor, "Address," *Proceedings* of the 24th Annual Convention of the National Association of Manufacturers of the United States, 1919, pp. 361-368; *Proceedings* of the 25th Annual Convention . . ., 1920, p. 297. See also Robert E. Park, *The Immigrant Press and Its Control* (New York, 1922), pp. 451-457.

[53] See, for example, the correspondence between F.L.I.S. Director Josephine Roche and Assistant Commissioner of Naturalization Crist, file E7571, RG 85, NA.

[54] See "Proposed Four Minute Speech," file 27671/4938, ibid. The "Four Minute Men" were volunteers who delivered brief patriotic addresses at movie and vaudeville theaters and the like. Examination of the bureau's files relating to Creel-sponsored ethnic organizations reveals sporadic contacts with the American Friends of German Democracy, file 27671/6098, ibid.; and the committee's Italian, Polish, and Russian Bureaus (all located in New York City), files 27671/6425, 6752, 6753, ibid.

[55] Council of National Defense, Bulletin no. 86, "Americanization of Aliens, Exhibit B, Some Americanization Agencies Now in the Field," box 106, RG 12, NA.

Sons of aliens who registered to become citizens became subject to the draft. Here a throng of a thousand women protesting the draft is rushed by New York police. The woman were allegedly urged on by anarchists Emma Goldman and Alexander Berkman.

merce indicated that *they* did not regard the N.A.C. as speaking for the national chamber, and he complained that Kellor's letter had seemed to close the door on cooperation between the bureau and the chamber.[56]

Out of all this persistence came a letter from the chairman of the chamber's Immigration Committee, Frank Trumbull, to some 130 local chambers urging them to cooperate with the work of the Bureau of Naturalization.[57] Campbell chose to regard this as a victory; but inasmuch as the national chamber continued to ignore his bureau's program, it makes more sense

to regard it as a measure of just how eager the bureau was for business support. It had taken Campbell more than six months to get a single letter. A comparable effort with the Creel Committee might well have produced a flood of publicity for the bureau.

Ignored by the rest of the bureaucracy and given only token recognition by the business community, the Bureau of Naturalization started in the immediate postwar period to take advantage of its position in the Department of Labor to cultivate the unions. It sent a circular letter to the locals of the United Mine Workers and another to those of the International Iron Moulders Union of North America. Initial responses were encouraging. Most of the locals responding seemed eager to cooperate. But the bureau abandoned this campaign almost immediately.[58] The reason is by no means clear, and not much exists in the bureau's files to suggest why it decided not to follow up on the unions' willingness to cooperate. However, there is some evidence to suggest that working with the unions might have put the bureau in potential conflict with the courts. For some judges in naturalization proceedings denied citizenship to strikers. Several U.M.W. locals

[56] Campbell to Elliot H. Goodwin, May 19, 1917, Joseph Mayper [executive secretary, Committee on Immigration, Chamber of Commerce] to Campbell, June 16, 1917, Campbell to Goodwin, Aug. 8, 1917, Kellor to Campbell, Sept. 5, 1917, Campbell to Goodwin, Sept. 8, 1917, Goodwin to Campbell, Sept. 15, 1917, file 27671/1832, RG 85, NA.

[57] See Campbell to Goodwin, Dec. 29, 1919, ibid., in which Campbell expressed his satisfaction with this result.

[58] File E36 U.C., ibid.

complained of this, and the bureau itself verified the charges in at least one case.[59]

This placed the bureau in a ticklish position. On the one hand, it had recommended to the courts, before these complaints, that no objection be made to the citizenship applications of striking aliens. On the other hand, as Commissioner Campbell informed one disgruntled U.M.W. official, "the admissability of an alien to citizenship is a matter reposed by law exclusively within the discretion of the courts."[60] It may be that bureau officials were unwilling to cultivate the unions if it meant jeopardizing the good will of the courts. It may be too that the coincidence of the bureau's campaign with the high water mark of the Red Scare left Naturalization officials less than eager to solicit labor support. Unfortunately, the records of the Bureau of Naturalization simply do not contain enough information to permit confident conclusions. What is clear is that the bureau did not pursue unions with the ardor that it courted the United States Chamber of Commerce.[61]

Outmaneuvered in the bureaucracy, bereft of business support, unwilling to seek the blessing of organized labor, the Bureau of Naturalization was nevertheless not without powerful allies, and it more than held its own in its struggle with Education. The bureau gained these allies largely through the activities of its eleven chief naturalization examiners in major cities across the country. The chief duty of these examiners was to represent the government at naturalization hearings; this brought them into close and cooperative contact with state and federal courts. Judges and court clerks were, as a result, familiar with and favorably disposed to the bureau's Americanization efforts. On the local level judges would address rallies and sign public appeals for the bureau's public school activities. On the national level, court officers, who were often important figures in local politics, would lobby congressmen and senators on the bureau's behalf. This happened in 1917 when the bureau sought a $30,000 increase in its annual appropriation.[62] Rarely have so many written so much for so little. Although Congress adjourned without giving Naturalization the money, the bureau and its allies were back in 1918, and this time they succeeded in obtaining approval for the bureau to use its surplus revenues (naturalization fees exceeded administrative costs) to finance its textbook program.[63]

This was a small matter when considered in terms of the 1918 federal budget, but it was a crucial victory for Naturalization since it provided it with a secure source of funds. This became all the more important when Congress failed to pass the Smith-Bankhead and Kenyon bills for their failure left the Bureau of Education with no funds for Americanization after June 30, 1919. By that date too the Creel Committee had dissolved and the Council of National Defense was winding up its affairs. Simply by surviving, in other words, Naturalization finally triumphed over its rivals.

Bureau of Naturalization officials, however, were by no means content with the terms of the 1918 law. They had used it, in 1919, to set up a Division of Citizenship Training under Raymond Crist, but two years later the Comptroller General's Office held that they had exceeded their statutory authority in so doing. The adverse decision did not bring the bureau's work to a halt; Crist continued it in his new capacity as chief naturalization examiner. But it left the bureau people longing for, in Commissioner Campbell's words, "plain, specific, and intelligible" authority.[64]

[59] George L. Mercer [secretary, District no. 12, U.M.W.] to Crist, Dec. 24, 1919, Muir Frew [secretary, U.M.W., Dixonville, Pa., no local or district number available] to Crist, Jan. 1, 1920, files E979 U.C. and E1836 U.C. Pittsburgh C.N.W., W. M. Ragsdale, report, Jan. 15, 1920, ibid.

[60] Campbell to Frew, Jan. 31, 1920, ibid.

[61] It did manage to have its Americanization work endorsed by the American Federation of Labor in 1919. A.F.L., *Report of Proceedings*, June 17, 1919, p. 6. The resolution, no. 124, was introduced by William Green of the U.M.W. A year earlier, Samuel Gompers endorsed the work of the Bureau of Education. See Gompers to Hon. Franklin K. Lane, May 18, 1919, box 106, RG 12, NA. There seems no reason to attach much significance to either endorsement.

[62] File E2243, RG 85, NA.

[63] The bureau used this authorization to establish, on April 1, 1919, a Division of Citizenship Training headed by Raymond Crist. On September 7, 1921, the U. S. comptroller general abolished the division on the grounds that the May 1919 act did not authorize it; *Decisions of the Comptroller General of the U. S.*, vol. 1, pp. 127-129. According to "Report on Series Identification Sheets," (p. 1), however, "the Director [Crist] . . . assumed the title of Chief Examiner and the work continued under the same organization unidentified by name as a divisional unit. There was supposedly no change in function or activities, but the work assumed a position of lesser importance."

[64] U. S. Department of Labor, *Annual Report of the Commissioner of Naturalization to the Secretary of Labor* (Washington, 1922), pp. 17-18.

Ironically, the authority the bureau sought was embodied in an alien registration bill originally suggested by Frances Kellor in 1917.[65] The following year, as noted above, Rep. B. F. Welty introduced the measure, but in his formulation Naturalization would have had charge of the work rather than Education as Kellor originally proposed. The Welty measure died, but James J. Davis, secretary of labor in the Harding and Coolidge administrations and himself an immigrant from Wales, enthusiastically revived the idea in 1921 after the comptroller general killed off the Division of Citizenship. Davis boosted registration as a panacea for the nation's problems with immigration. While its purpose, said Davis, was "primarily to provide for the education of the registrant [registration of course would be compulsory], to assign to him educational facilities and to furnish him such information as would be helpful in promoting Americanization," it would "nevertheless automatically bring into notice the alien who declares himself or is known to be an anarchist, whose intentions are hostile or resistive [sic] or who is for any reason undesirable." An enlarged Bureau of Naturalization, renamed the Bureau of Citizenship, would undertake all of this and would also, Davis claimed, coordinate the efforts, now "haphazard," "unsatisfactory," and "wasteful," of private Americanization programs. It would also use "constructively" the foreign-language press by running "Americanization articles . . . and, along side of them, the English translation."[66]

The registration scheme, in brief, was the last serious attempt to create a coherent federal Americanization program, and Secretary Davis proved an indefatigable campaigner. He worked so energetically, and lined up so much support for his bill, that its failure[67] cannot be easily explained. Some explanation, however, is necessary not only because no account of the Americanization movement would be complete without one but also because Davis's inability

to get his bill passed epitomizes the failure of all of the foregoing agencies and individuals to coordinate and control the movement.

As has been seen, Davis believed registration could solve the whole range of "dangers" immigration represented, from illiteracy to anarchy and espionage. He was no less creative in conjuring up reasons why various interest groups should support it. To several score of steel executives at a White House dinner[68] he emphasized that foreign-born labor was essential to the country's industrial development and that such labor had to be educated to citizenship.[69] To Simon Wolf, chairman of the Board of Delegates on Civil Rights, Union of American Hebrew Congregations (which had bitterly condemned registration as "patterned on the unpopular Alien and Sedition Acts of 1798, and the harsh and oppressive Chinese Exclusion Law," and which Davis credited with leading the opposition to his measure), he spelled out — somewhat disingenuously perhaps — his plan's benefits for the "Hebrew race." Wolf knew, Davis wrote, "there is considerable race prejudice in America against the Jews," a prejudice Davis attributed to "misunderstanding among the foreign born, and the hatreds which they have brought with them." Registration would give Jews "a chance to combat constructively this active prejudice" and "would be your most fertile field for developing understanding between the Hebrew and the other races in America."[70]

The Union of Hebrew Congregations remained unpersuaded, but Davis did succeed in lining up an impressive array of endorsements. In addition to the steel executives, supporters included District of Columbia Supreme Court Chief Justice Walter I. McCoy, Robert DeCourcey Ward of the Immigration Restriction League, John L. Lewis of the United Mine

[65] *New York Times,* July 15, 29, 1917.

[66] James J. Davis to Hon. Samuel M. Shortridge, Dec. 3, 1921, file 163/127, RG 174, NA. Senator Shortridge (R-Calif.) and Rep. Albert Johnson (R-Wash.) sponsored the registration bill.

[67] Aliens were not required to register with the federal government until the coming of the Second World War raised some of the same concerns we have been examining in connection with the first.

[68] Guest list in file no. 163/127B, RG 174, NA.

[69] No text of Davis's remarks has been preserved. The summary is from one of the executives present. George W. Niedringhaus [president, National Enameling and Stamping Co., Granite City, Ill.] to Davis, June 1, 1922, file 163/127C, ibid.

[70] "Copy of Resolution Adopted by the Union of Hebrew Congregations," Jan. 26, 1923, ibid. Davis to Simon Wolf, Mar. 5, 1923, "I have talked with the leaders of many of the racial groups and with the larger publishers of foreign language papers. They are practically unanimous in favor of the registration program with the exception of . . . the Hebrew interests." Davis to Wolf, Mar. 28, 1923, files 163/127C and 163/127D, ibid.

Workers, the American Legion, and the National Industrial Council of the N.A.M.[71] Moreover, the measure's sponsor in Congress was Albert Johnson, chairman of the House Committee on Immigration. The opposition was weak, consisting for the most part of alarmed immigrant groups, aided by an occasional liberal journalist, who saw registration as part of the nativist crusade.[72] Why then did the bill fail?

Opposition from ethnic associations could not have counted for much with a Congress that passed the Johnson-Reed Restriction Act. It is to Congressman Johnson, and to restriction, that we must look. For the simple fact is that Johnson sponsored registration but pushed restriction.[73] The two measures were logically compatible. In fact, Davis promoted registration as a complement to restriction. As he pointed out on many occasions, restriction would do nothing to Americanize the millions of immigrants already in the country or the hundreds of thousands admitted annually under the quota.[74] Logic was on Davis's side, but logic had never controlled the national response to immigration[75] and Congress had consistently favored restriction and repression as solutions to the immigrant problem. Both were irrational, emotional responses, the one based upon racial stereotypes, the other upon

exaggerated fears of alien anarchists and Bolsheviks. Both, that is, tapped the deep well springs of historic nativism.[76] And while, as we have seen, Americanizers also belonged to the nativist camp, they represented its more sedate and pacific wing.

The failure of the registration proposal signaled the end of the federal Americanization effort though the Bureau of Naturalization's public school program continued into the late 1920s.[77] That effort, disorganized and rancorous, lacking executive leadership and congressional authorization, nonetheless represents the most important chapter in the history of Americanization. For it was at the federal level that the major struggles for power within the movement took place. A thoroughgoing assessment of Americanization will require more studies on the local level of the sort being pioneered by A. Gerd Korman, Raymond Mohl, and Daniel Weinberg, and such studies will have to include, as they have not thus far, analyses of the federal role. It is possible now, however, to attempt a preliminary assessment of the federal programs. This may at least have the virtue of providing future scholars with a series of hypotheses they can test.

What follows is a tentative analysis of the degree of success the Bureaus of Naturalization and Education had in influencing state and local officials to follow their lead. Two areas of influence will be considered: the bureaus' efforts to provide model Americanization legislation for the states and to work with state councils of defense and state and local school authorities. These two scarcely exhaust the range and variety of the bureaus' activities, but they should provide the basis for a reasonable preliminary judgment since few of their other programs could have succeeded if these had failed.

Some time in late 1918 or early 1919 the Bureau of Naturalization drew up a model bill to try to give some consistency to the flood of state legislation on Americanization.[78] To estimate

[71] See Walter I. McCoy to M. E. Aiton [principal, Americanization School, Washington, D. C.], May 8, 1923, file 163/127D, ibid.; Robert D. Ward to Davis, Aug. 22, 1922, file 163/127C, ibid.; John L. Lewis to Davis, July 22, 1921, file 163/127, ibid.; John Thomas Taylor [vice-chairman, National Legislative Committee, American Legion] to Davis, Nov. 17, 1921, ibid.; and N.A.M., "Report of Committee," 26th annual meeting, May 1921, pp. 2-3.

[72] For examples of immigrant opposition, see "Immigrant Register!", *Amerikaki Magyar Ujsag* in "Exhibits," American Press Bureau of the Foreign Language Information Service, "An Editorial Digest of the Foreign Language Press in America," Feb. 21, 1922, file 163/127A, RG 174, NA; and "Resolution, March 14, 1926," Cleveland Council for the Protection of the Foreign Born Workers, file 163/127D, ibid. See also Walter Lippman, "Some Remarks on Alien Registration," *The Immigrant* [Bulletin of the Department of Immigrant Aid of the National Council of Jewish Women], pp. 5-7, file E1659, RG 85, NA.

[73] See Johnson to Arthur E. Cook [Secretary's Office, Department of Labor], Dec. 9, 1921, file 163/127, RG 174, NA.

[74] See Davis, draft of "A Century of Immigration," file 164/14, ibid.; Davis to Lyman Abbott [editor, *The Outlook*], Apr. 11, 1922, file 163/127A, ibid.; and Lima (Ohio) *News*, Feb. 23, 1922.

[75] See Billington, *Protestant Crusade*, pp. 1-31; and Higham, *Strangers in the Land*, pp. 300-301.

[76] Higham, *Strangers in the Land*, pp. 3-11.

[77] In his annual report for 1925 the new commissioner of naturalization, Raymond Crist, lamented that the personnel engaged in this work in the bureau were further reduced to "what is now an irreducible minimum." Little was done thereafter. See also National Archives and Records Service, "Report on Series Identification Sheets."

[78] For the model bill, undated, see file E1989, RG 85, NA. This file also contains copies of the state laws. Of 27 such

the impact of this model, I selected eight states which passed laws in 1919 and one, Illinois, which passed no law at all, and searched the bureau's files for any indication of influence.[79] In six cases the files make it plain that the bureau had nothing whatever to do with the drafting of the state measures.[80] In one state, Connecticut, the director of the Department of Americanization did seek the bureau's help in 1923. His goal was to revise the 1919 legislation, and Raymond Crist wrote to State Commissioner of Education A. B. Meredith at his behest. The Connecticut legislature, however, rejected the revisions.[81]

Only in California could the bureau claim real success and here, as in Connecticut, at issue was a 1921 revision of the 1919 statute. According to her own account, Ednah Aiken, an educational assistant attached to the C.N.E.'s office in San Francisco, played a very active role in lobbying for and even redrafting the 1921 Badarocco law.[82] Illinois was the only state with a large foreign-born population to pass no Americanization legislation, and the bureau's efforts in this regard were unavailing.[83]

This rather unimpressive record can be attributed to several factors. One, suggested by the dates of the legislation, is that state laws were largely responses to the popular fears of alleged alien radicalism generated by the Red Scare. The bureau's efforts were too little and too late to have much impact. A second, suggested by the California success, is that whatever leverage the bureau could exert was through local C.N.E. personnel working quietly behind the scenes. And none of the other C.N.E. offices, apparently, had a lobbyist with Mrs. Aiken's skills.

Education necessarily made less of an effort because the termination of its N.A.C. subsidy coincided with the flurry of state action. Even so, it influenced some states. In New Hampshire the House Committee on Education drew up a very sweeping law after "the recent serious investigation into the educational conditions in this state [which] arose out of the work of the Americanization Committee, appointed in April 1918, at the insistence of the federal government acting through Secretary Lane of the Department of the Interior."[84] But the bureau had no hand in drafting this measure. It was in New York that Education played the sort of role that both bureaus coveted for themselves. There three laws were passed, all clearly bearing the bureau's imprint. The first required all illiterate and non-English-speaking persons between the ages of 16 and 21 to attend some school until they had achieved the equivalent of a fifth-grade knowledge of English. The second required cities and towns to maintain night schools where a sufficiently large immigrant population existed. Both bills were originally drafted by H. H. Wheaton, chief of the bureau's Division of Immigrant Education. The third, which established teacher-training institutes for Americanization instructors, was drawn up by W. C. Smith, director of the New York State Americanization program in the State Office of Education. Smith was also chairman of the Legislative Committee of the National Committee of One Hundred, discussed above, which the bureau had established to coordinate Americanization efforts. Director Wheaton drew the lesson of this: "Their [the three bills] passage illustrates the wisdom and value of having a National Committee of One Hundred acting as an advisory council. Through it, steps are possible in a cooperative way with State legislatives and other institutions and organizations which are not possible did it not exist."[85]

Whether the bureau could have replicated this success in other states was a question foreclosed by the loss of its subsidy and the failure of the Smith-Bankhead and Kenyon bills. There is ample basis for believing, however, that its Committee of One Hundred provided an ex-

---

laws, for which the date of enactment is given, only 7 were passed before 1919. A full 15, more than half, were passed in 1919 during the height of the Red Scare.

[79] The states were California, Connecticut, Massachusetts, New Hampshire, New York, Ohio, Pennsylvania, and Rhode Island. All had substantial numbers of foreign-born residents.

[80] For Massachusetts, New Hampshire, New York, Ohio, Pennsylvania, and Rhode Island, see file E1989, RG 85, NA.

[81] Robert C. Deming to Crist, Jan. 31, 1923, Crist to Meredith, Feb. 2, 1923, Meredith to Crist, Feb. 5, 1921, Deming to T. S. Shoemaker, July 3, 1923, ibid.

[82] Aiken to Crist, Apr. 16, 1921, Crist to Aiken, Apr. 27, 1926, ibid.

[83] Crist to Harold K. Kesinger [chairman, Education Committee, Illinois State Senate], May 8, 1919, Crist to Chicago C.N.E. Fred J. Schlotfeldt, Mar. 21, 1921, Schlotfeldt to Crist, July 16, 1921, ibid.

[84] "Statement of Committee on Education" [to accompany their report on House Bill no. 262 (1919)], quoted in "New Hampshire Public School Legislation," Naturalization Bureau memo, n.d., ibid.

[85] H. H. Wheaton to Claxton, Apr. 16, 27, 1918, box 106, RG 12, NA.

AMERICANIZATION 39

cellent basis for lobbying in state legislatures. And it is clear that the combined influence of Education and Naturalization on state Americanization laws was not inconsiderable.

Under the aegis of the Council of National Defense, Education had the inside track to state councils. Only an examination of the records of these councils would allow a definitive judgment on how well it used this advantage. All that the bureau's records contain is an extensive outline of the activities it wanted the state councils to undertake. These ranged from the appointment of a state committee on Americanization, a campaign to "Make English the Language of Your State," and support for English and civics classes to "cooking, knitting and similar classes for alien women" because the "Alien man is often best reached through the Alien woman." [86] The degree of cooperation the bureau received varied, no doubt, from state to state and may have been greatest where the Committee of One Hundred provided it with local contacts.

The Bureau of Naturalization, for its part, was able to undermine Education's efforts in several states where its local C.N.E.s made determined and persuasive efforts to work with the state councils. In Idaho, for example, the chairman of the state Americanization Committee wrote to the state Council of Defense that "Americanization work is being conducted very largely by the Naturalization officers who have realized as no other officials . . . the gravity of the situation with respect to the foreign element in our midst." [87] The bureau achieved some success in Pennsylvania as well. There the Philadelphia C.N.E. office spent several years lobbying with state Americanization officials. Finally, Examiner Gurnett could report that the state Director of Americanization had "berated the Bureau of Education" and had said "it had nothing to offer" and had done little or nothing.[88] The field staff of the Bureau

of Naturalization were once again the key to whatever success it enjoyed over its rival; it would seem that the absence of field personnel in the Bureau of Education was its greatest weakness.

A similar pattern characterized the bureaus' public school programs. Education sought to capitalize on the Council of National Defense's endorsement [89] and sent out reams of printed material.[90] What effect these materials had can only be determined from public school records, since the bureau apparently received no reports from state or local officials. The Bureau of Naturalization, on the other hand, undertook a survey of states, cities, towns, and communities cooperating with its public school program for fiscal year 1921. All told, some 3,526 communities took part that year.[91] In Illinois, Massachusetts, Michigan, New Jersey, New York, Ohio, and Pennsylvania alone more than 90,000 aliens received free textbooks. And while it is impossible to calculate the total number of immigrants who participated during the life of the program, the number clearly exceeded five hundred thousand and perhaps topped one million.

So the bureau's impact on local education was, to say the least, considerable — so considerable that a number of state officials protested. Most vociferous was John J. Mahoney, Massachusetts state supervisor of Americanization. He wrote that in his judgment:

The Bureau of Naturalization has, in law, no authority whatever over the Americanization work so-called, that is being carried on in this state through the cooperation of local school departments and the State Department of Education. . . . It is a work strictly educational in character and has no necessary connection with the process of naturalization. The federal government has nothing to do with it whatsoever. . . . I

[86] "Outline of National and State Programs of the United States Bureau of Education and of the Work of State Councils and State Divisions of the Woman's Committee in Regard to Americanization," in Council of National Defense, *Bulletin no. 86, Americanization of Aliens* (Feb. 12, 1918), ibid. Exhibit A contains a list of 27 bureau pamphlets and 12 Committee of One Hundred publications available to the state councils. Exhibit B is a list of some 32 "Americanization Agencies Now in the Field." The Bureau of Naturalization was not included.

[87] G. A. Axline to State Council of Defense of Idaho, Oct. 25, 1918, file 27671/5000, RG 85, NA.

[88] Report of Henry B. Hazard [Philadelphia C.N.E.] to

Campbell, Aug. 5, 22, 1918, E. E. Bach [Pennsylvania director of Americanization] to Crist, Oct. 3, 1918, report of J. M. Gurnett [Philadelphia C.N.E.], July 31, 1919, file 27671/5006, ibid.

[89] See Claxton to "City Superintendents of Schools," undated [Jan. or Feb. 1918], circular letter, box 106, RG 12, NA.

[90] See, for example, "The Kindergarten and Americanization," Bureau of Education Kindergarten Circular no. 3 (Nov. 1918), ibid.

[91] Not all states supplied full data. Nor can the accuracy of the data supplied be easily checked. Thus my estimates are tentative. See "List by states and cities and towns, of communities cooperating with the [Bureau of Naturalization] in education work through their public schools during the fiscal year ending June 30, 1921," file E16132, RG 85, NA. The survey upon which the list is based is in file E16075-1, ibid.

am making such a point of this matter because I have viewed with increasing alarm the very evident desire on the part of the Federal Department of Labor to control the education of the adult immigrant.[92]

Mahoney claimed he was "only expressing the sentiment of all the State Directors of Immigrant Education that I know," but it is almost impossible to gage how common these feelings were by reading the bureau's official correspondence since few experienced bureaucrats were candid in answering a form letter. Certainly Mahoney was not the only state official to resent the bureau's activities.[93] Whether such state and local fears of federal intrusion worked to hamper the bureau's efforts or simply testify to its effectiveness is, for the moment, an open question.

Beyond question, however, is the fact that thousands of school programs took much of their materials and curriculum from federal agencies. This and similar evidence of federal influence on state legislation and on state councils of defense, limited though that evidence is,

should make us question as overly simplistic the traditional view that the Americanization movement was too diverse for any central control.[94] That interpretation is literally accurate. There was no single center of the movement, and the heads of both private and public programs often strove to retain operational independence. But, and it is a big one, the interconnections between public and private organizations, at all levels, were far more numerous and significant than has previously been recognized. And these connections help to explain the striking uniformity of most Americanization efforts. The bureaucratic rivalries did not involve serious disagreements over how aliens should be Americanized or what Americanization should mean. The quarrels were over which agency should predominate. None ever achieved preeminence, but that was small comfort to the millions of foreign-born Americans who struggled through an era of nativist-inspired conformity.

---

[92] Mahoney to Campbell, May 2, 1922, file E16075-1, ibid.

[93] See memo from Margaret D. Moore to Campbell, Jan. 24, 1923, in which she explains the bureau's difficulty in obtaining information from state officials to carry out its "Survey of Immigrant Education," ibid.

[94] See Higham, *Strangers in the Land*, p. 257; Hill, "The Americanization Movement," p. 626; and Hartmann, *Movement to Americanize the Immigrant*, p. 205. I have helped perpetuate this view myself; McClymer, "Scientific Nativism."

ADAPTING THE IMMIGRANT TO THE LINE:
AMERICANIZATION IN THE FORD FACTORY, 1914-1921

Americanization involved the social and cultural assimilation of immigrants into the mainstream of American life. However, the process also constituted a unique, and distinctly American, method for the resolution of a key industrial problem — the problem of work-discipline and of the adjustment of new workers to the factory environment. In the early twentieth century, the Ford Motor Company established an Americanization program in order to adapt immigrant workers to its new system of mass production. This paper will examine the Americanization policies and practices of the Ford Sociological Department, a novel experiment in welfare capitalism, and the Ford English School, an institution which taught immigrant workers the English language. It will treat both institutions in relation to the problem of the adaptation of an immigrant workforce to new conditions of production.

For the most part, Americanization has not usually been the concern of labor or industrial historians. Historians of Americanization have generally emphasized the differences between American and immigrant cultures. Edward G. Hartmann, the movement's principal historian, examined the early Americanization campaign from this perspective. According to his investigation, American middle-class and business elites, "the intelligentsia, the educators and social workers, the industrialists, and . . . business and civic groups," were the leaders and organizers of this "educative movement." He concluded that:

> the Americanization effort stressed the desirability of the rapid assimilation of the millions of immigrants who had come to America during the pre-war decades, through the attendance of the newcomers at special classes, lectures, and mass meetings, where they might be instructed in the language, the ideals, and on the life which had come to be accepted as the American way of life.

In this form, the Americanization campaign was voluntary, benevolent, and educational. Nevertheless, when the programs emanated from within factory gates, they had their darker side. The issue was not simply different national or ethnic cultures, but also pre-industrial and industrial cultures, and even class cultures. Americanization was an important movement for the adjustment of immigrant workers to a new industrial environment and to American urban and industrial conditions, not just to American society in the abstract.[1]

In recent years, historians have become more and more aware of the importance of culture as a concept for the examination of the history of the working class and industrialization. In their investigations of the original eighteenth-century industrial Revolution, British historians first raised the idea of culture as a significant dimension in the adaptation of workers to the new factory system. In his ground-breaking essay, Sidney Pollard noted that the new industrial worker "entered a new culture as well as a new sense of direction . . . ." Preindustrial artisans, laborers, and peasants faced a strange and alien world in the factory. In his brilliant outline of the cultural parameters of the new industrial capitalism, E.P. Thompson detailed the cultural adjustment which modern forms of production required. Utilizing the concepts of time-thrift and work-discipline, he stressed that "the transition to mature industrial society entailed a severe restructuring of working habits — new disciplines, new incentives, and a new human nature upon which these incentives could bite effectively . . . ." Other British historians have continued this tradition and have delineated the cultural boundaries of social class in industrial society.[2]

More recently, American historians have borrowed from and added to this new body of work on working-class and industrial history. Under the strong influence of Thompson, Herbert Gutman has examined the impact of preindustrial cultures on an industrializing American society. He suggested that the continuous influx of new workers from preindustrial and rural areas of Europe and American "brought into industrial society ways of work and other habits and values not associated with industrial necessities and the industrial ethos." In fact, he concluded that "the changing composition of the American working class caused a recurrence of the 'preindustrial' patterns of collective behavior usually associated with the early phases of industrialization." In other words, American industrialization was unique, because successive waves of immigrant workers continuously recreated the conflict between preindustrial and industrial values and habits with each generation of American workers. In addition to Gutman, David Montgomery has explored the shop culture of industrial veterans fully acquainted with the regimen of factory life and Daniel Rodgers has investigated the nature of the work ethic in industrial America and the attitudes of workers toward factory life.[3]

All of this analysis suggests the critical importance of culture as a concept for understanding working-class and industrial history. Indeed, the adaptation of a new industrial workforce involved a complex matrix of interrelationships between industrialization, social class, and culture. The new industrial worker needed a new culture, i.e., a new set of attitudes, values, and habits, for his survival and for his very existence in the factory and in industrial society. In the United States, the Americanization movement sought to provide the necessary industrial culture for immigrant workers in American factories. Imposed from above, it was a middle-class industrial ethos for immigrant workers. While the Ford Americanization program was unique in some of its elements, it typified the experiences of many other American manufacturers and industrialists for the period.

Even before the development of the modern system of mass production, Ford officials and managers proposed their industrial ethos to a predominantly German and American workforce. For example, in 1908, the *Ford Times* provided a model New Year's resolution for Ford employees. "Of my own free will and accord, I sincerely covenant with myself," the resolution began. It later continued:

> To exalt the Gospel of Work, and get action here and now. To keep head, heart, and hand so busy that I won't have time to think about my troubles.
> Because idlesness is a disgrace, low aim is criminal, and work minus its spiritual quality becomes drudgery.

Over and over again, in anecdotes, homilies, and stories, Ford literature for workers reiterated similar outlines of the American work ethic with the prospect of upward mobility as a reward for patience, self-denial, and hard work. Later, as more and more immigrants streamed into the newly mechanized Highland Park factory, the Ford Americanization program propounded similar socio-cultural themes for the new workers.[4]

Modern mass production profoundly altered the character of the Ford factory and the Ford workforce. Developed from 1910 to 1914, the new methods and techniques of production drastically diluted the skills necessary for factory operations. Consequently, as the physical plant expanded to meet the growing demand for the Model T Ford, thousands of unskilled Southern and Eastern European immigrants swarmed into the Highland Park factory. By 1914, the Ford Motor Company employed 12,880 workers and the overwhelming majority (9,109) were foreign-born. The five largest nationality groups — Poles, Russians, Romanians, Italians and Sicilians, and Austro-Hungarians — constituted a majority of the workforce and came from the least industrialized areas of Europe. Generally, American industrial leaders and factory managers rated these nationalities low in their "racial efficiency," as they defined industrial skill and efficiency in terms of work-habits and work-discipline. In addition, the immigrant workers' non-American styles and standards of living compounded the problems of their preindustrial origins and preindustrial attitudes and habits. In their homes, their neighborhoods, and their separate networks of economic, social, and cultural interaction, immigrant workers maintained residues of their former cultures and remained in isolation from the broader American society. Finally, middle-class and other Americans believed that the isolation and autonomy of immigrant communities generated alien and radical social philosophies.[5]

Ford officials, managers, and engineers expressed the most concern about the immigrants' poor and inefficient habits of work. These men, who used numbers to measure the success of their highly coordinated productive operations, found that productivity under actual factory conditions fell far short of anticipated levels derived from ideal laboratory conditions. In the phraseology of period, they discovered "the human element of production." Ford manager John R. Lee recalled:

> . . . we began to realize something of the relative value of men, mechanism, and manufacturing, so to speak, and we confess that up to this time we believed . . . that somehow or other the human element of our men were taken care of automatically and needed little or no consideration.

In the new Ford factory, the rates of absenteeism and labor turnover steadily rose with the completion of the new productive system. In 1913, "daily absences" amounted to a staggering ten per cent of the entire workforce. This meant that an average of from 1,300 to 1,400 workers were absent from their work stations each day. For the same year, the rate of labor turnover reached a phenomenal 370 per cent. In order to maintain a workforce of about 13,600 workers, the company hired over 52,000 workers in the course of a year. The numbers indicated a complete lack of work-discipline. Yet the new methods and techniques of production required new and more severe forms of work discipline. It needed workers more closely attuned to the coordinated regimen of the machines and assembly lines. The preindustrial culture of immigrant workers had to be restructured to meet the requirements of new and more sophisticated industrial operations.[6]

At this point, Ford inaugurated his grand experiment in welfare capitalism. Announced in January 1914 and popularly known as the Five Dollar Day, it was an ingenious profit-sharing scheme to induce Ford workers to alter their attitudes and habits to meet the rigorous requirements of mass production. Under the Ford

Profit Sharing Plan, the company divided an unskilled worker's income into two approximately equal parts — his wages and his profits. Each worker received his wages for work done in the factory. But he received his profits, and, hence, the Five Dollar Day, only when he met specific standards of productive efficiency and specific standards and conditions of domestic life. The "work standard" for a particular job and the pace of the assembly line determined the standard of efficiency.[7]

In addition a new institution, the Ford Sociological Department, later named the Ford Educational Department, examined the Ford worker's domestic life and attempted to elevate him and his family to a proper "American" standard of living. Ford and his managers held the progressive notion that environment shaped and molded men's attitudes, values, and habits. Their new institution sought to improve the worker's home and neighborhood environment in order to improve his ideas and behavior toward the factory. The Sociological Department investigated each worker and interviewed his family, friends, and neighbors. If the worker met specified requirements — "thrift, honesty, sobriety, better housing, and better living generally" — he received the Five Dollar Day. If not, the company withheld his profits and a Ford advisor periodically counselled on how to mend his ways. If after six months, the worker did not raise himself to Ford standards, the company discharged him.[8]

The Ford Profit Sharing Plan was deeply paternalistic. In this feature, it captured the Progressive Era's contradictory attitude toward the unskilled immigrant worker. On the one hand, it attempted to assist the worker and to elevate him to a better standard of life. On the other hand, it sought to manipulate or to coerce the worker to match a preconceived ideal of that better life. John R. Commons, the progressive labor historian, noted the double edged character of the Ford program. The Ford plan, he reported, "is just old fashioned industrial autocracy tempered by faith in human nature." A benevolent end — the uplift of the unskilled and unschooled immigrant worker — justified a manipulative and coercive means.[9]

From the very beginning, the Ford Profit Sharing Plan attempted to fit the immigrant worker into its preconceived mold of the ideal American. An early memorandum clarified the objectives of the Ford plan to a branch manager. "It is our aim and object," the Home Office noted, "to make better men and better American citizens and to bring about a larger degree of comforts, habits, and a higher plane of living among our employees . . . ." Henry Ford expressed his concern about non-American workers to an interviewer: "These men of many nations must be taught the American ways, the English language, and the right way to live." He then elaborated on the "right" life for the foreign-born worker. Married men "should not sacrifice family rights, pleasure, and comfort by filling their homes with roomers and boarders." Single men should live "comfortably and under conditions that make for good manhood and good citizenship." A company report on progress among immigrant workers noted that the Ford ideal was to create "a comfortable and cozy domesticity."[10]

In its literature for workers, the Ford Motor Company repeatedly advised them where and how to live. A pamphlet pointed toward "right" living conditions:

> Employees should live in clean, well conducted homes, in rooms that are well lighted and ventilated. Avoid congested parts of the city. The company will not approve, as profit sharers, men who herd themselves into overcrowded boarding houses which are menaces to their health . . . .

> Do not occupy a room in which one other person sleeps, as the company is anxious to have its employees live comfortably, and under conditions that make for cleanliness, good manhood, and good citizenship.

Ford and his managers deeply believed that tenement life in the immigrant neighborhoods of the city polluted body and soul. They also considered physical and moral cleanliness important attributes for work in modern industrial society. A clean home reduced the chances for illness and absenteeism. A clean mind provided the sound foundation for the construction of good work habits.[11]

The Ford Sociological Department even extended its interest and attention to the children of immigrant workers. It prescribed a strong dose of Victorian morality for them in order to promote and develop good bodies and souls. "Choose a home," a pamphlet advised:

> where ample room, good wholesome surroundings, will enable the children to get the greatest benefit possible from play, under conditions that will tend to clean helpful ideas, rather than those likely to be formed in the streets and alleys of the city.

Particularly in adolescence, young men and women "should be guarded well, and not allowed to contract habits and vices injurious to their welfare and health."[12]

S.S. Marquis, who headed the Ford Sociological Department, recalled Ford's own reason for this concern about the morality of children. "By underpaying men," Ford told the Episcopalian minister:

> we are bringing up a generation of children undernourished and underdeveloped morally as well as physically; we are breeding a generation of workingmen weak in body and mind, and for that reason bound to prove inefficient when they come to take their places in industry.

The good worker was both physically fit to perform his tasks in the factory and morally fit to perform these tasks diligently.[13]

Often, Ford's paternalistic advice on the care of the home and family contained overt manifestations of middle-class arrogance towards the new immigrant workers. In one instance, a Ford pamphlet advised:

> Employees should use plenty of soap and water in the home, and upon their children, bathing frequently. Nothing makes for right living and health so much as cleanliness. Notice that the most advanced people are the cleanest.

Again, the advice cut in two directions. On the one hand, health and cleanliness were important for immigrant workers. On the other hand, the assumption was that lower classes were generally unclean. Indeed, these sentiments typified upper- and middle-class American attitudes towards Southern and Eastern European immigrants.[14]

Boris Emmett examined the Ford Profit Sharing Plan for the U.S. Bureau of Labor Statistics. He discovered a class and ethnic bias in the administration of the Ford program. Although the rules and standards of the plan were "strictly applied," he reported that the "rigidity of application" depended on "the specific character of the group of employees concerned." Overall, the Sociological Department and its investigators tended to favor the life-style and the culture of American workers and office employees. "The company," Emmett wrote, "pays very little attention to the manner of life, etc., of their office employees." It believed that "the employees of the commercial and clerical occupations, who mostly are native Americans with some education, need not be told how to live decently and respectably." Consequently, the Ford welfare program concerned "chiefly the manual and mechanical workers, many of whom are of foreign bith and unable to speak the English language."[15]

Additionally, the instructions to the Ford investigators indicated that even American factory workers received preferential treatment. For example, as part of the sociological investigation, the worker who lived with a woman had to furnish proof of marriage. Yet, "especially in American homes," the company left "the question to the discretion of the investigator." If the worker lived in an exemplary American home environment, he need not embarass the worker with this question. He simply assumed marriage. "If it is the opinion of the investigator," the instructions noted, "that the surroundings and the atmosphere of the home are such as to be above reflecting suspicion on the marriage relation, it is not necessary to obtain documentary proof."[16]

In 1915, several Ford investigators wrote a number of "Human Interest" stories and other reports to describe the Sociological Department's welfare work among Ford workers. Two of these Horatio Alger style stories told how Southern and Eastern European immigrant workers met their good fortune in the form of the Five Dollar Day. One story involved a Russian immigrant and his family; the other a Turkish workman. While certainly not the average or typical Ford sociological case, the stories served as models for the work of Ford investigators and as examples of Ford welfare to the general public.[17]

F.W. Andrews, a Ford investigator, wrote his story on Joe, a former peasant, his wife, and their six children. Three years earlier, they left Russia for the United States. "Life was an uphill struggle for Joe since landing in America," Andrews reported. However, he had a positive trait — his willingness to work hard. "He was a willing worker and not particular about the kind of employment he secured." In the recent past, he dug sewers and worked as an agricultural laborer. When work ran out, he moved to Detroit with his family. "And here," Andrews noted, "for five long months he tramped with the 'Army of the Unemployed' — always handicapped by his meager knowledge of the English language, and was unable to find anything to do." As a result, his wife bore the "burden of supporting the family." She "worked at the washtub or with the scrubbing brush when such work could be found."

Fortunately, the tale continued, Joe applied for and received a job at the Ford factory. After the company hired him, Andrews went to Joe's home to determine his eligibility for the Ford Five Dollar Day. The scene could have been from a Dickens novel. He discovered "an old, tumbled down, one and a half story frame house." The family's apartment, Andrews related, "was one half of the attic consisting of three rooms, which were so low that a person of medium height could not stand erect — a filthy, foul-smelling hole." It had virtually no furniture, only "two dirty beds . . . , a ragged filthy rug, a rickety table, and two bottomless chairs (the five children standing up at the table to eat)." The family led a precarious hand-to-mouth existence and ate only when the wife earned enough to purchase food for the evening meal. They owed money to the landlord, the grocer, and the butcher. The oldest daughter went to a charity hospital a few days earlier. The wife and the other five children "were half clad, pale, and hungry looking."

This scene of poverty and misery set the Sociological Department's paternalistic programs into motion. Through special arrangements, the pay office issued Joe's wages each day instead of every two weeks. The company provided him with an immediate loan from its charity fund for "the family's immediate start toward right living." However, the investigator, and not Joe, took the fifty-dollar loan and paid the bills and rented a cottage. He also purchased inexpensive furniture and kitchen utensils, provisions, and cheap clothes for the wife and children. (Andrews reported that he bought "a liberal amount of soap" and gave the family "instructions to use freely.")

After Andrews arranged for this initial assistance for Joe and his family, a remarkable ritual followed. The Ford investigator:

> . . . had their dirty, old, junk furniture loaded on a dray and under the cover of night moved them to their new home. This load of rubbish was heaped in a pile in the back yard, and a torch was applied and it went up in smoke.
> There upon the ashes of what had been their earthly possessions, this Russian peasant and his wife, with tears streaming down their faces, expressed their gratitude to Henry Ford, the FORD MOTOR COMPANY, and all those who had been instrumental in bringing about this marvelous change in their lives.

In this ritual of fire, an old life went up in smoke as Joe and his family testified to their loyalty to Henry Ford.

In time, the children were well dressed and clean. They attended public school. The wife wore "a smile that 'won't come off.'" Joe soon repaid his loan and expected "to soon have a saving for the inevitable 'rainy day.'"[18]

Another investigator, M.G. Torossian, reported on the case of Mustafa, a young Turkish worker. He also was a former peasant. In his homeland, Mustafa "was the sole help of his father in the field." Nevertheless, he had positive virtues and the potential for right living even in an industrial job. "Young Mustafa," Torossian related, "unlike his race, who mostly wander in the mountains and make money quickly robbing others, had a natural intuition for an honest living." He learned about "this land of wealth and happiness" from friends, left his young wife and child with his parents, and went to Canada. Again, through friends, he learned about work with the Ford Motor Company. He came to Detroit and obtained work in the Ford factory before the announcement of the Five Dollar Day.

As in the case of so many other Southern and Eastern European workers, Mustafa lived in an immigrant boarding house. Torossian noted that he lived "with his countrymen in the downtown slums in a squalid house . . . ." However, even in this atmosphere, Mustafa demonstrated his abilities and his potential to change and to live in accordance with American standards. The Ford investigator pointed out that "he used to wash his hands and feet five times a day, as part of their religion before praying." But even in his native religion, the Turkish worker learned and accepted American social and cultural norms. In America, he only prayed three times a day. "This," said Torossian, "was modified from five times a day washing on account of time being too valuable."

With the announcement of the Five Dollar Day, Mustafa's "almost unimaginable dream came true." At first, he did not receive the "big money," because he did not speak English and did not comprehend "his trouble." Among other things, the investigator "advised [him] to move to a better locality." The Turkish worker even demonstrated his initiative and "voluntarily took out his first naturalization papers." In the end, he too received the Ford Five Dollar Day.

With the prospect of doubling his income, Mustafa readily abandoned his traditional customs and values for American ones. Torossian concluded:

> . . . Today has put aside his national red fez and praying, no baggy trousers anymore. He dresses like an American gentlemen, attends the Ford English School and has banked in the past year over $1,000.00. Now he is anxious to send for his young wife and child to bring her to America and to live happily through the grace of Mr. Henry Ford.

Moreover, the Turkish worker also dutifully expressed his gratitude for Ford's paternalism. Torossian related Mustafa's words: "Let my only son be sacrificed for my boss (Mr. Ford) as a sign of my appreciation for what he has done for me. May Allah send my boss Kismet."[19]

Against these uplifting cases, a single and revealing incident demonstrated the motives of the company's concern for the ways in which immigrant traditions affected industrial efficiency. In January 1914, a few days after its impressive gesture — the announcement of the Five Dollar Day — the Ford Motor Company dismissed "between eight and nine hundred Greeks and Russians, who remained from work on a holiday celebration." The holiday happened to be Christmas. Using the Julian calendar, the Greek and Russian Orthodox Christian workers celebrated Christmas thirteen days later than the rest of the Ford workforce. As justification for this large-scale dismissal, which amounted to about six per cent of the Ford workforce, a Ford official stated that "if these men are to make their home in America they should observe American holidays." The absence of this many workers disrupted production in the mechanized Highland Park plant. "It causes too much confusion in the plant," the official concluded, ". . . when nearly a thousand men fail to appear for work."[20]

The Ford English School extended the Ford Americanization program into the classroom. Its exclusive concern was the Americanization of the immigrant worker and his adaptation to the Ford factory and to urban and industrial society. In the English School, as adult immigrant workmen struggled to learn and to comprehend the strange sounds of a new language, they also received the rudiments of American culture. In particular, they learned those habits of life which resulted in good habits of work. In 1916, S.S. Marquis defended the objectives of the Ford educational program before an audience of American educators. The Ford English School, he noted, "was established especially for the immigrants in our employ." It was one part of a total program to adapt men to the new factory system. "The Ford School," he reported:

provides five compulsory courses. There is a course in industry and efficiency, a course in thrift and economy, a course in domestic relations, one in community relations, and one in industrial relations.

Later, using the Ford factory as a metaphor for the entire educational program, he added:

This is the human product we seek to turn out, and as we adapt the machinery in the shop to turning out the kind of automobile we have in mind, so we have constructed our educational system with a view to producing the human product in mind.

The Ford managers and engineers devised a system wherein men were the raw materials which were molded, hammered, and shaped ito products which had the proper attitudes and habits for work in the factory.[21]

In April 1914, the Ford Motor Company called upon Peter Roberts, a Young Men's Christian Association educator, to develop a program of English language instructor for immigrant workers in the Highland Park factory. In 1909, as the result of his activities among immigrant coal miners in Pennsylvania, Roberts published a preparatory course of English language instruction, *English for Coming Americans.* This course provided a complete package of materials to teach the basic elements of the English language. The core of the program centered around a Domestic, a Commercial, and an Industrial Series of lessons. Each series applied the English language to different aspects of the immigrant worker's life. This Roberts package formed the basis of language instruction in the Ford English School.[22]

The Domestic Series provided specific English lessons for the immigrant worker in his role as the head of an "American" family unit. This series, Roberts explained, identified "the experiences common to all peoples reared in the customs of western civilization." The ten lessons included such topics as "Getting Up in the Morning," "Table Utensils," "The Man Washing," and "Welcoming a Visitor."[23]

The Commercial Series supplied the immigrant worker with the vocabulary to serve in his role as a consumer. In particular, it attempted to break the economic power of immigrant bosses, who sold goods and services, who served as employment, travel, and shipping agents, and who functioned as bankers in the immigrant neighborhoods. Moreover, the lessons emphasized and encouraged the virtues of thrift and property ownership, which created stable and reliable citizens. "These lessons," Roberts noted:

> describe the acts which foreigners in a strange land daily perform. When they are mastered the pupils will be able to transact their business outside the narrow circle of places controlled by men conversant with their language.

The lessons intended to make the immigrant worker a consumer of American goods and services from American merchants. In this series, the subject matter included "Buying and Using Stamps," "Pay Day," "Going to the Bank," "Buying a Lot," "Building a House."[24]

Finally, the Industrial Series provided flexible lessons to meet the immigrant worker's needs as a producer in the factory. The aim of this series was "to meet the need of thousands who have common experience in industrial life." Here, the lessons included "Beginning the Day's Work," "Shining Shoes," "A Man Looking for Work," and "Finishing the Day's Work."[25]

The lessons in each series had characteristically prosaic titles. And, indeed, the lessons provided helpful and useful information for the immigrant worker. Nevertheless, each lesson contained specific social and cultural norms for life in urban and industrial America. Ford workers learned the value of time in their personal and working lives. They learned the importance of cleanliness and health. The learned self-discipline through regular habits of saving and work. The learned to invest in and to purchase property and to become responsible citizens. These positive virtues — timeliness, cleanliness, thrift, self-discipline, regularity, and citizenship — represented the Ford, and generally the American middle-class, ideal for remaking former European peasants into reliable and efficient factory workers. The English language was an important means for the adaptation of immigrant workers to the regimen and the discipline of the mechanized factory.

As part of its instructional program, the Ford English School also taught immigrant workers not to offend their social betters in their manner and their behavior. For this reason, table manners and etiquette were important parts of the curriculum. "Last, but not least," S.S. Marquis reported, "must be mentioned our professor of table manners who with great dramatic art teaches the use of napkins, knife and fork and spoon." The Ford instructor taught the immigrant worker "the art of eating a meal in a manner that will not interfere with the appetite of the other fellow." In addition, Marquis continued: "We also have a professor of etiquette, such as is required for the ordinary station in life." Moreover, Ford English instructors expected their students to dress properly for the classes. "A by-product of the classes," a report noted, "was a rise in the 'standard of living' by making men conscious of their personal appearance." Instead of going directly from work to school, the instructors required that "class members first go home, wash, and change clothes."[26]

In 1919, Clinton C. DeWitt, the Director of the Ford English School, defended the Ford system of industrial Americanization with its practical teachers from the shop floor before an unfriendly audience of American educators. He argued that "a real live American born man, who is a leader among the fellows of his department" would make "in a short time out of Europe's downtrodden and outcasts, good Americans." He also catalogued the advantages of the industrial teacher:

> . . . both teacher and student have so many things in common. He works for the same employer, he works the same hours, he has the same pay day, he has the same environment, he has the same legal holidays, he refers to the same head office, the same pay office, the same superintendent's office, the same safety department, the same Americanization school. The main doorway, the different buildings, and all the printed signs are thoroughly common to teacher and student.

From DeWitt's perspective, the factory hierarchy facilitated instruction. The foreman, the natural leader in his shop, instructed his subordinates in the English language, American values and customs, and Ford shop practices.[27]

In 1915, Oliver J. Abell, an industrialist journalist, praised Ford's "benevolent paternalism" in industry. He maintained that the "greater must care for the less." Furthermore, he continued:

> We provide schools for the child. Instruction and discipline are compulsory, and it is well. But we forget that measured in the great scale of knowledge, there are always children and grownups, pupils and teachers, and age is nothing.

Here, Abell captured the essence of Ford paternalism and of the relationship between dominant and subordinate groups in American society. Superiors considered their inferiors — Blacks, servants, women, and even workers — as no more than children. Indeed, the Ford immigrant worker was no more than a child to be socialized, in this case, Americanized, to the reigning social and cultural norms of American society.[28]

S.S. Marquis, the liberal clergyman, explained how the company coerced workers into attending their English lessons. "Attendance," he reported:

> is virtually compulsory. If a man declines to go, the advantages of the training are carefully explained to him. If he still hesitates, he is laid off and given uninterrupted meditation and reconsideration. When it comes to promotion, naturally preference is given to the men who have cooperated with us in our work. This, also, has its effect.

In the early twentieth century, Ford officials duplicated the disciplinary patterns which early industrialists utilized in eighteenth-century England. The carrot and the stick rewarded or punished the worker as though he were an errant child.[29]

Gregory Mason, a strong advocate of Americanization programs, questioned "the grotesquely exaggerated patriotism in the Ford plant." In the course of the English lessons, "the pupils are told to 'walk to an American blackboard, taken a piece of American chalk, and explain how the American workman walks to his American home and sits down with his American family to their good American dinner.'" "The first thing we teach them to say," Marquis related, "is 'I am a good American,' and then we try to get them to live up to that statement." "It is a very common thing," DeWitt noted, "to have a fellow born in Austria yell to a teacher passing by, 'We are all good Americans!'" In this period, Ford and other employers began to give good citizenship and Americanism their own definition. A Ford pamphlet noted:

> Automatically, upon graduation, the English school alumni become members of the American Club. At weekly meetings they practice speaking, reading, debating, and discuss points of history, civil government, and national problems of current interest.

By the end of the First World War, Americanism countered those social and economic philosophies which threatened managerial prerogatives of production, namely Bolshevism, socialism, and even trade unionism.[30]

The mass ritual of graduation was the most spectacular aspect of Americanization in the Ford factory. Ford English School graduates underwent a symbolic ritual which marked the transformation from immigrant to American. DeWitt describes the ceremony as:

> a pageant in the form of a melting pot, where all men descend from a boat scene representing the vessel on which they came over; down the gangway . . . into a pot 15 feet in diameter and 7-1/2 feet high, which represents the Ford English School. Six teachers, three on either side, stir the pot with ten foot ladles representing nine months of teaching in the school. Into the pot 52 nationalities with their foreign clothes and baggage go and out of the pot after vigorous stirring by the teachers comes one nationality, viz, American.

Marquis enriched this image and emphasized the conformity of the one nationality: "Presently the pot began to boil over and out came the men dressed in their best American clothes and waving Americn flags.[31]

Following this pageant, teachers and community leaders gave speeches which praised the virtues of American citizenship. When the graduation ceremony ended, all went on "a trip to some park, where American games are played by teachers and students for the rest of the day." In the evening, the company rewarded its volunteer teachers for their time and their efforts. It held "an entertainment and banquet for the volunteer instructors and their wives. The expense, of course, being paid by the company." At this celebration, DeWitt reported, "the teachers meet with Mr. Ford and other high officials of the company, and a great spirit of one for all and all for one predominates the entire evening."[32]

Americanization in the Ford factory was important for a number of reasons. First, the Ford programs touched the lives of tens of thousands of Ford workers in its effort to influence those institutions which shaped working-class culture — the home, the neighborhood, and the factory. From 1914 to 1917, Ford statistics, derived from the reports of sociological investigators, revealed that bank accounts, home and property ownership, neighborhoods, home conditions, and habits of Ford workers either increased or improved. In addition, from 1915 to 1920, the company reported that some 16,000 workers graduated from the Ford English School. Moreover, statistics indicated that while 35.5 per cent of the workforce did not speak English in 1914, only 11.7 per cent did not speak the language in 1917. Second, the Ford Americanization programs indirectly captured the American imagination in the prewar years. They served as the model for a city-wide Americanization campaign in Detroit. And, in 1915, Detroit in turn became the model for the National Americanization Day Committee and its national campaign for the assimilation of immigrants into American society.[33]

Finally, Ford was neither alone nor entirely unique in its attempt to adapt immigrant workers to factory and industrial life. In fact, American industrial leaders and managers developed a new and different strategy for the management of an immigrant workfoce in this period. Whereas the traditional managerial practice divided ethnic groups and played their national and cultural rivalries against one another, the new one emphasized conformity with American social, cultural, and industrial values. During the First World War, as manufacturers and managers became increasingly apprehensive about aliens in their midst, they viewed Americanization as a means to remake immigrant workers into their image of efficient and productive American workers. Through cooperative efforts with industry, Peter Roberts and other Y.M.C.A. educators established programs which employed thousands of instructors and taught tens of thousands of foreign workers. And, in the postwar labor upsurge, industrial leaders considered Americanization as the cure for the ills of industrial society. In 1919, George F. Quimby, the keynote speaker of the National Conference on Americanization in Industries, emphasized that the conference should be "based on the fundamental principles of American life — a sound social order." In 1920, Peter Roberts gave citizenship a broad social and economic definition. "Good citizenship," he noted, "means each one in his sphere keeping busy, doing honest work, and contributing to the sum total of wealth for the support of the nation."[34]

In the end, Ford paternalism failed, and, perhaps, even proved irelevant. Its success rested on the monetary incentive of the Five Dollar Day. Even for unschooled immigrants, money, and not patronizing benevolence, talked in the industrial age. Wartime economic conditions undermined the Ford high income policy. As the new methods of production rapidly diffused to Detroit's other automobile and machine shops, Ford lost the technological and financial advantage over its competitors. In addition, a severe war-induced inflation eroded the incentive of the Five Dollar Day. Gradually, the company shifted the differential between wages and profits. Wages became a larger and larger proportion of the worker's income. In 1914, approximately 50 per cent of the unskilled worker's income was profits; in 1918, only 20 per cent. In 1919, Ford established the Six Dollar Day in order to maintain an adequate incentive. However, at the time, it needed a Ten Dollar Day to provide the same incentive as in 1914. For all practical purposes, the Ford welfare programs began their decline in the post-war period. In the recession of 1920 to 1921, the company faced a serious financial crisis as loans for the River Rouge expansion came due. The Ford enterprises underwent a ruthless phase of cost-cutting and officials terminated the sociological and Americanization programs. Through the 1920s, the hard-nosed and pragmatic production managers gained control of and directed Ford personnel relations.[35]

After the First World War, American society demanded a more rigid social, cultural, and political conformity from its members. For immigrant and other American workers, the war marked a transition from the reform-minded "Progressive Era" to the tougher "Lean Years." Other societal institutions took up the crusade for Americanization. With the Red Scares of 1919 and 1920 and with state criminal syndicalism legislation, the federal and state governments delineated the boundaries of political tolerance for immigrant radicals. In the post-war period, local public school systems became the principal agents for the adaptation of immigrants to American industrial society. The American Legion and other patriotic organizations preached their vision of the American social order. The Inter-Racial Council used its influence over advertisers to direct the foreign-language press to stress American values and ideals. The Americanism Committee of the Motion Picture Industry utilized the tremendous popular appeal of the new medium to produce films on American themes for immigrants. And, in 1921 and 1924, restrictive federal legislation limited the number of new immigrants and reduced the dimension of the problem of assimilation. As a result of these and other activities, employers no longer needed to pay so much attention to the Americanization of immigrant workers. Some directed more time and energy towards the scientific examination of the human element of production. Others, like Ford, shifted their attention towards some variation of the American Plan and its more repressive and intransigent factory environment.[36]

Despite the brevity of the Ford Americanization program and aside from its undoubted impact on some workers, the program offers a most interesting insight into the managerial mentality for an important period in the development of the American workforce. It draws attention to Gutman's conclusion that American industrialization involved a series of wave-like adaptations to changing factory conditions. In efforts such as Ford's, entrepreneurs and managers revived and suitably restyled the earlier industrial strategies for new industrial situations. For example, Ford and his managers utilized the classic forms of industrial discipline for the adaptation of immigrant workers — "the proverbial stick, the proverbial carrot, and thirdly, the attempt to create a new ethos of work, order and obedience." The relatively modern Ford program followed patterns which Sidney Pollard and Reinhard Bendix described for late eighteeenth- and early nineteenth-century England and which Peter Stearns described for nineteenth-century France. The Bendix schema of successive managerial ideologies suggests in fact that altered forms of the earliest, the theory of dependence, and the latest, the human relations approach, were coexisting in the Ford factory in the early twentieth century.[37]

Perhaps the most significant feature of the Ford Americanization program was its failure and eventual termination. It signalled a halt to a manipulative and optimistic approach in favor of a tougher and conflict-oriented approach to the problem of labor relations. In the end, this may have been more realistic, because management meant the control of the factory workforce, and the conflict that dominance generated could not be entirely glossed over. Real worker adaptations, in fact, differed considerably from the outdated patterns of the Americanization program. As preindustrial immigrants and industrial veterans intermingled in the shop, they often created their own attitudes and modes of behavior for urban and industrial life. Even green immigrant hands readily acquired a taste for the American worker's high standard of living and quickly learned the importance of the monetary incentive to achieve it. At the same time, a class dimension developed as more experienced workers taught their less experienced workmates the rules of the game on the shop floor. Management could not use Americanization to create a fully malleable workforce.

In 1920, Myron W. Watkins, a political economist, who donned worker's clothing and who worked in Detroit's automobile factories, related a revealing incident. He reported that "dissatisfaction was well-nigh universal" and described one of "[s]cores of incidents." In one auto factory, fifteen minutes before quitting time, the entire shop slackened the pace, put away tools, and removed aprons "in preparation for an instantaneous getaway at the first stroke of the gong." "Irish," a Russian-born shopmate, inspected an almost finished batch of carburetor valves. Instead of completing the batch, he fumbled "over one piece so as not to draw the attention of the foreman to his idleness." Watkins asked: "Why not finish up the job tonight?" The Russian industrial veteran replied: "Why finish it? It do no good. You never get all those boxes cleared off the floor. As soon as you finish one box, they bring 'nother down. Don't hurry. You never get done anyway."[38]

University of Wisconsin — Milwaukee Stephen Meyer

FOOTNOTES

The author wishes to thank Margo Conk, Nathan Miller, David Montgomery, Carl Torgoff and Peter Stearns for their reading of and comments on this paper.

1. Edward G. Hartmann, *The Movement to Americanize the Immigrant* (New York, 1948), p. 7. Other important works on immigrants and immigrant workers include: Gerd Korman, *Industrialization, Immigrants, and Americanizers: The View from Milwaukee* (Madison, 1967), Herbert Gutman, "Work, Culture, and Society in Industrializing America, 1815-1915," *American Historical Review,* 78 (1973), pp. 531-87, and John Higham, *Strangers in the Land: Patterns of American Nativism* (New York, 1973). On Ford and the Ford Motor Company, the most detailed account is Allan Nevins' multivolume history, especially the first two volumes, *Ford: The Times, the Man, the Company* (New York, 1954) and *Ford: Expansion and Challenge* (New York, 1957). Other important works include Keith Sward, *The Legend of Henry Ford* (New York, 1972), Anne Jardim, *The First Henry Ford: A Study in Personality and Business Leadership* (Cambridge, Mass., 1970), Samuel S. Marquis, *Henry Ford: An Interpretation* (Boston, 1923), and Charles C. Sorenson, *My Forty Years with Ford* (New York, 1956). On the development of the Ford system of mass production, see Nevins, *Ford: The Times,* Horace Lucien Arnold and Fay Leone Faurote, *Ford Methods and Ford Shops* (New York, 1916), and Stephen Meyer, "Mass Production and Human Efficiency: The Ford Motor Company, 1908-1921" (Ph.D. dissertation Rutgers University, 1977). On the attitudes and the activities of factory managers and engineers, see David Noble, *American by Design: Science, Technology, and the Rise of Corporate Capitalism* (New York, 1977), Daniel Nelson, *Managers and Workers: Origins of the New Factory System in the United States, 1880-1920* (Madison, 1975), Samuel Haber, *Efficiency and Uplift: Scientific Management in the Progressive Era, 1890-1920* (Chicago, 1964), and Loren Baritz, *The Servants of Power* (Middletown, Conn., 1960).

2. Sidney Pollard, "Factory Discipline in the Industrial Revolution," *Economic History Review,* 16 (1963), p. 254; E.P. Thompson, "Time, Work Discipline, and Industrial Capitalism," *Past and Present,* 38 (1967), p. 57. See also Raymond Williams, *The Long Revolution* (New York, 1961) and *Marxism and Literature* (New York, 1978), Richard Hoggart, *The Uses of Literacy* (New York, 1961), and Gareth Stedman Jones, "Working Class Culture and Working Class Politics in London, 1870-1900," *Journal of Social History,* 6 (1974), pp. 460-508.

3. Gutman, "Work, Culture, and Society," pp. 541 and 543; David Montgomery, "Workers' Control of Machine Production in the Nineteenth Century, *Labor History,* 17 (1976), pp. 486-7; Daniel Rodgers, "Tradition, Modernity, and the American Industrial Worker," *Journal of Interdisciplinary History,* 7 (1977), pp. 655-81.

4. *Ford Times,* 2 (Dec. 1908), p. 1.

5. On the numbers of immigrant workers, see "Automobile Trade Notes," *New York Times,* November 15, 1914, sec. 7, p. 6; on the "racial efficiency" of immigrants, see Nelson, *Managers and Workers,* pp. 81-2; on American attitudes towards the immigrant, see Higham, *Strangers in the Land,* pp. 158-63.

6. John R. Lee, "The So-Called Profit Sharing System in the Ford Plant," *Annals AAPSS,* 45 (May 1916), pp. 299 and 308; O.J. Abell, "The Making of Men, Motor Cars, and Profits," *Iron Age,* 95 (Jan. 7, 1915), p. 37.

7. Lee, "Profit Sharing," pp. 297-310; John A. Fitch, "Ford of Detroit and his Ten Million Dollar Profit Sharing Plan," *Survey* 31 (Feb. 7, 1915), pp. 545-50; Oliver J. Abell, "The Ford Plan for Employees' Betterment," *Iron Age,* 93 (Jan. 20, 1916), pp. 306-9; Harold Whiting Slausson, "A Ten Million Dollar Efficiency Plan," *Machinery* (Oct. 1914), pp. 83-7.

8. Ford Motor Company, *Helpful Hints and Advice to Employes to Help them Grasp the Opportunities which Are Presented to them by the Ford Profit Sharing Plan* (Detroit, 1915) and *A Brief Account of the Educational Work of the Ford Motor Company* (Detroit, 1916); Fitch, "Ford of Detroit," pp. 545-50; and Meyer, "Mass Production and Human Efficiency," pp. 156-216.

9. John R. Commons, "Henry Ford: Miracle Maker," *Independent*, 102 (May 1, 1920), p. 161.

10. Letter to Omaha, Jan. 29, 1914, Accession 683, Ford Motor Company Archives, Dearborn, Michigan; Henry Ford quoted in *New York Times*, Apr. 19, 1914, sec. 3, p. 12; and "Progress Among Foreigners," Box 17, Accession 940, F.M.C.A., Dearborn, Michigan.

11. Ford Motor Company, *Helpful Hints*, p. 13.

12. Ford Motor Company, *Helpful Hints*, p. 15.

13. Marquis, *Henry Ford*, p. 151.

14. Ford Motor Company, *Helpful Hints*, p. 13.

15. Boris Emmett, "Profit Sharing in the United States," *Bulletin of the Bureau of Labor Statitistics*, 208 (1916), p. 106.

16. "Sociological Department Instructions, Verifying Marriage," Box 17, Accession 940, F.M.C.A., Dearborn, Michigan.

17. "Human Interest Stories," Box 17, Accession 940, F.M.C.A., Dearborn, Michigan. The Ford investigators seem to have been instructed to search their memories and their records for those cases which best reflected the objectives and the successes of Ford sociological work. Only fourteen of these stories have survived. However, the ones which exist are numbered from 1 to 38. They are scattered throughout box 17. See "Human Interest Stories" numbered 9 and 39.

18. "Human Interest Story, Number 9."

19. "Human Interest Story, Number 38."

20. *New York Times*, Jan. 10, 1914, sec., p. 6.

21. S.S. Marquis, "The Ford Idea in Education" in National Education Association, *Addresses and Proceedings . . . 1916*, vol. 64 (1916), p. 911, 915, and 916.

22. Peter Roberts, *English for Coming Americans* (New York, 1909).

23. Roberts, *English*, p. 20.

24. Roberts, *English*, p. 22-3.

25. Roberts, *English*, p. 20-1.

26. "Ford Profit Sharing Plan," Accession 293, F.M.C.A., Dearborn, Michigan; Marquis, "Ford Idea in Education," p. 912; "Preliminary Report of Work Done Teaching the English Language to Employees of the Ford Motor Company at Stevens School, Highland Park, Mich., June 12, 1914," Accession 940, F.M.C.A., Dearborn, Michigan.

27. Clinton C. DeWitt, "Industrial Teachers" in United States Bureau of Education, *Proceedings Americanization Conference . . .1919*(Washington, D.C., 1919), p. 116.

28. Abell, "Men, Motor Cars, and Profits," P. 39.

29. "Ford Profit Sharing Plan." See also, Marquis, "Ford Idea in Education," pp. 911-2.

30. Gregory Mason, "Americans First: How the People of Detroit Are Making Americans of the Foreigners in their City," *Outlook*, 114 (Sept. 27, 1915), p. 200; Marquis, "Ford Idea in Education," p. 915; DeWitt, "Industrial Teachers," p. 118; and Ford Motor Company, *Facts from Ford* (Highland Park, Mich., 1920), p. 33.

31. DeWitt, "Industrial Teachers," p. 119; "Ford Profit Sharing Plan."

32. DeWitt, "Industrial Teachers," p. 119.

33. "Ford Sociological Statistics," Jan. 12, 1914 and Jan. 12, 1917, pp. 1-6; Ford Motor Company, *Facts from Ford*, p. 32; Mason, "Americans First," pp. 193-201; and Esther Everett Lape, "The English First Movement in Detroit," *Immigrants in America Review*, 1 (Sept. 1915), pp. 46-50.

34. George Quimby in *Proceedings of the National Conference on Americanization in Industries . . . 1919* (n.p., n.d.), pp. 4-5; Peter Roberts, *Problems of Americanization* (New York, 1920), pp. 226-7. See also Fred. H. Rindge, Jr., "Developing the Human Side of Industry," *Iron Age*, 97 (May 25, 1916), pp. 1264-5; J.D. Hackett, "Breaking Down the Language Barrier," *Iron Age*, 97 (Feb. 3, 1916), pp. 293-4; Winthrop Talbot, "The Illiterate Workers in War Time," *Iron Age*, 100 (Aug. 16, 1917), pp. 372-3; United States Bureau of Education, *Proceedings Americanization Conference . . . 1919*; and Inter-Racial Council, *Proceedings National Conference on Immigration . . .*(New York, 1920).

35. Meyer, "Mass Production and Human Efficiency," pp. 181-7; Nevins, *Ford: Expansion*, pp. 324-54.

36. Higham, *Strangers in the Land*, pp. 242-63 and 300-30; Joel Spring, *Education and the Rise of the Corporate State* (Boston, 1972); Edward A. Krug, *The Shaping of the American High School* (New York, 1964), pp. 417-27; Lawrence A. Cremin, *The Transformation of the School: Progressivism in American Education, 1876-1957* (New York, 1963), pp. 66-75; Raymond Moley, *The American Legion Story* (New York, 1966), pp. 125-50 and 167-89; Marquis James, *History of the American Legion* (New York, 1923), pp. 293-5; Richard S. Jones, *A History of the American Legion* (Indianapolis, 1946), pp. 283-44; Roberts, *Problems of Americanization*, p. 149; and Robert E. Park, *The Immigrant Press and Its Control* (New York, 1922), pp. 359-76.

37. Pollard, "Factory Discipline," p. 260; Sidney Pollard, *The Genesis of Modern Management* (Baltimore, 1968); Reinhard Bendix, *Work and Authority in Industry: Ideologies of Management in the Course of Industrialization* (New York, 1963), see pp. 435-6 for his periodization; and Peter N. Stearns, *Paths to Authority: The Middle Class and the Industrial Labor Force in France, 1820-1848* (Urbana, 1978).

38. Myron W. Watkins, "The Labor Situation in Detroit," *Jouranl of Political Economy*, 28 (Dec. 1920), pp. 850-1.

Ethnic Adjustment in the Industrial City: The International Institute of Gary, 1919–1940

by Raymond A. Mohl and Neil Betten*

The traditional American response to immigrants has emphasized either Americanization or assimilation. As Milton M. Gordon has suggested, the principles of "Anglo-conformity" and the "melting pot" remained prevailing ideologies until after World War II. These ideas demanded that immigrants with foreign and "different" ways, traditions, languages, and customs be brought into the mainstream of American culture, be made over into Americans, be assimilated and homogenized. American institutions (schools, churches, factories, settlement houses, political parties, government) approached immigrants with those fundamental assumptions. Thus, teachers and educators used the schools as a primary agent of Americanization, advancing a laudatory view of American culture and history which implied inferiority of the old country. Schools, churches, and industries sponsored English classes and government lessons, exhorting foreigners to adopt American ways. Social workers sometimes showed an excessive, moralistic concern for indoctrinating newcomers, especially children, with middle-class American values. Most people dealing with immigrants assumed cleanliness, sobriety, industriousness, honesty, patriotism, and piety as inseparable from the "American way."[1]

Unique among agencies working with immigrants were the International Institutes established in more than sixty American cities by the YWCA in the years after 1918. At the end of World War I, the YWCA's War Work Council transformed itself into the Department of Immigration and Foreign Communities with the initial intention of aiding foreign-born women and girls in the United States. To carry out its program, the National Board of the YWCA sponsored local affiliates named International Institutes, primarily in industrial cities with heavy ethnic populations like Buffalo, Boston, Bridgeport, Detroit, Chicago, New York, Philadelphia, Milwaukee, Pittsburgh, St. Louis, McKeesport, St. Paul, Du-

* Raymond A. Mohl, Department of History, Florida Atlantic University. Neil Betten, Department of History, Florida State University.

[1] Milton M. Gordon, "Assimilation in America: Theory and Reality," *Daedalus*. 90 (Spring 1961), 263–285. For more general studies elaborating the American response to immigrants, see Maldwyn Allen Jones, *American Immigration* (Chicago, 1960); Oscar Handlin, ed., *Immigration as a Factor in American History* (Englewood Cliffs, N.J., 1959); Ray Allen Billington, *The Protestant Crusade. 1800–1860: A Study of the Origins of American Nativism* (New York, 1938); John Higham, *Strangers in the Land: Patterns of American Nativism. 1860–1925* (New Brunswick, N.J., 1955).

361

luth, Trenton, Toledo, Akron, and San Francisco. The Institutes rapidly broadened their objectives and soon engaged in traditional settlement house tasks—handling immigrant problems and attempting to ease the transition to American society. Beyond this, Institute workers aided in the citizenship process and served as mediators between immigrants and government agencies.

But despite such practical work, each Institute found its most important task in helping various ethnic groups to maintain cultural identity and a positive self-image. Often immigrants themselves, Institute workers with multiple language skills tried to build consciousness and pride in the immigrant heritage, fostered inter-ethnic cooperation and understanding, and emphasized ethnic contributions to American life. They urged newcomers to retain their language and their customs while simultaneously learning American ways. At the same time, they worked among Americans to develop understanding of immigrant traditions. These were especially significant objectives during the post-World War I years, when nativism, the "Great Red Scare," and the movement for immigration restriction added impetus to demands for complete Americanization and speedy assimilation. The activities of the International Institute of Gary, Indiana, typified YWCA work among the foreign-born.[2]

Gary began as a city of steel mills and immigrants. Founded in 1906 by the United States Steel Corporation, it grew rapidly, eventually becoming the largest planned company town in the United States. U.S. Steel officials found the sand barrens on the southern shore of Lake Michigan an ideal industrial location—well situated for lake transport, traversed by the trunk lines of five major railroads, and available land cheap enough to permit construction of an extensive industrial establishment and a residential community. Steel could be produced more cheaply in Gary than in Pittsburgh, which was further from the raw materials of the Minnesota mines, or in Chicago, where industrial congestion, high land prices and taxes, and competition for transportation facilities reduced efficiency and raised costs.[3]

---

[2] Although the first International Institute—that in New York City—was founded as an experiment in 1911, only after World War I did the Institutes proliferate as the YWCA channeled effort and money from war work to aid to the foreign-born. See Edith T. Bremer, "Development of Private Social Work with the Foreign Born," American Academy of Political and Social Science, *Annals,* 262 (March 1949), 141–142; Mary S. Sims, *The Natural History of a Social Institution—the Young Women's Christian Association* (New York, 1936), 60, 64, 213. For some of the assumptions underlying the International Institute movement, see Edith T. Bremer, "The Foreign Language Worker in the Fusion Process: An Indispensable Asset to Social Work in America," National Conference on Social Work, *Proceedings* (1919), 740–746.

[3] The founding of Gary is treated in Powell A. Moore, *The Calumet Region: Indiana's Last Frontier* (Indiana Historical Collections, XXXIX; Indianapolis, 1959), 257–303; Raymond

Through its subsidiary, the Gary Land Company, U.S. Steel laid out streets on a rectangular pattern, provided essential utilities, subdivided the area directly south of the lake-shore mills into lots, and built houses, apartments, and boarding houses for executives, supervisors, foremen, and some skilled workers, primarily American. At the outset, the immigrant laborers who made up the bulk of the work force found housing only in "Hunkyville" (a group of shabby, company-owned boarding houses near the mills on the east side) and in the "Patch" (a slum of hovels, tin and tar paper shacks, and dingy rooming houses beyond U.S. Steel property to the south). Within four years, Gary grew from uninhabited sand dunes and swampland to a busy industrial metropolis of twenty thousand; it was, Charles P. Burton wrote enthusiastically in *The Independent*, "the most remarkable city ever known." Numerous national magazine articles predicted greatness for the "Magic City" and workers flocked to the mills in search of employment. By 1930, Gary's population had surpassed 100,000.[3]

Immigration gave Gary its special character. The immediate task of city building and factory construction attracted foreign-born workers from the Chicago area. Many later secured jobs in the new steel mills. Wide publicity surrounding Gary's creation attracted other newcomers, mainly recent immigrants from southern and eastern Europe who poured into the United States in ever-increasing numbers during the first decade of the twentieth century. Steel's labor recruiters also brought workers to Gary to meet burgeoning labor needs in the mills. Labor shortages during World War I and in the mid-1920's encouraged migration of southern Blacks and Mexicans to Gary, adding further to the ethnic and racial diversity of the

---

A. Mohl and Heil Betten, "The Failure of Industrial City Planning: Gary, Indiana, 1906–1910," *Journal of the American Institute of Planners*, XXXVIII (July 1972), 203–215; Isaac James Quillen, "Industrial City: A History of Gary, Indiana to 1929" (unpublished Ph.D. dissertation, Yale University, 1942), 46–149; Richard J. Meister, "A History of Gary, Indiana: 1930–1940" (unpublished Ph.D. dissertation, University of Notre Dame, 1966), 1–19. See also Raymond A. Mohl and Neil Betten, "Gary, Indiana: The Urban Laboratory as a Teaching Tool," *The History Teacher*, IV (January 1971), 5–17.

---

[3] Charles P. Burton, "Gary—A Creation," *The Independent*, 70 (February 16, 1911), 337. See also Henry B. Fuller, "An Industrial Utopia: Building Gary, Indiana, to Order," *Harper's Weekly*, 51 (October 12, 1907), 1482–1483, 1495; John K. Mumford, "This Land of Opportunity: Gary, the City that Rose from a Sandy Waste," *ibid.*, 52 (July 4, 1908), 22–23, 29; "Gary—Pittsburg's Future Rival," *The American Review of Reviews*, 39 (February 1909), 236–237; Elliott Flower, "Gary, the Magic City," *Putnam's Magazine*, V (March 1909), 643–653; Graham Romeyn Taylor, "Creating the Newest Steel City," *The Survey*, 22 (April 3, 1909), 20–36; Eugene J. Buffington, "Making Cities for Workmen," *Harper's Weekly*, 53 (May 8, 1909), 15–17; Graham Romeyn Taylor, "Satellite Cities: Gary," *The Survey*, 29 (March 1, 1913), 781–798.

Mexicans to Gary, adding furter to the ethnic and racial diversity of the city's population. The stream of new immigrants swelled once again in immediate post-war years until slowed by restrictive laws in 1921 and 1924. Throughout this period, U.S. Steel and other large industrial corporaticns vigorously opposed immigration restriction, preferring the obvious advantages of foreign-born laborers who worked long hours at relatively low wages and could be easily coerced to resist industrial unionism. By the 1920's, Steel's demand for labor had made Gary an immigrant city.

Gary's ethnic diversity astonished observers as early as 1908, only two years after construction of the city had begun. "As for the laboring element southeastern Europe seems almost to have emptied itself here," journalist John K. Mumford wrote in *Harper's Weekly*. "There is every class, stratum, and substratum of the Slav; there are Croats, Huns, Sicilians, Neapolitans, Servians, Bulgarians, Roumanians, Rumelians, and even a colony of Turks." A census taken by the Gary Land Company in November 1908, showed a substantial majority of foreign-born in the city's total population of 10,246 (see Table 1).[5] By 1920, more than fifty-two nationalities added to the "babel of tongues" in Gary; immigrants and

TABLE 1

Gary Land Company's Census, November 1908

Slavonians	300	Belgians	15
Hungarians	325	French	6
Croatians	950	Norwegians	75
Bohemians	125	Swedes	125
Serbians	1,000	Danes	15
Montenegrans	375	Finns	20
Turks	40	Italians	350
Macedonians	100	Japanese	10
Armenians	25	Negroes	250
Greeks	40	Welsh	50
Russians	150	Jews	150
Poles	1,100	Irish, Scotch, English,	
Germans	150	Canadian, and American	4,500

Graham Romeyn Taylor, "Creating the Newest Steel City," *The Survey*, 22 (April 3, 1909), 33. The last category is confusing, for there is no way to separate foreign-born from American-born.

---

[5] Mumford, "This Land of Opportunity," 23; Taylor, "Creating the Newest Steel City," 33.

Blacks together totalled seventy-nine percent of the city's population.[6] According to an annual survey made in 1927 by the International Institute, Gary's major ethnic enclaves contained more than 55,000 foreign-born residents and their children. Most numerous were Poles, Russians, Czechs, Serbs, Croatians, Greeks, Italians, Germans, and Mexicans (see Table 2). By the end of the twenties, Gary also had about 18,000 Blacks.[7]

Immigrants in Gary faced difficult problems of adjustment. Most newcomers were transplanted rural laborers and small farmers unfamiliar with urban life or factory work. Surveying Gary's foreign-born communities in 1929, International Institute workers found that ninety percent of Polish immigrants came from villages or agricultural districts of Russia and Austria. Similarly, most Greek immigrants came from small villages on the islands of Greece, where they had been fishermen, spongemen, fruit-growers, and farmers. The Mexicans imported to work on the railroads and in the mills also came primarily from agricultural backgrounds. Other nationality groups had similar origins. The harsh

TABLE 2

Major Immigrant Groups in Gary, 1927

Poles	10,000	Lithuanians	1,500
Croatians	6,000	Romanians	1,500
Czechoslovakians	6,000	Bulgarians	800
Germans	5,000	Ukranians	800
Greeks	4,000	Assyrians	500
Serbians	4,000	Spanish	300
Mexicans	3,500	Albanians	200
Italians	3,000	Macedonians	200
Russians	3,000	Welsh	100
Hungarians	2,500	Syrians	50
Swedes	2,000	Chinese	50

These estimated figures are contained in "Report to Department of Immigration and Foreign Communities of the National Board of the YWCA," 1927, I.I. Papers.

[6] Emerson Hough, "Round Our Town," *The Saturday Evening Post*. 192 (February 14, 1920), 19; Agnes B. Ewart to Elin S. Phinney, November 31, 1919, Correspondence, 1919–1929, Gary International Institute Papers (hereafter referred to as I.I. Papers).

[7] "Report to Department of Immigration and Foreign Communities of the National Board of the YWCA," 1927, I.I. Papers; Emma Lou Thornbrough, "Segregation in Indiana during the Klan Era of the 1920's," *Mississippi Valley Historical Review*. XLVII (March 1961), 595. The rate of Black population increase in Gary during the 1920's amounted to 238.2 percent, a rate higher than that of any other city of 100,000 or more except for one borough of New York City (Manhattan). Monthly Report, September 1931, I.I. Papers.

reality of the twentieth-century industrial city confronted the rural immigrant. The traditional ways of the sparsely populated villages of fishermen or farmers became anachronistic in a city of steel mills and ethnic slums. "Peasant immigrants," as Oscar Handlin has suggested so well in *The Uprooted,* became conscious of their differentness and suffered the "shock of alienation." As native Americans demanded conformity from newcomers, the industrial city itself forced immigrants into new patterns of life and work.[8]

Mill work was dangerous and physically exhausting. The typical steel worker labored twelve hours a day, seven days a week, but some jobs required longer hours. Every two weeks men worked a twenty-four hour "swing shift," as day and night shifts rotated. Occasionally men on special projects worked as long as thirty-six hours without rest. Industrial accidents were common, particularly for unskilled newcomers with language difficulties performing unaccustomed tasks. Mill workers also experienced relatively high rates of respiratory disease, especially tuberculosis and pneumonia. Before the successes of CIO industrial unionism in the 1930's, unorganized laborers in the Gary steel mills received wages insufficient to sustain a minimum American standard of living. According to U.S. Labor Department statistics for 1912, common laborers in thirty-nine mid-west steel plants earned an average wage of 16.7 cents per hour. In the same year weekly earnings for laborers in blast furnace departments averaged $11.15, in Bessemer converter departments $12.64, in open hearth furnaces $12.10, in blooming mills $12.13, in plate mills $11.04, in rail mills $12.07, in bar mills $10.52, in sheet mills $10.72, and in tinplate mills $10.37. Although wages improved somewhat in the 1920's, the standard of living of unskilled steel workers remained relatively low. In addition, steel workers had no protections against unemployment during frequent business fluctuations and depressions.[9]

Immigrant laborers faced equally trying living conditions in the "Magic City." The earliest workers in Gary, those who built the city and

---

[8] "Study of the Foreign-Born in Gary," 1929, I.I. Papers; Oscar Handlin, *The Uprooted* (New York, 1951), 259–285.

[9] John A. Fitch, "Steel and Steel Workers in Six American States, Part VI: The Labor Policies of Unrestricted Capital," *The Survey,* 28 (April 6, 1912), 17–27; Taylor, "Satellite Cities: Gary," 790; U.S. Department of Labor, *Wages and Hours in the Iron and Steel Industry in the United States, 1907–1912* (Bureau of Labor Statistics Bulletin No. 151; Washington, 1914), 15, 28, 101, 171, 212, 246, 285, 330, 520, 533; Irving Bernstein, *The Lean Years: A History of the American Worker, 1920–1933* (Boston, 1960), 63–74. See also John A. Fitch, "Labor in the Steel Industry—The Human Side of Large Outputs," American Academy of Political and Social Science, *Annals,* 33 (March 1909), 307–315; David Brody, *Steelworkers in America: The Nonunion Era* (Cambridge, Mass., 1960), 27–49, 96–111.

the factories, lived in flimsy tents and primitive sheds and shacks around construction sites. Three years later, the same hovels still housed most immigrant laborers, three-room shacks often housing as many as twenty persons. A few fortunate new arrivals found quarters in the fifty four-room houses built by the Gary Land Company in "Hunkyville" in the northeast part of the city. Designed for individual families and rented at twelve to thirteen dollars per month, these "double drygoods boxes," as they were called, quickly filled with lodgers. Low-paid laborers by necessity turned their homes into overcrowded boarding houses to supplement meager wages. When "Hunkyville" soon became unsightly, insanitary, garbage-strewn, and run down, the company evicted tenants and boarders, replacing them with American families who agreed to take no lodgers. In the absense of any industry provision for housing unskilled laborers, private builders and real estate developers constructed cheap frame houses and barracks in the "Patch" and on the "south side," both within the corporate limits of Gary but beyond U.S. Steel property. The housing scarcity caused exploitative rents. Two-room apartments without running water, toilets, or any other modern conveniences rented for as much as nine dollars a month; most occupants took in boarders as well, for, as Graham Romeyn Taylor wrote in *The Survey* in 1913, "throughout the south side the immigrant family which does not have borders is an exception." One social worker reported an immigrant family with twenty-five borders in seven rooms. As late as 1936, according to a WPA survey, at least twenty-five percent of Gary's homes had no baths or toilets. Gary may have been an "industrial utopia" for U.S. Steel, but it hardly seemed so promising to most immigrant workers.[10]

Foreign-born workers in Gary also suffered the consequences of nativist hostilities. For Gary's immigrants the "shock of alienation" was very real, the frequent calls for Americanization occasionally oppressive. Unionism, for example, was condemned as radical and un-American. The belief that foreigners (that is, labor radicals, socialists, and I.W.W. agitators) stirred up the 1919 steel strike seemed to justify repressive police tactics, martial law, and 1,500 federal troops in Gary. The "Red" headquarters, according to the military authorities, lay "on the south side of the city in the midst of a foreign section." The post-war threat of "Bolshevism" and the reality of the 1919 strike generated an aggressive Americanization campaign. Gary sported a "Loyal Legion," which defended the principle of "America for Americans," and a Ku Klux Klan with 500 members by

---

[10] Taylor, "Creating the Newest Steel City," 24, 29, 31; Taylor, Satellite Cities: Gary," 786–788; *Recovery in Indiana* (Governor's Commission on Unemployment Relief, August 1936), 7; Fuller, "An Industrial Utopia," 1495.

1921. Some nativists demanded the end to Gary's foreign-language newspapers. Gary's mayor, W. F. Hodge, urged deportation as "the answer" to labor radicalism among immigrants.[11] In analysing the impact of the strike, an Institute worker in Gary wrote that "the foreign-born are being greatly antagonized, and the number of radicals, naturally, grows as the result of undeserved unfriendliness on the part of Americans. They were considered Americans during the war, they are considered foreign—and only foreign—now."[12]

Anti-immigrant feelings did not subside with Steel's victory in 1919 and the consequent repression of labor radicalism. Throughout the twenties, Gary's newcomers felt scorn, ridicule, discrimination, and exploitation. The depression of the thirties brought a resurgence of anti-immigrant hostility, even demands for deportation. Nativists blamed immigrants for the depression, for depriving Americans of jobs when working, and for increasing relief costs when unemployed. The Mexican "repatriation" movement of the early thirties—the involuntary return of Mexican immigrant families to Mexico—typified twentieth-century nativism in Gary and nationwide.[13]

The YWCA designed the International Institutes to deal with the immigrants' multiple problems. Under the direction of Agnes B. Ewart, and later of Maude Cooley Polk, Gary's Institute began in 1919 in the basement of a library branch on the west side. Four nationality workers (as the Institute called its immigrant social workers) made up the staff—one each for the Polish, Czechoslovakian, Bulgarian, and Italian communities of Gary. All the workers spoke several languages and handled other ethnic groups as well as their own. By the mid-twenties, an expanded staff included Mexican, Serbian, and Greek nationality workers. These workers attempted to serve immigrant needs, preserve ethnic identity, and "internationalize" the community by promoting mutual understanding and respect among ethnic groups and between natives and newcomers.[14]

---

[11] Graham Taylor, "At Gary: Some Impressions and Interviews," *The Survey*, 43 (November 8, 1919), 65–66; Emerson Hough, "Round Our Town," *The Saturday Evening Post*, 192 (February 21, 1920), 102, 106; Kenneth T. Jackson, *The Ku Klux Klan in the City, 1915–1930* (New York, 1967), 97.

[12] Agnes B. Ewart to Elin S. Phinney, November 31, 1919, I.I. Papers.

[13] Typical examples of anti-immigrant hostility in the 1930's can be found in Isaac F. Marcosson, "The Alien in America," *The Saturday Evening Post*, 207 (April 6, 1935), 22–23, 110, 112–113; Raymond G. Carroll, "The Alien on Relief," *ibid.*, 208 (January 11, 1936), 16–17, 100–101; Raymond G. Carroll, "Alien Workers in America," *ibid.*, 208 (January 25, 1936), 23, 82, 84–86, 89. See also Louis Adamic, "Aliens and Alien-Baiters," *Harpers Magazine*, 173 (November 1936), 561–574.

[14] "Notes on the Early History of the International Institute of Gary, 1919–1937," I.I. Papers; Annual Report, 1921, *ibid.*

Although old-stock American settlement house leaders had advanced such ideas in earlier years, language difficulties, immigrant opposition, and insufficient understanding of ethnic traditions had frustrated all but a few immigrant-oriented settlement house programs.[15] Gary's Institute staff recognized their objectives and the use of immigrant social workers as new and unusual. "Existing social workers had never approached the problem from our angle," Bulgarian nationality worker Luba Tzvetanova wrote in her monthly report for September 1919. "Their basis has been plain charity, very often with utter lack of sympathetic understanding for the party concerned." The Institute worker hoped to be "a friend in every day life first, and then a friend in need."[16]

During the twenties, Gary's International Institute channeled considerable energies into individual service and case work. Contacts with church and community leaders in ethnic neighborhoods served to introduce nationality workers to immigrant families. During the Institute's first decade, nationality workers handled as many as five and six hundred individual cases each month. Most of these dealt with legal problems or paper work involved in immigration and citizenship. Typical cases were recorded in the monthly report for September 1920: Institute workers helped prepare necessary affidavits to bring workers' families to the United States; aided families in getting "their kinsfolk off from Ellis Island"; visited a Chicago jail to assist a Bulgarian woman sentenced to deportation; secured payment for a woman in Lithuania on property owned in the United States by her dead husband; helped several immigrants settle affairs in America so they could return to Europe. In addition, they visited people in hospitals, directed those in need to physicians and free medical clinics, found employment for men and women, got college scholarships for boys and girls (mainly at American International College in Springfield, Massachusetts), assisted in income tax difficulties, located relatives in Europe, made application for passports, citizenship, and soldier's compensation, interceded with immigration authorities on behalf of immigrants, wrote and translated letters in many languages, even secured a divorce for an immigrant woman whose husband loved "good times," which "he carried in a bottle in one of his big coat pockets." Serving the varied needs of immigrants with diligence and respect, the International Institute soon made itself an indispensable community agency.[17]

---

[15] George Cary White, "Social Settlements and Immigrant Neighbors, 1886–1914," *Social Service Review, XXXIII (March 1959), 55–66;* Allen F. Davis, *Spear heads for Reform: The Social Settlements and the Progressive Movement, 1890–1914* (New York, 1967), 86–90. The best example of a successful immigrant-oriented settlement program—the Hull-House Labor Museum—is described in Jane Addams, *Twenty Years at Hull-House* (Signet ed., New York, 1961), 169–185.

[16] Monthly Report, September 1919, I.I. Papers.

[17] Monthly Reports, September 1920, March 1921, I.I. Papers.

In addition to individual case work, the Institute promoted ethnic group activities which sometimes helped immigrants adjust to life in the United States. For instance, nationality workers organized English classes, mainly for foreign-born women and girls at first. Such classes were established at the Institute and in immigrant homes for Italians, Russians, Poles, Greeks, Mexicans, Romanians, and others. Polish and Greek women were reported as the most ambitious and eager English students. Institute workers attributed the reluctance of others to opposition from husbands. The Institute's annual report for 1922 typically recorded one husband's feeling about education for his wife: "She old, she no learn nothing, she hard head." Despite such attitudes, English classes for women continued into the 1930's. Essay contests on such topics as "My Life in America," "My Experiences at Ellis Island," and "What I Think about Immigration" generated enthusiasm for English classes, as did the five-dollar prizes awarded to winners. By the mid-twenties, the Institute sponsored classes for men as well. U.S. Steel and its several subsidiaries helped finance Institute classes for workers. During the Depression, when the Gary public schools discontinued free adult English classes, the Institute expanded its educational program. Later, New Deal programs provided the Institute with FERA and WPA instructors. While the International Institute resisted full-blown Americanization, it saw only advantages in teaching immigrants the language skills needed to adjust to life in the industrial city.[18]

Although the Institute considered English an important tool for survival in a new environment, it regarded preservation of the immigrant heritage as equally important. Thus, building ethnic consciousness through group activities became one of the organization's most significant tasks. The Institute opened its facilities to existing immigrant clubs, mutual aid societies, and social organizations, while nationality workers helped organize new ethnic associations throughout the city. Gary affiliates of such national ethnic organizations as the Polish National Alliance, the Sons of Italy, and the Croatian Catholic Union worked with the Institute. Other Institute-based organizations sprouted locally and included the Czechoslovak Liberty Club, the Polish Mechanics Society, the Free Poland Society, the Hungarian Benevolent Society, the Bulgarian Society, the Russian-Slavonic Mutual Aid Society, the Lithuanian Political Club, the League of Italian Families, the Serbian Society, the Albanian Society, the Mexican Sociedad Protectora, and the Hidalgo Society. Some emphasized

---

[18] Monthly Reports, September 1919, March 1921, October 1921, May 1923, February 1924, I.I. Papers; Annual Report, 1922, *ibid.;* "Notes on Early History," *ibid.; Gary Post-Tribune,* April 9, September 27, 1923.

a particular avocation or served women and children: the Serbian Dramatic Club, the Russian Independent Musical and Dramatic Club, the Mexican Knitting Club, the Polish Women's Club, the Mexican Women's Club, the Assyrian Women's Society, the Polish Children's Club, and the Sokol Gymnastic Union. In 1924, seventy-two different groups used Institute facilities for 472 meetings, with a total attendance of 14,582. Immigrant groups and families also used Institute rooms for weddings, receptions, christenings, dancing, card parties, holiday celebrations, and Christmas parties. The Institute encouraged such group activities as a means of maintaining ethnic ties and immigrant culture.[19]

If the Institute served as a gathering place for Gary's immigrants, nationality workers also kept in close touch with happenings in ethnic neighborhoods. They attended immigrant churches, met with community leaders to discuss common problems, and worked closely with schools and teachers. During a two-month period in 1919, in addition to all their other activities, nationality workers attended the dedication of the Greek church and a Russian cemetery; made contacts with Russian, Serbian, and Croatian priests; attended services at a Serbian church and Temple Israel and visited classes at several schools; went to a Croatian glee club rehearsal, a Russian dance, a Russian concert, an Italian Columbus Day celebration, and five Greek, Mexican, and Bulgarian coffee houses; and accepted invitations to parties given by Russians and Bulgarians. Group work within the immigrant neighborhoods made other Institute programs successful.[20]

To build ethnic pride and to cushion cultural shock, every International Institute emphasized cultural programs based on immigrant traditions. From the outset, the Institutes rejected prevailing demands for complete assimilation and conformity. Through concerts, dances, festivals, plays, and exhibits, Institute nationality workers sought to preserve and enhance the immigrant heritage while simultaneously broadening American culture. An undated memorandum from the National Board of the YWCA presented Institute assumptions:

> America has an opportunity no other country has ever had—the opportunity of assimilating the old traditions of many lands into a new tradition of her own. The International Institute, because of its geographical situation in the heart of the foreign section of our great industrial towns, is afforded a uniquely favorable chance for devel-

---

[19] The Monthly Reports of the International Institute nationality workers are full of references to work among the various ethnic groups of Gary. See also "Notes on Early History," I.I. Papers.

[20] Monthly Reports, September 1919, October 1919, I.I. Papers.

oping this new tradition based on the festivals and songs, the art and handicraft, the folklore and customs of other races.

Accepting the need for Institutes to deal realistically with the social and economic problems of immigrants, the memo further urged nationality workers to be alive to possibilities for "capturing the beauty of earlier civilizations in order to preserve it for future generations in America." For newcomers, involvement in immigrant community activities and programs would build pride in one's heritage and provide a "wholesome outlet" for "excess energy" previously expended "in the stifling dance hall, the movie theater, or on the street corners of the crowded cities." Special emphasis was placed on working with immigrant children, who too often "scornfully cast aside the colorful language and symbolic customs of their forefathers" and "all too rapidly assimilated the movie, jazz and the gutter speech of the modern American city."[21]

Nationality workers at the Gary Institute accepted the principles of the YWCA memo and enthusiastically promoted immigrant cultural programs. Each year the Institute sponsored festivals, "harvest pageants," Christmas plays, concerts, folk singing, folk dancing, exhibits of arts and handicrafts, international banquets and dinners, and special affairs on immigrant holidays. Occasionally, immigrant clubs held lectures on the art, literature, and history of native countries. Institute-sponsored foreign-language classes for American-born children of immigrants sought to maintain ethnic culture.[22] The National Board of the YWCA in New York continuously distributed books, pamphlets, handbooks, bibliographies, and mimeographed materials to aid the cultural activities of local nationality workers.[23] Beyond building immigrant pride and self-respect, such group programs, because they often involved many different nationalities in a single project, helped promote inter-ethnic understanding. Institute workers considered the establishment of mutual respect among nationality groups one of their most important objectives. Thus, they brought immigrant women together for "international" luncheons and teas and helped

---

[21] "A Year's Plan for Community Programs," undated mimeo from National Board of YWCA, I.I. Papers.

[22] "Notes on Early History," I.I. Papers; Monthly Reports, November 1920, April 1925, September 1931, ibid; Annual Report, 1931, ibid; Gary Evening Post, November 13, 1920.

[23] See, for example, YWCA, Handbook on Racial and Nationality Backgrounds (New York, 1922); YWCA, A Brief Reading List on Immigration. Immigrant Backgrounds and Attitudes toward the Foreign-Born (New York, 1932); YWCA, National Costumes of the Slavic Peoples (New York, 1920); Marion Peabody, Music Suggestions for the Christmas Season (New York, 1934); and the following mimeos in I.I. Papers: YWCA, "The Value and Technique of Foreign Handicraft Exhibits," 1927; YWCA, "Organization Hints for a Play, Pageant or Festival," 1927; YWCA, "Czecho-slovakia—Holidays for 1927," 1927; YWCA, "Some Helpful Books on Folk Dances, Games, and Songs," 1927; YWCA, "Holidays and Festivals of Ancient Mexico and Modern Mexicans," 1928.

organize an International Girls Club. Numerous other Institute activities had the same goal, as when a Hungarian Gypsy Orchestra provided music for an Italian Club affair or when the Polish Girls Club made costumed dolls for Mexican children as a Christmas project. A "hard times dance" in 1921 included people from eight different nationalities. Such Institute programs eased adjustment to industrial America for immigrants from rural villages while simultaneously helping them resist total orthodoxy and Americanization.[24]

The Institute also tried to temper nativist bigotry by familiarizing Americans with immigrant traditions and contributions. The task was far from easy in the intolerant twenties. In her annual report for 1921, executive director Maude Polk wrote "we often feel that our biggest job is in educating American-born Americans in knowing and appreciating the foreign-born American." The Institute invited the public to most of its festivals and exhibits, while local newspapers publicized Institute activities. In addition, nationality workers spoke on Institute work at meetings of the PTA and other Gary organizations. When hostility to Mexicans intensified with soaring immigration in the 1920's, the Institute engaged in a "constant effort to break down prejudice against Mexicans through talks before various groups." The goal of establishing mutual understanding and respect between natives and newcomers made the International Institute an important force for progress and social welfare in the Steel City.[25]

The Institute worked for progress and reform in other areas as well. It developed a recreational program, for example, designed especially to take advantage of the rapidly diminishing natural beauties of the area. By 1919 U. S. Steel had appropriated for industrial use twelve unbroken miles of Lake Michigan beachfront, effectively preventing Gary residents from using the lake for recreational purposes. Yielding to pressures during the 1919 steel strike, the company donated 116 acres to the city for a lake shore park. But because it was located about six or eight miles from the center of town, few workers used its facilities. Indeed, in 1920 Institute workers reported numerous immigrants who had lived and worked in Gary for as long as twelve years and had never seen Lake Michigan. The Institute established a summer camp on the beach at Miller, then a small village east of Gary. Immigrant clubs and supervised groups of boys and girls used the camp for beach parties, picnics, swimming, and overnight outings.[26]

---

[24] Monthly Reports, February 1921, October 1921, November 1924, December 1926, I.I. Papers.

[25] Annual Report, 1921, I.I. Papers; "Report to Department of Immigration and Foreign Communities of the National Board of the YWCA," 1931, *ibid.*

[26] Taylor, "At Gary: Some Impressions and Interviews," 65; Monthly Reports, July-September 1920, I.I. Papers.

In addition to family case work, educational programs, and group activities, nationality workers became involved in a multiplicity of community affairs during the Institute's first decade. They encouraged "Big Sister" work to prevent female delinquency. They promoted public health with baby clinics, hygiene courses for immigrant women, and posters listing good health habits. They raised funds for numerous social welfare projects (on one occasion collecting money to purchase cribs for an Ellis Island nursery). They circulated petitions in 1923 calling for introduction of the city manager plan in Gary. In 1925 nationality workers cooperated with settlement houses and other social agencies in a study of housing in the Black ghetto on the "unlovely south side of Gary." In one of its most ambitious projects, the Institute in 1929 made a detailed survey of Gary's immigrant communities. Focusing on Greeks, Poles, and Mexicans, nationality workers interviewed neighborhood leaders and residents on their European backgrounds and American experiences, compiling the information in a detailed report for the National Board of the YWCA (other Institutes throughout the country made simultaneous surveys of immigrant communities). Throughout the twenties, the International Institute combined social welfare goals with social reform fervor.[27]

The Great Depression of the 1930's brought observable changes of emphasis to some Institute programs. The Institute continued its cultural activities and ethnic group work. However, with massive unemployment in the steel mills in the early thirties, the Institute took on some of the characteristics of a welfare agency as well. The Institute's report for December 1932 poignantly described the immigrant's plight: "men who have not yet brought their families to this country can neither bring them nor send money for their support; lack of proper food and medical attention has resulted in serious health problems; homes which were only partially paid for are being lost; clothing is wearing out and cannot be replaced; gas, electricity and water have been shut off." Many transient workers, men thrown out of jobs elsewhere, flocked to Gary in search of employment, compounding welfare needs.[28]

The Institute saw its main task as giving a "psychological lift" to those suffering "the long strain of discouragement and diminishing resources." But, recognizing that "moral support is quite indigestible on an empty stomach," the Institute also provided some relief. It distributed milk and second-hand clothing to the immigrant poor. Rummage sales, dances and other affairs raised small sums for relief. During winter months, the Institute secured permits for dependent families to cut fire-

[27] Monthly Reports, February 1921, April 1923, January 1925, January 1926, February 1929, October 1929, I.I. Papers; Annual Report, 1929, *ibid.;* Maude Cooley to Minnie M. Newman, August 18, 1920, Correspondence, *ibid.;* "Study of the Foreign-Born in Gary," 1929, *ibid.;* "Good Daily Health Practices," n.d., poster in *ibid.*
[28] Monthly Reports, October 1930, December 1932, I.I. Papers.

wood on Gary Land Company property. The Institute distributed candles to those whose electricity had been shut off for non-payment of bills. On behalf of immigrants, Institute workers interceded with local relief officials, who too often discriminated against the foreign-born. As the New Deal programs began in 1933, the Institute arranged jobs for young men in the Civilian Conservation Corps and later secured work for unemployed laborers on public projects. In addition, it helped provide free transportation for Mexicans and Europeans who wanted to return to their native lands.[29]

As the depression deepened, nativist hysteria mounted. Voluntary departure soon became forced expulsion. Newspapers and articles in national periodicals demanded deportation of aliens to reduce relief rolls or widen job opportunities for American workers. Gary's relief agencies frequently denied aid to men with foreign or "communistic" ideas. Immigrants who had never become American citizens were especially vulnerable to the new intolerance of the thirties. High naturalization fees prevented many unemployed aliens from becoming citizens during the depression. Much of the Institute's work in the thirties dealt with naturalization problems. The Institute helped those who had entered the United States under false names, who had lost entry papers, who could furnish no proof of residence prior to 1906 (when the United States government began registering immigrants), or who could not remember the date of their arrival or the name of the ship which brought them. With typical ingenuity, Institute workers solved the difficulties of a man who "left Europe when it was time to dig potatoes and landed in New York on a rainy Saturday." Special citizenship classes, even radio programs, speeded the naturalization process for aliens who might otherwise have been deported. As the Institute noted in its report for December 1932, "we have had to be on guard constantly to see that the foreign people secured the justice and fair treatment which they deserved. . . . This is especially true of the Mexicans."[30]

The experience of the Gary Mexican community reflected the resurgence of intolerance in the United States during the trying depression years. Economic pressure caused ninety percent unemployment in the steel mills and heavy demands on local welfare agencies. A local American Legion post first promoted the idea of "repatriation." Many Mexican immigrants had retained Mexican citizenship; indeed, many had been imported illegally by labor recruiters from railroad and steel companies, making naturalization all but impossible. Mexicans thus had few defenses against involuntary deportation. To speed the removal process, public officials denied

---

[29] Monthly Reports, November 1930, February 1931, May 1931, October 1932, November 1932, April 1933, December 1933, I.I. Papers; Annual Report, 1931, *ibid.*
[30] Carroll, "Alien on Relief," 16–17, 100–101; Carroll, "Alien Workers in America," 23, 82, 84–86, 89; Monthly Reports, October 1931, December 1932, December 1933, February 1934, March 1934, March 1936, June 1936, I:I. Papers; Radio Scripts, 1936, *ibid.*

relief to needy Mexican families and the steel mills refused to rehire Mexican workers without citizenship papers. In the early thirties, as many as 1,500 Gary Mexicans were returned to Mexico by truck and train under intolerable conditions, while another 1,800 were sent back from East Chicago, a nearby community with a similarly large Mexican population. Local welfare officials and native Americans viewed the repatriation movement as "an example of constructive relief," but International Institute workers soon saw it for what it really was—a new expression of nativist bigotry and racism. The Institute sought to protect Mexican interests as much as possible, aiding in the citizenship process and seeking relief and jobs for those discriminated against by public welfare agencies and steel mills.[31]

Institute support of Gary's troubled Mexican community typified the organization's efforts over two decades after its founding in 1919. Throughout the twenties and the thirties, nationality workers fought against open intolerance and nativism. They developed programs to give newcomers the tools they needed to adjust to life in urban America, but they simultaneously countered insistent demands for rapid assimilation. Most important, the Institute encouraged immigrants to retain their traditions, languages, and customs, to be proud of their backgrounds. At a time when most Americans denigrated immigrants and condemned their different ways and "un-American" habits, Institute cultural programs helped the foreign-born maintain a sense of worth and importance. Like similar agencies in more than sixty American cities, Gary's International Institute eased the transition from the old world village to the new world metropolis. Rather than assimilating the immigrant, it helped him retain his old culture. Rather than Americanizing him, the Institute helped the immigrant adjust to the urban and industrial environment of twentieth-century America. Like few other organizations during the decades of intolerance and depression, the Institutes affirmed the values of a democratic, pluralistic society.[32]

---

[31] Walter J. Riley, *The Story of Unemployment Relief in Lake County, Indiana* (n.p., 1932), 2, 9–11; Monthly Reports, December 1930, May 1931, September 1931, May 1932, September 1932, January 1933, May 1933, I.I. Papers; *Gary Post-Tribune*, January 14, February 27, March 16, April 20, May 11, 16, 1932.

[32] Although no longer connected with the YWCA, Gary's International Institute remains active, serving immigrant communities from its current location, 725 East 5th Avenue. During 1969 the Institute served 3,321 individuals from 50 nationalities (Annual Report, 1969). The authors would like to express their appreciation to the present executive director, Mrs. Marcella L. Otasevich, who permitted examination of the Institute's correspondence, reports, and other records in preparation for this article. This Institute, and others like it, are now affiliated with an independent national organization, the American Council for Nationalities Service, whose headquarters are in New York City.

paternalism and pluralism

immigrants and social welfare
in gary, indiana, 1906-1940

raymond a. mohl and neil betten

In recent years, some historians have identified inherent contradictions in the history and practice of American social welfare. Ostensibly created to aid the poor and provide for the needy, social welfare agencies and institutions have often served other and sometimes opposite purposes—indoctrinating or socializing children, Americanizing immigrants, serving up heavy doses of religion or morality, enforcing social order among the poor and in general acting as instruments of social control. In 1959, historian Ralph E. Pumphrey suggested this dual thread in American social welfare history. Both "compassion" and "protection," he noted, had traditionally motivated philanthropists and reformers; humanitarian concern for the poor and suffering was often balanced by "fear of change or . . . fear of what may happen if existing conditions are not changed." Several studies of nineteenth-century social welfare developments have offered similar conclusions, suggesting that benevolence had very important latent functions in a society undergoing rapid social change. More recently, social work scholars Frances Fox Piven and Richard A. Cloward have conceived of the contemporary welfare system in similar terms. In their book, *Regulating the Poor: The Functions of Public Welfare*, they contend that historically relief systems have served two crucial purposes: first, to maintain social and civil order, and second, to force the poor to work. Denying that government welfare policies have become progressively more liberal and humane, the authors argue that relief has simply been an effective way of manipulating the poor, keeping them orderly, and pushing them into low-income, menial jobs.[1] The conflicting patterns and purposes suggested by these studies have not yet been fully explored by historians of American social welfare. We would like to offer here, however, some evidence which sub-

5

stantiates the divergent themes sketched out above—conclusions based upon an analysis of the ideologies and programs of several social agencies working with immigrants in Gary, Indiana, during the first four decades of the twentieth century.

Much like other institutions, social welfare agencies working with immigrants in Gary and elsewhere usually reflected the predominant values of American society. In many cities, the urban settlement house provided the newcomer with his first contact beyond the ethnic community. Yet because of the particular value orientation of the people who ran such institutions—a value orientation which prized sobriety, industriousness, thrift, obedience, honesty, cleanliness, piety, patriotism and the "American way"—settlement house work generally served the interests of American society more than those of the immigrants themselves. In vigorously promoting Americans ideals and values, these institutions, to borrow from Pumphrey's analysis, served "protective" goals, often under the guise of "compassionate" programs. To be sure, professionally trained settlement workers in nationally known agencies like Hull House, the Chicago Commons and the Henry Street Settlement displayed a humane and sympathetic attitude toward the newcomers; but the typical settlement was a religious mission staffed by church personnel and non-professionals. Immigrants often regarded these settlement workers with suspicion, language barriers frequently proved insurmountable, and the Protestant missionizing of such settlements undermined social work among a primarily non-Protestant clientele.[2] In working among the steel city's immigrants, Gary's several settlement houses typified the nativist paternalism inherent in the history of American social welfare.

By contrast, the work of another local institution—the International Institute of Gary—reflected the humanitarian thrust of immigrant social welfare. In a city where nativist and Americanization demands established the public parameters of immigrant life, the International Institute's uniqueness lay in its efforts to support and preserve immigrant cultures and traditions. Seeking opportunity or escaping oppression, the immigrants brought little with them but their cultural heritage. Confronted with harsh demands for conformity and submission to American ways, newcomers found adjustment to the American city an exceedingly difficult process. Most of Gary's immigrants were transplanted rural laborers or small farmers, fruit growers and fishermen unfamiliar with urban life or factory work. They faced severe language problems as well as a kind of cultural shock. Like many industrial cities with large communities of foreign-born residents, Gary became an arena of cultural and ethnic conflict. Challenging established opinion and practice, the International Institute countered the nativist-dominated Americanization policies of the settlements, offering instead an early program of cultural pluralism.[3] Thus, Gary—and the distinctly different immi-

6

grant-helping agencies it spawned—provides an ideal laboratory to examine the functions of immigrant social welfare.

i

Founded in 1906 by the United States Steel Corporation on the southern shore of Lake Michigan, Gary grew rapidly as an industrial city. Although it was the largest planned company town in the United States, Gary nevertheless developed a sprawling slum of shacks, boarding houses, tenements, and bungalows on its unplanned "south side"—a section within the city limits but owned by private and speculative real estate interests rather than the steel company. The eastern and southern European immigrants who thronged into this section before the restrictive quota laws of the 1920's gave Gary its special character. They came largely from Poland, Austria, Hungary, Russia, Italy, Greece and the Balkan nations. When European immigration slowed during the twenties, Gary experienced large influxes of Mexicans and southern Blacks as well. By 1930, the city's population surpassed 100,000; 48.7 percent of the city's residents in that year were immigrants, or had one or more foreign-born parents; Blacks, primarily from the lower South, comprised another 17.8 percent of the population (see Table 1).[4]

Within a decade of its founding, Gary had two social settlements in crowded immigrant neighborhoods on the south side. One of these, the Gary Neighborhood House, began in 1909 as a Presbyterian-sponsored kindergarten for immigrant children. The program quickly expanded to handle the community's multiple social needs, while construction of a large new building in 1912 provided facilities for traditional settlement house activities. Methodist women in Gary supplied the initial impetus for the second agency, the Campbell Friendship House, which opened in 1914, a few blocks away. Located amid "dreary shacks and tenements

TABLE I
Population of Gary, Indiana

	1910 Number	%	1920 Number	%	1930 Number	%
Native White _____	4,480	26.7	16,519	29.8	33,635	33.5
Foreign-born White _____	8,242	49.0	16,460	29.7	19,345	19.3
Native White, one or more Foreign-born Parents _____	3,681	21.9	17,065	30.8	26,012	25.9
Other races _____	16	.1	35	.1	3,512*	3.5
Black _____	383	2.3 ·	5,299	9.6	17,922	17.8
Totals _____	16,802	100.0	55,378	100.0	100,426	100.0

* Mexican immigrants made up 3,486 of the total listed under "other races" in 1930.

Sources: U.S. Bureau of the Census, **Thirteenth Census of the United States, II, Population** (Washington, D.C., 1913), 568; U.S. Bureau of the Census, **Fourteenth Census of the United States, III, Population** (Washington, D.C., 1922), 297; U.S. Bureau of the Census, **Fifteenth Census of the United States: 1930. Population, III, Part I** (Washington, D.C., 1932), 715.

7

stretching away for blocks in every direction," each settlement hoped to become a kind of "social lighthouse" in the "polyglot and congested" neighborhood it served.[5]

Religious purposes and missionary programs strongly marked both settlements. Methodist and Presbyterian ministers usually served as directors of the two institutions.[6] Despite the overwhelming number of non-Protestants among Gary's newcomers, many Neighborhood House and Campbell House programs sought to Americanize immigrants by making them Protestants. The Neighborhood House, for instance, conducted Bible study classes and Protestant Sunday schools in several languages for immigrant children. Week-day church schools, established in the settlements under a public school release-time plan, served many nationalities but taught Protestant doctrines. By the 1920's the settlement held Presbyterian services weekly in English, Italian, Slovak, Hungarian, Spanish and Russian. The settlement's workers distributed Bibles among immigrants on the south side. When the house created an employment agency, people attended week-day religious services while waiting at the settlement for jobs.[7] At Campbell House—which promoted what one observer described as "Christian Americanization of foreign peoples"—settlement residents held Sunday schools, vacation Bible schools and weekly church services.[8]

Beyond Protestant proselytizing, both settlements began a number of practical social programs for south side immigrant families. Thus, the Neighborhood House provided day and night nurseries for working mothers, playground facilities, legal aid, employment assistance, a savings bank program, laundry facilities, "much used" public baths, and free drinking water to those without it at home. To promote public health in the community, the settlement developed a visiting nurse program, medical and dental clinics, and classes in home hygiene, sanitation, diet and nutrition, and child training. It also fostered "enrichment" activities for children and adults: recreational programs, team sports, hobby clubs, and classes in cooking, sewing, dressmaking, wood working, metal working and various crafts. Vacant lots adjacent to the house supplied plots for neighborhood vegetable gardens. During the Great Depression of the 1930's, the house served as a neighborhood relief center. In addition, the settlement served as a temporary shelter for new arrivals in the city, renting small rooms to those without friends or relatives until they found permanent housing.[9]

Campbell House had similar programs, including day nurseries, home visiting, health clinics, vaccination stations, library and gymnasium activities, and classes in domestic science, cooking, sewing, music, crafts and other subjects. The settlement provided weekly movies, encouraged community singing programs, held occasional neighborhood picnics, and supplied baths, work, even hair cuts. During the Depression, Campbell House functioned as a community relief center and conducted a sub-

8

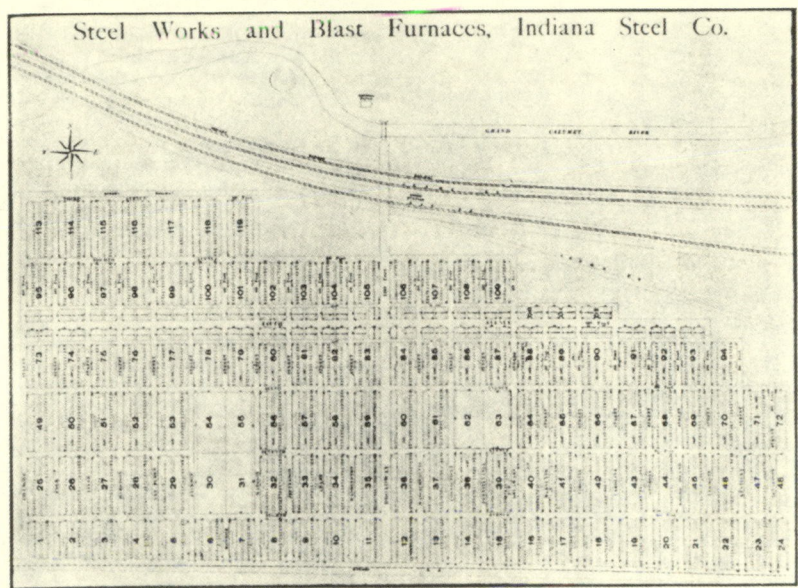

Steel Works and Blast Furnaces, Indiana Steel Co.

PLAN OF GARY'S FIRST SUBDIVISION, 1906: Laid out by the Gary Land Company, a subsidiary of the United States Steel Corporation, Gary's First Subdivision reveals close adherence to the traditional gridiron plan. Two major traffic arteries— Broadway running north-south and Fifth Avenue running east-west—served as the axis of the company plan. And while the names of these two streets reflected the pretentions of the town's builders, the rigid gridiron pattern ignored current and innovative thinking about city planning, imposed a dreary uniformity on the city, and determined its future physical form (Source: Gary Public Library).

sistence garden program for about 500 families. By 1931 the settlement also sponsored five separate Boy Scout troops for Polish, Russian, Croatian, Greek and Black youths.[10] The practical programs of the Neighborhood House and Campbell House generally eased adjustment of immigrant newcomers to the new and sometimes frightening conditions of the industrial city. Unquestionably, the settlements provided essential and needed services.

Yet, these very same programs, in many instances, sought to Americanize the immigrant, to wean adults and children—especially children—away from the old culture by introducing them to and indoctrinating them with American customs, values and ideals. English classes became opportunities for "special instruction . . . in the duties of American citizenship."[11] Campbell House was founded, according to a short history of the settlement written in 1943, as a center "where the work of Americanization could be carried on."[12] Children in the Neighborhood House day nursery assisted the "matron" in sweeping, cleaning, setting the table, washing dishes and other tasks. "In this way," wrote the settlement head in 1920, "many are learning habits of industry and thrift

9

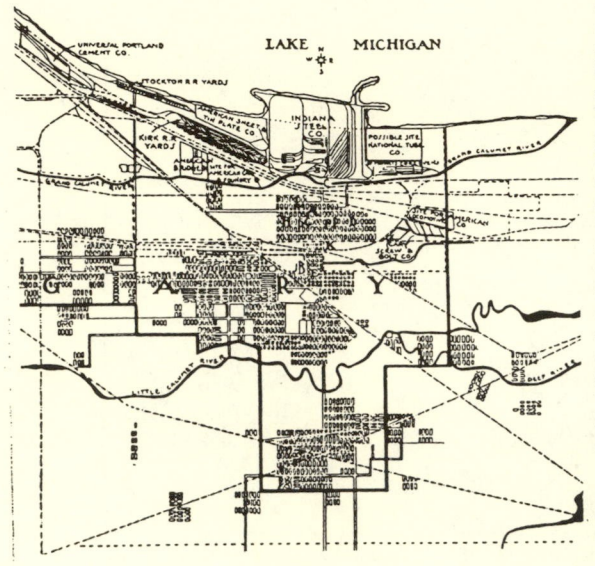

at a very impressionable age." A similar rationale underlay the settlement's employment bureau; immigrant women hired as domestics could "get a glimpse into American homes and are able to learn from them [American housewives] as well as receive pay for their services."[13] A short historical sketch of the Neighborhood House written in 1945 declared that the main purpose of the settlement has always been "to furnish educational, religious and moral training." Nursery schools in the settlements, conducted under WPA auspices during the late 1930's and early 1940's, were labeled "institutes of social behavior to develop habit patterns for good citizenship." Cooking classes taught immigrant women how to prepare only American foods.[14] The missionary zeal of Sunday schools, Bible classes and Protestant church services in the settlements revealed disregard and contempt for traditional immigrant religions. Aware of poverty, disease, bad housing and social disorganization in immigrant communities, the settlement workers sponsored programs to counter these difficulties. But too often the goal of Americanization turned these same programs into forces of cultural destruction.

In contrast to many non-denominational settlements in the United States during the progressive era, Gary's social centers did little to preserve immigrant culture and traditions. To be sure, some ethnic associations met regularly at the settlements. However, few of these groups fell under the supervision or guidance of settlement workers; they simply used the house as a convenient gathering place and had no other formal

10

connection with the settlements.[15] Occasionally, the settlements sponsored concerts of immigrant music and singing, but these events were few and far between. Although settlement religious activities were often organized along ethnic lines, these can hardly be construed as efforts at cultural preservation. Rather, they attacked traditional immigrant religions. Thus, in their pervasive paternalism, in their continual efforts at immigrant assimilation, and in their implict denial of the worth of old world cultures in the new world environment, Gary's Protestant settlements became active and rigorous forces for Americanization.[16]

As zealous in pursuing religious and Americanization goals, the Catholic-sponsored Gary-Alerding Settlement originated in 1917 with the aid of a $100,000 contribution from the United States Steel Corporation. (It might be noted that U.S. Steel made numerous similar, but smaller, donations to immigrant churches and other community agencies as a means of fostering American values among newcomers and promoting their own form of social order.) The steel company also donated a large lot on the south side, on which a forty-room settlement house went up in the mid-twenties, complete with bowling alleys, gymnasium, auditorium, medical center, game and craft rooms, and a chapel. Headed from its beginning by a Gary Catholic priest, Father John B. DeVille, the house was jointly named after Elbert Gary of U.S. Steel and Bishop Henry Alerding of the Fort Wayne Catholic Diocese (which included Gary).[17]

The Gary-Alerding House had many programs similar to those of the Protestant settlements: recreational and educational activities, work with delinquents and orphans, and youth programs emphasizing music, dramatics and crafts. During the Great Depression, the house opened a soup kitchen and served hot lunches to school children. In its practical social services, the Gary-Alerding Settlement hardly differed from the Neighborhood House and Campbell House.[18]

The underlying rationale, however, for many of these various activities was distinctly religious. Jessie M. Vogt, a YWCA worker from New York who surveyed Gary's social agencies in 1933, described the settlement this way: "the work seems to be rather largely of a religious nature, at least the emphasis is decidedly Catholic." Nuns from the order of the Poor Handmaids of Jesus Christ handled the teaching and social work of the settlement, along with a few paid workers. The settlement's St. Anthony's Chapel accommodated separate Italian, Mexican, Spanish and English-speaking Catholic congregations. In the 1920's Father DeVille formed the Catholic Instructional League at the Gary-Alerding House to conduct week-day church schools under the public school release-time plan. By the mid-twenties, ten centers staffed by settlement teachers handled more than six thousand students each week.[19] If the Protestant settlements would Americanize Gary's newcomers by making them Presbyterians and Methodists, the Gary-Alerding

11

House pursued the same goal by reaffirming and strengthening the immigrants' Catholicism. Since many immigrants, including Roman Catholics, had fallen away from traditional religious affiliations and many—Mexicans, for example—had strong anti-clerical traditions in the old country, missionary goals in the settlements represented imposition of American authority, and therefore American values, upon the center's Catholic clientele.

The Gary-Alerding House also had a vigorous and undisguised Americanization program. Founder and director Father DeVille headed Gary's city-wide Americanization campaign during the nativist hysteria of the Great Red Scare. He guided the settlement along the same path. As late as 1924, according to DeVille's monthly newsletter, *The Good Samaritan*, the settlement spent much of its energy in "counteracting the socialistic and bolshevistic tendencies of certain elements among the foreigners." Dedicating the new settlement building in 1924, Jesuit Father Frederick Siedenburg noted the special duty of social workers "to lead these foreign-born brothers into the path of patriotism and true Americanism." Americanization classes were held at the settlement from the beginning for Hungarians, Poles, Italians, Mexicans and other Catholic immigrants. Nor did the nativist emphasis on Americanization end with the intolerant twenties. In a 1938 newspaper report, settlement director Father Frederick Westendorf repeated the goal of character building, citizenship and conformity, this time for second-generation children: "the sooner the boy accepts the civil and social customs in this new country of his parents adoption, the sooner he will become a sober, responsible citizen." Religious and political aims clearly predominated at the Gary-Alerding Settlement.[20]

Gary's settlements, then, differed markedly from the non-denominational social centers in large American cities well-described in Allen Davis' *Spearheads for Reform*. In contrast to Chicago's Hull House, New York's Henry Street Settlement or Boston's South End House, Gary's Protestant and Catholic settlements consciously promoted immigrant cultural destruction; they sought to erase ethnic backgrounds and make newcomers into Americans. Workers at each steel city settlement often responded in humane and sympathetic fashion to immigrants and their problems; many settlement programs dealt with very practical concerns. But, the emphasis on religious proselytizing made the Gary settlements more urban missions than altruistic immigrant social centers. At the same time, the excessive concern for Americanization tempered sympathies, denied the worth of old country traditions and values, and encouraged, even demanded, conformity and submission to American ways.

By the 1930's, Gary's settlements had become ineffective as agents of immigrant assimilation. By that time, immigration restriction laws of previous years almost entirely cut the flow of new arrivals. During the

12

"HUNGARY ROW" about 1910. Among the earliest houses in Gary, fifty wooden-frame structures of the type shown here were built by the Gary Land Company on the northeast corner of the First Subdivision for immigrant workers. In order to meet the twelve to thirteen dollar per month rent the steel company charged for these houses, poorly paid immigrants with families soon turned these structures into boarding houses serving the overwhelmingly male population. In 1909, one critical observer reported that thirty-eight of these dwellings (containing 152 rooms) housed 428 people, most of them lodgers sleeping in shifts. As the population of the area soared, "Hungary Row" soon became unsanitary, run-down and garbage-strewn. The company promptly evicted immigrant tenants and boarders, replacing them with more prosperous American families who agreed to take no lodgers. In 1916, these structures were torn down and replaced with more substantial residential dwellings for officials of the adjacent American Locomotive Company factories (Source: above, Gary Public Library; below, Taylor, **Satellite Cities**, 191).

early twenties, European immigration had slowed, Mexico providing the largest single group of newcomers during that decade. Even more significant in undermining immigrant activities in the settlements, Black migration from the south had displaced immigrant communities on Gary's south side, now called the "central district" as Poles, Serbs, Greeks, Russians and others moved further south to the Glen Park section of the city, or to emerging ethnic enclaves on Gary's northeast side.

War-time steel mill labor demands stimulated Black migration after 1914, while national prosperity during the twenties sustained high levels of steel production and thus the Black movement as well. By 1930 the Black population of Gary reached about 18,000. Excluded from the better housing on the north side, Blacks moved into the slums, shacks, and tenement apartments on the south side where most immigrants had

13

lived since the city's origin in 1906. Common poverty created integrated neighborhoods. Unlike the city's present segregated residential pattern, for a time European immigrants, Mexicans, and Blacks lived side by side. Yet continued Black migration through the 1920's, although it brought temporary integration to immigrant districts, eventually speeded the dispersal of ethnic whites south to Glen Park and nearby suburbs.[21]

Neighborhood changes resulting from these migration patterns caused consequent alterations in settlement house participation. During the mid-twenties, settlement constituencies became increasingly Black. Gary's fourth settlement—the John Stewart House—although strangely located in a Polish neighborhood, had been founded by Methodists in 1920 exclusively for Blacks. With the exception of Americanization activities, its programs matched those of the other three social centers.[22] As Blacks moved into the south side, and as white immigrant groups moved out, the other settlements opened their programs to Blacks as well. By 1926, for instance, sixty-six per cent of the Campbell House district was Black, and the settlement had hired a Black social worker. When Jessie Vogt of the National Board of the YWCA visited Gary in 1933, Blacks predominated in the activities of each of the three formerly immigrant-oriented settlements.[23]

Despite these changes beginning in the mid-twenties, the settlements tried to retain their hold on the declining numbers of immigrants and immigrant children in their neighborhoods. At first, because of the racist attitudes of early settlement leaders and, as a consequence, developing hostilities of east and south Europeans against Blacks and Mexicans, classes, team sports and other activities were segregated. In the 1930's, according to Jessie Vogt, the Neighborhood House tried to limit the proportion of Blacks in settlement activities, "in order that they might have time for work with the people of the different nationalities."[24] By the late thirties, these efforts had been abandoned, a change typified by the Campbell House decision in 1940 to terminate some older programs (the Sunday school was closed, for instance) and emphasize "a Christian solution to Gary's race problem."[25] Unlike settlements in some cities, Gary's social centers did not follow immigrant constituencies to new neighborhoods; rather, they eventually adjusted to a new clientele and worked for racial cooperation and harmony.

During the years of Gary's early growth—also the years of heaviest immigration—the social settlements became important institutions in ethnic neighborhoods. Their health, educational and recreational programs aided immigrant adjustment. But paternalism undermined many positive activities. Settlement workers tried to foster cleanliness, thrift, industriousness, sobriety and other socially desirable traits. They promoted adherence and submission to established American ideals and values. They did nothing to encourage ethnic pride or preserve immigrant heritages. Unlike settlements elsewhere, ideas of conformity and

14

assimilation rather than those of "cultural pluralism" underlay the social settlement rationale in Gary. Until migration patterns altered the ethnic make-up of south side neighborhoods, the settlements served simultaneously as conscious agents of cultural destruction and Americanization.

ii

If Gary's settlements urged immigrants to become Americans, another institution—the International Institute of Gary—encouraged them to retain their languages and cultures, to be proud of their heritage. The Gary Institute was one of nearly sixty such agencies established by the YWCA in the years after 1910.[26] For two decades after its founding in 1919, the Gary organization worked actively in the immigrant communities, promoted cultural pluralism and defended newcomers against nativist attacks. The Institute became less effective by the 1940s;[27] but during its most active years, it countered the blatant and denigrating Americanization programs of the settlements and fostered immigrant cultural preservation.

The first International Institute—that in New York City—began as a YWCA experiment in 1910 under the direction of settlement worker Edith Terry Bremer. Within five years additional Institutes had sprouted in Trenton, Los Angeles, Pittsburgh and Lawrence, Massachusetts. The Institute movement proliferated at the end of the war, when the YWCA's War Work Council transformed itself into a Department of Immigration and Foreign Communities, with the initial objective of assisting immigrant women and girls in the United States. The National Board of the YWCA urged formation of local Institutes in industrial cities with heavy ethnic populations, and by 1920 fifty-five Institutes had been established.[28]

Over several decades, Edith Terry Bremer became the national spokesman for the International Institutes and for immigrant welfare generally. Her writings established the philosophy and the goals of the Institute movement. Drawing upon Progressive Era thinking, she envisioned every Institute "as a conscious venture in the new democracy." The purpose of the movement was "the cultivation of a new social class —the class of mankind, which finds its alikeness transcending its unalikeness of nationality or race." Rather than demanding assimilation or Americanization, Bremer promoted an early form of cultural pluralism. "We believe," she wrote in an important statement of purpose in 1923, "there is no richer material for cultural growth than that which can be saved for the foreigner out of his own inheritance." Thus, programs had to be devised to preserve the immigrant heritage, transmit the old culture to the second generation in America, and foster good will and understanding between newcomers and native Americans.[29]

15

IMMIGRANT HOUSING in the Shack Colonies of the South Side, circa 1920: Housing for the work force—the great bulk of it from eastern and southern Europe —became a serious problem early in Gary's history. Excluded from the better housing of the more fashionable north side by company policy and high rents, many immigrant families set up housekeeping in the numerous shack colonies which sprouted on the unregulated south side. These typical scenes suggest the tenuousness of America's promise as a land of opportunity (Source: Above: Elizabeth Hughes and Lydia Roberts, **Children of Preschool Age in Gary, Ind.** [U.S. Department of Labor, Children's Bureau, Publication No. 122, 1925], facing pages 20, 21. Facing: Gary Public Library).

The work of the Institutes generally conformed to the objectives articulated by Edith Terry Bremer. Institute workers went beyond the original idea of aiding foreign-born women and girls and began working with immigrant communities as a whole. They engaged in traditional settlement house tasks, handled immigrant problems as case workers and attempted to ease the transition to American society. They aided in

16

the citizenship process, serving as mediators between newcomers and government agencies. And they paid special attention to the "second generation problem"—the family disorganization which prevailed when immigrant children became caught between loyalties to the old culture and the appeal of the new.[30]

Beyond these practical tasks, Institute workers—usually immigrants themselves—saw their most important function as fostering cultural identity and a positive self-image among immigrant newcomers. They built consciousness and pride in the immigrant heritage and encouraged inter-ethnic cooperation and understanding. They urged newcomers to retain their language and their customs while simultaneously learning American ways. At the same time, they encouraged Americans to understand immigrant traditions and recognize ethnic contributions to American life. These were especially significant objectives during the post-World War I years, when nativism, the "Great Red Scare" and the movement for immigration restriction intensified ruthless Americanization demands.[31]

Under the direction of social worker Agnes B. Ewart, Gary's Institute began in 1919 in a south side library basement. Four nationality workers (as the Institute called its immigrant social workers) made up the

17

staff—one each for the Polish, Czechoslovakian, Bulgarian and Italian communities of Gary. Mexican, Serbian and Greek nationality workers were added by the mid-twenties. These workers, who spoke several languages and handled other ethnic groups as well as their own, attempted to serve immigrant needs, preserve ethnic identity and promote mutual understanding and respect among ethnic groups and between natives and newcomers.[32] International Institutes objectives and methods, especially the use of immigrant social workers, were recognized as new and unorthodox. "Existing social workers had never approached the problem from our angle," Gary's Bulgarian nationality worker Luba Tzvetanova wrote in her monthly report for September 1919. "Their basis has been plain charity, very often with utter lack of sympathetic understanding for the party concerned." The Institute worker hoped to be "a friend in every day life first, and then a friend in need." Even so, immigrants at first regarded the Institute with the same suspicion the social settlements had received. As one nationality worker in Gary put it in 1920, "the people can't understand why we should come here to help them, and not expect to get anything out of it."[33] Gradually overcoming suspicions, the Gary International Institute soon made itself an indispensable community agency.

The work of the Institute fell into several general categories: individual and family case work, group activities, cultural programs, educational work, recreational programs and social reform efforts. Throughout the Institute's first twenty years, nationality workers spent the largest part of their time doing case work in the immigrant communities, handling as many as five or six hundred individual cases each month. These cases dealt primarily with legal and technical difficulties in connection with immigration and citizenship. But the whole range of human problems became the domain of Institute workers, as their monthly reports show. During September 1920, for instance, nationality workers visited immigrants in jails and hospitals, served as a clearing house for information about legal needs and social services, acted as employment agents, located relatives in Europe and the United States, wrote and translated letters in many languages, interceded with immigration authorities and other governmental agencies at every level on behalf of newcomers, even secured a divorce for an immigrant woman whose husband loved "good times," which "he carried in a bottle in one of his big coat pockets." Except in a very tangential way, these case work activities did not overlap with those of the church-related settlement houses. They were addressed to real immigrant needs and they displayed none of the paternalism evident in the programs of other social welfare agencies.[34]

While case work took up most of the Institute's attention, group work in Gary's immigrant communities followed closely. The Institute movement built on the belief that preservation of the immigrant heritage

18

was crucially important in the creation of a more democratic American society. Thus, building ethnic consciousness through group activities became one of the organization's most significant tasks. Gary's Institute worked closely with local affiliates of such national organizations as the Polish National Alliance, the Sons of Italy, the Serb National Federation and the Croatian Catholic Union. Nationality workers also went out into the community to help organize a host of local ethnic associations: mutual aid societies, dramatic and musical groups, and political, women's and children's clubs. The Institute threw open its facilities to these groups, serving as a central gathering place for organized ethnic activities on the south side. In 1924, seventy-two different groups held 472 meetings at the Institute, with a total attendance of 14,582.[35] In addition, the Institute provided rooms for immigrant weddings, christenings, parties and holiday celebrations. Moreover, Institute workers attended immigrant churches, participated in numerous activities in the ethnic communities and met regularly with immigrant leaders. Through these group activities, the Institute fostered a sense of ethnic identification and promoted immigrant culture.[36]

To achieve these same objectives, each International Institute emphasized cultural programs based on immigrant traditions. Rejecting prevailing demands for conformity and submission to American ways, the Institutes sought to preserve and enhance the immigrant heritage by sponsoring ethnic concerts, dances, festivals, pageants, plays and exhibits. Such programs were considered important for several reasons: American culture would be broadened and enriched; for the immigrants themselves, participation in these activities built pride in one's heritage; and for the second generation—the American-born children of the immigrants who too often "scornfully cast aside the colorful language and symbolic customs of their forefathers" and "all too rapidly assimilated the movie, jazz and the gutter speech of the modern American city"— these programs could provide a bridge to the past.[37] Along the same lines, the Gary Institute sponsored lectures on the art, literature and history of native countries, as well as foreign-language classes for American-born children of immigrants. Ethnic cultural programs at the Institute eased adjustment to industrial America for newcomers from rural villages while simultaneously helping them resist total orthodoxy and Americanization.[38]

A series of educational programs supplemented Institute cultural programs, case work and group activities. Some of these educational programs were designed to help immigrants adjust to life in the United States. Thus, nationality workers organized English classes, both at the Institute and in immigrant homes, for Italians, Russians, Poles, Greeks, Mexicans, Romanians and others. Conducted throughout the twenties, these classes multiplied during the depression years when immigrant workers lost their jobs in the idled steel mills. While the Institute re-

19

sisted rigorous Americanization, it saw only advantages in teaching immigrants helpful language skills.[39]

Other Institute programs sought to build harmony and understanding in the community by educating immigrant groups about one another. Considering the establishment of mutual respect among nationality groups one of their most important aims, Institute workers brought men, women and children of different backgrounds together for a variety of activities: dances, dinners, concerts and the like. When the Institute formed an Advisory Council in 1930, leaders from various nationalities met regularly to share in Institute decision-making. In the 1930's, the Institute sponsored a series of "Nationality Nights," the avowed purpose being "to break down nationality antagonisms" and to create "a just pride" in ethnic heritages. Institute programs, therefore, not only built immigrant pride and self-respect, but encouraged toleration and inter-ethnic understanding—a formidable task given long traditions of hostility based on old country religion, politics and regional loyalties.[40]

Throughout the intolerant twenties, the Institute also tried to temper nativist bigotry by familiarizing Americans with immigrant traditions and contributions. As executive director Maude Polk wrote in her annual report for 1921, "We often feel that our biggest job is in educating American-born Americans in knowing and appreciating the foreign-born American." Thus, the Institute sponsored regular gatherings of American and immigrant women and invited the public to festivals and exhibits, local newspapers publicized Institute activities, and nationality workers spoke on Institute work at meetings of the PTA and other Gary organizations.[41] During the early thirties the Institute sponsored a series of "Know Your City Tours" in a major effort to temper nativist intolerance and build community solidarity. Seeking to explain immigrants and their customs to others, each tour focused on a single na-

21

tionality; groups covered included Greeks, Lithuanians, Mexicans, Russians, Romanians, Hungarians, Italians, Serbians, Croatians, Czechs, Poles and Assyrians. A typical tour began at the YWCA with a talk by one of the community leaders, went to the ethnic neighborhood by bus, visited immigrant churches, listened to speeches by priests and other spokesmen, and ended at one of the immigrant association halls for songs, folk dances and native food specialties. Aware that most of the "tourists" were native Americans, immigrant leaders often used their speaking opportunities to build a positive image of the newcomers in Gary. On the Greek tour, for example, lawyer George P. Rose described Gary's Greeks in terms nativists could understand: "there are no communists among them. They work long hours. They don't believe in unions." On the other hand, a few tours revealed bitter inter-ethnic divisions, sometimes defeating the Institute's aim of creating sympathetic understanding of immigrant groups. During the Russian tour, a speaker at the Russian Orthodox Church defended the czarist regime as a "democratic monarchy," while radical speakers at the Gary Workers' Center argued the case for soviet communism. Despite these occasional debates and shouting matches between immigrant splinter groups, the Institute considered the "Know Your City Tours" successful and continued to sponsor them periodically.[42]

Beyond these varied educational programs, Gary's International Institute actively promoted a number of urban political and social reforms. Nationality workers combined reform fervor with social welfare goals, for example, by openly fighting widespread political corruption in municipal administration and campaigning for introduction of the city manager plan. They cooperated with other social agencies in public health and recreation efforts, encouraged "Big Sister" work as an antidote to delinquency among second-generation girls and made several significant social surveys, including an extensive study of housing in the growing Black ghetto on Gary's "unlovely south side."[43] During the Great Depression, the Institute became a relief center of sorts as well, providing immigrants with food, clothing, employment and legal assistance. Notably, the Institute interceded with local relief officials, who too often discriminated against the foreign-born.[44]

The Depression caused some observable changes of emphasis in Institute programs. As the economic crisis worsened, nativist hysteria intensified. Using the press and national magazines like the *Saturday Evening Post* as a soapbox, anti-alien spokesmen simultaneously blamed immigrants for the depression, for depriving American workers of jobs and for driving up relief expenses.[45] These national patterns were duplicated in Gary, where unnaturalized immigrants became vulnerable to the new forces of intolerance. Mexican aliens in Gary were particularly targeted as an objectionable group by Gary's new nativists. Denied welfare and deprived of jobs in the steel mills, the Mexican community

22

faced an American Legion sponsored drive for "repatriation"—a forced and involuntary expulsion to the homeland. Gary's native American population, led by the local press, the steel company, municipal government, and welfare officials, all supported repatriation as a method of "constructive relief." International Institute workers fought this new expression of nativist bigotry and racism.[46]

Not surprisingly, most of the Institute's work during the thirties focused on naturalization. By 1936, seventy percent of all Institute cases dealt with such problems. But financial difficulties beset the Institute; in contrast to the 1920's, when as many as seven full-time nationality workers staffed the Institute, the agency had only one full-time and a few part-time workers during most of the thirties. Many Institute activities were curtailed during these years. Group work and cultural programs languished, as citizenship and naturalization problems absorbed almost the total energies of the Institute's limited staff. As executive secretary Esther Tappan noted in 1939, "We have been so overwhelmed with requests for assistance on naturalization that everything else gets pushed in the background." Nevertheless, the Institute served as a clearing house for information on citizenship, publicized new alien legislation, explained the laws to confused immigrants and handled the complicated paperwork connected with the naturalization process.[47] Special efforts were made to protect the harried Mexican community, although with limited success (about half of Gary's Mexicans—some 1,500—were sent back to Mexico).[48] The Depression, therefore, significantly altered International Institute programs, for limited finances undermined what had been one of the agency's most innovating tasks—the promotion of ethnic identity and cultural pluralism.

The renewed nativism of depression years served to consolidate immigrant defenders on the national level, resulting in changes in institutional affiliation for the Gary Institute. Early in 1933 the national board of the YWCA approved dissolution of its Department of Immigration and Foreign Communities (which had supervised the work of International Institutes) and helped sponsor formation of a new independent national organization for work with immigrants—the National Institute of Immigrant Welfare. The reasons for the split seemed logical and compelling. The YWCA had designed its programs, largely group activities, for women; but the International Institutes dealt with families, rather than with foreign-born women exclusively, and by the 1930's group activities had virtually been abandoned in favor of case work. Moreover, the YWCA had a distinctly Protestant rationale, while the clientele of the Institutes was almost entirely non-Protestant. Finally, spokesmen for the Institutes on the national level like Edith Terry Bremer argued that the immigrant cause was too important to be submerged as a partial concern of a women's organization. An independent organization could consolidate pro-immigrant forces, lobby for favorable

23

Congressional legislation, funnel information to local agencies, and perhaps secure foundation support for Institute work.[49]

Bremer and others connected with the new National Institute of Immigrant Welfare urged International Institutes to sever ties with their local YWCA and affiliate with the new organization. By the end of 1933, ten Institutes had done so, including the one in Gary. The arguments which justified creation of the National Institute of Immigrant Welfare swayed Institute people in Gary, particularly Irma Wagner, executive director after 1931. A simultaneous financial dispute with local YWCA officials catalyzed the Gary Institute's drive to independence. Looking upon the Institute as a financial drain, the Gary YWCA quickly approved the plan of separation and the International Institute officially became independent January 1, 1934.[50]

Independence hardly solved all the Institute's difficulties. As an independent organization the Institute had greater visibility, but donations from the immigrant people served by the agency supplied only a small part of the funds formerly obtained from the YWCA. U.S. Steel made its usual contribution each year, but it was considerably smaller ($1,500 in 1936, for instance) than the $5,000 to $10,000 annual donations previously shared by the YWCA and the Institute. The organization of a Community Chest in Gary in 1936 rationalized voluntary giving and assured the Institute of basic funding annually.[51] But the Institute's budget remained small throughout the thirties and, as noted earlier, many important programs had to be abandoned. By 1940, as naturalization work absorbed the attention of nationality workers, well-established ethnic churches had begun to replace the Institute as a cultural, associational and recreational center for Gary's immigrant communities. Passage of the Alien Registration Act by Congress in 1940 kept naturalization work at a heavy level throughout the war years, and continued financial strains prevented the Institute from restoring its group and cultural activities in later years.[52]

iii

Irrespective of its limited role after 1940, the International Institute had served important functions during the twenties and thirties—functions quite different from those of the religious settlement houses. In contrast to other social welfare agencies, which promoted the values of the steel city's native white establishment, the Institute fostered the more traditional cultures of Gary's numerous ethnic groups. Like the settlements, the Institute sponsored activities such as language classes to help immigrants adjust to industrial and urban life; but the agency rejected the second thrust of the settlements' programs—the very obvious denigration of the newcomers' traditions and customs and the simultaneous demands for conformity, submission and speedy assimilation. While

24

other social agencies sought to Americanize the immigrant, the Institute helped him retain his old cultures and traditions, eased his transition from the old world village to the new world metropolis. Unlike the missionary, paternalist, nativist-dominated settlement houses which consciously sought to destroy immigrant cultures, Gary's Institute promoted an emerging doctrine of cultural pluralism.

The sources of the different approaches of the settlements and the International Institute are not difficult to find. The concentration by historians on nationally known settlements such as Hull House has created a distorted picture of the entire movement. The social workers in such settlements had been trained as professionals in the new schools of social work, such as the Chicago School of Civics and Philanthropy or the New York School of Social Work. As Allen Davis points out in his study of the settlement movement, *Spearheads for Reform*, people such as Jane Addams, Lillian Wald, Graham Taylor, Raymond Robins and others were genuinely progressive or even radical in their political and social orientation; and most of these settlement leaders accepted the immigrants on their own terms and practiced some degree of cultural pluralism.[53] But Hull House was not a typical settlement. As suggested earlier, most settlements were religious missions, either attached to a particular church or sponsored by some religious body. In a study of social Catholicism, for instance, historian Aaron Abell noted that the Catholic Church had established some 2,500 settlements by 1915.[54] Those who directed and worked in such mission settlements were either priests, ministers, church employees or pious volunteers; few were trained professionals, and fewer still accepted the radical orientation of such leaders of the settlement movement as Raymond Robins. Thus, settlements such as those in Gary did not become the buffer between the ethnic communities and American society envisioned by the movement's leaders. Rather, they reflected, acted upon, and transmitted the values and attitudes of the larger society; beyond their proselytizing activities, they adopted a derogatory view of ethnic traditions and assumed that their proper role was that of Americanizing the immigrant with all possible speed. Indeed, spokesmen for Gary's native white establishment such as the newspapers routinely expected the settlements to perform this function.[65]

The radically different orientation of the International Institute stemmed from a variety of circumstances. Founder Edith Terry Bremer provided overall leadership for the Institute movement from its beginnings in 1910 through the 1930s. She articulated the ideals of cultural pluralism and, through a stream of memos and policy statements sent out from the national office to each Institute, constantly reiterated the humanistic goals of the movement. On the local level, professionally trained social workers headed the Institutes; the Gary Institute's first director, for example, graduated from the Chicago School of Civics and

25

Philanthropy. More important, perhaps, in maintaining the consistent pro-immigrant policy of the Institute was the practice of staffing the agency with immigrants themselves. Familiar with immigrant languages and traditions and known in the ethnic communities, these professionally educated foreign-born or second-generation social workers approached their tasks in Gary with a knowledge and a sensitivity virtually unobtainable for most settlement house workers. They did not accept the paternalism and nativism which prevailed in the settlements, nor did they consider rigorous Americanization a proper goal. The Gary Institute also had an advisory board composed entirely of leaders from the ethnic communities, which only reinforced the pluralistic character of the agency's work. Further, part of the financial support for the Institute's work had always come from individuals and associations in the immigrant communities. And finally, even though originally sponsored by the YWCA, the Institute had no religious or missionary purpose; rather, serving multiple immigrant needs became the agency's task from the very beginning. The kinds of goals they set for themselves, and the kinds of people hired to achieve those goals, insured that the Institutes would be agencies whose functions differed markedly from the mission settlements.[56]

Thus, social agencies working in Gary's ethnic communities exhibited clearly contradictory purposes and programs. Combined with the conclusions of some other recent studies, these findings suggest possible lines of inquiry for social welfare historians. The settlement movement, for instance, generally pictured as a progressive force for social change, should be carefully reexamined. We know quite a bit about the Hull Houses and the University Settlements. But we need to know considerably more about the less well known but more typical settlement—the church-related and missionary agencies such as those in Gary. Too many historians for too long have accepted uncritically the positive image of social welfare institutions, an image which easily emerges from a narrow or unimaginative study of institutional records. At the same time, we need additional individual studies of the fifty-odd International Institutes. Was the Gary Institute unique in its early advocacy of cultural pluralism? Or, did other Institutes successfully implement on the local level the national policies worked out by Edith Terry Bremer? Like most institutions, social welfare agencies reflected the value orientation of the particular society in which they operated. It seems implicit, therefore, that such institutions and the functions they served can be understood fully only when considered within the larger social and cultural milieu.

Florida Atlantic University
and Florida State University

26

INDUSTRIAL POLLUTION Hides the City of Gary to the South, circa 1950. The quality of urban life in industrial cities like Gary has never even approached the ideal. Despite the best intentions of its planners, Gary developed a large, sprawling slum in its early years. The city's physical form has changed little over the years, although population movements have transformed Gary from an immigrant city to a Black ghetto, as the descendents of original immigrants moved to outlying suburbs. But despite these changes, the puffing smokestacks of the steel mills—of which Gary's early boosters were so proud—remain a constant feature of the environment and cast a threatening pall over a decaying city (Source: Gary Public Library).

footnotes

1. Ralph E. Pumphrey, "Compassion and Protection: Dual Motivations in Social Welfare," *Social Service Review*, XXXIII (March 1959), 22; Clifford S. Griffin, "Religious Benevolence as Social Control, 1815-1860," *Mississippi Valley Historical Review*, XLIV (December 1957), 423-444; Raymond A. Mohl, "Poverty, Pauperism, and Social Order in the Preindustrial American City, 1780-1840," *Social Science Quarterly*, LII (March 1972), 934-948; David J. Rothman, *The Discovery of the Asylum: Social Order and Disorder in the New Republic* (Boston, 1971); Frances Fox Piven and Richard A. Cloward, *Regulating the Poor: The Functions of Public Welfare* (New York, 1971).

2. On settlements, see Allen F. Davis, *Spearheads for Reform: The Social Settlements and the Progressive Movement, 1890-1914* (New York, 1967); George Cary White, "Social Settlements and Immigrant Neighbors, 1886-1914," *Social Service Review*, XXXIII (March 1959), 55-66; Alvin Kogut, "The Settlements and Ethnicity: 1890-1914," *Social Work*, XVII (May 1972), 22-31.

3. This analysis of the International Institute draws upon preliminary findings published in Raymond A. Mohl and Neil Betten, "Ethnic Adjustment in the Industrial City: The International Institute of Gary, 1919-1940," *International Migration Review*, VI (Winter 1972), 361-376.

4. Population statistics are drawn from U.S. Bureau of the Census, *Fifteenth Census of the United States: 1930. Population*, III, Part 1 (Washington, D.C., 1932), 715. For the early planning of Gary and an analysis of its failures, see Raymond A. Mohl and Neil Betten, "The Failure of Industrial City Planning: Gary, Indiana, 1906-1910," *Journal of the American Institute of Planners*, XXXVIII (July 1972), 203-215.

5. Henry David Jones, *Twenty Years of Neighborliness* (Gary, n.d., ca. 1933), unpaginated; Bess Sheehan, *History of Campbell Friendship House; Gary, Indiana, 1912-1940* (Gary,

27

1943), 1, 5-6; Neighborhood House, *Eleventh Annual Report of the Superintendent, April 1, 1920* (Gary, 1920), unpaginated; Gary *Post-Tribune*, March 20, 1940.

6. Jones, *Twenty Years of Neighborliness*; Sheehan, *History of Campbell House*, 1-2.

7. Clifford T. Stewart, *Historical Sketches: Gary Neighborhood House* (Gary, 1945), 3, 8-9, 15, 20; Gary *Daily Tribune*, September 5, 1914; *Neighborhood House Visitor*, ·I (March 20, 1916); Gary *Evening Post*, April 2, 1919; Neighborhood House *Annual Report, 1924-25* (Gary, 1925), unpaginated; Neighborhood House, Annual Report, 1938-39, mimeo in Settlement File, Indiana Room, Gary Public Library (hereafter cited as GPL); Jones, *Twenty Years of Neighborliness*.

8. "Activities of Friendship House, 1925-1926," publicity card, n.d., GPL; Gary *Post-Tribune*, May 29, 1942.

9. Stewart, *Historical Sketches*, 3-5, 10, 19; *Neighborhood House Visitor*, I (May 20, 1916); Gary *Evening Post*, April 2, 1919; Neighborhood House, *Eleventh Annual Report*, unpaginated; Gary *Post-Tribune*, February 1, 1935. On the need for such services as public baths and drinking water, see Governor's Commission on Unemployment Relief, *Recovery in Indiana*, August 1936, 7, which reported on a WPA survey showing that at least twenty-five percent of Gary's homes had no baths, toilet facilities or running water.

10. Sheehan, *History of Campbell House*, 4-5, 15, 17; *Annual Report of Activities at Friendship House, Gary, Ind., August 1, 1922* (Gary, 1922), unpaginated; *Annual Report of Campbell Settlement, 1922-1923* (Gary, 1923), unpaginated; Campbell House, *Annual Report, October 1931* (Gary, 1931), unpaginated; Gary *Post-Tribune*, February 1, 1935; Gary *Post-Tribune*, February 1, 1938.

11. Neighborhood House, *Eleventh Annual Report*. See also *Neighborhood House Visitor*, I (December 8, 1916).

12. Sheehan, *History of Campbell House*, 1.

13. Neighborhood House, *Eleventh Annual Report*.

14. Stewart, *Historical Sketches*, 19-20; Gary *Post-Tribune*, March 5, 1941; Jones, *Twenty Years of Neighborliness*.

15. Campbell House, *Annual Report . . . 1922*; Neighborhood House, *Eleventh Annual Report*. Interestingly, as late as 1946, when the Neighborhood House constituency had become entirely Black, groups of Lithuanians and Ukrainians still drove from various suburbs to the meeting place they had used for thirty-five years. Neighborhood House, Annual Report, April 1946, mimeo in GPL.

16. Jones, *Twenty Years of Neighborliness*.

17. Gary *Post-Tribune*, February 1, 1935; Gary *Post-Tribune*, undated clipping, Settlement File, Indiana Room, GPL.

18. Gary-Alerding House, *The Good Samaritan*, II (April 1924), unpaginated; Gary *Post-Tribune*, March 30, April 12, 1940.

19. Jessie M. Vogt, "Memorandum Regarding Social Settlements and Other Agencies in Gary, Indiana," July 6, 1933, typescript in Gary International Institute Papers (hereafter referred to as I.I. Papers); Gary *Post-Tribune*, March 30, 1940; *The Good Samaritan*, II (April 1924).

20. *The Good Samaritan*, II (April 1924); Gary *Post-Tribune*, April 27, 1938.

21. On these trends, see Neil Betten and Raymond A. Mohl, "The Evolution of Racism in an Industrial City: A Case Study of Gary, Indiana," *Journal of Negro History*, LIX (January, 1974), 51-64.

22. See, for example, *The Eighth Annual Report of the Activities and Anniversary Program of the John Stewart Memorial Settlement House* (Gary, 1928); Gary *Post-Tribune*, February 14, 1936.

23. Sheehan, *History of Campbell House*, 12-13; Vogt, "Memorandum Regarding Social Settlements."

24. Stewart, *Historical Sketches*, 20; *Neighborhood House Visitor*, I (March 20, 1916); Gary *Post-Tribune*, March 20, 1940; Vogt, "Memorandum Regarding Social Settlements."

25. Gary *Post-Tribune*, April 1, 1940.

26. On the International Institute movement, see Mary S. Sims, *The First Twenty-Five Years: Being a Summary of the Work of the Young Women's Christian Associations of the United States of America, 1906-1931* (New York, 1932), 17, 33; Mary S. Sims, *The Natural History of a Social Institution—the Young Women's Christian Association* (New York, 1936), 60, 64, 213; Grace H. Wilson, *The Religious and Educational Philosophy of the Young Women's Christian Association* (New York, 1933), 30; Edith T. Bremer, "Development of Private Social Work with the Foreign-Born," American Academy of Political and Social Science, *Annals*, 262 (March 1949), 141-142.

27. As will be noted later, financial difficulties stemming from the depression, the outbreak of war in Europe, Congressional legislation on aliens and changes within Gary's ethnic communities caused a reduction of Institute functions and activities.

28. YWCA, *After War Program of the Department on Work for Foreign-Born Women and Americanization Work of the War Work Council of the National Board of the YWCA* (New

28

York, 1918); YWCA, *An International Institute for Young Women through which the YWCA Helps New Americans* (New York, 1918); YWCA, *Foreign-Born Women and Girls* (New York, 1920), 10. International Institutes were established in Buffalo, Boston, Bridgeport, New Haven, Detroit, Philadelphia, Milwaukee, St. Louis, McKeesport, St. Paul, Duluth, Akron, Toledo, San Francisco and San Antonio, among other cities.

29. Edith T. Bremer, *The International Institutes in Foreign Community Work: Their Program and Philosophy* (New York, n.d., ca. 1923), 7, 10, 12. See also Edith T. Bremer, "Foreign Community and Immigration Work of the National Young Women's Christian Association," *Immigrants in America Review*, I (January 1916), 73-82; Edith T. Bremer, "The Foreign Language Worker in the Fusion Process: An Indispensable Asset to Social Work in America," National Conference on Social Work, *Proceedings* (1919), 740-746.

30. Bremer, *International Institutes in Foreign Community Work*, 4-6. See also Edith T. Bremer, *The Field of the International Institute and its Place in Social Work* (reprint of paper given at Seventh Annual Conference of International Institutes, 1925; New York, 1926); Esther Tappan, "Case Work with the Foreign Born," *Public Welfare in Indiana*, LV (August 1945), 10-12.

31. Bremer, *International Institutes in Foreign Community Work*, 5-7, 10; Allen H. Eaton, *Immigrant Gifts to American Life* (New York, 1932), 92-94.

32. "Notes on the Early History of the International Institute of Gary, 1919-1937," typescript, I.I. Papers; Annual Report, 1921, *ibid.*; *Indianapolis Star*, November 30, 1919, clipping, International Institute File, GPL.

33. Monthly Report, September 1919, I.I. Papers; Chicago YWCA, *Central Field Notes*, I (April 1920), 1.

34. Staff Minutes, October 24, 1921, I.I. Papers; Monthly Reports, September 1920, March 1921, *ibid.*

35. Institute-based ethnic organizations included the Czechoslovak Liberty Club, the Polish Mechanics Society, the Free Poland Society, the Hungarian Benevolent Society, the Bulgarian Society, the Russian-Slavonic Mutual Aid Society, the Lithuanian Political Club, the League of Italian Families, the Serbian Society, the Albanian Society, the Mexican Sociedad Protectora, the Hidalgo Society, the Serbian Dramatic Club, the Russian Independent Musical and Dramatic Club, the Mexican Knitting Club, the Polish Women's Club, the Mexican Women's Club, the Assyrian Women's Society, the Polish Children's Club and the Sokol Gymnastic Union. The Monthly Reports of the International Institute nationality workers are full of references to work among the various ethnic groups of Gary. See also "Notes on Early History," I.I. Papers.

36. Typifying Institute community activities beyond actual casework, nationality workers during a two-month period in 1919 attended the dedication of a Greek church and a Russian cemetery; made contacts with Russian, Serbian and Croatian priests, attended services at a Serbian church and Temple Israel and visited classes at several schools; went to a Croatian glee club rehearsal, a Russian dance, a Russian concert, an Italian Columbus Day celebration and five Greek, Mexican and Bulgarian coffee houses; and accepted invitations to parties given by Russians and Bulgarians. See Monthly Reports, September 1919, October 1919, I.I. Papers.

37. "A Year's Plan for Community Programs," undated mimeo from National Board of YWCA, I.I. Papers.

38. "Notes on Early History," I.I. Papers; Monthly Reports, November 1920, April 1925, September 1931, *ibid.*; Annual Report, 1931, *ibid.*; Gary *Evening Post*, November 13, 1920.

39. Monthly Reports, September 1919, March 1921, October 1921, May 1923, February 1924, I.I. Papers; Annual Report, 1922, *ibid.*; "Notes on Early History," *ibid.*; Gary *Post-Tribune*, April 9, September 27, 1923.

40. Monthly Reports, February 1921, October 1921, November 1924, December 1926, I.I. Papers; Committee of Management Minutes, February 13, 1931, *ibid.*; Annual Report, 1939, *ibid.*

41. Annual Report, 1921, I.I. Papers; "Report to Department of Immigration and Foreign Communities of the National Board of the YWCA," 1931, *ibid.*; Gary *Daily Tribune*, April 12, 1921, clipping, International Institute File, GPL.

42. Undated clippings, Clipping File, I.I. Papers; Annual Report, 1930, International Institute File, GPL.

43. Monthly Reports, July-September 1920, February 1921, April 1923, January 1925, January 1926, February 1929, October 1929, I.I. Papers; Annual Report, 1929, *ibid.*; Maude Cooley to Minnie M. Newman, August 18, 1920, Correspondence Files, *ibid.*; "Good Daily Health Practices," n.d., poster in *ibid.*; "Study of the Foreign-Born in Gary," 1929, *ibid.*

44. Monthly Reports, November 1930, February 1931, May 1931, October 1932, November 1932, April 1933, December 1933, I.I. Papers; Annual Report, 1931, *ibid.*; Gary *International Institute News*, October 1931, mimeo newsletter, *ibid.*

45. See, for example, Isaac F. Marcosson, "The Alien in America," *The Saturday Evening Post* (April 6, 1935), 22-23, 110, 112-113; Raymond G. Carroll, "The Alien on Relief," *ibid.*

29

(January 11, 1936), 16-17, 100-101; Raymond G. Carroll, "Alien Workers in America," *ibid.* (January 25, 1936), 23, 82, 84-86, 89.

46. On the Mexican repatriation movement in Gary, see Neil Betten and Raymond A. Mohl, "From Discrimination to Repatriation: Mexican Life in Gary, Indiana, During the Great Depression," *Pacific Historical Review*, XLII (August 1973), 370-388.

47. Monthly Reports, October 1931, December 1932, December 1933, February 1934, March 1934, March 1936, June 1936, I.I. Papers; Annual Report, 1936, International Institute File, GPL; Gary *Post-Tribune*, March 17, 1934; International Institute Radio Scripts, 1936, I.I. Papers; Esther Tappan to Marie S. Wilkins, November 17, 1939, Correspondence Files, *ibid.*

48. Walter J. Riley, *The Story of Unemployment Relief in Lake County, Indiana* (n.p., 1932), 2, 9-11; Monthly Reports, December 1930, May 1931, September 1931, May 1932, September 1932, January 1933, May 1933, I.I. Papers; Committee of Management Minutes, April 15, 1932, *ibid.*; Gary *Post-Tribune*, January 14, February 27, March 16, April 20, May 11, 16, 1932.

49. Theresa M. Paist (President of National Board of YWCA) to International Institutes, April 23, 1933, mimeo, Correspondence Files, I.I. Papers; Edith T. Bremer to International Institutes, May 8, 1933, *ibid.*; "Emergence of International Institute from the YWCA," undated memo, *ibid.*; *The Continuing Responsibility of the Young Women's Christian Association for Work with Women and Girls of Foreign Background* (New York, 1934), 3, 6.

50. Edith T. Bremer to Irma Wagner, undated (ca. 1933), Correspondence Files, I.I. Papers; Irma Wagner to Edith T. Bremer, July 19, 1933, August 16, 1933, January 15, 1934, *ibid.*; Irma Wagner to Ethel Bird, December 12, 1933, *ibid.*; Committee of Management Minutes, May 4, 1932, March 10, 1933, April 14, 1933, *ibid.*; Gary *Post-Tribune*, January 17, 1934, Clipping File, *ibid.*

51. Board of Directors Minutes, February 19, March 25, April 23, June 25, 1935, January 21, 1936, I.I. Papers.

52. Esther Tappan to Marie S. Watkins, November 17, 1939, Correspondence Files, I.I. Papers; Esther Tappan to Katharine H. Johnson, July 3, 1942, *ibid.*; Annual Report, 1940, I.I. File, GPL; *International Community News*, No. 1 (January 1941), mimeo newsletter, *ibid.*; Gary Council of Social Agencies, "Committee Report on International Institute of Gary," 1945, *ibid.*

53. Davis, *Spearheads for Reform*. See also John Higham, *Strangers in the Land: Patterns of American Nativism, 1860-1925* (New Brunswick, N.J., 1955), 119-121, 236. On the professionalization of social work, see Roy Lubove, *The Professional Altruist: The Emergence of Social Work as a Career, 1880-1930* (Cambridge, Mass., 1965).

54. Aaron I. Abell, *American Catholicism and Social Action: A Search for Social Justice, 1865-1950* (Garden City, N.Y., 1960), 163.

55. For a sampling of this opinion, see Gary *Daily Tribune*, February 14, May 9, 1910, October 31, November 1, 1911, October 5, 1915, July 20, November 24, 1916.

56. A study of records of the International Institute in Boston made by one of the present authors revealed an agency with similar programs, a staff made up of immigrants and trained professionals, and an identical set of goals.

30

COMPASSION AND PROTECTION: DUAL MOTIVATIONS IN SOCIAL WELFARE[1]

THE range of "causes," activities, and institutions which make up the overlapping fields of philanthropy and social welfare is so vast, and the different parts are so isolated from each other, that it is difficult to comprehend the whole. This is equally true for the historian and the professional practitioner, such as the educator or social worker. There is a lack of recognition of common elements that can be analyzed, whatever the form of organization or the object of the activity, regardless of the time or place at which they occur.

Historians have not attempted to relate such diverse items as the movement for universal education and the Social Security Act of 1935, the founding of the Pennsylvania Hospital and the research in the field of child labor once conducted by the Russell Sage Foundation. In this, they are merely reflecting the lack of unity between operating fields, but the result has been that existing histories, mostly institutional, usually fall short of their potentialities in relating their immediate subjects to the whole of American life.

Finding common elements in organizations and activities which, on the surface, have little relation to each other would not only forward historical research but would contribute to the philosophic understanding and perspectives of the professions and institutions that are responsible for current operations.

MOTIVATIONS FOR PHILANTHROPIC EFFORT

One thread running through much of our philanthropy is the effort of benefactors to make life in the immediate present better for the beneficiaries than would otherwise be the case. This is frequently accomplished through institutions which put those motives into slogans such as the Boy Scout injunction to "Do a Good Turn Daily" and the CARE appeal that "Hunger Hurts!" But these institutions are essentially extensions of such spontaneous individual acts as rescuing a child from a well, dropping a coin in a beggar's cup, or helping some young person through college. Examples of such individual efforts are found in very early colonial records. Winthrop noted in his journal during a smallpox epidemic among the Indians:

> Mr. Maverick of Winesmeet is worthy of a perpetual remembrance. Himself, his wife, and servants, went daily to them, ministered to their necessities, and buried their dead, and took home many of their children. So did other of the neighbors.[2]

This aspect of philanthropy may be designated as *compassion:* the effort to alleviate present suffering, deprivation, or other undesirable conditions to which a segment of the population, but not the benefactor, is exposed. It characteristically results in direct physical services to meet an obvious present need without necessarily relating the services to the

[1] Paper presented at a meeting of the Mississippi Valley Historical Association, Minneapolis, April 25, 1958.

[2] *Winthrop's Journal*, ed. James Kendall Hosmer (New York: Charles Scribner's Sons, 1908), I, 115 (December 5, 1633).

21

extent of the need or to ways of preventing it.

Another thread found in the pattern of philanthropy is typified in current life by such commonplaces as school crossing guards, chlorinated water, and the Scout motto: "Be Prepared!" This, too, can be found in the earliest colonial records, as when, during the "starving time" in Jamestown, John Smith found it necessary to tell his disorderly band:

I will take a course you shall provide what is to be had. The sick shall not starve, but equally share of all our labours; and he that gathereth not every day as much as I doe, the next day shall be set beyond the river, and be banished from the Fort as a drone, till he amend his conditions or starve.[3]

This is *protection,* in which the promoters, not only on their own behalf, but on behalf of their group or of the whole community, endeavor to prevent unwanted developments. It may result either from fear of change or from fear of what may happen if existing conditions are not changed. Characteristically it involves reasoning, and it results in institutionalized action designed to forestall the need for compassion.

Compassion and protection represent two more or less consciously determined purposes that may be served by any given philanthropic enterprise. They become crystallized in institutional patterns, and hence are precursors of social policy. They are usually found in combination, rather than in pure form. John Smith, for instance, probably felt compassion for the sick who could not care for themselves. But his greatest concern appears to have been for the survival of the entire company; and he may well,

too, have wished to insure himself not only against starvation but against bodily harm from his followers and against the wrath of the promoters in London who would hold him accountable for failure.

Some problems in using compassion and protection to analyze the inception, development, and impact of philanthropic enterprises may be mentioned. One may well be confused by the wide differences in the objects of concern of the benefactors. Disaster relief calls forth a compassionate outpouring on behalf of utter strangers. At the other extreme is the self-protective benevolence of real estate promoters who give land for schools, churches, and parks to increase the attractiveness of their developments. Consider, too, the mixture of motives of persons who give buildings to colleges and have them adorned with their own names.[4]

Time and place also occasion confusion. In the mid-nineteenth century, most associations for improving the condition of the poor had as a major objective the financial protection of givers and society at large through better coordination of the activities of the many small relief agencies of that day. Yet, over the years, these associations tended to minimize their protective function while maximizing the compassionate activity of almsgiving.[5] Also, Charles

[3] John Smith, *The Generall Historie of Virginia, New England and the Summer Isles* (London: Printed by I. D. and I. H. for Michael Sparkes, 1624), p. 87.

[4] An extreme example of this is Ogden Hall, Miami University, Oxford, Ohio, where each entrance bears a brass tablet reading: "Laura Louise Ogden Whaling, donor of Ogden Hall, named this apartment thereof ...., in honor of ...." One entrance is modestly named "Whaling, in honor of herself."

[5] See annual reports of the New York Association for the Improvement of the Condition of the Poor, 1845–1900, esp. first (1845), pp. 14, 15; ninth (1852), p. 43; and fifty-sixth (1899), pp. 90–105. See also annual reports of the Baltimore Associ-

Loring Brace and the promoters of the New York Children's Aid Society were apparently largely influenced by an urge to protect society against the "dangerous classes."[6] However, in placing the children snatched from the streets of New York in homes throughout the middle west, the agency relied upon the very different motivations of compassion and cupidity on the part of the receiving families.[7]

The sponsoring group itself may be an artificial assemblage representing a variety of individual and group motivations converging on a single objective. The published appeals of a community chest, directed to groups of givers, may be quite distasteful to those dealing directly with recipients of service. An intensive historical analysis of the different groups which have been involved in chests—big and small givers, boards and staffs of beneficiary agencies, public officials, the combined giving and beneficiary group represented by labor unions—might well reveal that the variety of their motivations has been a major source of internal conflicts in the movement for unified fund-raising.

Disparity between what people do

and what they say is a familiar phenomenon to behavioral scientists. Often it is an indication of deep-seated emotional involvements. Even in those expressions of motivation which find their way into institutional pronouncements and behavior, usually on a quite conscious level, people may talk compassion and act out self-protection, or vice versa. A desirable campsite was made available rent free to a struggling youth organization in a northern city. The public saw youngsters who otherwise would have been on the city streets given a chance for a camp experience. But suppose the donor had required the agency, which had a substantial number of Negro members, to refuse to permit any Negro to set foot on the camp grounds. Would this raise the question whether the donor was using a gift with compassionate elements to erect a dike against an unwanted social change, while the agency, in its compassionate desire to provide camping opportunities to some of its members, was allowing economic pressure to force it into a partial negation of some of its objectives?[8]

One further problem is the danger of false identification of differences in motivational concepts with such familiar dichotomies as conservative and liberal, public and private, treatment and prevention, or services to individuals as against services to the community at large. Motivational concepts are entities in themselves, and examples of both compassion and protection can be found aligned with both elements of all these dichotomies. The basic distinction is that in compassion the benefactor identifies with and seeks to alleviate the present pain which another person feels; in pro-

---

ation for the Improvement of the Condition of the Poor, 1851–1900.

[6] This term, which was later made famous by the title of Brace's best-known book, *The Dangerous Classes of New York,* was emphasized from the start. See *First Annual Report of the Children's Aid Society* (New York, 1854), p. 12. The idea had been expressed in the "First Circular of the Children's Aid Society" (1853): "These boys and girls . . . will help to form the great multitude of robbers, thieves, and vagrants who are now such a burden upon the law-respecting community." Quoted in Emma Brace, *The Life of Charles Loring Brace Chiefly Told in His Own Letters* (New York: Charles Scribner's, 1894), Appendix A, p. 490.

[7] Hastings Hart, "Placing Out Children in the West," *Proceedings of the National Conference of Charities and Correction, 1884,* pp. 143–50.

[8] Such a situation has come within the professional cognizance of the author.

tection he guards against painful consequences to himself, his group, or his community in the future.

THE COMPASSION OF DOROTHEA DIX

How may these ideas be applied? The story of Dorothea Dix and her campaign for the humane treatment of the insane is a familiar one.[9] Her memorials to one state legislature after another were masterpieces in the art of assembling incontrovertible facts calculated to shock and shame lawmakers into taking the action demanded. Ultimately, in 1854, her clamorous appeals led Congress to authorize the distribution of public lands to the states for the care of the insane. This measure was vetoed by President Pierce on the grounds that if Congress could provide for the indigent insane it could provide for all indigent, and thus the federal government would "enter into a novel and vast field of legislation, namely, that of providing for the care and support of all those, among the people of the United States, who, by any form of calamity, become fit objects of public philanthropy."[10]

The Pierce veto may be regarded as a significant turning point in American constitutional history. For eighty years, until the passage of the Social Security Act, the country was bound by its identification of the care of the indigent as compassionate activity and therefore a matter of individual and local, rather than federal, concern. One might speculate on the "ifs" of social welfare and the effect on national life had the Dix bill been enacted, but it is not speculation that Miss Dix's essentially compassionate motivation and her appeal to the compassion of others fixed the form for the provision of care to the insane throughout most of the country down to the present. Miss Dix saw suffering human beings inhumanly confined in jails, barns, and sties. When asked if she had investigated the causes of insanity, she said: "I have not. . . . Shall man be more just than God? . . . Have pity on those who . . . 'unto themselves are more grievous than the darkness.' "[11] She promoted institutional care on a state-wide basis as the means of providing clean, warm, safe surroundings, whether or not the patients were treatable.

It would have been entirely possible for her to direct her energies to the furtherance of efforts to find and extend the use of improved methods of treatment in order to reduce future suffering, but she responded to the compassionate urge to see that the immediate conditions of the victims were more comfortable, and she impressed this pattern on the country. Protection through research and treatment received secondary attention. It was two generations later before another crusader,[12] with a compassionate focus on treatment, began to alter the pattern, but it persisted.

[9] Albert Deutsch, *The Mentally Ill in America* (2d ed.; New York: Columbia University Press, 1949), chap. ix; Helen E. Marshall, *Dorothea Dix, Forgotten Samaritan* (Chapel Hill: University of North Carolina Press, 1937), esp. pp. 87–91; Francis Tiffany, *Life of Dorothea Lynde Dix* (Boston: Houghton Mifflin Co., 1891).

[10] James B. Richardson, *A Compilation of the Messages of the Presidents, 1789–1897* (Published by Authority of Congress, 1901), V, 249.

[11] *Memorial to the Legislature of Massachusetts, 1843* (Old South Leaflets, Vol. VI, No. 148), p. 17.

[12] Clifford Whittingham Beers, *A Mind that Found Itself* (New York: Longmans, Green & Co., 1908), pp. 295–96; Albert Deutsch, "The History of Mental Hygiene," in *One Hundred Years of American Psychiatry* (New York: Published for the American Psychiatric Association by Columbia University Press, 1944), pp. 356–59; Deutsch, *The Mentally Ill in America*, chap. xv.

In recent years those concerned with mental hygiene have emphasized protection. In contrast to the pattern which Miss Dix bequeathed to us, the amount of purely custodial care is being minimized, while increasing effort is being put into research into the causes and cures of mental illness and into education and auxiliary services designed to prevent the expansion of the problem. In 1945 a federal official stated:

Neuropsychiatric disorders constitute one of our most serious health problems, and call for prompt and energetic action if we are to avoid an even more serious situation than that in which we find ourselves. . . . It is necessary to find the cause, provide treatment for those who are ill, reduce the incidence of new cases, and show the public how they can help in combatting the disease.[13]

After such testimony Congress enacted the National Mental Health Act and launched the government on its present vigorous protective mental hygiene program.

Many other institutions and movements started out as purely or largely compassionate responses to immediate need. There were the movements for the institutional care of other groups of the handicapped. For example, Samuel Gridley Howe's education of the blind, deaf Laura Bridgman stands out as one of the great examples of individual compassionate action within an institutional setting.[14] Orphanages throughout the land were expressions of compassion, as

such a name as "New England Home for Little Wanderers"[15] still testifies. Sarah Josepha Hale, working through the Boston Seaman's Aid Society, was far ahead of her time in the quality of the compassion which she bestowed on the women whom she employed at living wages instead of giving them alms.[16] The travelers'-aid and the visiting-nurse movements, as well as disaster relief,[17] are other examples.

It seems probable that historical examination would show that, when they have endured, institutions originating in compassion have changed their programs usually to reflect a protective urge to forestall the need for the sort of service which they had been providing.

JOHN GRISCOM EXEMPLIFIES PROTECTION

The motivation of a person like John Griscom, on the other hand, was primarily protection. An older contemporary of Dorothea Dix, he is known as "the father of all chemistry teachers."[18]

---

[13] Letter from Watson Miller, acting administrator, Federal Security Agency, September, 1945, in *Hearings before a Subcommittee of the Committee on Interstate and Foreign Commerce, on H.R. 2550, National Neuropsychiatric Institute Act, September 18, 19, and 21, 1945* (House [79th Cong., 1st sess.], Washington, D.C.: Government Printing Office, 1945), p. 5. The National Mental Health Act (outgrowth of these hearings) was enacted in 1946.

[14] Harold Schwartz, *Samuel Gridley Howe, Social Reformer, 1801–1876* (Cambridge: Harvard University Press, 1956), chaps. v, vi, x.

[13] A prominent Boston agency. For the development of orphanages, see Henry W. Thurston, *The Dependent Child* (New York: Published for the New York School of Social Work by Columbia University Press, 1930), chap. v, esp. pp. 45, 53, 61.

[16] Mrs. Hale, president of the Seaman's Aid Society, Boston, 1833–37, wrote the annual reports of the agency during that period. This phase of her career is dealt with briefly in Isabelle Webb Entrikin, *Sarah Josepha Hale and Godey's Lady's Book* (Philadelphia, 1946), pp. 39, 40, 54, 56, 106.

[17] Bertha McCall, "History of the National Travelers Aid Association, 1911–1918" (mimeographed; New York: National Travelers Aid Association, 1950), pp. 206; Lillian D. Wald, *The House on Henry Street* (New York: Henry Holt & Co., 1915), esp. pp. 7 ff. and 40 ff.; J. Bryon Deacon, *Disasters* (New York: Russell Sage Foundation, 1918), pp. 60–67, 83–89, 137, 151.

[18] Edgar F. Smith, *John Griscom, Chemist* (Philadelphia: University of Pennsylvania Press, 1925), p. 14, cited in Araminta W. Anthony, "John Griscom, His Life Experiences, Philosophy, and Contribution to Social Work" (unpublished Master's

He devoted considerable time to teaching science to people not ordinarily reached by such education. As a redoubtable advocate of free, universal public education, he made notable contributions to the philosophy and techniques of education; as a philanthropist, he was the founder of the New York Society for the Prevention of Pauperism, a short-lived organization which cast a long shadow. When he moved to New York, Griscom, appalled to find poverty and ignorance on a scale such as he had never experienced, saw the two—poverty and ignorance—as interrelated threats to the well-being of the whole social structure. While he expressed his compassion in many ways, including his science lectures, his concern for the individual was, in large part, subordinated to his protective concern for society.

In his *Discourse on the Importance of Character and Education in the United States,* he asked:

Where learning is only a thing of patrician acquirement . . . is it surprising that these [chosen few] should be crushed by the tumultuous passions which impel the vulgar breast?

. . . .

Not only does the safety of our form of government depend upon . . . universality of instruction, but the wisdom of its measures and the whole concatination of its policy. . . . If then Americans are wise, will they not cherish with peculiar affection, and with surpassing liberality, their seminaries of learning, and every institution which renders useful knowledge accessible to all.[19]

In the same protective vein, in his "Report on the Subject of Pauperism," prepared in 1818, he said:

We were fully prepared to believe, that without a radical change in the principles upon which public alms have been usually distributed, helplessness and poverty would continue to multiply—demands for relief would become more and more importunate, the numerical difference between those who are able to bestow charity and those who sue for it, would gradually diminish, until the present system must fall under its own irresistible pressure, prostrating, perhaps, in its ruin, some of the pillars of the social order.[20]

Having this sort of background, Griscom saw as principles for systematic charity:

First, amply to relieve the unavoidable necessities of the poor; and *Secondly,* to lay the powerful hand of moral and legal restriction upon every thing that contributes . . . to introduce an artificial extent of suffering; and to diminish . . . a reliance upon . . . powers of body and mind for an independent and virtuous support.[21]

Thus, Griscom saw the importance of relieving the immediate needs of the poor, but, unlike Miss Dix who made care an end in itself, he saw this as only one aspect of a total program of protection, on behalf of which he appealed to the fear of what might otherwise happen to society. Here Griscom utilized his own scientific background to attempt an approach to the problems of poverty. Throughout the rest of the century, in England and America, we see these same ideas recurring—in Thomas Chalmers, the Scottish divine whose writings so greatly influenced the charity organization movement; in Robert Hartley and the New York Association for the Improvement of the Condition of the Poor; in Charles Loch and the London Charity

project, New York School of Social Work, Columbia University, February, 1958), p. 8. See also John H. Griscom, *Memoir of John Griscom, L.L.D.* (New York: Robert Carter & Bros., 1859).

[19] John Griscom, *Discourse on the Importance of Character and Education in the United States* (New York: Mahlon Day, 1823), pp. 11, 13.

[20] "Report on the Subject of Pauperism, on Behalf of the Committee, John Griscom, Chairman," in *First Annual Report of the New York Society for the Prevention of Pauperism* (New York, 1819), p. 12.

[21] *Ibid.,* p. 13.

Organisation Society; and in such American charity organization leaders as Josephine Shaw Lowell and Mary Richmond. In its essence, Griscom's concept of the twofold protection of society through adequate relief and through environmental controls is deeply embedded in most modern American social welfare legislation and organization.

However, every generation has had difficulty maintaining this protective approach. Griscom himself, after a trip to Europe during which he imparted to Dr. Chalmers his ideas about the necessity to protect society against pauperism,[22] became eager to do something for the poor waifs who were getting into trouble on the streets of New York. The Society for the Prevention of Pauperism took up his ideas, and the energies of that organization were soon drained off into the establishment and operation of a new institution, the House of Refuge, the first home for delinquents in this country. From the start, and throughout the hundred years of its history, this agency, which had its nurture in protection, functioned primarily according to the concept of compassion.[23]

The historian who examines institutions from this point of view may well find even more clear-cut illustrations of institutions in which protection was the primary motivation. Such a possibility seems to be particularly good with re-

spect to the social hygiene, tuberculosis, and Americanization movements; such specialized police activities as the Police Athletic League and juvenile aid bureaus; and such ideological efforts as the American Heritage Foundation appeals on behalf of Radio Free Europe.

A BLENDING OF MOTIVATIONS

The founding of the Pennsylvania Hospital in 1750 shows the combination of compassion and protection from the start. There was no American precedent for Franklin and his friends when, moving beyond a merely ameliorative infirmary in which the ill might be cared for, they envisioned an institution that would supplement the "many compassionate and charitable provisions for the relief of the poor" and would make it possible for the ill, "by the judicious assistance of physick and surgery . . . to taste the blessings of health, and be made in a few weeks useful members of the community, able to provide for themselves and families."[24]

Note the identification with both the poor person and the donor which is conveyed in this excerpt from the 1761 report:

Let it be considered that . . . poor people are maintained by their labour, and, if they cannot labour they cannot live, without the help of the more fortunate. We all know, many mouths are fed, many bodies clothed, by one poor man's industry and diligence: should any sudden hurt happen to him, which should render him incapable to follow the business of his calling, unfit him to work, disable him to labour but for a little time; or should his duty to his aged and diseased parents or his fatherly tenderness for an afflicted child, engross his attention and care, how great must be the calamity of such a family! How pressing their wants! How moving

---

[22] John Griscom, *A Year in Europe: Comprising a Journal of Observations* [1818–19] (New York: Collins & Hannay, 1824), p. 261.

[23] *House of Refuge for Vagrant and Depraved Young People: Report of a Committee Appointed by the Society for the Prevention of Pauperism in the City of New York on the Expediency of Erecting an Institution for the Reformation of Juvenile Delinquents* (New York: Mahlon Day, 1824); "Vacating the House of Refuge," *Correction Magazine* (Albany: New York State Department of Correction, March, 1935).

[24] Benjamin Franklin, *Some Account of the Pennsylvania Hospital* (Philadelphia: B. Franklin & D. Hall, 1754), p. 5. This quotation is from the petition to the provincial House of Representatives.

their distress! And how much does it behove the community to take them immediately under their guardianship and have the causes of their misfortunes as speedily remedied as possible! Experience shows, this will be more effectually and frugally done in a publick hospital than by any other method whatever.[25]

Whereas the uncured sick person and his family were a drain, the one who was restored to health was a contributing member of the community. The corollary, that the best results would come from the best physicians and that opportunity should be afforded to train them, was embodied in the rules for the operation of the hospital.[26] Hence, from the start, this was no mere custodial institution, but one for cure, research, and training—an embodiment of compassion that also extended protection to the donor and the community at large. Further, the fact that the hospital was to be open to paying patients only if there were beds available after all public cases were taken care of[27] established a relationship that was salutary to the standards of public service.

For such an institution it was possible to appeal to people with many different motivations—pity for the afflicted, worry over the expense to the taxpayer of inadequate care, concern over danger from little-understood diseases, and self-seeking publicity. To get the colonial assembly to provide the building, Franklin played on all of these, proposing a contingent appropriation requiring private subscription of a like sum. He tells us the result in his autobiography:

[25] *Continuation of the Account of the Pennsylvania Hospital* (Philadelphia: B. Franklin & D. Hall, 1761), pp. 113–14.

[26] Franklin, *Some Account of the Pennsylvania Hospital*, p. 49.

[27] *Ibid.*, pp. 47–48.

This condition carried the bill through; for the members who had opposed the grant, and now conceived they might have the credit of being charitable without the expense, agreed to its passage; and then, in soliciting subscriptions among the people, we urged the conditional promise of the law as an additional motive to give since every man's donation would be doubled; thus the clause worked both ways.[28]

USE AS ANALYTICAL TOOLS

There are other significant motivations, such as religion, and other concepts, such as responsibility, which might be developed similarly. Here compassion and protection have been developed in a very limited way as samples of the sorts of unifying ideas that need to be identified and utilized in the analysis of historical materials in the wide area of philanthropy and social welfare, just as nationalism and the frontier have been identified and utilized in other aspects of history. Their usefulness can only be suggested.

First, the historian of a single agency is likely to be puzzled by sudden modifications in program, frequently associated with new leadership. In such cases, did motivation change and, if so, did the new leadership reflect or precipitate the shift in emphasis between protection and compassion? Did internal struggles reflect changing attitudes in society at large? What changes in skill and training of staff were required as the agency's prevailing purposes changed?

On the other hand, in the study of the long-range effects of new technical skills or institutional mechanisms, one may find instances in which, with little change in form, the technique is used to accomplish varying purposes at differ-

[28] *The Life of Benjamin Franklin, Written by Himself*, ed. John Bigelow (Philadelphia: J. B. Lippincott & Co., 1874), I, 298.

ent times. For example, the idea of the exchange of information about individual clients, represented in institutional form in most cities by the social service exchange, has been a battleground for generations between those who see this device as a way of protecting givers and taxpayers against fraudulent appeals for help, those who see it from the compassionate point of view of providing more information about, and therefore better service to, the individual client, and those who see it as an undesirable activity because of their compassionate desire to shield the person in trouble from any intrusion into his affairs.[29]

Again, in the analysis of relations between agencies, and indeed between major fields, such as education, medicine and social welfare, the historian might find the ideas of compassion and protection helpful in understanding some of the recurring affinities and rivalries such as those seen in the current acrimonious exchanges between courts, police, schools, social agencies, and other groups dealing with juvenile delinquency. Would this type of analysis help to explain some of the fratricidal criticism of each other among philanthropic groups as "hard boiled," "impersonal," or "soft," a well-known aspect of the

competition for the philanthropic and tax dollar?

For the biographer, who may wish to probe rather deeply the inner motivations of his subject, external manifestations such as compassion or protection still provide focuses for analysis. What was there about Mrs. Hale that led her to direct her great compassion for the families of sailors toward enabling them to be as much like other people as possible, rather than toward providing alms or institutionalization? What, on the other hand, made Mrs. Lowell, in her urge to protect society against pauperism, feel it necessary to set relief recipients completely apart from other people?[30]

Finally, might not historical examination of compassion and protection give some further clue to philanthropists and professional workers regarding the nature of the components of a successful institution? A hypothesis that might well be tested is that no matter what their auspices or sources of support, those social welfare institutions which have proved enduringly useful to society as a whole have embodied in a balanced relationship both compassion, that is, a desire to do something for the benefit of unfortunate people in the present, and protection, a concern for the well-being of the donor's group both now and in the future.

GRADUATE SCHOOL OF PUBLIC ADMINISTRATION
AND SOCIAL SERVICE
NEW YORK UNIVERSITY

Received April 30, 1958

---

[29] For the evolution of social service exchange philosophy see Associated Charities of Boston, *First Annual Report* (1880), p. 5; *Third Annual Report* (1882), pp. 12–13; Margaret F. Byington, *The Confidential Exchange: A Form of Social Cooperation* (New York: Charity Organization Department of the Russell Sage Foundation, Publication No. 28, 1912); Beatrice R. Simcox, "The Social Service Exchange, Part II: Its Use in Casework," *Journal of Social Casework*, XXVIII (1947), 388–90; Stephen L. Angell and Frank T. Greving, "A New Look at the Social Service Exchange," *Social Work Journal*, XXXVI (1955), 16–17.

[30] Seaman's Aid Society, Boston, *Third Annual Report* (1836), pp. 12–13; Josephine Shaw Lowell, *Public Relief and Private Charity* (New York: G. P. Putnam's Sons, 1884), pp. 67, 106.

The American Jewish Response to Nineteenth-Century Christian Missions

Jonathan D. Sarna

Kenneth Scott Latourette properly characterized the nineteenth century as the "Great Century" of Christian expansion: the age when missionary activities spread to cover all corners of the world. Numerous facets of this development have been investigated.[1] We know a great deal about the origins, growth, and impact of the missionary movement. But the immediate response of the missionized, their counteractive programs and battle for cultural survival, has received surprisingly scant attention. Most scholars continue to view the "unenlightened" only as objects of history, shaped by others.[2]

In some cases, written native evidence concerning missionaries simply does not exist. Folklore, travel diaries, and missionary reports must be employed, resulting in inevitable distortion. In the case of Jewish missions, however, responses exist in abundance. The special nature of missions to the Jews, particularly in America, militate against glib cross-cultural generalizations. Still, the range, diversity, and surprising result of the American Jewish response invite critical comparative study.[3] The basic theme, after all, is a universal one:

Jonathan D. Sarna is assistant professor of history at Hebrew Union College—Jewish Institute of Religion in Cincinnati. The American Jewish Archives, National Foundation for Jewish Culture, and Memorial Foundation for Jewish Culture generously funded parts of the research upon which this paper is based.

[1] Kenneth Scott Latourette, *The Great Century: A.D. 1800–A.D. 1914, Europe and the United States of America* (New York, 1941); this is volume IV of his *A History of the Expansion of Christianity* (7 vols., New York, 1937–1945). See also Stuart Piggin, "Assessing Nineteenth-Century Missionary Motivation: Some Considerations of Theory and Method," in *Religious Motivation: Biographical and Sociological Problems for the Church Historian*, ed. Derek Baker (Oxford, Eng., 1978), 327–37; John K. Fairbank, ed., *The Missionary Enterprise in China and America* (Cambridge, 1974); James P. Ronda and James Axtell, *Indian Missions: A Critical Bibliography* (Bloomington, Ind., 1978); John McCracken, *Politics and Christianity in Malawi, 1875–1940: The Impact of the Livingstonia Mission in the Northern Province* (Cambridge, Eng., 1977).

[2] An important exception is Louise H. Hunter, *Buddhism in Hawaii* (Honolulu, 1971). See also James P. Ronda, "'We Are Well as We Are': An Indian Critique of Seventeenth-Century Christian Missions," *William and Mary Quarterly*, XXXIV (Jan. 1977), 66–82.

[3] The closest comparison is to missions directed at American Catholics. See Maxine S. Seller, "Protestant Evangelism and the Italian Immigrant Woman," in *The Italian Immigrant Woman in*

the struggle of a minority group to maintain its religious and cultural identity in the face of pressures to convert and conform.

Efforts to convert American Jews date far back into the colonial period. Increase Mather labored and prayed for Jewish national conversion throughout his life. His son, Cotton Mather, dedicated a conversionist tract to the Jews (1699) and—until he changed his opinions—fervently prayed "for the conversion of the Jewish Nation, and for my own having the happiness, at some time or other, to baptize a Jew, that should by my ministry, bee brought home unto the Lord." Even the mild-mannered Ezra Stiles lamented that the "sincere, pious, & candid mind" of one of his friends, Aaron Lopez of Newport, could not "have perceived the Evidences" of Christianity. He hoped that others would see the light.[4]

These, it must be emphasized, were individual and spontaneous efforts undertaken by well-meaning people eager to extend heavenly blessings to those whom they saw as good-hearted but misguided. The small number of Jews in the country, probably less than 0.1 percent of the population, made more grandiose undertakings unnecessary. Besides, the theological foundation of later missions—the notion that man by his own actions could speed redemption—had not yet found acceptance outside of limited circles. The basis for a special missionary society aimed at Jews did not exist.[5]

Organized Protestant efforts to convert American Jews began only in the nineteenth century. *Annus mirabilis* was 1816, a year that saw the establishment both of the Female Society of Boston and the Vicinity for Promoting Christianity among the Jews and of the American Society for Evangelizing the Jews. Post-Edwardsian theology, the Second Great Awakening, the growth of the London Society for Promoting Christianity amongst the Jews, and the Peace of Ghent form the background for these developments. In addition, a man sailed into New York harbor in 1816 who had become famous for the leading role he had played in founding the London conversionist society: Joseph Samuel Christian Frederick Frey.[6]

North America, ed. Betty Boyd Caroli, Robert F. Harney, and Lydio F. Tomasi (Toronto, 1978), 124–36; Angelo Olivieri, "Protestantism and Italian Immigration in Boston in Late Nineteenth Century: The Mission of G. Conte," in *The Religious Experience of Italian Americans*, ed. Silvano M. Tomasi (Staten Island, 1975), 73–103; Salvatore Mondello, "Protestant Proselytism among the Italians in the USA as Reported in American Magazines," *Social Science*, 41 (April 1966), 84–90; and Theodore Abel, *Protestant Home Missions to Catholic Immigrants* (New York, 1933).

[4] Lee M. Friedman, *Jewish Pioneers and Patriots* (Philadelphia, 1942), 95–106; Mel Scult, *Millennial Expectations and Jewish Liberties: A Study of the Efforts to Convert the Jews in Britain, up to the Mid Nineteenth Century* (Leiden, Neth., 1978), 47–55; Jacob R. Marcus, *The Colonial American Jew, 1492–1776* (3 vols., Detroit, 1970), III, 1135–48; Arthur A. Chiel, "Ezra Stiles and the Jews: A Study in Ambivalence," in *A Bicentennial Festschrift for Jacob Rader Marcus*, ed. Bertram Wallace Korn (New York, 1976), 63–76.

[5] Oliver Wendell Elsbree, *The Rise of the Missionary Spirit in America, 1790–1815* (Williamsport, Pa., 1928); Ernest A. Payne, "Introduction," to William Carey, *An Enquiry into the Obligations of Christians to Use Means for the Conversion of the Heathens* (London, 1961), iii–xx; Charles L. Chaney, *The Birth of Missions in America* (South Pasadena, Calif., 1976). For population statistics, see Marcus, *Colonial American Jew*, I, 388–90.

[6] *Religious Intelligencer*, I (Jan. 25, 1817), 555–58. On early American Jewish missions generally, see David Max Eichhorn, *Evangelizing the American Jew* (New York, 1978); Max Eisen,

Frey (1771–1850), a native of Franconia, converted in 1798 and immigrated to London in 1801. Though originally slated to work for the London Missionary Society in Africa, he soon commenced labors among his "brethren and kinsmen according to the flesh." In 1809, he helped organize the London Society for Promoting Christianity amongst the Jews. Seven years later, following the publication of his best-selling autobiography and in the wake of an ugly scandal (according to one source Frey seduced a convert named Mrs. Josephson), Frey came to the United States.[7]

Frey's arrival, and the initial attention lavished upon him in New York, brought about the first American response to missionary activities directed at Jews. European polemics and counter-polemics, including the works of David Levi in London, had appeared in New York bookstores earlier—thanks in part to Jewish printers. George Bethune English's idiosyncratic, eccentric, and highly Judeophilic *The Grounds of Christianity Examined, by Comparing the New Testament with the Old* (1813), had also stirred up a predictable storm of controversy.[8] But *Tobit's Letters to Levi; or A Reply to the Narrative of Joseph Samuel C. F. Frey* (1816) was different. Personalities rather than theologies dominated its pages. It sought to puncture the halo around Frey—whose original name was Levy—and tried to prove from "common sense" that money should not be "squandered in America, in . . . the conversion of the Jews." "Tobit" claimed both membership in a Christian church and adherence to "the doctrine of Jesus Christ as contained in the New Testa-

"Christian Missions to the Jews in North America and Great Britain," *Jewish Social Studies*, X (Jan. 1948), 31–66; Marshall Sklare, "The Conversion of the Jews," *Commentary*, 56 (Sept. 1973), 44–53; Lee M. Friedman, "The American Society for Meliorating the Condition of the Jews and Joseph S.C.F. Frey," in Lee M. Friedman, *Early American Jews* (Cambridge, 1934), 96–112; Lorman Ratner, "Conversion of the Jews and Pre-Civil War Reform," *American Quarterly*, XIII (Spring 1961), 43–54; and Louis Meyer, "Hebrew-Christian Brotherhood Unions and Alliances of the Past and Present," *Minutes of the First Hebrew-Christian Conference of the United States. Held at Mountain Lake, Md., July 28–30, 1903* (Pittsburgh, 1903), 16–31. On British missions to the Jews, see Todd M. Endelman, *The Jews of Georgian England, 1714–1830: Tradition and Change in a Liberal Society* (Philadelphia, 1979), 71–76, 285–86; Harvey W. Meirovich, "Ashkenazic Reactions to the Conversionists, 1800–1850," *Transactions of the Jewish Historical Society of England*, 26 (1979), 8–25; and Bill Williams, *The Making of Manchester Jewry, 1740–1875* (Manchester, Eng., 1976), 45–48, 148–50. On German missions, see David C. Smith, "The Berlin Mission to the Jews and its Ecclesiastical and Political Context, 1822–1848," *Neue Zeitschrift für Missionswissenschaft*, XXX (1974), 182–90. The only general survey of the field remains A. E. Thompson, *A Century of Jewish Missions* (Chicago, 1902).

7 On Joseph Samuel Christian Frederick Frey see, in addition to works already cited, George Harvey Genzmer, "Joseph Samuel Christian Frederick Frey," *Dictionary of American Biography* (20 vols., New York, 1928–36), VII, 28–29; George J. Miller, "David A. Borrenstein: A Printer and Publisher at Princeton, N.J., 1824–28," *Papers of the Bibliographical Society of America*, 30 (1936), 1–6; and Harry Simonhoff, *Jewish Notables in America, 1776–1865: Links of an Endless Chain* (New York, 1956), 176–80.

8 *Christian Disciple*, IV (Aug. 1816), 249–52; (New York) *Jewish Chronicle*, 10 (March 1854), 248; David Levi, *Letters to Dr. Priestly, in Answer to Those He Addressed to the Jews; Inviting Them to an Amicable Discussion of the Evidences of Christianity* (New York, 1794); David Levi, *A Defence of the Old Testament, in a Series of Letters Addressed to Thomas Paine* (New York, 1797); George Bethune English, *The Grounds of Christianity Examined, by Comparing the New Testament with the Old* (Boston, 1813); and Edward Everett, *A Defence of Christianity, against the Work of George B. English* (Boston, 1814).

ment."[9] Be this as it may, his work—especially in its attacks on Christian divisions and prejudices—reads like one that was Jewish-inspired. European Jews often subsidized philo-Semitic tracts. The same may well have been true in America.[10]

Four years after Tobit's publication, the American Society for Evangelizing the Jews received a state charter. The organization's list of officers reads like a Who Was Who of New York: Elias Boudinot, former president of the Continental Congress, stood at the helm. Below him sat many, obviously honorific, vice presidents, including John Quincy Adams, Jeremiah Day, Ashbel Green, Philip Milledoler (presidents respectively of Yale, Princeton, and Rutgers), William Phillips, and Stephen Van Rensselaer. Rounding out the list of officers was the treasurer, Peter Jay, son of diplomat John Jay. Even this formidable assembly, however, failed to convince the legislature to grant the desired charter. Disturbed by the implications of state-sanctioned evangelization, and embarrassed by the presence in Albany of Mordecai Noah, the Jewish editor of the *National Advocate*, New York City's Tammany newspaper, the legislature insisted on a new name for the evangelization society. From 1820 onward, the organization was known as the American Society for Meliorating the Condition of the Jews.[11]

Open and direct American Jewish responses to Christian missions properly date to this 1820 incorporation. Only then did the melioration society become an active force, funded by hundreds of auxiliary organizations that poured money into its coffers and promised full support to its activities.[12] Though the society initially claimed to be interested only in "melioration," and only in those already converted abroad, American Jews understandably took fright. They feared for their survival. Being small in number (about 3,000), they could ill afford to lose adherents to the majority faith.[13] But fear was not the whole of

[9] *Tobit's Letters to Levi; or A Reply to the Narrative of Joseph Samuel C. F. Frey* (New York, 1816), 1,36. See also the American reprint of a Liverpool polemic, Jacob Nikelsburger, *Koul Jacob In Defence of the Jewish Religion: Containing the Arguments of the Rev. C. F. Frey* (New York, 1816).

[10] Alexander Altmann, *Moses Mendelssohn: A Biographical Study* (University, Ala., 1973), 449–61, 512; and more generally Hans Joachim Schoeps, *Philosemitismus im Barock: Religions-und geistgeschichtliche untersuchungen* (Tübingen, Ger., 1952).

[11] American Society for Meliorating the Condition of the Jews, *Constitution of the American Society for Ameliorating the Condition of the Jews; with an Address from the Hon. Elias Boudinot . . . And the Act of Incorporation Granted by the Legislature of the State of New York* (New York, 1820); Joseph Samuel C. F. Frey, *Judah and Israel: Or, the Restoration and Conversion of the Jews and the Ten Tribes* (New York, 1840), 81–93; Joseph L. Blau and Salo W. Baron, eds. *The Jews of the United States, 1790–1840: A Documentary History* (3 vols., New York, 1963), III, 714–73; Jonathan D. Sarna, *Jacksonian Jew: The Two Worlds of Mordecai Noah* (New York, 1981), 56–57.

[12] The early support for the American Society for Meliorating the Condition of the Jews is chronicled in its annual reports (especially 1820–1825) and in its *Israel's Advocate* (1823–1827). For details of the Philadelphia auxiliary, see Marion L. Bell, *Crusade in the City: Revivalism in Nineteenth-Century Philadelphia* (Lewisburg, Pa., 1977), 137–59.

[13] Ira Rosenswaike, "The Jewish Population of the United States as Estimated from the Census of 1820," *American Jewish Historical Quarterly*, LIII (Dec. 1963), 148; Bertram W. Korn, "Factors Bearing upon the Survival of Judaism in the Ante-Bellum Period," *American Jewish Historical Quarterly*, LIII (June 1964), 341–51; and more generally, Malcolm H. Stern, "The 1820s: American Jewry Comes of Age," in *Bicentennial Festschrift for Jacob Rader Marcus*, ed. Korn, 539–49.

it. Historically, Christianity posed a menacing challenge to the Jewish people. By undertaking active missions, Christians forced Jews back into an age-old battle. Not only live souls were at stake; centuries of martyred souls were too. In Jewish eyes, the war against missionaries became a war of affirmation, a war to prove that eighteen hundred years of Jewish civilization had not been in vain.[14]

The symbolic importance of the missionary battle explains the magnitude of the Jewish response. Beginning in 1820 with a work entitled *Israel Vindicated* (allegedly authored by "An Israelite" but probably written by the non-Jewish George Houston with the help and financial assistance of Jews)[15] and continuing down through the nineteenth century, the small Jewish community devoted a substantial portion of its resources to various forms of polemics. Solomon Jackson devoted his entire *The Jew* (1823–1825), the first Jewish periodical in America, to "a defence of Judaism against all adversaries."[16] Later Jewish works, if less single-minded, never strayed far from "the challenge." As far as Jews were concerned, nothing was more important.

The most traditional form of Jewish polemic dealt with theology—specifically, the wearisome arguments over the meaning of the Hebrew Bible and the validity of the Christian one. The points of contention scarcely changed over time.[17] As a result, Jews freely borrowed from past masters. A work composed in eighteenth-century England but first printed in nineteenth century America, *A Series of Letters on the Evidences of Christianity* by Benjamin Dias Fernandes, proved spectacularly popular. Its arguments drew heavily from the classic polemical works of Isaac Troki (1533–1594) and Isaac Orobio de Castro (1620–1687).[18] A later American volume, Selig Newman's *The Challenge Accepted*, was completely derivative:

The following work does not profess to be original as the subjects on which it treats, have been already fully and ably discussed by former writers, defenders of Judaism. Therefore, the learned reader will here find nothing that is new. . . . It is for the use of the less informed of our co-religionists who are almost strangers to all but the English language, that the discussions and writings of the ancient and modern defenders of our

---

[14] On the background of the Jewish-Christian encounter in the United States, see Hans Joachim Schoeps, *The Jewish-Christian Argument: A History of Theologies in Conflict,* trans. David E. Green (New York, 1963); Oliver Shaw Rankin, *Jewish Religious Polemic of Early and Later Centuries, a Study of Documents Here Rendered in English* (Edinburgh, 1956); Kenneth R. Stow, "The Church and the Jews: From St. Paul to Paul IV," in Lawrence V. Berman, et al., *Bibliographical Essays in Medieval Jewish Studies* (New York, 1976), 109–65; and Frank Ephraim Talmage, *Disputation and Dialogue: Readings in the Jewish-Christian Encounter* (New York, 1975), especially the bibliographic essay, 361–83.

[15] Jonathan D. Sarna, "The Freethinker, the Jews and the Missionaries: George Houston and the Mystery of *Israel Vindicated,*" *AJS Review,* 5 (1980), 101–14.

[16] *The Jew,* I (March 1823), 1.

[17] See, in addition to works cited in note 14, Daniel J. Lasker, *Jewish Philosophical Polemics against Christianity in the Middle Ages* (New York, 1977).

[18] Benjamin Dias Fernandes, *A Series of Letters on the Evidences of Christianity* (Philadelphia, [1853]), 2,250–58. Isaac Leeser briefly traces the history of these letters in his introduction to the 1853 edition. See also *The Jew,* I (July 1823), 85. Reprints of this polemic appeared in 1858 and in 1869, and a "revised and enlarged" edition was printed serially in *Israelite,* 14–15 (1868–1869). See Isaac Mayer Wise's praise of the book as "one of the best polemical works on this topic ever published by a Hebrew in the English language." *Israelite,* 12 (1864), 149.

Faith have herein been collected and exhibited in an English dress, to enable them to stand in self-defence, when challenged respecting certain predictions of our Prophets, and perverted constructions of Scripture are sought to be forced upon them.

Like others of its genre, *The Challenge Accepted* explained crucial biblical passages, mostly in Genesis and Isaiah, and then moved on to question the authenticity of the gospel literature based on alleged inner contradictions.[19]

Works like these demonstrated their modern character through their emphasis on reason. No standard of truth stood higher. Following Moses Mendelssohn, the great eighteenth-century Jewish philosopher, most insisted that nothing in Judaism was "contrary to, or above, reason." Noah called Judaism "the religion of nature—the religion of reason and philosophy." Isaac Mayer Wise, the pioneer of American Reform Judaism, entitled his first theological polemic "Reason and Faith," and he later stated as a principle that "nothing which reason rejects is to be accepted." By invoking reason Jews proclaimed themselves blissfully modern. They relegated Christianity to a lower level, one reserved for religions repugnant to reason: "The credo which establishes this doctrine is so full of contradictions and inconsistencies, that I challenge any person to compose, within the same compass of words, anything equal to it, or more repugnant to reason and common sense." They implied that Judaism would win out in the end.[20]

A variant form of theological polemic, while dependent on reason, departed from Jewish arguments and relied instead on enlightenment, deistic, and freethought ones: works by John Toland, Anthony Collins, and Paul Henry Thiry, Baron d'Holbach. *Israel Vindicated* falls into this category—not surprisingly, since its presumed author, Houston, had translated Holbach's *Ecce Homme*. English's *The Grounds of Christianity Examined* drew from similar sources. Both employed the same arguments: "Christians . . . adopt, without examination, the most contradictory facts, the most incredible actions, the most amazing prodigies, the most unconnected system, the most unintelligible doctrine, and the most revolting mysteries." Judaism, by contrast, was thoroughly reasonable. Jews promoted and printed these volumes, just as later they publicized the "heretical" findings of David Strauss and Ernest Renan. They aimed to show, as Wise admitted, that Christians and infidels had already "shorn the Christian story of the last prestige." The polemical cor-

[19] Selig Newman, *The Challenge Accepted; a dialogue between a Jew and a Christian: The Former Answering a Challenge Thrown Out by the Latter, Respecting the Accomplishment of the Prophecies Predictive of the Advent of Jesus* (New York, 1850), iii. On Selig Newman, see Endelman, *Jews of Georgian England*, 244, 285. For another example of a theological polemic from this period, see the unpublished manuscript of Jacob Mordecai, Mordecai Family Papers (American Jewish Archives, Cincinnati, Ohio).

[20] Moses Mendelssohn to Elkan Herz, July 22, 1771, quoted in Altmann, *Moses Mendelssohn*, 249; Mordecai M. Noah, *Discourse Delivered at the Consecration of the Synagogue K. K. Shearith Israel in the City of New York* (New York, 1818), 24; James G. Heller, *Isaac M. Wise: His Life, Work, and Thought* (New York, 1965), 140–41, 535; Dias Fernandes, *Series of Letters*, 149; see generally, Schoeps, *Jewish-Christian Argument*, 103–05; and Arthur Hertzberg, *The French Enlightenment and the Jews* (New York, 1968), 256–58.

ollary was obvious: if Christians could not even convince their own adherents, why should Jews pay them heed?[21]

By employing for polemical purposes non-Jewish, anti-Christian works, Jews courted great danger. The impious and nonbeliever held low esteem in America; irreligion and immorality were assumed to go hand in hand.[22] Furthermore, many of the authors whom Jews happily quoted in attacks on the Gospels had on other occasions attacked Judaism with equal vehemence. Why would Jews want to associate with such people? The needs of the hour, however, took precedence over due caution. As had been true in the Middle Ages and in eighteenth century Germany, Jews risked temporary alliances with outcast dissenting Christians for the sake of their more urgent battle against onslaughts from mainstream missionaries. In times of religious war, polemics made strange bedfellows.[23]

Jews stood on safer terrain when they employed a third kind of theological polemic, one that might be called Mendelssohnian or even antipolemical. These works invoked the spirit of Mendelssohn's *Jerusalem* and his letter to Lavater, both of which were known in America, and they professed a "disinclination to enter into religious controversy" of any sort. Isaac Leeser, a leading Jewish minister, editor, and publicist in the antebellum period, employed this type of argument in his *The Jews and the Mosaic Law* (1834) and *The Claims of the Jews to an Equality of Rights* (1841). In both volumes he condemned Christian missionaries without specifically attacking Christianity itself. Though his later synagogue discourses were at times full of theological polemics, Leeser in these early works acknowledged and praised the kind treatment he had received at non-Jewish hands. If only Jews could disabuse their neighbors of "any unfounded suspicions they might be induced to adopt concerning us," he mused, conversionist efforts might lose public support.[24] Leeser did his best

[21] An Israelite [George Houston], *Israel Vindicated; Being a Refutation of the Calumnies Propagated Respecting the Jewish Nation* (New York, 1820), 30; Sarna, "The Freethinker, the Jews and the Missionary," 105–06. Abraham De Sola republished George Bethune English's work in 1852, and readers were urged to buy it in *Occident*, 11 (Sept. 1853), 324. For Wise, see Heller, *Isaac M. Wise*, 641; and *Israelite*, 12 (1866), 396.

[22] Robert T. Handy, *A Christian America: Protestant Hopes and Historical Realities* (New York, 1971), 30–42; see also John Webb Pratt, *Religion, Politics, and Diversity: The Church-State Theme in New York History* (Ithaca, N.Y., 1967), 121–57.

[23] Hertzberg, *French Enlightenment and the Jews*, 268–313; Jacob Katz, *From Prejudice to Destruction: Anti-Semitism, 1700–1933* (Cambridge, 1980), 23–33; S. Ettinger, "Jews and Judaism as Seen by English Deists of the Eighteenth Century" [in Hebrew], *Zion*, XXIX (no. 3–4, 1964), 182–207; Moshe Pelli, "The Impact of Deism on the Hebrew Literature of the Enlightenment in Germany," *Journal of Jewish Studies*, XXIV (Autumn 1973), 127–46; David Berger, "Christian Heresy and Jewish Polemic in the Twelfth and Thirteenth Centuries," *Harvard Theological Review*, 68 (July–Oct. 1975), 287–303; Lasker, *Jewish Philosophical Polemics*, 164–65.

[24] Moses Mendelssohn, "Letter to Johann Casper Lavater," in *Disputation and Dialogue*, ed. Talmage, 266; Isaac Leeser, *The Claims of the Jews to an Equality of Rights* (Philadelphia, [1841]), 4, 8–13, 92–97; Isaac Leeser, *The Jews and the Mosaic Law* (Philadelphia, [1834]), 228; *Occident*, 9 (1852) supplement, iii–xx, 1–115; *Israelite*, 1(1854), 132–33; and, for a later example, *Sabbath Visitor*, 22 (1893), 324. More generally, see Bertram Wallace Korn, "German-Jewish Intellectual Influences on American Jewish Life, 1824–1972," in *Tradition and Change in Jewish Experience*,

to educate Christians, but as a strategy his proved thoroughly unsuccessful—
which perhaps led him to abandon it in later years. By not challenging Christian arguments, he had unwittingly opened himself to the charge of being
unable to challenge them. Missionaries claimed victory by default.[25]

The failure of the Mendelssohnian approach points up a more general dilemma that American Jews met in their missionary encounters. If they ignored
missionaries, they faced charges of cowardice or tacit acquiescence. If, on the
other hand, they debated missionaries, they risked angering and offending all
Christians, even those with whom they had established social relations. Civil
society frowned on religious disputations. It viewed Jews who undertook them
as medieval, insular, and intolerant. It made no provisions, however, for how
Jews should respond when attacked. Jews did not know either.[26]

By the end of the nineteenth century, some Jews had found a way out of this
dilemma. They employed special antimissionary crusaders, like Adolph
Benjamin, who defended Judaism with all necessary weapons. These crusaders
scorned civility and accepted on their own heads the "medieval taint." Meanwhile, the wealthy, socially active Jews who secretly supported them—men
like the banker Jacob Schiff—could proclaim themselves progressively modern
and thoroughly tolerant.[27] The compromise may look hypocritical. In fact, it
was an effort by some Jews to assimilate socially while simultaneously holding
fast to their Jewish identities. The result was ambivalence: manners went one
way, money the other.

Historical polemics, those that dealt with the medieval and modern worlds
rather than with the biblical one, proved less risky than theological disputes.
Furthermore, Jews' relative success in America made these polemics particularly effective. To view the Jewish experience, as many Christians had, as
a "tedious succession of oppressions and persecutions" or as "a standing
monument of the truth of the christian religion"[28] did not square with obvious
facts of American Jewish history. "In this country," as Tobit pointed out, "a
Jew is equally as proud a man as a Christian . . . [nor] is it incompetent for a

ed. A. Leland Jamison (Syracuse, N.Y., 1978), 106–40; and Maxine S. Seller," Isaac Leeser: A
Jewish-Christian Dialogue in Antebellum Philadelphia," *Pennsylvania History*, XXXV (July
1968), 231–42.

[25] See the bound compendium of issues from *The Jew*, S. H. Jackson, ed., *The Jew; Being a
Defence of Judaism against All Adversaries, and Particularly against the Insidious Attacks of
Israel's Advocate* (New York, 1824), vii. "In the present enlightened age, not to defend Judaism,
would be considered a tacit acknowledgment that it was indefensible, or at least that we thought
so."

[26] For this theme in a different context, see John Murray Cuddihy, *The Ordeal of Civility: Freud,
Marx, Lévi-Strauss, and the Jewish Struggle with Modernity* (New York, 1974), 13–14.

[27] Eichhorn, *Evangelizing the American Jew*, 178–80.

[28] Hannah Adams, *The History of the Jews from the Destruction of Jerusalem to the Nineteenth
Century* (2 vols., Boston, 1812), I, iii, iv. See *Christian Disciple*, IV (Aug. 1816), 250; Blau and
Baron, eds., *Jews of the United States*, I, 88–89; Anita Libman Lebeson, "Hannah Adams and the
Jews," *Historia Judaica*, VIII (Oct. 1946), 113–34; and C. Conrad Wright, "Hannah Adams,"
Notable American Women: 1607-1950: A Biographical Dictionary, ed. Edward T. James, Janet
Wilson James, and Paul S. Boyer (3 vols., Cambridge, 1971), I, 9–11. Hannah Adams's view of
Jewish history can be traced back to Jacques Basnage. See Hertzberg, *French Enlightenment and
the Jews*, 47.

Jew to be the first magistrate, the President of these United States."[29] It followed that past persecutions were not divinely inspired at all, but rather the products of human intolerance. While Christians blamed Jewish intransigence and God's wrath for medieval persecutions, Jews blamed the church "whose principles, condensed into a small compass, appear to be, all who are one way are legitimized; all not are cut off."[30] Jews and Christians agreed on the basic facts of medieval Jewish history; only their interpretations differed.

For a while, Jews had more trouble when Christians pointed to the Jewish diaspora as proof of divine wrath, an argument easily buttressed by Jewish sources. In the late nineteenth century, however, Jews, particularly Reform Jews, provided an answer for this claim as well: "We do not look upon this dispersion as a curse; on the contrary, we regard it as a blessing—a blessing for you and all mankind." This account viewed the diaspora as God's means of spreading his message to the world. Far from being a cursed figure, the wandering Jew had been transformed into a hero: an authentic Jewish missionary.[31]

Jewish historical polemics depended on Jewish current events. The more Jews succeeded, the easier it was to claim that God still loved his people Israel and had never rejected them. In boasting of their success, however, Jews sometimes overstated their case—disastrously. Such claims as "there are upwards of seven millions of Jews, known to be in existence, throughout the world; a number greater than at any period of our history; and possessing more wealth, activity, influence and talents than any body of people of their number on earth" provided grist for the anti-Semite's mill. The same claims to power which negated an old stereotype—"the ever-persecuted Jew"—confirmed a new one—"the all-powerful Jew." Polemics had Jews caught in a double-bind.[32]

As a result, some Jews reworded this argument and substituted a new phrase: "the accepted Jew." Prestige replaced power as a mark of success. The new answer to the myth of the accursed, wandering Jew was a proud, well-mannered and well-groomed Jew who "enjoy[ed] excellent social positions."[33]

Historical polemics based on Christian history posed considerably less danger and shifted the argument to the enemy's turf. Consequently, Jews

[29] *Tobit's Letters to Levi*, 55. Christians themselves realized that "America was different," but this had little bearing on their arguments. See *Israel's Advocate*, I (Feb. 1823), 29; American Society for Meliorating the Condition of the Jews, *Interesting Documents* [New York, 1822], 11; and Aaron Bancroft, *A Discourse Delivered before the Worcester Auxiliary Society for Meliorating the Condition of the Jews, April 28, 1824* (Worcester, Mass., 1824), 11.

[30] "Honestus," *A Critical Review of the Claims Presented by Christianity for Inducing Apostacy in Israel* [New York, 1852], 30.

[31] Bernhard Felsenthal, *The Wandering Jew: A Statement to a Christian Audience, of the Jewish View of Judaism* [Chicago, 1872], 5. Cf. Haim Hillel Ben-Sasson, "Galut," *Encyclopaedia Judaica* (16 vols., Jerusalem, 1971), VII, 275-94. See also Max Wiener, "The Conception of Mission in Traditional and Modern Judaism," *Yivo Annual of Jewish Social Sciences*, II-III (1947-1948), 9-24.

[32] Abraham Collins, *The Voice of Israel, Being a Review of Two Sermons Preached in the City of New York* [New York, 1823], 20. See also "Honestus," *Critical Review*, 21; and Sarna, *Jacksonian Jew*, 122.

[33] Felsenthal, *Wandering Jew*, 4.

employed them as often as possible. A hardy perennial, deeply rooted in medieval disputations, was the proof from world events. Writers on this theme borrowed liberally from Troki's list of twenty "prophecies which are unfulfilled, and are yet to come to pass in the days of the expected Messiah." These included everything from "the ingathering of the Ten Tribes" and "the rise of Gog and Magog" to "peace and harmony" and the rebuilding of the temple. Dias Fernandes reprinted these unfulfilled prophecies in their entirety, with full attribution. Others reduced them to their barest essence: "great events are contingent on the appearance of the Messiah which have not yet been realized."[34] In either case, Jews forced missionaries to respond. Without explicitly saying so, they warned that missions could ultimately backfire, as Christians exposed to Jewish arguments began to question their own faith.

Similarly well rooted in the past was the argument from Christian divisions. A variety of denominations missionized simultaneously among American Jews, each claiming truth for its own views. Noah and other Jews posed the obvious question: "how are we to choose?" The question was rhetorical. Since Christians "contradict each other on vital principles and condemn each other most recklessly," Jews like Wise argued that they were better off keeping to their own firmly held convictions. Wise suggested, as others had before him, that Christianity put its own house in order before daring to venture into Jewish-held territory.[35]

In this defensive strategy Jews did not merely refer to Christian divisions. Being thoroughly familiar with the Christian scene, they knew, in Leeser's words, of "multitudes in America who never enter a church, who never have been in Sunday School, who never had a preacher's voice reaching their ears."[36] Jews urged missionaries to attend to these unfortunates and to leave them alone. In some cases, though not that of Wise, they even supported Christian foreign missions and Bible societies. They did not care where the Christian army marched, so long as it kept out of Jewish domains.[37]

Jews trumpeted two other Christian problems. In these cases, however, they aimed not to deflect Christianity, but rather to demonstrate its waning influence in order to deter potential newcomers from signing up. First, they pointed to the "rapid progress of Unitarianism." To Abraham Collins this indicated the indubitable quality of Unitarian arguments and the abiding power

[34] [Isaac Troki], *Faith Stengthened*, trans. Moses Mocatta (New York, 1970), 32–36; Dias Fernandes, *Series of Letters*, 250–58; *New York Sunday Times and Noah's Weekly Messenger*, April 14, 1850, p. 2. See also Collins, *Voice of Israel*, 80.

[35] M. M. Noah, *Discourse on the Restoration of the Jews: Delivered at the Tabernacle, Oct. 28 and Dec. 2, 1844* (New York, 1845), 27; F. C. Gilbert, *From Judaism to Christianity and Gospel Work among the Hebrews* (Concord, Mass., 1911), 85; *Israelite*, 1 (1854), 36; *ibid.*, 4 (1857), 4. See also M. M. Noah in *New York Evening Star*, June 14, 1836, p. 2; Isidor Kalisch, *A Guide for Rational Inquiries into the Biblical Writings* (Cincinnati, 1857), ix; [Houston], *Israel Vindicated*, 9; Leeser, *Claims of the Jews*, 14.

[36] *Occident*, 3 (May 1845), 99. See also *ibid.*, 6 (May 1848), 101; *Israelite*, 3 (1856), 172.

[37] Abraham Collins, "Introduction," to John Oxlee, *Three Letters Humbly Submitted . . . on the Inexpediency and Futility of Any Attempt to Convert the Jews to the Christian Faith* (Philadelphia 1843), ii; Mordecai M. Noah, *Travels in England, France, Spain, and the Barbary States, in the Years 1813–14 and 15* (New York, 1819), 56; Noah, *Discourse Delivered at the Consecration of the Synagogue*, 43; S. M. Isaacs in *London Voice of Jacob*, Aug. 4, 1853, p. 214B.

of its reason—as contrasted with that of the missionaries. To the typically more exuberant Noah, the same evidence showed broader influences at work, ones that might ultimately lead to the reunification of Christianity with Judaism—largely on Jewish terms. Both men thought that Unitarianism was on the rise and evangelical Protestantism on the decline. Neither hesitated to exploit this "fact" for its polemical possibilities. After the Civil War this argument largely died. Unitarianism became a threat to Judaism, luring away those on the fringes of the Reform movement.[38] But there remained another sign of weakness for Jews to exploit: Christian conversions to Judaism.

The fact that Christian conversions to Judaism took place at all in early America is remarkable. In England, through most of the nineteenth century, synagogues refused to accept proselytes because of fear of popular, clerical, and government reaction. Where converts found acceptance, as in Holland, nobody boasted about them. Jews rather took pride in their lack of evangelical zeal. They made a positive virtue of historical necessity and stressed the ethnic aspects of the faith.[39] Logically, however, no Jewish argument had better polemical potential than proselytism. Converts demonstrated that Judaism was a vibrant religion, one worth leaving Christianity to join. Why then, Jews asked, should anyone want to leave Judaism? By no coincidence, Christians often trumpeted Jewish conversions for the opposite reason: to stimulate backsliding Christians.

The centuries-old taboo on discussing proselytization did not break easily. Strategic considerations, however, finally won out. Jackson admitted in *The Jew* to having on file "a score or more" names of converts to Judaism. He revealed no particulars. Leeser also overcame early hesitations. By 1844 he justified reports of proselytization as an "offset to the occasional apostasy of Jews to Christianity." Wise hardly hesitated at all. He enjoyed taunting missionaries with tales of proselytization and went so far as to inform his readers that if non-Jews mastered his *Essence of Judaism*, he would consider their "confessions." Unfortunately, we have no record of how many confessions he heard. At least one missionary, however, sadly admitted that conversions of Gentiles to Judaism were "not uncommon."[40]

The argument from proselytization stands as one of American Jewry's most original and important contributions to counter-missionary polemics. Its significance lies primarily in its daring. By trumpeting conversions, American Jews insisted on their right to battle Christianity on equal terms—no holds barred. If Christians could convert Jews, Jews could convert Christians.

[38] Collins, *Voice of Israel*, iv; Sarna, *Jacksonian Jew*, 131; Benny Kraut, "Judaism Triumphant: Isaac Mayer Wise on Unitarianism and Liberal Christianity," unpublished typescript, 1980 (American Jewish Archives), 49.

[39] "Proselytes," *Encyclopaedia Judaica*, XIII, 1182–93; Joseph R. Rosenbloom, *Conversion to Judaism: From the Biblical Period to the Present* (Cincinnati, 1978), 67–89.

[40] *The Jew*, I (Dec. 1823), 222; *ibid.*, II (April 1824), 294; *Occident*, 2 (July 1844), 216; *Israelite*, 12 (1868), 76; *Israelite Indeed*, 7 (March 1864), 213. For other examples, see *Occident*; 3 (May 1845), 42; *ibid.*, 6 (Dec. 1848), 456–67; *ibid.*, 8 (May 1850), 59; *Israelite*, 3 (1856), 52, 412; *ibid.*, 6 (1860), 210, 259; *ibid.*, 9 (1863), 220. For comparable Catholic arguments, see Aaron I. Abell, ed., *American Catholic Thought on Social Questions* (Indianapolis, 1968), xvi–xvii, 13, 14.

Religious liberty, according to this view, meant nothing less than religious anarchy. All sects had the right to fight among themselves for new members. The same "voluntary system" that permitted Protestant denominations to compete with one another, and permitted Catholics to make converts, must allow Jews to proselytize as well.[41]

Earlier, some Jews had propounded a different view. *Israel Vindicated* considered missions to American Jews "contrary to the true spirit and meaning of the *constitution*." Leeser used a similar phrase, arguing that it was "contrary to the spirit of the constitution of the country for the many to combine to do the smallest minority the injury of depriving them of their conscientious conviction by systematic efforts."[42] According to this understanding of the First Amendment, all sects, Christian and non-Christian, had the right to exist unmolested and unmissionized. The "spirit of the constitution," however, never became enshrined into law. By the mid-1840s at the latest, most American Jews realized this. They understood that they had to fight missionaries, and they proceeded to do so with all means at their disposal.

Polemics formed only one means of countering missionaries. They covered a broad range of subjects—often borrowing arguments from both theology and history—and they aimed at a wide variety of audiences. Still, something was missing. Missions aroused the deepest of passions in American Jews: intellectual arguments, no matter how forceful, did not give them vent. Jews needed a vituperative outlet, a place where they could rage, roar, and respond with feeling. They employed for this purpose their Jewish newspapers.

Angry rebuttals consumed many pages of the Jewish press. *The Jew* specialized in point-by-point refutations of the melioration society's missionary sheet, *Israel's Advocate*. Leeser, who promised in the first issue of the *Occident* to keep "a watchful eye" on missionaries, picked his targets more selectively. He once devoted six passionate pages to a minute examination of the thirty-sixth annual report of the London Society for Promoting Christianity in order to prove that the magnitude of the society's expenses stood in stark contrast to the insignificance of its achievements. On other occasions, he found friends and relatives eager to watch missionaries for him. They furiously denied the alleged deathbed conversions of such people as Charleston's "Dr. D" (De La Motta) and Savannah's "Miss H."[43] Perhaps Leeser's greatest coup came in 1853 when Rabbi E. Marcussohn personally took to the *Occident*'s columns to refute missionary claims of his conversion. The private record suggests that Marcussohn, a heavy drinker, may not have been nearly so innocent as he maintained. In the antimissionary battle, however, propaganda

[41] The *London Voice of Jacob*, Sept. 29, 1843, p. 7B, viewed American Jews' daring with trepidation, and hoped "that forbearance will continue to characterize the English Jews." Anglo-Jewish passivity was attacked in *Israelite*, 3 (1856), 147.

[42] [Houston], *Israel Vindicated*, v; *Occident*, 3 (May 1845), 42. See also *New York Evening Post*, March 15, 1829, p. 2.

[43] *The Jew*, 1 (Nov. 1823), 191; *Occident*, 7 (July 1849), 223; *ibid.*, 2 (Aug. 1844), 255–56; *ibid.*, 4 (Oct. 1846), 355–57. Cf. (New York) *Jewish Chronicle*, 3 (Nov. 1846), 142, (May 1847), 346.

needs took precedence over fine points of fact. Leeser and his readers enjoyed their victory.[44]

No editor vented more rage at missionaries than Wise. He considered it a "sacred duty" to expose missionaries' "rascality" and wasted no opportunity to catch them at their "lying." Wise's passionate diatribes, however, by no means confined themselves to defensive rebuttals. By his own admission, he assumed the role of "malicious, biting, pugnacious, challenging, and mocking monster of the pen." His "peeps into the missionary efforts" conveniently summarize the major accusations made against missionaries by large numbers of Jews throughout the nineteenth century.[45]

Bribery and fraud held pride of place in Wise's standard litany of charges. Hyprocrisy, deception, impertinence, imposition, laziness, immorality, and false piety rounded out the sordid picture. When Wise opened his columns to a non-Jew, Theodore Norman, the message did not change. Norman dutifully revealed that missionaries "deceive, cheat and impose on mankind in general."[46] A single aim underlay all of these charges: the desire to prove missionaries depraved. If Christians considered them miscreants—evil, immoral, and corrupt—then they might refuse them support. They might even succumb to fallacious logic by deciding that the quality of missionary arguments was no better than the quality of the missionaries themselves. By the same token, if Jews considered them miscreants, then they would have more reason than ever to battle against them. They could rest secure that in opposing missionaries they were patriotically working to bring about moral reform.

Mighty as American Jewish pens were in the battle against missionaries, they still could not substitute for concrete actions. Christians, after all, had foot soldiers, tracts, institutions, and funding on their side. Jews needed to respond with more than printed words alone. And they did. At the most passive level, they attempted to talk with missionaries—especially the converts among them—hoping to show them the errors of their way. Occasionally this succeeded, and converts returned.[47] Most often, however, the tactic backfired. Reports of the conversations would appear in the missionary press as evidence that Jews had begun to "see the light." When he realized this, Leeser urged his

[44] *Occident*, 10 (Oct. 1852), 352–60; E. R. McGregor to Isaac Leeser, Oct. 5, 1852, Dec. 6, 1852, microfilm 200, Isaac Leeser Papers (American Jewish Archives); C. D. Oliver to Leeser, Oct. 20, 1853, *ibid.*; S. Cellner to Leeser, Aug. 23, 1852, *ibid.*; E. Marcussohn to Leeser, Jan. 1, 1853, *ibid.*; Stephen A. Speisman, *The Jews of Toronto: A History to 1937* (Toronto, 1979), 26–27.

[45] *Israelite*, 4 (1858), 237; Isaac M. Wise, *Reminiscences*, trans. David Philipson (New York, 1973), 273; Isaac Mayer Wise "The World of My Books," trans. Albert H. Friedlander, in *Critical Studies in American Jewish History: Selected Articles from American Jewish Archives*, ed. Jacob R. Marcus, (3 vols., Cincinnati, 1971), I, 173–75; Heller, *Isaac M. Wise*, 652–57. See also Samuel Sandmel, "Isaac Mayer Wise's 'Jesus Himself,'" in *Essays in American Jewish History: To Commemorate the Tenth Anniversary of the Founding of the American Jewish Archives under the Direction of Jacob Rader Marcus* (New York, 1975), 325–58.

[46] *Israelite*, 1 (1854), 36; *ibid.*, 3 (1856), 12, 268; *ibid.*, 5 (1859), 302. For the Theodore Norman exposés, see *ibid.*, 1 (1854), 39, 52, 68. Leeser employed proselyte Warder Cresson for a similar purpose. See *Occident*, 6 (Dec. 1858), 456–60.

[47] (New York) *Jewish Chronicle*, 3 (June 1847), 370; *Israelite Indeed*, 1 (July 1857), 7–8; *Israelite*, 10 (1864), 347.

readers to desist from conversations: "refrain from holding intercourse in any measure with these renegadoes." Many Jews apparently heeded his call. Missionaries increasingly reported finding Jews uncooperative and unwilling to open their doors.[48]

Snubbing may have functioned as a form of Jewish passive resistance to missionaries. Still, Jews yearned for more active strategies—ones that promised to have far greater impact. Back in the 1820s, Noah intimidated the melioration society by appearing at their annual meetings. His presence, eloquent in its silence, served as indubitable public testimony of missionary failure. In 1843, Joseph Simpson attempted to invoke the president's aid against the melioration society. He asked John Tyler to censure Gen. Winfield Scott for presiding at a missionary conference while on the public payroll. Tyler, who considered the matter a private one, refused.[49] A few Jews may have found other creative or political means of frustrating the hated missionary, but the average Jew could not always control his feelings. He viewed missionaries, especially if they were converts, as traitors and provocateurs, yet found no one in government interested in protecting him. So he lashed out on his own. In most cases, situations did not develop beyond the stage of malicious language and angry threats. At that point missionaries generally left the scene. As early as 1864, however, a stone-throwing incident took place at the New York City Mission School. More serious and widespread violence and rioting came later, in the 1890s, after the immigrant population grew and missionaries opened up conversionist centers in ghetto storefronts.[50]

Jewish leaders never encouraged antimissionary violence. They feared for the Jewish image and for Jews' acceptance into civil society. They also understood, however vaguely, that in the long run defensive actions—those aimed at strengthening the Jewish community internally—held far more promise of solving the missionary problem once and for all. Leading Jews preferred analysis to violence. They studied missionary successes to learn where their own society had failed. They saw how missionaries met needs that the Jewish community had ignored. Then, they imitated missionaries in order to defeat them. They created Jewish functional alternatives to missionary activities— alternatives that would keep Jews firmly within the fold.[51]

The most obvious weaknesses pointed up by pre-Civil War missionaries were Jewish ignorance and communal disunity. Before the rise of the meliora-

[48] Occident, 7 (July 1849), 223. Cf. ibid., 1 (April 1843), 43–47; (New York) Jewish Chronicle, 1 (Dec. 1844), 142; Israelite Indeed, 2 (Dec. 1858), 125.

[49] Sarna, Jacksonian Jew, 56–57; N. Taylor Phillips, "Items Relating to the History of the Jews of New York," Publications of the American Jewish Historical Society, 11 (1903), 158–59.

[50] Notices of violence include, (New York) Jewish Chronicle 1 (Aug. 1844), 43, (Jan. 1845), 177, (April 1845), 270, 274–75, (May 1845), 306; ibid., 4 (May 1848), 336; ibid., 8 (Aug. 1851), 45; Israelite, 2 May 24, 1868, p. 4; Israelite Indeed, 8 (July 1864), 10–11; Church Society for Promoting Christianity amongst the Jews, Annual Report, 1 (1879), 24; New York Evening Post, June 17, 1899, in Portal to America: The Lower East Side, 1870–1925, ed. Allon Schoener (New York, 1967), 63–65. See also Speisman, Jews of Toronto, 131–44; R. Gruneir, "The Hebrew-Christian Mission in Toronto," Canadian Ethnic Studies, IX (no. 1, 1977), 18–28.

[51] The contrast to the situation in Germany is striking; see Eleonore Sterling, "Jewish Reaction to Jew-Hatred in the First Half of the Nineteenth Century," Leo Baeck Institute Year Book, III (1958), 103–21.

tion society, the Jewish community had no newspaper, no certified rabbi, few textbooks, and no central leader. All of this changed once missionaries began their work. Within months of the appearance of their *Israel's Advocate, The Jew* rose up to answer it. Though neither lasted more than a few years, a pattern was set. In 1843, it repeated itself: the missionaries issued the *Jewish Chronicle*; Leeser responded with his *Occident*. Leeser may have been planning his newspaper for some time and for different reasons. The missionary challenge, however, transformed his ideas into action. From the very beginning the two periodicals functioned, in Leeser's words, as "two such little planets revolving around their peculiar axis, the former to malign Jews and to report all their faults and apostacies, the latter to be in a measure their *advocate* and to reprove without hesitation and reserve when errors and wrongs are discovered."[52]

The *Occident* benefited the Jewish community in two ways: it drew disparate settlements together, and it armed Jews with the kinds of information they needed to rebut missionary claims. The periodical could not substitute, however, for the textbooks, tracts, and English-language Bibles that missionaries provided Jews for free. Jews needed educational volumes of their own, and, thanks largely to the work of Leeser, these volumes came into being. Leeser personally translated into English catechisms, readers, even the Bible, and what he did not do himself, he urged others do do. The resulting books always mirrored Christian ones in form and style. But though outwardly the same, they differed in content. In a sense, this is symbolic of all Jewish counter-missionary activities: outwardly Jews conformed, inwardly they maintained their identity.[53]

The American Jewish Publication Society (1845–1851) expanded on Leeser's work, but kept only adult needs in mind. Rather than textbooks, the society printed popular literature—exclusively the kind, however, that challenged "the secret attacks and open assaults by specious arguments of those whose darling object is to break down the landmarks of Judaism." The society's first book, *Caleb Asher*, typifies the rest: it was an antimissionary satire.[54]

Other developments in the antebellum Jewish community—the publication of new books and periodicals, the creation of Jewish schools, hospitals, and synagogues, the appointment of foreign rabbis to be American religious

[52] *Occident*, 6 (Oct. 1848), 362. Cf. *ibid.*, 1 (April 1843), 43–44; and (New York) *Jewish Chronicle*, 1 (July 1844), 1. The *Jewish Chronicle* appeared in a newsletter format before 1844. Leeser issued a prospectus for the *Occident* in 1842. See Nathan M. Kaganoff, "Supplement III: Judaica Americana Printed before 1851," in *Studies in Jewish Bibliography, History and Literature in Honor of I. Edward Kiev*, ed. Charles Berlin (New York, 1971), 193.

[53] Moshe Davis, *The Emergence of Conservative Judaism: The Historical School in Nineteenth Century America* (Philadelphia, 1963), 34–64; Hyman B. Grinstein, "In the Course of the Nineteenth Century," in *A History of Jewish Education in America*, ed. Judah Pilch (New York, 1969), 25–50; Lloyd P. Gartner, ed., *Jewish Education in the United States: A Documentary History* (New York, 1969), 50–79. For a related problem, see Lloyd P. Gartner," Temples of Liberty Unpolluted: American Jews and Public Schools, 1840–1875," in *Bicentennial Festschrift for Jacob Rader Marcus*, ed. Korn, 157–89.

[54] *Occident*, 2 (Jan. 1845), 511–14; *Caleb Asher* (Philadelphia, 1845). See also Davis, *Emergence of Conservative Judaism*, 51–53, 367–69; and Solomon Grayzel, "The First American Jewish Publication Society," *Jewish Book Annual*, 3 (1944–45), 42–44.

leaders, and the drafting of plans for Jewish colonies in America and Palestine—also relate to the missionary challenge.[55] In each case, other motivating factors were at work, particularly the growth of Jewish immigration. "The activity and missionary zeal of all the [Protestant] sects," however, always played a part in Jewish planning.[56] Indeed, the conversionist threat frequently proved the decisive argument—the one that convinced thrifty Jews to contribute their hard-earned money.

The only weapon that Jews refused to employ in their anticonversionist war was the missionary weapon itself. Leeser, imitating "the activity and the missionary zeal of all the sects which surround us," once called for "Israelites of every degree to become missionaries," but only to carry the good tidings to "the bosom of their own families, to their neighbors, to their friends"—not, apparently, to Christians. A decade later, he suggested the creation of a Jewish missionary organization for the same purpose.[57] Leeser also advocated a Hebrew Foreign Mission Society aimed at sending Jews to China and "other quarters of the globe" that required "the presence of enlightened Israelites" to ward off "Christian soldiers." The philanthropist Judah Touro willed this society $5,000 in capital, and Julius Eckman, followed by the traveler I. J. Benjamin, agreed to undertake the arduous journey. In the end, however, no missionaries ever set out. Apathy, internal squabbling, charges that the society acted "contrary to Judaism," and the outbreak of Civil War brought the whole Jewish foreign missionary enterprise to a premature conclusion.[58]

After the Civil War, Jewish missions never received serious consideration. "Missionizing" became something that Christians did and Jews did not do.[59] Otherwise, the antebellum dynamic remained the same. Missionaries probed

[55] *Occident*, 1 (December 1843), 411; Hyman B. Grinstein, *The Rise of the Jewish Community of New York, 1654–1860* (Philadelphia, 1945), 156, 234, 386; S. Joshua Kohn, "Mordecai Manuel Noah's Ararat Project and the Missionaries," *American Jewish Historical Quarterly*, LV (Dec. 1965), 162–96; S. Joshua Korn, "New Light on Mordecai Manuel Noah's Ararat Project," *ibid.*, LIX (Dec. 1969), 210–14; Allan Tarshish, "Jew and Christian in a New Society: Some Aspects of Jewish-Christian Relationships in the United States, 1848–1881," in *Bicentennial Festschrift for Jacob Rader Marcus*, ed. Korn, 565–87; Allan Tarshish, "The Rise of American Judaism (A History of American Jewish Life from 1848 to 1881)" (Ph.D. diss., Hebrew Union College, 1938), 321–83.

[56] *Occident*, 2 (May 1844), 63.

[57] *Occident*, 2 (May 1844), 63; *ibid.*, 11 (Aug. 1853), 245. Cf. *Israelite*, Aug. 23, 1867, p. 4.

[58] *Occident*, 10 (March 1853), 583; *ibid.*, 11 (May 1853), 83–84, (June 1853), 180–84, (Aug. 1853) 275–76, (Nov. 1853), 409–13, (Jan. 1854), 510–15, (March 1854), 597; *ibid.*, 18 (June 7, 1860), 66, (June 14, 1860), 71, (June 26, 1860), 108; *Asmonean*, 7 (Jan. 14, 1853), 149, (March 11, 1853), 245, (March 18, 1853), 257; *Israelite*, 7 (1860), 14; Leon Huhner, *The Life of Judah Touro (1775–1854)* (Philadelphia 1946), 172; H. G. Reissner, "The German-American Jews (1800–1850)," *Leo Baeck Institute Year Book*, X (1965), 105; Davis, *Emergence of Conservative Judaism*, 78–79; I. J. Benjamin, *Three Years in America: 1859–1862*, trans. Charles Reznikoff (2 vols., Philadelphia, 1956), I, 318–33; Gershon Greenberg, "A German-Jewish Immigrant's Perception of America, 1853–54," *American Jewish Historical Quarterly*, LXVII (June 1978), 338; and Michael Pollak, *Mandarins, Jews, and Missionaries: The Jewish Experience in the Chinese Empire* (Philadelphia, 1980), 176–86.

[59] *Israelite Indeed*, 12 (July 1868), 10–16; Jacob J. Weinstein, *Solomon Goldman: A Rabbi's Rabbi* (New York, 1973), 267; Ida Cohen Selavan, "The Founding of Columbian Council," *American Jewish Archives*, XXX (April 1978), 32–33; Joseph R. Rosenbloom, "Intermarriage and Conversion in the United States," in *Bicentennial Festschrift for Jacob Rader Marcus*, ed. Korn, 496.

the underside of the Jewish community and uncovered areas of Jewish need. Alarmed Jews, in turn, probed the missionaries. Having learned about Jewish needs secondhand, they then proceeded to fill them. In so doing, they subverted the missionaries by imitation. The New York example is typical. Missionaries created schools, dispensaries, and ghetto charities designed to meet immigrant needs. This led to a Jewish survey of ghetto conditions. Ultimately, Jews created free schools, dispensaries, and philanthropies of their own.[60] And then the cycle began all over again.

By the end of the nineteenth century, missionaries actually posed only a petty threat to American Jewry. They continued to ply their trade, and American Jewry continued to battle them. But outsiders knew that widespread conversions would never take place. Eight decades of struggle had sensitized Jews to their own identities and past history. They had learned the value of education, organization, and leadership. They had even discovered how to use the missionary threat as a specter—an evil portent menacing enough to frighten the community into undertaking defensive actions, self-analyses, and constructive new projects. Occasionally, missionaries did succeed in luring a few troubled souls away. In the final analysis, however, their impact was precisely the opposite of what they intended.[61] Instead of converting the American Jewish community, they helped transform it into a more cohesive and more secure body than it had ever been before.

[60] Alexander M. Dushkin, *Jewish Education in New York City* (New York, 1918), 54, 468-69; *Year Book of the Central Conference of American Rabbis, 1890-91* (Cincinnati, 1891), 122; Moses Rischin, *The Promised City: New York's Jews, 1870-1914* (Cambridge, 1962), 101, 107, 199; Lloyd P. Gartner, "The Jews of New York's East Side, 1890-1893," *American Jewish Historical Quarterly*, LIII (March 1964), 264-81.

[61] For what may have been the first understanding of this impact, see Isaac M. Wise, "Had a Contrary Effect," *Israelite*, 7 (1861), 300.

ACKNOWLEDGMENTS

Neil Betten, "Polish American Steelworkers: Americanization Through Industry and Labor," *Polish American Studies*, 33:2 (Autumn 1976), 31–42. Reprinted with the permission of *Polish American Studies*. Courtesy of Yale University Library.

John J. Bukowczyk, "The Transformation of Working-Class Ethnicity: Corporate Control, Americanization, and the Polish Immigrant Middle Class in Bayonne, New Jersey, 1915–1925," *Labor History*, 25:1 (Winter 1984), 53–82. Reprinted with the permission of *Labor History*. Courtesy of Yale University Library.

Robert L. Buroker, "From Voluntary Association to Welfare State: The Illinois Immigrants' Protective League, 1908–1926," *Journal of American History*, 58:3 (December 1971), 643–660. Reprinted with the permission of *Journal of American History*. Courtesy of Yale University Library.

Robert A. Carlson, "Americanization as an Early Twentieth-Century Adult Education Movement," *History of Education Quarterly*, 10:4 (Winter 1970), 440–464. Reprinted with the permission of *History of Education Quarterly*. Courtesy of *History of Education Quarterly*.

Reinhard R. Doerries, "The Americanizing of the German Immigrant: A Chapter from U.S. Social History," *American Studies*, 23:1 (1978), 51–59. Reprinted with the permission of *Association of American Studies*. Courtesy of *Association of American Studies*.

Mario T. Garcia, "Americanization and the Mexican Immigrant, 1880–1930," *Journal of Ethnic Studies*, 6:2 (Summer 1978), 19–34. Reprinted with the permission of the *Journal of Ethnic Studies*. Courtesy of the *Journal of Ethnic Studies*.

Philip Gleason, "Americans All: World War II and the Shaping of American Identity," *Review of Politics*, 43:4 (October 1981), 483–518. Reprinted with the permission of the *Review of Politics*. Courtesy of George E. Pozzetta.

Gerd Korman, "Americanization at the Factory Gate," *Industrial and Labor Relations Review*, 18 (1965), 396–419. Reprinted with the permission of the *Industrial and Labor Relations Review*. Courtesy of the *Industrial and Labor Relations Review*.

Rivka Lissak, "Liberal Progressives and 'New Immigrants': The Immigrants' Protective League of Chicago, 1908–1919," *Studies in American Civilization*, XXXII (1987), 79–103. Courtesy of George E. Pozzetta.

Rivka Lissak, "Myth and Reality: The Pattern of Relationship Between the Hull House Circle and the 'New Immigrants' on Chicago's West Side, 1890–1919," *Journal of American Ethnic History*, 2:2 (Spring 1983), 21–50. Reprinted with the permission of the *Journal of American Ethnic History*. Courtesy of Yale University Library.

John F. McClymer, "The Federal Government and the Americanization Movement, 1915–1924," *Prologue: The Journal of the National Archives*, 10 (Spring 1978), 22–41. Reprinted with the permission of *Prologue*. Courtesy of the Library of Congress.

Stephen Meyer, "Adapting the Immigrant to the Line: Americanization in the Ford Factory, 1914–1921," *Journal of Social History*, 14 (1980), 67–82. Reprinted with the permission of the *Journal of Social History*. Courtesy of George E. Pozzetta.

Raymond A. Mohl and Neil Betten, "Ethnic Adjustment in the Industrial City: The International Institute of Gary, 1919–1940," *International Migration Review*, 6:4 (Winter 1972), 361–376. Reprinted with the permission of the *International Migration Review*. Courtesy of *International Migration Review*.

Raymond A. Mohl and Neil Betten, "Paternalism and Pluralism: Immigrants and Social Welfare in Gary, Indiana, 1906–1940," *American Studies*, 15 (Spring 1974), 5–30. Reprinted with the permission of *American Studies*. Courtesy of Yale University Library.

Ralph E. Pumphrey, "Compassion and Protection: Dual Motivations in Social Welfare," *Social Service Review*, 33:1 (March 1959), 21–29. Courtesy of Yale University Library.

Jonathan D. Sarna, "The American Jewish Response to Nineteenth-Century Christian Missions," *Journal of American History*, 68:1 (June 1981), 35–51. Reprinted with the permission of the *Journal of American History*. Courtesy of Yale University Library.